VINO
ITALIANO
BUYING GUIDE

Copyright © 2004 by Joseph Bastianich
and David Lynch

Photographs on pages 4, 6, and 288 by Alessandro Puccinelli

Published by Clarkson Potter/Publishers, New York,
New York.
Member of the Crown Publishing Group, a division of
Random House, Inc.
www.crownpublishing.com

CLARKSON N. POTTER is a trademark and POTTER
and colophon are registered trademarks of Random
House, Inc.

Printed in the United States of America

Design by Jennifer K. Beal

Library of Congress Cataloging-in-Publication Data
Bastianich, Joseph.
Vino italiano buying guide : the ultimate quick reference
to the great wines of italy / by Joseph Bastianich and
David Lynch.
        p.   cm.
    Includes bibliographical references.
1. Wine and wine making—Italy. I. Lynch, David, 1967–
II. Title.
    TP559.I8B37   2004
    641.2'2'0945—dc22   2004006190

ISBN 1-4000-5287-4

10   9   8   7   6   5   4   3   2   1

First Edition

VINO ITALIANO
BUYING GUIDE

THE ULTIMATE QUICK
REFERENCE TO THE
GREAT WINES OF ITALY

Joseph Bastianich and David Lynch

Clarkson Potter/Publishers
New York

CONTENTS

PREFACE

WE'RE OBVIOUSLY BIASED, but Italian wine is where it's at right now. Advances in winemaking technology have leveled the worldwide playing field, and Italy recently enjoyed an unprecedented run of successful vintages from 1995 to 2001 that included some of the best years of the last *century*. Today there is so much great Italian wine at every price, from every corner of the peninsula, that it is impossible to taste it all—although we're doing our best, every day. What follows are the results so far: a listing of top Italian wine producers whose wines are distributed in the United States, and which of their wines to buy. In the spirit of our first book, *Vino Italiano: The Regional Wines of Italy,* the *Buying Guide* assumes that an intelligent buyer wants more than just a recommendation. It's easy for us to tell you that a wine is good; we hope the information included here will help you to make such determinations for yourself when faced with a row of unfamiliar bottles in a wine shop or on a wine list.

It may seem excessive, for example, to list all of Italy's wine appellations, but if you want to buy good wine, it helps to know what you're buying. Say you see a red wine labeled "Carignano del Sulcis" and have no idea what that means. Understanding that the designation means the wine is made from carignan grapes in southwestern Sardinia is a first step in understanding what that wine will taste like. If you know that Carignano del Sulcis is a denomination of controlled origin, or DOC, you might be further reassured about its quality.

Since most Americans have come to wine via California or France, the average Italian label can be as baffling as a signpost on a rural Tuscan road. But it doesn't have to be so tough. Italian wine laws and labeling practices are essentially the same as those used in France, so in reality, the only thing that makes an Italian label more confusing than a French one is lack of practice in deciphering it.

Aside from that, the big question that arose in the preparation of this guide was whether or not to rate individual wines. There are already a number of excellent publications that do this, and we had neither the resources nor the inclination to join the fray. We have, of course, given ratings to many of the wineries profiled here. As explained on page 16, we've created categories for Elite Wineries, Premier Wineries, Rising Star Wineries, and so forth, but ultimately, a winery's inclusion in this guide is a recommendation in itself. There are tens of thousands of wine producers in Italy and a little over a thousand in this guide, so you do the math. There's never been a better time than now to get into Italian wine, as the following pages attest.

J.B. & D.L.
New York, 2004

The listings in this guide are organized alphabetically by wine producer to facilitate ease of use. In the Producer Directory, there are quirks to be aware of when searching for a specific winery. The names of Italian wineries often include prefixes such as *Tenuta* (Tenuta Caparzo), *Fattoria* (Fattoria di Felsina), and *Podere* (Podere Grattamacco). These are traditional wine-estate terms in Italy that date back to the days of feudal estates: the *tenuta* was the estate as a whole; the *fattoria* was the central production facility of the feudal owner; and the *poderi* were the various sharecropper farms on the property, which all contributed a portion of their production to the owner as rent. In the Producer Directory, these prefixes are included selectively, in instances where we felt they were integral to the estate's brand name. This somewhat complicates the overall alphabetization. Another prefix, *Azienda Agricola* (agricultural firm), which appears on countless Italian wine labels, has been omitted in these listings. Although the actual label may read "Azienda Agricola Miani," it will be listed here under "Miani." Further, we've tried to include as many cross-references as we could to make your search for a particular brand as easy as possible. In the appendixes, particularly the one listing all of Italy's DOC(G) wine appellations, the listings are also alphabetical. The Cellar Selections section is a great source for wine suggestions by category.

Finally, the appendixes are a useful reference for the aficionado. There, you'll find extensive data that includes vintage ratings, grape characteristics, appellation classifications, and even a guide to Barolo and Barbaresco vineyards.

ITALIAN WINE LAWS AND LABELING

In 1963, Italy's Ministry of Agriculture drafted the country's modern laws governing wine production, creating the *Denominazione di Origine Controllata* (DOC). Its model was the decades-old French *appellation contrôlée,* which continues to regulate the production of wines from specific geographic areas.

The primary identifier of an Italian wine (or any European wine) is where it comes from. Barolo is a place in southeastern Piedmont, and for a wine to be called Barolo it must come from vineyards within a specific area defined by law. There are also prescriptions controlling most aspects of production, including which grape(s) can be used and how long the wine must be aged before release. Overall, Italian wines are classified in one of four ways.

VINO DA TAVOLA (VDT)

Vino da Tavola (table wine) may come from anywhere in Italy, from any grape or blend of grapes. The majority of VdT is sold in bulk, although many top-flight wines continue to carry this lowly designation because they are produced in a manner that doesn't entitle them to any "higher" classification. Producers use the VdT designation when they buy grapes (or wine) from another area to bolster their own production, but in many cases the choice has more to do with creative freedom: wines from official appellations carry with them official prescriptions on how to do things. In the same way that DOC is not a guarantee of high quality, VdT is hardly an indicator of poor quality; many of the most famous "super-Tuscan" wines got their start as VdTs.

INDICAZIONE GEOGRAFICA TIPICA (IGT)

The IGT, or "Typical Geographic Indication," was created in 1992 in an effort to increase the number of officially classified wines in Italy. The government's intention behind both IGT and DOC was to bolster consumer confidence in Italy's wine production and to create recognizable identities for wines to help them sell better. Essentially, an IGT regulates only the geographic production area, lending the wine regional cachet while leaving the producer free to experiment with grapes and production methods. IGT is a middle ground between VdT and DOC, similar to the French *vin du pays*.

DENOMINAZIONE DI ORIGINE CONTROLLATA (DOC)

The DOC, or "Denomination of Controlled Origin," is both a place-name and a production formula: it requires that a wine come from a specific place delimited by law and be made with a prescribed mix of grapes to carry the designation. Most DOC "disciplines" further require that a wine be vinified in the place where it is grown; that it be aged for a certain period and in certain types of vessels; and that grape production levels not exceed certain standards. Government tasting committees evaluate each year's production to ensure that the wines have the "tipicity" to carry the DOC name. Today, about 25 percent of all Italian wine is classified as DOC.

DENOMINAZIONE DI ORIGINE CONTROLLATA E GARANTITA (DOCG)

The first DOCG, or "Denomination of Controlled and Guaranteed Origin," was named in 1980 (it was Brunello di Montalcino), even though the classification was created along with the DOC in 1963. DOCG is nominally reserved for wines of the greatest historic or qualitative pedigree; wines labeled as such are the most tightly regulated of all classified wines. There are twenty-eight DOCG classifications as of this writing, but the fact that the number continues to grow says something about the system: ultimately, DOC(G)s are not truly quality designations, because the creation of a DOC, as well as the "elevation" of a wine to DOCG, has as much to do with the political will of a particular municipality as it does with the inherent quality of the wines.

DECODING LABELS

A CLASSIC

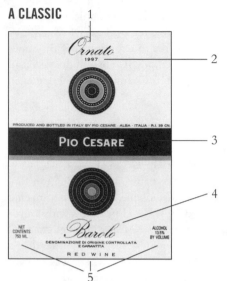

1. **Vineyard designation.** "Ornato" is the vineyard from which the wine is sourced. Sometimes a superfluous word like this may be a proprietary name.
2. **Vintage year.**
3. **Winery name.** There is little doubt as to the name of this winery, but in other cases, the emphasis may be on another name. To be certain, look for the fine print that reads "produced and bottled by . . ."
4. **Denomination.** As noted on pages 10–11, Italian wines are classified in one of four ways: VdT, IGT, DOC, or DOCG. The classification is always clearly indicated. In this case, you know that the wine is from a DOCG—Barolo—but you are not told that Barolo is in Piedmont and that the wine is made from the nebbiolo grape.
5. **Size, type, and alcohol content.** All required by the Bureau of Alcohol, Tobacco, and Firearms (ATF), which sets the parameters for labeling information and must approve the label.
6. **Proprietary information.** Explanatory information about the wine provided by the producer.
7. **Government warnings.** Required by the ATF.
8. **UPC code.** Used at all levels of the supply chain (importer, distributor, retailer) for inventory control, receiving, and purchasing.
9. **Importer name.** Usually found on the back label.

PIO CESARE The Pio Cesare winery near Alba in Italy's Piedmont was founded by its namesake in 1881. Great-grandson, Pio Boffa, continues the tradition of this internationally respected winery by emphasizing viticulture and innovative winemaking. Contemporary techniques applied to Piedmont's noble grape varietals result in wines of great character and distinction. — 6

GOVERNMENT WARNING: (1) ACCORDING TO THE SURGEON GENERAL, WOMEN SHOULD NOT DRINK ALCOHOLIC BEVERAGES DURING PREGNANCY BECAUSE OF THE RISK OF BIRTH DEFECTS. (2) CONSUMPTION OF ALCOHOLIC BEVERAGES IMPAIRS YOUR ABILITY TO DRIVE A CAR OR OPERATE MACHINERY, AND MAY CAUSE HEALTH PROBLEMS.

7 —

CONTAINS
SULFITES

— 8

0 86891 01570 5

IMPORTED BY 🍇 PATERNO® WINES INTERNATIONAL, LAKE BLUFF, IL — 9

WHAT THE LABEL DOESN'T SAY

1 — GRANATO

2 — 2001

3 — FORADORI

1. **Proprietary name.** This translates as "garnet," or, more specifically, the garnet color of pomegranates. It is not an official classification or vineyard designation.
2. **Vintage year.**
3. **Winery name.**
4. **Denomination or classification.** The wine is designated Indicazione Geografica Tipica (IGT). The Vigneti delle Dolomiti IGT applies to vineyards following the contours of the Dolomites, from Verona in the Veneto to Bolzano in Alto Adige. The label does not tell you that this is a wine made from the teroldego grape in Trentino.
5. **Winery name redux.** If you know that "TN" is the abbreviation for the province of Trento, this might help you determine that the wine is from Trentino.
6. **Importer name.** This U.S. contact can help get the information not contained on the label.

GRANATO

2001

4 — VIGNETI DELLE DOLOMITI ROSSO
INDICAZIONE GEOGRAFICA TIPICA

5 — ESTATE BOTTLED BY AZIENDA AGRICOLA FORADORI
MEZZOLOMBARDO (TN) ITALIA

6 — GOVERNMENT WARNING: (1) ACCORDING TO THE SURGEON GENERAL, WOMEN SHOULD NOT DRINK ALCOHOLIC BEVERAGES DURING PREGNANCY BECAUSE OF THE RISK OF BIRTH DEFECTS. (2) CONSUMPTION OF ALCOHOLIC BEVERAGES IMPAIRS YOUR ABILITY TO DRIVE A CAR OR OPERATE MACHINERY, AND MAY CAUSE HEALTH PROBLEMS.

CONTAINS SULFITES

SOLE U.S. IMPORTER VIN DIVINO Ltd CHICAGO ILLINOIS 60660

NET CONT. 750 ML · ALC. 13% BY VOL.   RED WINE · PRODUCT OF ITALY

PRINCIPAL GRAPES
OF EACH REGION

Abruzzo and Molise
Key Grapes: (w) Trebbiano. (r) Montepulciano.

Basilicata
Key Grapes: (r) Aglianico.

Calabria
Key Grapes: (w) Greco. (r) Gaglioppo (Cirò).

Campania
Key Grapes: (w) Falanghina, Fiano, Greco. (r) Aglianico.

Emilia-Romagna
Key Grapes: (w) Albana, Trebbiano. (r) Lambrusco, Sangiovese.

Friuli–Venezia Giulia
Key Grapes: (w) Tocai Friulano, Pinot Grigio, Sauvignon, Pinot Bianco. (r) Merlot, Cabernet family, Refosco.

Lazio
Key Grapes: (w) Malvasia, Trebbiano. (r) Cesanese, Merlot, Cabernet.

Liguria
Key Grapes: (w) Pigato, Vermentino. (r) Ormeasco (Dolcetto), Rossese.

Lombardia
Key Grapes: (w) Chardonnay, Pinot Bianco, Trebbiano. (r) Bonarda, Chiavennasca (Nebbiolo).

Marche
Key Grapes: (w) Verdicchio. (r) Montepulciano, Sangiovese.

Piemonte
Key Grapes: (w) Arneis, Cortese (Gavi), Moscato. (r) Barbera, Dolcetto, Nebbiolo.

Puglia
Key Grapes: (w) Bombino, Trebbiano. (r) Malvasia Nera, Negroamaro, Primitivo.

Sardegna
Key Grapes: (w) Nuragus, Vermentino. (r) Cannonau, Carignano.

Sicilia
Key Grapes: (w) Catarratto, Inzolia, Malvasia, Zibibbo. (r) Nero d'Avola.

Toscana
Key Grapes: (w) Trebbiano, Vernaccia. (r) Sangiovese.

Trentino–Alto Adige

Key Grapes: (w) Pinot Bianco, Pinot Grigio, Sylvaner, Gewürztraminer. (r) Lagrein, Teroldego, Schiava.

Umbria

Key Grapes: (w) Grechetto, Trebbiano. (r) Sagrantino, Sangiovese.

Valle d'Aosta

Key Grapes: (w) Blanc de Morgex, Muscat. (r) Fumin, Petit Rouge, Picotendro (Nebbiolo).

Veneto

Key Grapes: (w) Garganega (Soave), Trebbiano, Prosecco. (r) Corvina, Rondinella (Valpolicella), Cabernet family.

PRODUCER DIRECTORY

KEY TO SYMBOLS

WINERY CLASSIFICATIONS

ELITE WINERIES

The cream of Italy's crop, wineries designated as "Elite" have been in continuous production for more than twenty years; have a history of superior quality and critical acclaim across the whole of their portfolios; and produce a quantity significant enough to have a national market presence in the United States.

PREMIER WINERIES (LISTED IN ALL CAPS)

These estates are in the very top echelon of Italian wine but usually have shorter histories or more limited production compared with the Elite wineries. Premier estates consistently produce individual wines that rank among the best in Italy and, in many instances, have ranges of wine whose variety rivals those of the Elite. A winery that has been a standard-bearer in a sparse and/or historic production area will also be designated as a Premier winery, even if its wines aren't as critically acclaimed as those of other Premier estates.

RISING STAR WINERIES (★)

Wineries to watch. These are estates or brands of relatively recent origin that create significant buzz in the wine industry and press and demonstrate high quality and innovation.

VALUE WINERIES (⧉)

Wineries that offer exceptional value for the dollar across their entire range.

WINE PRICING*

€   inexpensive
€€   mid-to-high price range
€€€   most expensive

   * BASED ON WHOLESALE CASE COSTS OF A PRODUCER'S RANGE AND APPROXIMATE
      RETAIL VALUES OF THOSE WINES

WINE AVAILABILITY

- small/allocated production; difficult to find
- medium production; more challenging to find
- large production; widely distributed

SERVICES

- restaurant on premises
- accommodations or *agriturismo* available at winery

A Maccia LIGURIA

Via Umberto I 54, 18028 Ranzo (IM)
Tel.: 0183318003
DOC(G)s: Riviera Ligure di Ponente
Loredana Faraldi's tangy, herbaceous pigato is a distinctive white for about $15, though you're more likely to find it in a restaurant than at retail.

A-Mano PUGLIA

Fusione, Masseria Signorille, 74011 Castellaneta (TA)
Tel.: 0998493770/www.empsonusa.com
American Mark Shannon fell in love with Puglia and its primitivo grape. He created a value sensation with A-Mano ("made by hand") primitivo, always a dark, juicy, and affordable wine. A richer version called "Prima Mano" (closer selection, barrique aging) is pricier but still a value. There's also a second line of even less expensive wines called "Promessa."

Abbazia di Novacella ALTO ADIGE

Via dell'Abbazia 1, 39040 Varna/Vahrn (BZ)
Tel.: 0472836189/Fax: 0472837305
www.abbazianovacella.it
DOC(G)s: Alto Adige Valle d'Isarco/Südtirol Eisacktaler
Located in an Augustinian monastery founded in 1142. Aromatic, high-acid whites from sylvaner (theirs are some of the best) and gewürztraminer are a specialty. The smoky red lagrein is also good as is the rare dessert sipper from moscato rosa, a rare local grape with a rose-pink hue and lots of exotic berry flavor.

Abbazia di Rosazzo

See Filiputti, Walter.

★ Abbazia Santa Anastasia SICILIA

Contrada Santa Anastasia, 90013 Castelbuono (PA)
Tel.: 0921671959
Luscious reds with international flair, headlined by the 100% cabernet "Litra." Most interesting is the cabernet–merlot–nero d'avola–syrah blend "Montenero," which offers a nice combination of dark spice and sweetly ripe fruit. For every day, there's the smooth and fruity "Passomaggio" (a nero d'avola–merlot blend).

Abbona, Anna Maria PIEMONTE

Frazione. Moncucco 21, 12060 Farigliano (CN)
Tel.: 0173797228/www.amabbona.com
Dogliani is thought to be the birthplace of dolcetto, and Abbona's wines are inky, fat, fruity examples of the grape.

★ Abbona, Marziano ed Enrico PIEMONTE

Via Torino 242, 12063 Dogliani (CN)
Tel./Fax: 0173721317
DOC(G)s: Dolcetto di Dogliani; Barbaresco; Barbera d'Alba; Barolo; Langhe
  Although dolcetto is a specialty—from the fragrant, light "Vigneto Munta" to the denser "Papa Celso"—the real stars are the Barolo "Terlo Ravera" (from a small holding in Cherasco) and the Barbaresco "Faset." Both are lush and approachable on release, and great values.

Abrate, Luca PIEMONTE

Strada Orti 29/a, 12042 Brà (CN)
Tel.: 0172415254/Fax: 0172433350/www.abrate.com
DOC(G)s: Barbera d'Alba; Nebbiolo d'Alba; Roero
  Check out the powerful Barbera d'Alba "Ouitin." The Roero Arneis is a solid aromatic white, and the Langhe Nebbiolo is fleshy and fruity. Good prices.

Abrigo, Orlando PIEMONTE

Frazione Cappelletto, 5, 12050 Treiso d'Alba (CN)
Tel.: 0173630232/Fax: 017356120/www.orlandoabrigo.it
DOC(G)s: Barbaresco; Barbera d'Alba; Langhe Rosso
  Sturdy Barbaresco from several different single vineyards. Also worth trying are the well-structured Barbera d'Alba "Montersino" and the chocolaty, full-bodied Langhe Rosso "Livraie" (100% merlot).

Accordini, Stefano VENETO

Via Alberto Bolla 9, 37029 San Pietro in Cariano (VR)
Tel.: 0457701733
DOC(G)s: Amarone della Valpolicella; Recioto della Valpolicella; Valpolicella Classico
  The Accordini family makes excellent Amarone on a small scale. "Acinatico" is consistently silky, balanced, and of medium weight; "Il Fornetto" is a massive reserve wine.

Accornero e Figli PIEMONTE

Ca' Cima 1, 15049 Vignale Monferrato (AL)
Tel.: 0142933317
DOC(G)s: Barbera del Monferrato
  Monferrato is known for big barberas, and Accornero's juicy "Giulin" is a wine to buy by the case. The more expensive "Bricco Battista" is a barrel-aged bruiser, as is the cabernet-barbera blend "Centenario."

Ada Nada PIEMONTE

Via Ausario 12, 12050 Treiso (CN)
Tel.: 0173638127/www.adanada.it
DOC(G)s: Barbaresco, Barbera d'Alba, Dolcetto d'Alba, Langhe
  Barrique-aged Barbaresco from the Cichin and Valeirano vineyards in Treiso. Terrific textures and bright aromatics. "Bisbetica" is a silky nebbiolo-barbera blend.

Adanti UMBRIA

Vocabolo Arquata, 06031 Bevagna (PG)
Tel.: 0742360295/Fax: 0742361270
www.cantineadanti.com
DOC(G)s: Montefalco Rosso; Montefalco Sagrantino
  The best wines here are "Arquata Rosso" (cabernet sauvignon–cabernet franc–merlot-barbera) and "Nispero"

(sangiovese–cabernet sauvignon–barbera). The plush and well-priced Montefalco Rosso "Arquata" is a great start.

Adragna SICILIA
Via Regina Elena 4, 91100 Trapani
Tel.: 092326401

Solid varietal wines from nero d'avola to chardonnay. Also try the soft and fruity cabernet-merlot blend "Roccagiglio."

Agriverde ABRUZZO
Via Monte Maiella 118, 66020 Ortona (CH)
Tel.: 0859032101/www.agriverde.it
DOC(G)s: Montepulciano d'Abruzzo; Trebbiano d'Abruzzo

Part of the new wave of *Abruzzesi* turning the once-humble montepulciano grape into serious wine. This winery is best known for the superconcentrated (if a little expensive) Montepulciano d'Abruzzo "Plateo."

Ajello SICILIA
Contrada Giudeo, 91025 Mazara del Vallo (TP)
Tel.: 091309107

Here's one of many up-and-comers on Sicily: Ajello's inky "Furat" combines nero d'avola, cabernet, merlot, and syrah, and is a lot of wine for the money.

Alario, Claudio PIEMONTE
Via Santa Croce 23, 12055 Diano d'Alba (CN)
Tel.: 0173231808
DOC(G)s: Barolo; Dolcetto di Diano d'Alba

A specialist in light and fruity dolcetto. The dolcetto "Montagrillo" is a top choice, and the nebbiolo and Barolo are also well regarded.

Albano Carrisi PUGLIA
Contrada Bosco 13, 72020 Cellino San Marco (BR)
Tel.: 0831619211
DOC(G)s: Salice Salentino

This producer has won raves for "Platone," a dense, chocolaty blend of negroamaro and primitivo. It's a robust southern wine, if a touch expensive (in the $40 range). Cheaper offerings include the "Nostalgia" primitivo.

Aleramici TOSCANA
Podere Il Galampio, 53024 Montalcino (SI)
Tel.: 0577816056/Fax: 0577849078
www.marchesatodeglialeramici.it
DOC(G)s: Brunello di Montalcino

A consistently good buy in Brunello—generally smoky and more traditional in style with great aromatics. The little-brother Rosso di Montalcino follows suit.

Alessandria, F.lli PIEMONTE
Via Beato Valfré 59, 12060 Verduno (CN)
Tel.: 0172470113
DOC(G)s: Barolo; Barbera d'Alba; Langhe

A small producer known for its "Monvigliero" cru Barolo. Well priced and fairly approachable when young.

Alessandria, Gianfranco PIEMONTE
Via Manzoni 13, 12065 Monforte d'Alba (CN)
Tel./Fax: 017378576
DOC(G)s: Barolo; Barbera d'Alba; Dolcetto d'Alba

A tiny estate that bottled its first vintage in 1991. The

barrique-aged Barolos (the single-vineyard wine is "San Giovanni") find a nice middle ground between the earthy "traditional" style and the more fruit-forward "modern" style. There's also a luxurious Barbera d'Alba ("Vittoria").

Alessandro di Camporeale SICILIA

Via Atrio Principe 8, 90043 Camporeale (PA)
Tel.: 092437238
  This estate is the place for fat, fruity wines for every day. Its "Kaid" Syrah is an Aussie shiraz-style powerhouse.

ALLEGRINI VENETO

Corte Giara, 37022 Fumane (VR)
Tel.: 0457701138/Fax: 0457701774/www.allegrini.it
DOC(G)s: Valpolicella Classico; Amarone della Valpolicella; Recioto della Valpolicella
  With one of the largest assemblages of vineyards in Valpolicella and a state-of-the-art winery, Allegrini is synonymous with great Amarone. The house style is superrich yet silky, with tons of forward fruit. This decadent Amarone is complemented by the dense and spicy "La Poja," a single-vineyard wine from 100% corvina. "La Poja" does not incorporate any dried fruit, nor does it employ *ripasso*. It is old-vine corvina from a prime site in Sant'Ambrogio. "Palazzo della Torre" (which uses 30% dried grapes for a "baby Amarone" feel) is always an incredible value, and the chunky "La Grola" (corvina-rondinella-sangiovese-syrah) is another consistent, well-priced red.

ALTARE, ELIO PIEMONTE

Frazione Annunziata 51, 12064 La Morra (CN)
Tel./Fax: 017350835
DOC(G)s: Barolo; Langhe; Barbera d'Alba; Dolcetto d'Alba
  Buy-and-hold Barolo. Elio Altare is now one of the elder statesmen of the Langhe, the kind of guy younger vintners go to for inspiration. Since the 1970s he has been a technological and viticultural pace-setter in a tradition-bound zone. Altare is best known for his intensely perfumed, tightly wound, long-aging Barolo from the Arborina vineyard, from which he also crafts a plusher Langhe Rosso based on nebbiolo. He's also begun bottling a dense Barolo from the Brunate cru, which is a little broader in style but still elegant and aromatic. In all, this is some of the longest-lived Barolo to be found, made in a modern—but moderated—style. His Barbera d'Alba and the "super-Piedmont" blend "L'Insieme" are fat and fruity pleasures.

ALTESINO TOSCANA

Località Altesino, 53024 Montalcino (SI)
Tel.: 0577806208/Fax: 0577806131
DOC(G)s: Brunello di Montalcino; Rosso di Montalcino
  One of the longer-established estates in Montalcino, whose powerful Brunellos toe a slightly more traditional line (the basic Brunello and the single-vineyard "Montosoli" are aged in larger Slavonian oak, though there's no shortage of cleanliness or intensity). These are smoky, tightly wound wines designed for long aging, but there are a number of plush, oak-kissed super-Tuscans to drink while you're waiting, such as "Alte d'Altesi" (sangiovese-cabernet) and "Borgo d'Altesi" (cabernet).

Ambra TOSCANA

Via Lombarda 72, 59015 Carmignano (PO)
Tel.: 055486488/Fax: 0552335318
DOC(G)s: Carmignano

One of the best wineries in Carmignano. Giuseppe Rigolli specializes in single-vineyard wines, including the powerful "Elzana" (almost all sangiovese) and the perfumed "Le Vigne Alte" (made with grapes from his highest-elevation sites). Structured, high-toned wines at fair prices.

Ambrosini, Lorella TOSCANA

Località Tabaro, 96, 57028 Suvereto (LI)
Tel./Fax: 0565829301
DOC(G)s: Val di Cornia

This estate's top red is the deep and juicy "Riflesso Antico" (100% montepulciano). Also solid is the Val di Cornia DOC "Subertum" (sangiovese-merlot).

★ Anselma PIEMONTE

Località San Giuseppe 38, 12065 Monforte d'Alba (CN)
Tel./Fax: 0173787217/www.anselma.it
DOC(G)s: Barolo

Although the winery was established in 1993, the Anselmas have been acquiring vineyards since the seventies: they're now one of Barolo's largest landowners, with vineyards in several key villages, ensuring consistent production of their basic Barolo and special selection "Adasi." Their style is plush and modern, with a judicious use of oak that doesn't mask the perfume of nebbiolo.

Anselmet, Renato VALLE D'AOSTA

Frazione La Crete 194, 11018 Villeneuve (AO)
Tel.: 016595217
DOC(G)s: Valle d'Aosta

This little producer in the Valle d'Aosta makes a light, bright Torrette (from the petit rouge grape) that is nice with a chill. The chardonnay is done in a fresh, clean, minerally style that is reminiscent of Chablis.

ANSELMI VENETO

Via San Carlo 46, 37032 Monteforte d'Alpone (VR)
Tel.: 0457611488
DOC(G)s: Recioto di Soave

Roberto Anselmi shuns the Soave designation for his wines because of flaws he sees in the DOC production discipline. From "San Vincenzo"—a classic Soave, if not in name—to "Capitel Foscarino" (a richer single-vineyard wine) and "Capitel Croce" (the richest, barrel-fermented wine, also from a single vineyard), Anselmi has helped to make a name for Soave's garganega grape. "I Capitelli" is an unctuous *passito* (dried-grape wine).

★ Antano, Milziade UMBRIA

Località Colle Allodole, 06031 Bevagna (PG)
Tel.: 0742360371
DOC(G)s: Montefalco; Sagrantino di Montefalco

The Montefalco Rosso is more aromatic and structured than most, and the Sagrantino di Montefalco wraps the wintry spiciness of sagrantino in a tannic package. The *riserva*-level wine is the Sagrantino di Montefalco "Colleallodole," which is well built for aging.

Antiche Cantine PIEMONTE

Viale Mazzini 33-35, 28078 Romagnano Sesia (NO)
Tel.: 0163833108/Fax: 0163831200
DOC(G)s: Gattinara
   Inexpensive Gattinara in an earthy, rustic style.

AnticoTerrenOttavi MARCHE

Frazione Cagnore 6, 62027 San Severino (MC)
Tel.: 0733637804/www.vinocagnore.it
DOC(G)s: Vernaccia di Serrapetrona
   A fairly new winery near Macerata in the Marche.
Consultant Giancarlo Soverchia helps craft four interesting
reds, including two that incorporate the black and spicy
vernaccia nera grape. The base-level wine is the soft and
succulent "Cagnore" (montepulciano–sangiovese–
vernaccia nera), but the deeply concentrated "Pianetta di
Cagnore" (vernaccia nera only) is the one to find.

ANTINORI TOSCANA

Piazza degli Antinori 3, 50123 Firenze
Tel.: 05523595/Fax: 0552359884/www.antinori.it
DOC(G)s: Bolgheri; Brunello di Montalcino; Chianti
Classico; Orvieto Classico; Vino Nobile di Montepulciano
   The Antinoris have made wine since the 1300s, and
today theirs is arguably the biggest name in Italian wine.
Piero Antinori has been a dynamic force, having helped
launch the super-Tuscan category with the introduction of
the luxurious yet woodsy "Tignanello" (80% sangiovese,
20% cabernet) in 1971, and having shaken up Chianti
Classico by challenging the DOCG's long-established
norms. Both "Tignanello" and the opulent "Solaia" (80%
cabernet, 20% sangiovese) come from single vineyards on
the Santa Cristina estate, one of three properties the
Antinoris own in Chianti Classico (Santa Cristina is also
home to the benchmark Tenute Marchese Antinori Chianti
Classico Riserva). There are also estates in Bolgheri
(Guado al Tasso), Montalcino (Pian delle Vigne),
Montepulciano (La Braccesca), Umbria (Castello della
Sala), Piedmont (Prunotto), and Puglia (Tormaresca). The
Tuscan wines run the gamut from bargain-priced quaffers
like the white "Galestro" and "Péppoli" Chianti Classico to
collector wines such as "Solaia," which has the elegance
and longeity of a first-growth Bordeaux.

★ Antonelli UMBRIA

Località San Marco 59, 06036 Montefalco (PG)
Tel.: 0742379158/Fax: 0742371063
www.antonellisanmarco.it
DOC(G)s: Sagrantino di Montefalco (also Passito); Rosso
di Montefalco; Colli Martani
   One of Montefalco's best (if underregarded) producers.
Antonelli's rich, silky Sagrantinos and Port-like Sagrantino
passito are tough to find but well worth the search.

★ Antoniolo PIEMONTE

Corso Valsesia 277, 13045 Gattinara (VC)
Tel.: 0163833612/Fax: 0163826112
DOC(G)s: Gattinara
   One of the best wineries in Gattinara, with several crus:
"Osso San Grato" is considered the most powerful, and
the superb "San Francesco" is typically a little more

accessible and pinot noir–ish. The basic Gattinara and white Erbaluce di Caluso are excellent values.

Antonutti FRIULI–VENEZIA GIULIA

Via d'Antoni 21, 33030 Pasian di Prado (UD)
Tel.: 0432662001/www.antonuttivini.it
DOC(G)s: Friuli Grave

The tocai friulano is fat, slick, and modern. Barrique-aged merlot, cabernet sauvignon, and chardonnay are made as well, in a full-blown international style.

Apollonio PUGLIA

Via San Pietro in Lama 7, 73047 Monteroni di Lecce (LE)
Tel.: 0832327182/Fax: 0832325238/www.apolloniovini.it
DOC(G)s: Copertino; Salice Salentino

Superripe value reds from negroamaro and primitivo. Check out the "Divoto" Copertino or the Salice Salentino for a supple, spicy southern sensation.

ARGIANO TOSCANA

Località Argiano 74, 53024 Montalcino (SI)
Tel.: 0577844037/Fax: 0577844210/www.argiano.net
DOC(G)s: Brunello di Montalcino

This historic Montalcino estate is now owned by the Countess Noemi Marone Cinzano. The estate's tarry and toasty Brunello (aged part in second-pass barrique and part in large cask) has proved to be a graceful ager; the super-Tuscan "Solengo" (cabernet-syrah-merlot) is in the top rank and has become highly sought after.

ARGIOLAS SARDEGNA

Via Roma 56/58, 09040 Serdiana (CA)
Tel.: 070740606/Fax: 070743264
www.cantine-argiolas.com
DOC(G)s: Cannonau di Sardegna; Monica di Sardegna; Nuragus di Cagliari; Vermentino di Sardegna

Argiolas makes some of Sardinia's best wines. Using the full range of funky local grapes—cannonau (grenache), carignano (carignan), bovale (similar to mourvèdre), and monica—Argiolas is best known for the dense and slightly savage "Turriga," an excellent blend of cannonau, malvasia, carignano, and bovale. "Costamolino" vermentino is a reliable light white, and "Perdera" is a brightly aromatic red from monica.

Armani, Albino VENETO

Località Ceradello 401, 37020 Dolce (VR)
Tel.: 0457290033/Fax: 0457290023
www.albinoarmani.com

Located north of Verona, near Trentino. The top wine is the IGT Corvara Rosso (corvina-cabernet-merlot), and for those seeking adventure, "Foja Tonda" is a tartly fruity, exotically spicy red from the rare casetta grape.

Arrigoni LIGURIA

Via Sarzana 224, 19100 La Spezia
Tel.: 0187504060/Fax: 0187505264
DOC(G)s: Cinque Terre; Colli di Luni

A tiny producer based near La Spezia making fresh, briny Cinque Terre whites as well as the rare and more expensive sweet style of Cinque Terre called sciacchetrà.

Ars Poetica BASILICATA

Via Provinciale 8, 85028 Rionero in Vulture (PO)
Tel.: 097272517

DOC(G)s: Aglianico del Vulture

A private-label wine crafted by the D'Angelo family of Rionero. The specialty is smoky and fragrant aglianico. The spicy, tobacco-scented "Vulcano" is an excellent value, while the "Colline di Orazio" goes for deeper concentration of flavor (and a higher price).

Artimino TOSCANA

Viale Papa Giovanni XXIII 1, 59015 Artimino (FI)
Tel.: 0558751432/Fax: 0558751480

DOC(G)s: Carmignano; Chianti Montalbano

Spicy, more traditionally styled Carmignano wines with lots of brushy sangiovese aromas. A beautiful estate to visit.

Attems, Conte Douglas FRIULI–VENEZIA GIULIA

Via Giulio Cesare 36A, 34170 Gorizia (GO)
Tel.: 0481393619/www.frescobaldi.it

DOC(G)s: Collio

This historic Friulian estate was recently purchased by Tuscany's Frescobaldi family, who will surely give the wines a higher profile. Good, clean varietal whites from pinot grigio, chardonnay, tocai, etc., at reasonable prices.

Avide SICILIA

Corso Italia 131, 91000 Ragusa
Tel.: 0932967456/Fax: 0932731754/www.avide.it

DOC(G)s: Cerasuolo di Vittoria

Cerasuolo di Vittoria is always a good value and always interesting (it's a blend of nero d'avola and frappato that combines the fruity depth of the former with the bright acid and aroma of the latter). Avide has long been an anchor of the appellation. A soft summer red.

AVIGNONESI TOSCANA

Via di Gracciano nel
Corso 91, 53045 Montepulciano (SI)
Tel.: 0578757872/Fax: 0578757847/www.avignonesi.it

DOC(G)s: Vino Nobile di Montepulciano; Vin Santo

The Falvo family has four estates, with a home base in Montepulciano. Smooth and sleekly styled Vino Nobile di Montepulciano is still their calling card, but they're also famous for long-aged and very rare Vin Santo. Still, big reds are the specialty. After you've acquired a case of the Vino Nobile or the "Rosso Avignonesi" (sangiovese-cabernet-merlot) for everyday consumption, you might spring for the chocolaty super-Tuscan "<u>Desiderio</u>" (merlot) or the "50&50" (sangiovese-merlot), the latter made in collaboration with Chianti Classico's Capanelle (which supplies the sangiovese).

★ Azelia PIEMONTE

Via Alba-Barolo 53, 12060 Castiglione Falletto (CN)
Tel.: 017362859

DOC(G)s: Barolo; Barbera d'Alba; Dolcetto d'Alba

Luigi Scavino's small property makes weighty yet accessible Barolo, most notably the "Bricco Fiasco" (from the vineyard he shares with his cousin Enrico). The wines showcase the fruitier, more luxurious side of nebbiolo. Dolcetto d'Alba "Bricco Oriolo" is fresh and fragrant.

BADIA A COLTIBUONO TOSCANA

Località Badia a Coltibuono, 53013
Gaiole in Chianti (SI)
Tel.: 057774481/Fax: 0577749235/www.coltibuono.com
DOC(G)s: Chianti Classico

Roberto and Emanuela Stucchi run this historic estate—
housed in an eleventh-century abbey—in Chianti Classico.
Their reliable, value-priced Chiantis ("Roberto Stucchi,"
"Cetamura") complement their estate-labeled Chianti
Classico Riserva. There's also the powerfully built
"Sangioveto," one of Tuscany's great varietal sangioveses,
which shows off the woodsy, earthy flavors of the grape.

Badia di Morrona TOSCANA

Via di Badia, 8, 56030 Terricciola (PI)
Tel.: 0587658505/Fax: 0587655127
DOC(G)s: Chianti

This growing estate is best known for "N'Antia" (sangiovese-
cabernet-merlot) and "Vignalta" (sangiovese). Both have
super-Tuscan depth at a relatively reasonable price.

Balter TRENTINO

Via Vallunga II 24, 38068 Rovereto (TN)
Tel.: 0464430101
DOC(G)s: Trento Brut; Trentino

Nicola Balter makes a crisp *Champenoise* sparkler from
chardonnay. There's also an excellent sauvignon blanc
and a spicy and savory red blend, "Barbanico" (cabernet-
merlot-lagrein).

Baltieri VENETO

Villa Piatti 5, 37030 Mizzole (VR)
Tel.: 045557616/Fax: 0458869525/www.baltieri.it
DOC(G)s: Valpolicella; Amarone della Valpolicella

A small, family-run estate in Valpolicella. The limited-
production "Sortilegio" Amarone is high-acid and fairly
tannic. Built for long aging.

Banfi

See Castello Banfi and Vigne Regali.

Banti, Jacopo TOSCANA

Via Citerna 24, 57021 Campiglia Marittima (LI)
Tel.: 0565838802/www.jacopobanti.it
DOC(G)s: Val di Cornia

Val di Cornia, on the Tuscan coast, is a hot area (literally
and figuratively). Banti is one of a growing roster of wineries that are putting this place on the map. "Il Peccato" is
a red from sangiovese, cabernet, and ciliegiolo that has a
warm, juicy, Mediterranean savor. Other wines include a
tangy vermentino and a brightly fruity varietal ciliegiolo.

Baracchi TOSCANA

Via Giovanni Pascoli 7, 52042 Camuscia (AR)
Tel.: 0575612679/Fax: 0575612927
www.baracchiwinery.com

The winemaking arm of Riccardo and Silvia Baracchi's
estate outside Cortona, where they operate the Relais &
Châteaux hotel/restaurant Il Falconiere. Their bold reds
include "Smeriglio" (sangiovese-syrah-merlot) and the
bigger-boned "L'Ardito" (cabernet-merlot-sangiovese).

Barberani-Vallesanta UMBRIA

Via Michelangeli 14, 05018 Orvieto (TR)
Tel.: 0763341820/Fax: 0763340773/www.barberani.it
DOC(G)s: Orvieto Classico; Lago di Corbara

A top producer of Orvieto whites, best evidenced by "Calcaia." Other wines include a citrusy grechetto and a "super-Umbrian" red, "Foresco," which blends sangiovese and cabernet sauvignon and has some decent depth.

Barbi

See Fattoria dei Barbi and Decugnano dei Barbi.

Baroncini TOSCANA

Località Casale 43, 53037 San Gimignano (SI)
Tel.: 0577940600/www.baroncini.it
DOC(G)s: Vernaccia di San Gimignano; Chianti Colli Senesi; Morellino di Scansano

In addition to the light and flinty Vernaccia di San Gimignano "Apollonia" and several simple Chiantis, there's also a soft, fruity Morellino di Scansano "Le Mandorlae" from a satellite estate in the Maremma. The Baroncini family is both an estate bottler and a purchaser of fruit; the firm owns a number of Tuscan farms, including Poggio Castellare, Fattoria Sovestro, Tenuta Faggeto, and Il Puntone.

Barone Cornacchia ABRUZZO

Contruda Torri, 64010 Torano Nuovo (TE)
Tel.: 0861887412
DOC(G)s: Montepulciano d'Abruzzo; Trebbiano d'Abruzzo
Inexpensive Montepulciano d'Abruzzo. "Poggio Varano" is a supple and fruity by-the-case red to have around the house for everyday drinking.

Barone Pizzini LOMBARDIA

Via Brescia 3, 25050 Corte Franca (BS)
Tel.: 030984136/www.baronepizzini.it
DOC(G)s: Franciacorta; Terre di Franciacorta

Originally founded in 1870, this estate was sold to a group of investors in 1991, who brought in high-end consultants and spent heavily on vineyards and equipment. Their best wine right now is a red Bordeaux blend called "San Carlo"; the sparklers are good, too.

BARONE RICASOLI (CASTELLO DI BROLIO)

TOSCANA

Cantine del Castello di Brolio, 53013 Gaiole in Chianti (SI)
Tel.: 05777301/Fax: 0577730225
DOC(G)s: Chianti Classico

The Castello di Brolio winery had fallen out of family hands, but upon reclaiming it in 1993, Francesco Ricasoli (a descendant of Bettino Ricasoli, who created the original formula for Chianti in the 1870s) set out to make serious reds. Castello di Brolio Chianti Classico is truly a world-class red and a far cry from the thin, acidic Chiantis of decades ago. "Casalferro," once a hard-edged varietal sangiovese, has been retooled (with a little merlot and cabernet) to be more generous in its youth. "Torricella" is a sleek and serous white, and there are nice Chiantis at the low end, too.

Basilisco BASILICATA

DOC(G)s: Aglianico
Via Umberto I 129, 85028 Rionero in Vulture (PZ)
Tel.: 0972720032
   Michele Cutolo makes his Aglianico del Vulture in a highly extracted, barrique-aged style, so there is a formidable layer of sweet fruit and toasty oak to balance out the naturally smoky, earthy, almost ashy characteristics of Vulture-area aglianico. A little pricey but good.

★ Bastianich FRIULI–VENEZIA GIULIA

Frazione Casali Ottelio 7, 33040 Premariacco (UD)
Tel.: 0432675612; 0432655363/Fax: 0432655526
DOC(G)s: Colli Orientali del Friuli
   Owned by the coauthor of this book, this small property boasts a stand of 50-year-old tocai vines, which produce deeply concentrated fruit for "Tocai Plus," crafted by consultant Maurizio Castelli. Castelli uses some late-harvest fruit in the unctuous "Tocai Plus," whereas the "plus" in "Pinot Plus" comes from a touch of pinot bianco added to a pinot grigio base. The flagship is the powerfully built "Vespa Bianco," a mix of barrel-fermented chardonnay and picolit with sauvignon fermented in stainless steel. "Vespa Rosso" is a savory blend of merlot, refosco, and pignolo, and, in select vintages, there's the high-powered "Calabrone" (cabernet franc, merlot, pignolo, refosco), which incorporates some dried-grape wine for extra concentration.

Batasiolo PIEMONTE

Frazione Annunziata 87, 12064 La Morra (CN)
Tel.: 0173501130/Fax: 0173509258/www.batasiolo.com
DOC(G)s: Barolo; Barbera d'Alba; Dolcetto d'Alba; Langhe
   With more than 250 acres of vineyards, Batasiolo is one of the Langhe's largest estates, with a wide range of wines (and price points). Prime holdings include pieces of the Boscareto and Briccolina crus in Serralunga d'Alba, from which they source their top Barolos. The base-level Barolo and Barbaresco wines are great introductions to these styles. At the lower end, the tangy Barbera d'Alba "Sovrana" is a good choice for burgers on the grill.

Battistotti TRENTINO

Via III Novembre 21, 38060 Nomi (TN)
Tel.: 0464834145/Fax: 0464830528/www.battistotti.com
DOC(G)s: Trentino
   This house makes two Trentino oddities (among other wines): the dry red marzemino and the sweet moscato rosa. The marzemino is an exotic, jammy mix of red and black berry flavors, the moscato rosa a more ethereal after-dinner sipper.

Baudana, Luigi PIEMONTE

Frazione Baudana 43, 12050 Serralunga d'Alba (CN)
Tel.: 0173613354
DOC(G)s: Barbera d'Alba; Barolo; Dolcetto d'Alba; Langhe
   Barolo "Cerretta Piani" is the top wine of this artisan producer, which makes stylish, fragrant wines with lots of big fruit. The viscous "Sorì Baudana" Dolcetto d'Alba is a great buy. Overall, an excellent find and prices are terrific.

Bava PIEMONTE

Strada Monferrato 2, 14023 Cocconato d'Asti (AT)
Tel.: 0141907083/Fax: 0141907085/www.bava.com
DOC(G)s: Barolo; Barbera d'Asti; Gavi; Monferrato;
Moscato d'Asti

A large Piedmontese winery with a diverse production
that includes Asti, Gavi di Gavi, and Barolo. Barbera is a
specialty, with the inky "Stradivario" getting the most
attention ("Arbest" is also good, and cheaper). The Barolo
is tannic, earthy, and dry, in the classic "traditional" style.

BEA, PAOLO UMBRIA

Località Cerrete 8, 06036 Montefalco (PG)
Tel.: 0742378128/Fax: 0742371070
DOC(G)s: Montefalco

An artisan producer who makes both Montefalco Rosso
and Sagrantino di Montefalco in a deeply concentrated yet
extremely rustic style. Bea brings out the animal funk in
the sagrantino grape, whether in his inky, super-spicy
Sagrantino or in the velvet-textured Montefalco Rosso
Riserva, nearly as rich as the Sagrantino but incorporating
both sangiovese and montepulciano. Intense, very earthy
reds that capture the brackish intensity of sagrantino.

★ Begali, Lorenzo VENETO

Via Cengia 10, 37020 San Pietro in Cariano (VR)
Tel.: 0457725148/Fax: 0457725148
DOC(G)s: Valpolicella; Amarone della Valpolicella; Recioto
della Valpolicella

Deep, round, well-balanced Amarone (the base wine is
great, so don't worry if you can't afford the single-vineyard
"Ca' Bianca"). Begali's sweet Recioto is also a great
example of how a wine can have both intensity and
finesse. Also notable is an elegant, Bordeaux-inspired red
called "Tigiolo," which combines classic Valpolicella-area
grapes with cabernet and merlot.

Bel Colle PIEMONTE

Frazione Castagni 56, 12060 Verduno (CN)
Tel.: 0172470196/Fax: 0172470196
DOC(G)s: Barolo; Barbaresco; Barbera d'Alba; Dolcetto
d'Alba; Verduno Pelaverga

Barolo "Monvigliero" and Barbaresco "Roncaglie" are
traditionally styled, with lots of leathery, earthy notes. The
base-level Barolo is an affordable place to start if trying
Barolo for the first time.

Belguardo

See Tenuta Belguardo.

BELLAVISTA LOMBARDIA

Via Bellavista 5, 25030 Erbusco (BS)
Tel.: 0307762000
DOC(G)s: Franciacorta; Terre di Franciacorta

A beautiful winery specializing in superbly crafted *Champenoise* sparklers. Along with Ca' del Bosco, this estate
established the Franciacorta region as a serious player in
sparkling wine. "Gran Cuvée Brut" and the finely tuned
"Gran Cuvée Rosé" compare favorably with Champagnes.
Also try the "Convento dell'Annunciata" Chardonnay.

Bellenda VENETO

Via Giardino 90, 31010 Carpesica di Vittorio Veneto (TV)
Tel.: 0438920025/Fax: 0438920015

DOC(G)s: Prosecco di Conegliano-Valdobbiadene; Colli
Trevigiani
  A top maker of prosecco; a great party wine.

Beltrame

See Tenuta Beltrame.

Benanti SICILIA

Via Garibaldi 474, 95029 Viagrande (CT)
Tel.: 0957893438/Fax: 0957893436
www.vinicolabenanti.it

DOC(G)s: Etna
  Benanti has long been at the forefront of winemaking on
Mount Etna. "Pietramarina" is a light, flinty white from
carricante. The reds remain rustic and traditional.
"Rovittello" Etna Rosso is an earthy, spicy example.

Benincasa, Eredi UMBRIA

Località Capro 99, 06031 Bevagna (PG)
Tel.: 0742361307

DOC(G)s: Colli Martani, Montefalco Rosso, Sagrantino di
Montefalco
  A more classic, earthy-spicy take on Sagrantino di
Montefalco. More supple and modern in style is the "La
Fornace" (barbera-merlot-sagrantino).

Bera, F.lli PIEMONTE

Via Castellero 12, 12050 Neviglie (CN)
Tel.: 0173630194/Fax: 0173630394/www.bera.it

DOC(G)s: Asti; Barbera d'Alba, Langhe; Moscato d'Asti
  Among the best small-scale producers of Asti Spumante
and Moscato d'Asti. Also some seriously extracted reds,
including a juicy barbera and a monster Langhe Rosso
called "Sassisto" (barbera-nebbiolo-merlot). A great find.

Berlucchi, F.lli LOMBARDIA

Via Broletto 2, 25040 Corte Franca (BS)
Tel.: 030984451/www.berlucchifranciacorta.com

DOC(G)s: Franciacorta; Terre di Franciacorta
  One of two Berlucchis in Franciacorta; this one offers a
classy, often vintage-dated lineup of structured sparklers:
a basic nonvintage Brut, a Satén (made from all white
grapes in a *crémant* style), and a rosé.

Berlucchi, Guido & Co. LOMBARDIA

Piazza Duranti 4, 25040 Corte Franca (BS)
Tel.: 030984381/Fax: 030984293/www.berlucchi.it

DOC(G)s: Franciacorta; Terre di Franciacorta
  Back in the sixties, it was enologist Franco Ziliani, while
working for the Berlucchi estate (one of maybe five
commercial wineries in the zone at the time), who began
to craft Champagne-style sparklers from Berlucchi's pinot
noir grapes. Today, the Berlucchi wines remain Franciacorta staples, particularly the "Cuvée Imperiale Brut."

Bersano PIEMONTE

Piazza Dante 21, 14049 Nizza Monferrato (AT)
Tel.: 0141721273/Fax: 0141701706/www.bersano.it

DOC(G)s: Barbera d'Asti; Barolo; Barbaresco; Brachetto
d'Acqui; Gavi; Monferrato

A historic winery with a huge portfolio headlined by two big barberas: "Generala" and "Cremosina." The barbera-cabernet blend "Pomona" also gets high marks. Bersano is one of the classic Barolo houses—wines from the fifties and sixties are still found in the market—and produces a cru from the Badarina vineyard in Serralunga.

BERTANI VENETO

Località Novare, 37020 Arbizzano di Negrar (VR)
Tel.: 0456011211/Fax: 0456011222/www.bertani.net
DOC(G)s: Bardolino; Valpolicella; Amarone della Valpolicella; Lugana; Soave

Founded in 1857, Bertani is one of Italy's oldest wineries and was a pioneering producer of Amarone. Bertani Amarone is classically styled, aged in large casks for long periods (up to 10 years) before its release, resulting in a spicier wine with moderated sweetness and notes of dried fruits. Another classic is the Valpolicella Valpantena "Secco Bertani," a silky, fragrant, value-priced wine in the *ripasso* style. Bertani's Villa Novare estate produces more "international" wines, including the succulent "Ognisanti" Valpolicella and "Villa Novare" Cabernet Sauvignon.

Bertelli PIEMONTE

Frazione San Carlo 38, 14100 Costigliole d'Asti (AT)
Tel.: 0141966137
DOC(G)s: Barbera d'Asti; Monferrato
Earthy, spicy barberas and a smoky syrah-based red (yes, syrah in Piedmont) called "St. Marsan."

★ Berti, Stefano EMILIA-ROMAGNA

Località Ravaldino in Monte, Via La Scagna 18, 47100 Forlì (FO)
Tel.: 0543488074
DOC(G)s: Sangiovese di Romagna
Part of a new wave of producers in Romagna making sangiovese in a highly extracted, oak-influenced style. "Calisto" is superpowered sangiovese that needs some beef to tame it.

Bianchi, Giuseppe PIEMONTE

Via Roma 37, 28070 Sizzano (NO)
Tel.: 0321810004/Fax: 0321820382
www.bianchibiowine.it
DOC(G)s: Gattinara; Ghemme; others
If you see this organic winery's "Vigneto Valferana" Gattinara, buy it: it's a fantastic value. It's a smoky, complex, prettily perfumed nebbiolo to serve with mushroom- or truffle-dressed pastas.

Bianchi, Maria Donata LIGURIA

Via delle Torri, 16, 18010 Diano Castello (IM)
Tel.: 0183498233
DOC(G)s: Riviera Ligure di Ponente
Citrusy, herbaceous vermentino and pigato.

Bigi UMBRIA

Località Ponte Giulio 3, 05018 Orvieto (TR)
Tel.: 0763316291
DOC(G)s: Orvieto; Est! Est!! Est!!! di Montefiascone; Vino Nobile di Montepulciano

This historic property is one of Orvieto's staples. Orvieto Classico (especially the citrusy "Torricella") is the key wine. Good by-the-case white.

Bindella TOSCANA

Via delle Tre Berte 10/a, 53045 Acquaviva di Montepulciano (SI)

Tel.: 0578767777/Fax: 0578767255

DOC(G)s: Vino Nobile di Montepulciano; Rosso di Montepulciano

Swiss-born Rudolph Bindella acquired this small estate in 1984. He produces two wines: a perfumed, traditionally styled Vino Nobile and the super-Tuscan "Vallocaia," which combines sangiovese with a touch of cabernet.

BIONDI-SANTI (IL GREPPO) TOSCANA

Via dei Pieri 1, 53024 Montalcino (SI)

Tel.: 0577847121/Fax: 0577847131/www.biondisanti.it

DOC(G)s: Brunello di Montalcino

A legend. The birthplace of the "brunello" clone of sangiovese and of Brunello di Montalcino wine. Biondi-Santi's cellars contain vintages dating back to the late 1800s, and in tasting recent releases it's clear the house style hasn't changed much over time: this is austere Brunello built for long aging. Aside from the classic "Tenuta Il Greppo" Montalcino estate (hugely popular with visitors), the Biondi-Santi holdings include Villa Poggio Salvi, also in Montalcino (a maker of good Brunello) and the Castello di Montepò (silky sangiovese "Sassoalloro" and a potent sangiovese-cabernet blend, "Schidione").

Bisci MARCHE

Via Fogliano 120, 62024 Matelica (MC)

Tel.: 0737787490

DOC(G)s: Verdicchio di Matelica

Located in the foothills of the part of the Apennines that separates the Marche and Umbria. Steely, minerally whites from verdicchio, most notably "Vigneto Fogliano," a great choice for shellfish.

Bisol Desiderio & Figli VENETO

Via Fol 33, 31040 Santo Stefano di Valdobbiadene (TV)

Tel.: 0423900138/Fax: 0423900577/www.bisol.it

DOC(G)s: Prosecco di Valdobbiadene; Talento Brut

Well-structured Prosecco di Valdobbiadene that's a cut above most. The best buy is the "Crede."

Bisson, Enoteca LIGURIA

Corso Gianelli, 28, 16043 Chiavari (GE)

Tel.: 0185314462/www.bissonvini.it

DOC(G)s: Golfo del Tigullio

Piero Lugano started as a wine merchant but now divides his time between his shop and his winery, where he crafts pungent coastal whites from vermentino and pigato. Try the "Vigna Erta" Vermentino or the excellent rosé (made from ciliegiolo) the next time *zuppa di pesce* (fish soup) is on the menu. There's also a piquant red "Il Musaico," from ormeasco (dolcetto).

★ Boasso PIEMONTE

Via Gabutti 3/A, 12050 Serralunga d'Alba (CN)
Tel./Fax: 0173613165
DOC(G)s: Barolo; Dolcetto d'Alba

No barrique-aging for Boasso's excellent Barolos, though the wines don't lack for power. His wines include a bottling from the Gabutti vineyard in Serralunga and a multivineyard wine called "Serralunga." Great old-school Barolo aromatics—tar, roses, leather, dried cherry—will keep you swirling and sniffing. Best with some age.

★ Boccadigabbia MARCHE

Contrada Castelletta 56, 62012 Civitanova Marche (MC)
Tel.: 073370728/www.boccadigabbia.com
DOC(G)s: Rosso Piceno

Headquartered on the southern Marche coast and specializing in chunky, softly contoured reds like "Akronte" (cabernet sauvignon). The Rosso Piceno DOC wine is a good value.

Bocchino, Eugenio PIEMONTE

Località Serre 2, 12051 Alba (CN)
Tel.: 0173364226
DOC(G)s: Barbera d'Alba; Langhe; Nebbiolo d'Alba

Big-impact Langhe Rosso blend of nebbiolo and barbera called "Suo di Giacomo." Also good varietal wines from barbera and nebbiolo.

Boffa, Alfiero PIEMONTE

Via Leiso 50, 14050 San Marzano Oliveto (AT)
Tel.: 0141856115/www.alfieroboffa.com
DOC(G)s: Barbera d'Asti

Old-vine barbera from a variety of choice sites, including "La Riva," "Cua Longa," and "Vigna delle More."

★ Boglietti, Enzo PIEMONTE

Via Roma 37, 12060 La Morra (CN)
Tel.: 0173503330/Fax: 017350330
DOC(G)s: Barolo; Barbera d'Alba; Dolcetto d'Alba; Langhe

Since Enzo Boglietti took over his family estate in the early 1990s, he's found that middle ground between traditional and modern, using oak judiciously in Barolos that are plush, berried, and fairly accessible on release. His wines hail from prime vineyard sites in La Morra: Brunate, Case Nere, and Fossati.

Bogoni VENETO

Quartiere Aldo Moro 1, 37032 Monteforte d'Alpone (VR)
Tel.: 0456100385
DOC(G)s: Soave; Recioto di Soave

Fruity, fairly weighty Soave at a great price.

Bolla VENETO

Piazza Cittadella 3, 37122 Verona (VR)
Tel.: 0458670911/Fax: 0458670912/www.bolla.com
DOC(G)s: Bardolino; Soave; Valpolicella; Amarone della Valpolicella

Founded in 1883, this Veronese giant became one of the largest-selling Italian brands in the United States (it's now owned by Brown-Forman of Louisville, Kentucky). Bolla was the first producer to label and market an Amarone wine (in 1950), and continues to make very good (if not trendy) Amarone. The overall product line varies from supermarket-scale varietal wines and cheap classics like Bardolino to more serious (and pretty good) wines like the Soave "Tufaie" and a cabernet-corvina blend called "Creso," which has genuine depth.

Bologna, Giacomo
See Braida.

Bolognani, Nilo TRENTINO
Via Stazione 19, 38015 Lavis (TN)
Tel.: 0461246354
DOC(G)s: Trentino
One of the better-regarded red wine producers in Trentino, with a typically savory, smoky teroldego as well as a Bordeaux-style blend called "Gabàn." Good varietal whites from the fragrant müller-thurgau and the flinty nosiola grapes.

Bonci MARCHE
Via Torre 13, 60034 Cupramontana (AN)
Tel.: 0731789129/Fax: 0731789808
DOC(G)s: Verdicchio dei Castelli di Jesi
Clean, weighty, and brightly aromatic Verdicchio dei Castelli di Jesi, especially the "San Michele."

Bonfiglio EMILIA-ROMAGNA
Via Cassola 21, 40050 Monteveglio (BO)
Tel.: 051830758
DOC(G)s: Colli Bolognesi
The hills southeast of Bologna have become known for cabernet sauvignon, and this producer makes a nice, well-priced example with flavors that lean more toward Bordeaux than California.

Bongiovanni
See Cascina Bongiovanni.

Borgo Conventi FRIULI-VENEZIN GIULIA
Strada Colombara 13, 34070 Farra d'Isonzo (GO)
Tel.: 0481888004/www.borgoconventi.it
DOC(G)s: Collio; Friuli Isonzo
A Friulian lineup of fresh but substantial varietal whites, including tocai, sauvignon, chardonnay, riesling, and traminer. There's also a rich and meaty Bordeaux-style red blend called "Braida Nuova."

Borgo del Tiglio FRIULI–VENEZIA GIULIA
Via San Giorgio 71, 34070 Brazzano di Cormons (GO)
Tel.: 048162166/Fax: 0481630845
DOC(G)s: Collio
A rich, exotically aromatic tocai headlines a stylish lineup of mostly white wines, all of which can handle a few years' aging (atypical for Italian whites). The super-white "Studio di Bianco" uses both sauvignon and riesling, and the varietal wines have power and precise aromatics. Great malvasia also.

Borgo Magredo FRIULI–VENEZIA GIULIA
Via Bassaldella 5, 33090 Tauriano di Spilimbergo (PN)
Tel.: 042751444/Fax: 042750840/www.borgomagredo.it
DOC(G)s: Friuli Grave
A solid and inexpensive range of varietal wines. Good pinot grigio or chardonnay for a party.

Borgo Salcetino TOSCANA

Località Lucarelli, 53017 Radda in Chianti (SI)
Tel.: 0577733541

DOC(G)s: Chianti Classico

The basic Chianti Classico has serious depth for a wine of its price, while the *riserva* "Lucarello" is built to compete with the inky giants so common now in the Classico. "Rossole" is a sangiovese-merlot with over-the-top concentration.

Borgo San Daniele FRIULI–VENEZIA GIULIA

Via San Daniele 16, 34071 Cormons (GO)
Tel.: 048160552

DOC(G)s: Friuli Isonzo

A boutique estate in the Isonzo zone making powerful, extracted wines. The oily and exotic tocai friulano is a highlight, as is the viscous "Arbis Blanc," a mix of tocai, pinot bianco, chardonnay, and sauvignon. "Arbis Rosso" (pignolo–cabernet–cabernet franc) is one of the more luxurious Friulian reds to be found—if you can find it.

Borgo Scopeto TOSCANA

Frazione Vagliagli, 53010 Castelnuovo Berardenga (SI)
Tel.: 0577848390

DOC(G)s: Chianti Classico

Great value in Chianti Classico. Good depth and aromatics, particularly in the *riserva*.

Borgogno, Giacomo & Figli PIEMONTE

Via Gioberti 1, 12060 Barolo (CN)
Tel.: 017356108/Fax: 017356344

DOC(G)s: Barolo; Barbera d'Alba; Dolcetto d'Alba

Founded in the 1700s, this is one of Barolo's standard-bearers and one of its larger landowners. The supertraditional Barolos (lots of acid and barnyard funk) are blended from a variety of vineyard sites. Borgogno has a veritable bottled history of Barolo, having preserved stocks of vintages such as 1952, '64, and '67—which you can actually find in the U.S. market.

Borgogno, Lodovico PIEMONTE

Via Alba 73, 12060 Barolo (CN)
Tel./Fax: 017356120/www.virnabarolo.it

The name "Virna"—that of Lodovico Borgogno's daughter, the winery's enologist—is scrawled on these bottles. "Preda-Sarmassa" (from two crus in Barolo) and "Cannubi Boschis" Barolos see some time in new French *tonneaux*, but the oak influence is moderate; the wines have earthy, leathery tones and are priced well.

Bortoluzzi FRIULI–VENEZIA GIULIA

Via Roma 43, 34072 Gradisca d'Isonzo (GO)
Tel.: 048192250/Fax: 0481954364

DOC(G)s: Collio; Friuli Isonzo

Clean, correct, substantial varietals. The blend "Gemina" (pinot grigio–sauvignon–chardonnay–pinot bianco) has nice complexity for under $20.

Boscaini VENETO

Via Ca' de Loi 2, 37020 Marano di Valpolicella (VR)
Tel.: 0456832500

DOC(G)s: Soave; Valpolicella; Amarone della Valpolicella

Valpolicella "San Ciriaco" and *ripasso*-style "Santo

Stefano" are both solid. The Amarone "Ca' de Loi" is the top bottling, but "Marano" is also nice; both are aromatic, lighter-styled Amarones that can work on a table with food.

BOSCARELLI TOSCANA

Via di Montenero 28, 53045 Montepulciano (SI)
Tel.: 0578767277/Fax: 0578766882
www.poderiboscarelli.com
DOC(G)s: Vino Nobile di Montepulciano

The De Ferrari family quietly turn out some of Montepulciano's noblest wines. They don't make showy wines for the critics, but theirs are some of the most evocative sangioveses to be found. The Vino Nobile "Vigna del Nocio" is potent yet balanced and beautifully aromatic —a rare exercise in restraint in an extract-crazy world. The basic Vino Nobile is a consistent value: a gamy, *frutti di bosco*-scented red with good acid.

Botromagno PUGLIA

Via F.lli Cervi 12, 70024 Gravina di Puglia (BA)
Tel.: 0803265865/Fax: 0803269026/www.botromagano.it
DOC(G)s: Gravina

Perhaps the only Gravina Bianco you'll ever see in the United States. A clean, simple, and cheap blend of greco and malvasia that's perfect for whole grilled fish.

Bottega Vinaia

See Cavit.

Botter VENETO

Via Cadorna 17, Fossalta di Piave (VE)
Tel.: 042167194/www.botter.it
DOC(G)s: Prosecco di Valdobbiadene

A nice little prosecco producer. Great for Bellinis.

BOVIO, GIANFRANCO PIEMONTE

Frazione Annunziata 63, 12064 La Morra (CN)
Tel.: 017350667/Fax: 017350667
DOC(G)s: Barolo; Barbera d'Alba; Dolcetto d'Alba; Langhe

Although Gianfranco Bovio made his reputation as a restaurateur (Belvedere is still a prime destination), he has been making great Barolo since 1978. There seems to have been a shift to a plusher, more oak-kissed style in recent years, but in general Bovio Barolos are thought of as more traditional, long-aging wines. They come from the La Morra crus of Arborina (more berried and aromatic) and Gattera (more leathery and spicy). Look also for the barberas "Il Ciotto" and "Parussi."

BRAIDA DI GIACOMO BOLOGNA PIEMONTE

Via Roma 94, 14030 Rocchetta Tanaro (AT)
Tel.: 0141644113/Fax: 0141644584/www.braida.it
DOC(G)s: Barbera d'Asti; Brachetto d'Acqui; Dolcetto d'Alba; Langhe; Moscato d'Asti; Monferrato

Based in Rocchetta Tanaro, an area not known for nebbiolo, the late Giacomo Bologna instead focused on making great wines from barbera. Bologna showed how noble barbera could be when it was planted in choice sites and aged in small oak barrels to compensate for its lack of tannins. He launched single-vineyard barberas in the 1980s that continue to set the standard: "Bricco dell'Uccellone" (generous yet powerful), "Bricco della

Bigotta" (more spicy/savory/structured due to longer wood aging), and "Ai Suma" (softest and fruitiest due to shortest aging). There's also great Moscato d'Asti and Monferrato Rosso "Il Baciale," a silky blend of barbera and pinot nero. The Bologna family is also one of three partners in Serra dei Fiori, a vineyard in nearby Trezzo Tinella from which they produce a nice dolcetto and a terrific (and cheap) white blend called "Il Fiore" (chardonnay-riesling).

Brero, Alessandro PIEMONTE

Via Carlo Alberto 19, 12060 Verduno (CN)
Tel./Fax: 0172470179

DOC(G)s: Barolo; Barbera d'Alba; Dolcetto d'Alba; Verduno Pelaverga

Another great-value Barolo producer in Verduno. "Poderi Roset" Barolo has a nice balance of up-front fruit and darker, smokier, coffee-ground tones. Good wines across the board, including the muscular Barbera d'Alba "Poderi Roset" and the rare, tangy Verduno Pelaverga.

Brezza, Giacomo & Figli PIEMONTE

Via Lomondo 4, 12060 Barolo (CN)
Tel.: 0173560921/www.brezza.it

DOC(G)s: Barbera d'Alba; Barolo; Dolcetto d'Alba; others

This winery provides the full-service Barolo experience, from good wines to a restaurant and hotel for when you're done tasting. The fourth generation of Brezzas now oversees production of several cru Barolos (Catellero, Cannubi, and Sarmassa, all in the commune of Barolo). The style is hard-edged and spicy. Other wines include barbera, dolcetto, and Langhe chardonnay.

Bricco Mondalino PIEMONTE

Regione Mondalino 5, 15049 Vignale Monferrato (AL)
Tel.: 0142933204

DOC(G)s: Barbera d'Asti; Barbera del Monferrato

A small winery specializing in ripe and rich barberas. The biggest wine is the barrique-aged "Il Bergantino," but the basic Barbera del Monferrato is good, too.

BRICCO ROCCHE (BRICCO ASILI) PIEMONTE

Via Monforte 63, 12060 Castiglione Falletto (CN)
Tel.: 0173282582/www.ceretto.com

DOC(G)s: Barolo; Barbaresco

The Ceretto family makes Barolos and Barbarescos that are branded with the names of their most prized vineyard sites, each of which includes a winery. Bricco Rocche is the Barolo property, which produces three crus: the supercharged "Bricco Rocche," the round and leathery "Brunate," and the more austere "Prapò." At Bricco Asili, there are also three crus: the formidable (and expensive) "Bricco Asili" and the more delicate "Fasét" and "Bernardot" bottlings. All of the Ceretto wines tend to be tough and tannic in their youth. For a drink-now style, try the well-priced "Zonchera" Barolo and "Asij" Barbaresco (also see the listing for Ceretto).

Brigaldara VENETO

Via Brigaldara 20, 37029 San Pietro in Cariano (VR)
Tel.: 0457701055

DOC(G)s: Valpolicella; Amarone della Valpolicella; Recioto della Valpolicella

A gem of a winery. Check out the smooth and savory Amarone and the surprisingly rich Valpolicella.

Brigl, Josef ALTO ADIGE

Località Cornaiano Girlan, Via San Floriano 8, 39050 Appiano/Eppan (BZ)
Tel.: 0471662419/www.brigl.com
DOC(G)s: Alto Adige

Like many Alto Adige estates, Brigl makes three distinct "lines" of wine: a basic set of varietal wines ("Classic Line"), a second tier of wines from estate vineyards ("Estate Line"), and a high-end range ("Superior Line"). The top range carries the "Briglhof" designation and includes cabernet, lagrein, and chardonnay.

Broglia PIEMONTE

Località Lomellina 14, 15066 Gavi (AL)
Tel.: 0143642998/Fax: 0143645699
DOC(G)s: Gavi; Monferrato Rosso

Some of the better, more fruit-driven Gavi around. The "Bruno Broglia" bulks up the traditionally lean frame of Gavi by adding a percentage of barrel-fermented cortese, but "La Meirana" is the better buy. Also try the Monferrato Rosso (barbera-cabernet-merlot).

Brolio

See Barone Ricasoli.

Brovia PIEMONTE

Via Alba-Barola 54, 12060 Castiglione Falletto (CN)
Tel.: 017362852/Fax: 0173462049/www.brovia.net
DOC(G)s: Barolo; Barbera d'Alba; Dolcetto d'Alba; Roero

Pretty Piedmontese wines at palatable prices. Brovia's style emphasizes finesse and balance, whether it's Roero Arneis (flinty and floral), Barbera d'Alba "Sorì del Drago" (clean and fruity), or one of several Barolo/Barbaresco wines. There are muscular Barolos from the Rocche and Villero crus in Castiglione as well as Ca' Mia in Serralunga (the Rocche drinks great young), as well as a spicy Barbaresco from the Rio Sordo vineyard.

Brunelli, Gianni TOSCANA

Località Le Chiuse di Sotto, 53024 Montalcino (SI)
Tel.: 0577849342
DOC(G)s: Brunello di Montalcino

Gianni Brunelli is a chef/restaurateur in Siena, but he also makes wines at his small property in Montalcino. His Brunello is aromatic, intense, and slightly rustic; it's aged only in large casks for a more moderated, traditional feel.

Brunelli, Luigi VENETO

Via Cariano 10, 37029 San Pietro in Carano (VR)
Tel.: 0457701118/Fax: 0457702015
www.brunelliwine.com
DOC(G)s: Amarone della Valpolicella; Recioto della Valpolicella

Amarone in a decadent extracted style. The reserve "Campo dei Titari" is over the top—an Amarone for a stinky cheese course. Valpolicella "Pa Riondo" is also appealing, as is the white *passito* "Re Sol."

Brunori MARCHE

Viale della Vittoria 103, 60035 Jesi (AN)
Tel.: 0731207213
DOC(G)s: Verdicchio dei Castelli di Jesi; Rosso Piceno; Rosso Cònero

Fragrant whites from Verdicchio are a highlight.

Bucci MARCHE

Via Cona 30, 60010 Ostra Vetere (AN)
Tel.: 071964179/Fax: 071964179/www.villabucci.com
DOC(G)s: Verdicchio dei Castelli di Jesi

One of the best in the Jesi DOC, with a range of tightly structured verdicchios that emphasize elegance and bright aromatics. The "Villa Bucci" Riserva is a rare example of a verdicchio that ages well, holding on to its freshness for many years in the bottle.

Bucciarelli, Massimo TOSCANA ▬●

Località La Piazza, 53011 Castellina in Chianti (SI)
Tel.: 0577749756
DOC(G)s: Chianti Classico

Old-school Chianti, in a good way: lots of woodsy scents over black cherry fruit. No oak or heavy extract, but bright acid and smoky aromatics instead.

Buiatti, Livio e Claudio FRIULI–VENEZIA GIULIA

Via Lippe 25, 33042 Buttrio (UD)
Tel.: 0432674317/www.buiattivini.it
DOC(G)s: Colli Orientali del Friuli

Solid, inexpensive Friulian varietals, including pinot grigio, pinot bianco, tocai, and refosco. The whites are clean and correct, good for parties. The reds are light, spicy, more classic northeastern styles.

Burlotto, G. B. PIEMONTE

Via Vittorio Emanuele 28, 12060 Verduno (CN)
Tel.: 0172470122/Fax: 0172470322
DOC(G)s: Barolo; Barbera d'Alba

Great-value wines from the commune of Verduno in the Barolo zone, headlined by the Barolo "Monvigliero." The "Cannubi" (from the famed site in Barolo proper) is also deep yet drinkable on release, though you could certainly hold it. Solid and consistent wines from top to bottom.

Bussi-Mauro PIEMONTE

Via Roma 7, 12050 Treiso (CN)
Tel./Fax: 0173638305
DOC(G)s: Barbaresco; Barbera d'Alba; Dolcetto d'Alba

Lesser-known estate making barrique-aged dolcetto, barbera, and Barbaresco. The wines are ripe and round, fairly accessible when young, and although they'd qualify as "modern," the influence of oak is not overbearing.

Bussia Soprana PIEMONTE

Località Bussia 81, 12065 Monforte d'Alba (CN)
Tel./Fax: 039305182
DOC(G)s: Barolo; Barbera d'Alba

Named for one of the top vineyards in Monforte d'Alba. Single-vineyard wines include bottlings from the Colonello and Mosconi crus. They sinewy and finely tuned, with lots of penetrating aromas; give them time to show their best.

Busso, Piero PIEMONTE

Via Albesani 9, 12057 Neive (CN)

Tel./Fax: 017367156

DOC(G)s: Barbaresco; Barbera d'Alba; Dolcetto d'Alba; Langhe

Busso's "Vigna Borgese" Barbaresco is sourced from the Gallina and Santo Stefano crus in Neive and is aged only in large Slavonian casks, so the oak influence is very moderate; it typically shows good ripeness and depth and pure nebbiolo aromatics, a nice mix of traditional and modern. The Barbera "Vigna Majano" is a dense, barrique-aged beauty, in accordance with current fashion.

★ Bussola, Tommaso VENETO

Via Molino Turri 30, 37024 Negrar (VR)

Tel.: 0457501740

DOC(G)s: Valpolicella; Amarone della Valpolicella; Recioto della Valpolicella

A boutique producer of Valpolicella in a supercharged modern style. Bussola's "BG" line is more affordably priced, while the "TB" is a little higher-end; both lines offer luscious takes on Valpolicella, Amarone, and Recioto. The "TB Vigneto Alto" Amarone is one of the most highly sought-after Amarone wines on the market.

Ca' Bianca PIEMONTE

Regione Spagna 58, 15010 Alice Bel Colle (AL)

Tel.: 0144745420

DOC(G)s: Barolo; Barbera d'Asti; Dolcetto d'Acqui; Gavi; Moscato d'Asti

Piedmontese staples at reasonable prices. The Barolo, Barbaresco, and Gavi are all solid, traditional examples of their styles, and the flashy Barbera d'Asti "Chersi" has gotten lots of critical attention.

Ca' Bolani

See Zonin.

Ca' dei Frati LOMBARDIA

Via Frati 22, 25010 Sirmione (BS)

Tel.: 030919468/www.cadeifrati.it

DOC(G)s: Lugana

The fragant and fine Lugana "I Frati" is a terrific buy, vintage to vintage. The barrel-fermented "Brolletino" is richer but ultimately less appealing. The fat and fruity "Pratto" combines trebbiano di Lugana with chardonnay and sauvignon. Also a good spicy rosé (*chiaretto*) from an interesting blend of local grapes.

Ca' del Baio PIEMONTE

Via Ferrere 33, 12050 Treiso (CN)

Tel.: 0173638219/www.cadelbaio.com

DOC(G)s: Barbaresco; Barbera d'Alba; Langhe

Two plush, easy-drinking Barbarescos from the Asili cru: one is the earthier "Slavonia" (so named because it is aged in larger Slavonian oak); the other is a fruitier, more modern one named "Barrique." The varietal reds from nebbiolo and barbera have a similarly soft edge.

CA' DEL BOSCO LOMBARDIA

Via Case Sparse 20, 25030 Erbusco (BS)
Tel.: 0307766111/Fax: 0307268425
www.cadelbosco.com
DOC(G)s: Franciacorta; Terre di Franciacorta

The premier name in Franciacorta and one of the most
high-tech wineries in Italy. Maurizio Zanella's sparklers are
some of Italy's best answers to Champagne, from nonvintage Brut to the potent vintage cuvée "Annamaria
Clementi." Like all Franciacorta sparklers, Ca' del Bosco's
are made in the Champagne method and are based on
chardonnay grapes, although most include pinot noir and
pinot bianco as well. There's also an opulent chardonnay
and one of the better Italian pinot noirs ("Pinèro"), as well
as the savory Bordeaux blend "Maurizio Zanella." More
recent is "Carmenero," a deep and powerful red that
captures the menthol/camphor "greenness" of the rare
carmènere grape, and two terrific value wines: the bright
and creamy "Curtefranca Bianco" (chardonnay–pinot
bianco) and the smooth "Curtefranca Rosso" (cabernet-
merlot-nebbiolo-barbera).

Ca' del Tondo TOSCANA

Casanuova Paiolo, 53013 Gaiole in Chianti (SI)
Tel.: 3356074261/Fax: 0577744024
DOC(G)s: Chianti Classico

A tiny organic winery in Gaiole whose first commercial
vintage was 2000. Rising star Stefano Chioccioli consults.
Chianti Classico "Risoluto" is a deep, barrique-aged style,
and the "Sassi Chiusi" IGT ups the ante with some
cabernet sauvignon and more wood.

Ca' del Vispo TOSCANA

Via Fugnano 31, 53037 San Gimignano (SI)
Tel.: 0577943053

Based in San Gimignano, which is known for the white
vernaccia, but more focused on red wines. There's a
round and fruity merlot called "Cruter" and "Roval," a
cabernet-merlot-sangiovese blend. Not quite "super"
super-Tuscans, but priced right.

Ca' di Frara LOMBARDIA

Via Casa Ferrari 1, 27040 Mornico Losana (PV)
Tel.: 0383892299/Fax: 03838922752
DOC(G)s: Oltrepò Pavese

A leading winery in the Oltrepò Pavese. Look for the late-
harvest pinot grigio "V.T." for a supercharged take on that
variety, and for a minerally white from riesling renano. The
reds include a good, characteristically spicy bonarda, a
fragrant pinot nero, and several meaty blends.

Ca' La Bionda VENETO

Frazione Valgatara, Via Bonda 4, 37020 Marano di
Valpolicella (VR)
Tel.: 0456801198/Fax: 0456837097/www.calabionda.it
DOC(G)s: Valpolicella; Amarone della Valpolicella

An up-and-coming winery in Valpolicella with two
assertive single-vineyard Amarones, "Ravazzol" and "Le
Tordare." The base Amarone is more softly textured.

★ Ca' Marcanda TOSCANA

Località Santa Teresa 272, 57022, Castagneto Carducci (LI)
Tel.: 0565763809
DOC(G)s: Bolgheri

Angelo Gaja began planting this Bolgheri estate with cabernet sauvignon, merlot, cabernet franc, and syrah in 1996, and with the 2000 vintage he jumped into the super-Tuscan fray with several luscious reds. First came the plush "Promis" (55% merlot, 35% syrah, 10% sangiovese). He's since added "Magari" (50% merlot, 25% cabernet, 25% cabernet franc) and "Camarcanda" (50% merlot, 40% cabernet, 10% cabernet franc). As with all of his wines, Gaja's super-Tuscans are super-powerful, but also silken textured and elegantly aromatic.

Ca' Rome PIEMONTE

Via Rabajà 36, 12050 Barbaresco (CN)
Tel.: 0173635126/Fax: 0173635175/www.carome.com
DOC(G)s: Barbaresco; Barbera d'Alba; Barolo

The Marengo family's Barbarescos favor finesse and aromatics over dense extract. "Maria di Brun" (a special selection made in top years) is one to hold, while the single-vineyard "Rio Sordo" is a little more accessible when young. There are also two cru Barolos—"Rapet" and "Vigna Cerretta"—from holdings in Serralunga.

Ca' Ronesca FRIULI–VENEZIA GIULIA

Via Lonzano 27, 34070 Dolegna del Collio (GO)
Tel.: 048160034/Fax: 0481639941/www.caronesca.it
DOC(G)s: Collio; Colli Orientali del Friuli

The broad product line includes serious whites from tocai, malvasia, sauvignon, and a host of *riserva* selections, such as the red "Sariz" (pinot nero–cabernet franc–refosco) and the white "Sermar" (tocai–pinot bianco–ribolla gialla).

Ca' Rossa

See Cascina Ca'Rossa.

Ca' Rugate VENETO

Via Pergola 72, 37030 Montecchia di Crosara (VR)
Tel.: 0456175082; 0456176328/www.carugate.it
DOC(G)s: Soave; Valpolicella

Another source of serious Soave. Ca' Rugate brings out the fleshiness of garganega in a range of wines that includes the crisp and aromatic "Monte Fiorentine" and the richer, barrel-fermented "Monte Alto."

Ca' Viola PIEMONTE

Frazione San Luigi, 11, 12063 Montelupo Albese (CN)
Tel.: 017370547/Fax: 0173617935/www.caviola.com
DOC(G)s: Dolcetto d'Alba; Langhe

Beppe Caviola is a well-traveled consultant, but he also finds time to make his own wines. His style is over-the-top, exemplified by the black and viscous "Barturot" dolcetto (no wood, but plenty of power) and the chocolaty "Bric du Luv," a blend of 85% barbera and 15% pinot nero (aged more than a year in barrique). "Rangone" pinot nero is a superextracted take on that variety.

Cabreo

See Folonari, Tenute Ambrogio e Giovanni.

Cacchiano

See Castello di Cacchiano.

★ Caggiano, Antonio CAMPANIA

Contrada Sala, 83030 Taurasi (AV)
Tel.: 082774043/Fax: 082774043/www.cantinecaggiano.it
DOC(G)s: Taurasi

Antonio Caggiano only started bottling in 1990, but in a short time he's become one of the premier producers in Campania. Taurasi "Vigna Macchia dei Goti" showcases the woodsy, angular, tobacco-tinged ferocity of aglianico, while "Salae Domini" goes for more forward blackberry fruit. "FiaGre" is a round and creamy fiano-greco blend, and "Béchar" is a honeyed Fiano di Avellino.

Calatrasi SICILIA

Contrada Piano Piraino, 90040 Sancipirello (PA)
Tel.: 0918576767/Fax: 0918576041/www.calatrasi.it

The Micciché family founded this estate in 1980 and have created four brands: "Terrale" (IGT wines from Sicily and Puglia), "Terra di Ginestra" (Sicilian whites and reds), "Allora" (varietal Puglian wines, most notably negroamaro), and "D'Istinto" (the top line, with syrah being the highlight). The D'Istinto wines are produced in partnership with BRL Hardy of Australia. Calatrasi has a marketing arm in Vashon, Washington.

Calbello

See Costanti.

Calò, Michele PUGLIA

Via Masseria Vecchia 1, 73058 Tuglie (LE)
Tel./Fax: 0833596242/www.michelecalo.it
DOC(G)s: Alezio

Located in in southwest Puglia, with ancient bush vines that produce superripe fruit. Calò's warm southern reds, all based on negroamaro and malvasia nera, are headlined by the savory, concentrated "Vigna Spano."

Camigliano TOSCANA

Via d'Ingresso 2, 53024 Montalcino (SI)
Tel.: 0577816061/Fax: 0577844068 /www.camigliano.it
DOC(G)s: Brunello di Montalcino

Good Brunello and Rosso di Montalcino at very reasonable prices.

Campagnola, Giuseppe VENETO

Località Valgatara, Via Agnella 9, 37020 Marano di Valpolicella (VR)
Tel.: 0457703900/www.campagnola.com
DOC(G)s: Valpolicella; Amarone della Valpolicella; Soave

A reliable lineup that includes one of the few varietal corvina wines around: "Corte Agnela." The Amarone "Caterina Zardini" is reasonably priced and both the Valpolicella and Soave "Le Bine" wines are solid.

Campogiovanni TOSCANA

Frazione Sant'Angelo in Colle, 53020 Montalcino (SI)
Tel.: 0577864001/www.agricolasanfelice.it
DOC(G)s: Brunello di Montalcino

A Montalcino estate owned by the San Felice winery. A

legendary name with a long-lived Brunello and the exceptionally powerful *riserva* "Vigna del Quercione."

Canalicchio di Sopra TOSCANA

Località Casaccia 73, 53024 Montalcino (SI)
Tel./Fax: 0577848316/www.canalicchiodisopra.com
DOC(G)s: Brunello di Montalcino; Rosso di Montalcino
   At the turn of the century the Pacenti family were share-croppers here, and in the 1960s Primo Pacenti bought the land and began to make wine. These are powerfully structured, high-acid Brunellos aged in large casks, full of dark, smoky notes and in need of time to show their best.

Candido PUGLIA

Via A. Diaz 46, 72025 Sandonaci (BR)
Tel.: 0831635674
DOC(G)s: Salice Salentino
   Candido is a historic, relatively small Puglian winery; its wines are always ripe and ready (if a little cooked sometimes) and well priced. Try "Duca d'Aragona" (negroamaro-montepulciano). There's also "Cappello di Prete" (100% negroamaro) and the newer "Immensum" (negroamaro-cabernet). Salice Salentino DOC wine is one of the best examples of its type and a bargain.

Canevel Spumanti VENETO

Via Roccat e Ferrari, 31049 Valdobbiadene (TV)
Tel.: 0423975940/Fax: 0423975961/www.canevel.it
DOC(G)s: Prosecco di Valdobbiadene; Cartizze; Colli di Conegliano
   Bargain-priced prosecco.

Canonica a Cerreto TOSCANA

Frazione Vagliagli, 53019
Castelnuovo Berardenga (SI)
Tel.: 0577363261/www.canonicacerreto.it
DOC(G)s: Chianti Classico
   A small property in a former monastery in Castelnuovo Berardenga. The Chianti Classico has a good combination of depth and authentic sangiovese aromatics.

★ Cantalupo PIEMONTE

Via Michelangelo Buonarroti 5, 28074 Ghemme (NO)
Tel.: 0163840041
DOC(G)s: Ghemme
   Further proof that great nebbiolo isn't just from Barolo and Barbaresco. The base-level Ghemme from this estate is a terrific buy: all the leathery, smoky, cherry-scented sensations of nebbiolo are there. The single-vineyard "Collis Breclamae" is a denser, more structured wine—as impressive as many Barolos in fact—and surely benefits from at least short-term aging.

Cantele PUGLIA

Via Vincenzo Balsamo 13, 73100 Lecce (LE)
Tel.: 0832240962/Fax: 0832307018/www.cantele.it
DOC(G)s: Salice Salentino
   A large estate near Lecce that produces a variety of wines, usually at bargain prices. "Amativo" (primitivo-negroamaro) is probably the most serious of the reds.

Cantina Cooperativa di Oliena SARDEGNA

Via Nuoro 112, 08025 Oliena (NU)
Tel.: 0784297509
DOC(G)s: Cannonau di Sardegna

These are signature cannonau (also called grenache) wines, made in the Barbagia region of central Sardinia, the grape's prime territory. "Nepente di Oliena" Cannonau di Sardegna is as wild and funky as the place it comes from—a warm and tangy Mediterranean red for pizza or pasta with a spicy sauce.

Cantina dei Colli Amerini UMBRIA

Località Fornole di Amelia, 05020 Amelia (TR)
Tel.: 0744989721
DOC(G)s: Colli Amerini

A huge co-op in southern Umbria. Riccardo Cotarella consults, and the smooth and substantial red blend "Carbio" (sangiovese-ciliegiolo-montepulciano-barbera-merlot) is damn good for the money. "Torraccio" sangiovese has good weight and deep black cherry aromas.

Cantina dei Produttori Nebbiolo di Carema

See Produttori Nebbiolo di Carema.

★ Cantina del Pino PIEMONTE

Via Ovello 15, 12050 Barbaresco (CN)
Tel.: 0173635147
DOC(G)s: Barbaresco; Barbera d'Alba; Dolcetto d'Alba

A small winery run by father-son team Adriano and Renato Vacca, which began bottling in 1997. The family previously sold its grapes from the Ovello vineyard to Produttori del Barbaresco. The Vaccas' Barbaresco "Ovello" is very lush and silky, and the varietal reds from dolcetto and barbera are very balanced and stylish.

★ Cantina del Taburno CAMPANIA

Via Sala, 82030 Foglianise (BN)
Tel.: 0824871338/Fax: 0824878898

This cooperative near Benevento has climbed into Campania's elite ranks. The old-vine aglianico "Bue Apis" is as dense as motor oil, and "Delius" Aglianico del Taburno isn't far behind—serious aglianico for osso buco on a cold winter's night. The lighter "Fidelis" is a great value, and the whites are good, especially the minerally Taburno Falanghina.

Cantina di Venosa BASILICATA

Località Vignali, Via Appia, 85029 Venosa (PZ)
Tel.: 097236702/www.cantinadivenosa.it
DOC(G)s: Aglianico del Vulture

This co-op's "Carato Venusio" shows the brawny funk of Vulture wines, with a sheen of new oak on top to soften the blow. "Vignali" is a good, tobacco-tinged alternative at a lower price.

Cantina Produttori Nalles Niclara
Magrè ALTO ADIGE

Niclara Magre, Via Heiligenberg 2, 39012 Nalles/Nals (BZ)
Tel.: 0471678626
DOC(G)s: Alto Adige

Named for three towns in northern Alto Adige (most co-ops are named for the towns they're located in). We've actually seen these wines in the U.S. market. The wines from the "Baron Salvadori" line are quite good, most notably the chunky, smoky lagrein.

Cantina Produttori San Michele–Appiano/ St. Michael Eppan ALTO ADIGE

Via Circonvallazione 17/19, 39057 Appiano/Eppan (BZ)
Tel.: 0471664466/Fax: 0471660764/www.stmichael.it
DOC(G)s: Alto Adige/Südtirol

This winery was founded in 1907 and does everything well. A vast selection includes pinot bianco (try the impossibly cheap "Schulthauser"), chardonnay, and others, all of them distinctive. The "Classic" wines emphasize acidity and fruit, while the single-vineyard and "Sanct Valentin" wines ratchet up the intensity (try the minerally "Montiggl" riesling or the "Sanct Valentin" sauvignon). Sanct Valentin Pinot Nero is the star on the red side, along with a meaty lagrein.

Cantina Produttori Santa Maddalena/ St. Magdalener ALTO ADIGE

Piazza Gries 2, 39100 Bolzano (BZ)
Tel.: 0471270909/Fax: 0471289110/
www.kellereimagdalena.com
DOC(G)s: Alto Adige

Steely whites from chardonnay, sauvignon (try the "Mockhof"), and pinot bianco are complemented by reds from lagrein (especially the well-priced "Perl," which has plenty of bitter-chocolate lagrein kick), cabernet, and the schiava-based Santa Maddalena DOC. Reliable and varietally correct.

Cantina Produttori Valle Isarco ALTO ADIGE

Via Coste 50, 39043 Chiusa/Klausen (BZ)
Tel.: 0472847553/Fax: 0472847521/
www.cantinavalleisarco.it
DOC(G)s: Alto Adige

Racy, minerally whites from high-altitude vineyards. There's a veltliner (related to Austria's grüner veltliner), as well as pinot bianco, pinot grigio, and more exotically aromatic whites such as kerner, sylvaner (try the "Aristos"), and müller-thurgau.

Cantina Rotaliana TRENTINO

Corso del Popolo 6, 38017 Mezzolombardo (TN)
Tel.: 0461601010/Fax: 0461604323
www.cantinarotaliana.it
DOC(G)s: Teroldego Rotaliano; Trentino

If you like the oddly appealing sensations of the teroldego grape—huckleberry, road tar, violets—here's another good producer to try.

Cantina Sociale del Vermentino SARDEGNA

Via San Paolo 1, 07020 Monti (SS)
Tel.: 078944012/www.vermentinomonti.it
DOC(G)s: Vermentino di Gallura

Another of Sardinia's excellent co-ops, sourcing fruit from 250 growers. The specialty here is oily, herbaceous vermentino. "Funtanaliras" is a lot of wine for the money and a great wine for a *zuppa di pesce*.

Cantina Sociale della Trexenta SARDEGNA

Viale Piemonte 28, 09040 Senorbì (CA)

Tel.: 0709808863

DOC(G)s: Cannonau di Sardegna; Monica di Sardegna

A co-op founded in 1956 by 26 local farmers. Production is large and mostly middle-of-the-road, but there are some finds: Cannonau di Sardegna is a specialty (try the plush and minty "Corte Adua"), and the red blend "Tanca Su Conti," aged 18 months in barrique and 2 years in bottle before release, is noteworthy. Among whites, "Donna Eleonora" Vermentino has the most appeal, with all of the requisite herbal notes of Sardinian vermentino.

★ CANTINA SOCIALE DI SANTADI SARDEGNA

Via su Pranu, 12, 09010 Santadi (CA)

Tel.: 0781950127/www.cantinadisantadi.it

DOC(G)s: Carignano del Sulcis; Monica di Sardegna; Nuragus di Cagliari

One of southern Italy's premier wineries. Powerful reds from carignano are the specialty. "Terre Brune" Carignano del Sulcis is a perennial critics' favorite that brings to mind the inky wines of Priorato in Spain. The similarly well-structured "Rocca Rubia" Carignano del Sulcis is less expensive, and then there's "Shardana" (carignano-syrah), which can stand toe-to-toe with Aussie shiraz. The Vermentino di Sardegna "Cala Silente" is a value on the white side, adding a layer of fruity extract to the typically lean, herbal vermentino frame.

Cantina Sociale Dorgali SARDEGNA

Via Piemonte 11, 08022 Dorgali (NU)

Tel.: 078496143/www.c.s.dorgali.com

DOC(G)s: Cannonau di Sardegna

In the heart of Sardinia's Barbagia, ground zero for cannonau (also known as grenache), this co-op turns out a range of spicy, fleshy reds from that grape.

Cantina Sociale Gallura SARDEGNA

Via Val di Cossu 9, 07029 Tempio Pausania (SS)

Tel.: 079631241/www.cantinagallura.it

DOC(G)s: Vermentino di Gallura

Hefty vermentino from northern Sardinia. Three different Vermentino di Gallura wines are produced—the best is the intense, herb-laced "Canayli"—along with other specialties. The fatter, more tropically fruity "Balajana" is barrique-aged, non-DOC vermentino.

Cantina Sociale Il Nuraghe di Mogoro SARDEGNA

Strada Statale 131, Km. 62, 09095 Mogoro (OR)

Tel.: 0783990285

DOC(G)s: Nuragus di Cagliari; Monica di Sardegna; others

This co-op near Cagliari has an interesting range: from the Monica di Sardegna "San Bernardino," a light, berry-scented red that could replace Beaujolais at a picnic, to the juicy white semidano, one of the few wines made from that rare variety of grape.

Cantina Sociale Santa Maria La Palma SARDEGNA

Località Santa Maria La Palma, 07041 Alghero (SS)

Tel.: 079999008/Fax: 079999044

www.santamarialapalma.it

DOC(G)s: Cannonau di Sardegna; Vermentino di Sardegna

The herbal flavors and soft, sweet tannins of "Le Bombarde" cannonau make it a great wine for baked pastas or maybe sausages on the grill. Pinot noir–ish in scale, but with a Mediterranean feel. For white, try "Aragosta" vermentino with linguine and clams.

★ Cantina Terlano ALTO ADIGE
Via Colli d'Argento 7, 39100 Terlano/Terlan (BZ)
Tel.: 0471257135
DOC(G)s: Alto Adige
Another great Alto Adige co-op, one with a penchant for digging aged wines out of the cellar (they recently released a 1991 chardonnay that showed well). The sauvignon blanc "Quarz" is exceptional, and the gigantic "Porphyr" lagrein is one of the fullest-bodied lagreins around—a savory choice for braises or even southern barbecue.

Cantina Tollo ABRUZZO
Via Garibaldi 68, 66010 Tollo (CH)
Tel.: 087196251/Fax: 0871962122/www.cantinatollo.it
DOC(G)s: Montepulciano d'Abruzzo; Trebbiano d'Abruzzo
A large cooperative with bargain-priced wines. Our top pick is the Montepulciano d'Abruzzo "Cagiolo." Simple, fruity wines.

Cantine del Notaio BASILICATA
Via Roma 159, 85028 Rionero in Vulture (PZ)
Tel.: 0972717111
DOC(G)s: Aglianico del Vulture
The Giuratrabocchetti family always grew aglianico in northern Basilicata, but their Cantine del Notaio wines didn't debut until 1998. Hugely extracted and aged in new oak, the wines take the smoldering aglianico in a deeply fruity direction. "La Firma" is the top wine, and it is definitely big; "Il Repertorio" is a little more restrained and has more classic varietal character.

Cantine Due Palme PUGLIA
Via San Marco 130, 72020 Cellino San Marco (BR)
Tel.: 0831617865
DOC(G)s: Salice Salentino
A lot of Puglian wine is overripe and underwhelming, but this estate keeps the cooked-fruit flavors in check while delivering good concentration: try the excellent Salice Salentino "Selvarossa" or the Salento Rosso "Albrizzi" (cabernet-primitivo).

Cantine Farro CAMPANIA
Via Virgilio 30/36, 80070 Bacoli (NA)
Tel.: 0818545555/Fax: 0818545489/www.cantinefarro.it
DOC(G)s: Campi Flegrei
Tangy and refreshing falanghina from north of Naples. Good for pungent seafood like grilled sardines.

Cantine Sant'Agata PIEMONTE
Regione Mezzena 19, 14030 Scurzolengo (AT)
Tel.: 0141203186
DOC(G)s: Barbera d'Asti; Ruché di Castagnole Monferrato; Monferrato
Rich and ripe barberas that are complemented by bright, spicy, unusually aromatic reds from the ruché grape. The Monferrato Rosso "Genesi" combines barbera with ruché to tangy effect. Fruity, slightly rustic wines.

Capannelle TOSCANA

Località Capannelle, 53013 Gaiole in Chianti (SI)
Tel.: 0577749691

DOC(G)s: Chianti Classico

Deep and evocative Chianti Classico using only traditional grapes—sangiovese, colorino, canaiolo. This boutique estate was purchased by the owner of Orient Express hotels in the late nineties, but the wines still have an artisan feel: not too much oak, earthy/smoky flavors, good acidity. If you don't think Chianti can age, try some older vintages of this wine or of the super-Tuscan "Solare" (sangiovese-malvasia aged in barrique).

Caparzo

See Tenuta Caparzo.

CAPEZZANA TOSCANA ⚷

Via Capezzana 100, 59015 Carmignano
Tel.: 0558706091/Fax: 0558706673/www.capezzana.it

DOC(G)s: Carmignano

"Villa di Capezzana" Carmignano is a rich and elegant red that transcends its price category. Ditto for the fruity and fragrant Barco Reale di Carmignano. The Contini-Bonacossi family is a class act, and their winery is also famous for cooking classes at its Wine and Culinary Center. For a higher-end red, try the luscious "Ghiaie della Furba" (cabernet-merlot-syrah). For a party, the Conti Contini sangiovese is a steal at about $10.

Capichera SARDEGNA

Strada Statale Arzachena–San Antonio, Km. 6, 07021 Arzachena (SS)
Tel.: 078980800

DOC(G)s: Vermentino di Gallura; Carignano del Sulcis

Vermentino at its most intense, from old vines in the Gallura zone of northeast Sardinia. It's always been expensive—stick with basic Vermentino di Gallura and you'll be fine, although "Vendemmia Tardiva" (late-harvest, but not in a dessert style) is some potent stuff. There are also fruity reds from carignano (try "Assaje").

Cappellano PIEMONTE

Via Alba 13, 12050 Serralunga d'Alba (CN)
Tel.: 0173613103

DOC(G)s: Barolo; Barbera d'Alba; Dolcetto d'Alba; Langhe

Barolo and Barbera d'Alba "Gabutti" are the wines to look for, both of them crafted in a more earthy, high-acid "traditional" style. A historic property credited with the invention of Barolo Chinato, the bitter, aromatized *digestivo* made from a Barolo base.

CAPRAI, ARNALDO UMBRIA

Località Torre, 06036 Montefalco (PG)
Tel.: 0742378802/www.arnaldocaprai.it

DOC(G)s: Montefalco; Sagrantino di Montefalco; Colli Martani

The Caprai family invested heavily in their high-tech winery, and theirs is the highest-profile estate in the sleepy village of Montefalco. The exotic, sooty sagrantino grape is their specialty, whether it's blended with sangiovese in the Montefalco Rosso (a great everyday wine) or in the flashy Sagrantino di Montefalco. The reserve selection "25 Anni"

is one of a new generation of collectible reds from Italy; it will age for 10-plus years with ease.

Caputo CAMPANIA

Via Consortile, Zoni ASI, 81032 Carinaro (CE)
Tel.: 0815033955/www.caputo.it
DOC(G)s: Asprinio di Aversa; Sannio; Vesuvio
   A huge producer. Campanian classics such as red and white Lacryma Christi, along with varietal wines from the usual suspects: aglianico, greco di tufo, falanghina. Simple and cheap.

Carmignani, Fuso TOSCANA

Via della Tinaia 7, 55015 Montecarlo (LU)
Tel.: 058322038
DOC(G)s: Montecarlo
   Some interesting chunky reds from western Tuscany. "For Duke" is a sangiovese-syrah blend named for Duke Ellington. Montecarlo Rosso DOC "Sassonero" also includes syrah; Montecarlo Bianco "Stati d'Animo" ("Feelings") is a creamy, barrique-aged white.

Carobbio TOSCANA

Via San Martino a Cecione 26, 50020 Panzano in Chianti (FI)
Tel.: 055852136
DOC(G)s: Chianti Classico
   Panzano is known for powerful Chianti, and Carobbio's wines have that power without being overly "international." Woodsy sangiovese aromatics and silky textures abound in both the basic Chianti Classico and the *riserva*.

Carpenè Malvoti VENETO

Via A. Carpenè, 31015 Conegliano (TV)
Tel.: 0438364611/Fax: 0438364690
www.carpene-malvolti.com
DOC(G)s: Prosecco di Conegliano
   This winery is considered the birthplace of prosecco. Prosecco di Conegliano "Extra Dry" is a good house pour.

Carpineta Fontalpino TOSCANA

Frazione Monteaperti, Pod. Carpineta, 53019 Castelnuovo Berardenga (SI)
Tel.: 0577369219; 0577283228
DOC(G)s: Chianti Colli Senesi
   Gioia Cresti's small estate near Siena is a good source for Chianti Colli Senesi, always an affordable alternative to Chianti Classico with smooth, smoky sangiovese flavors. Her dense super-Tuscan "Do Ut Des" (cabernet-merlot-sangiovese) continues to grow in stature (and price).

Carpineto TOSCANA

Frazione Dudda, 50022 Greve in Chianti (FI)
Tel.: 0558549062/Fax: 0558549001/www.carpineto.com
DOC(G)s: Chianti Classico; Brunello di Montalcino; Vernaccia di San Gimignano; Vino Nobile di Montepulciano; Orvieto
   A large estate with holdings in Chianti Classico, Montepulciano, and elsewhere. Solid whites from San Gimignano and Orvieto, a good Vino Nobile, a value-priced super-Tuscan called "Dogajolo" (sangiovese-cabernet), and a line dubbed "Farnito," highlighted by a peppery cabernet sauvignon.

Casa alle Vacche TOSCANA

Località Lucignano 73/A, 53037 San Gimignano (SI)
Tel.: 0577955103
DOC(G)s: Chianti Colli Senesi; Vernaccia di San
Gimignano

This estate's "Cinabro" is a warm and well-concentrated red for around $20. "Crocus" Vernaccia di San Gimignano (like many producers' "top" wines in this area) is dosed with chardonnay and a healthy amount of oak.

Casa Emma TOSCANA

Strada Provinciale di Castellina in Chianti 3/5/7, 50021
Barberino Val d'Elsa (FI)
Tel.: 0558072859/www.casaemma.com
DOC(G)s: Chianti Classico

Not far from Isole e Olena, this small estate makes sleek, aromatic Chianti Classico. Try the *riserva* in particular. "Soloio" is a chunky merlot aged in barrique.

Casafrassi TOSCANA

Località Casafrassi, 53011 Castellina in Chianti (SI)
Tel.: 0577740621/Fax: 0577740805
DOC(G)s: Chianti Classico

The Vidali family purchased this property in 1980, first developing a country hotel then focusing on wines. The Chianti Classico is deep and smooth, while the "XXI Sec," a selection of sangiovese aged 15 months in barrique, has some sandy tannins and a plusher feel.

★ Casale del Giglio LAZIO

Strada per Isterna–Nettuno, Km. 13, 04010 Le Ferriere (LT)
Tel.: 0692902530/Fax: 0692900212

An up-and-coming estate making international varietals on a large scale. The chardonnay-viognier blend "Antinoo" is superripe and tropical. Good (and reasonably priced) reds from merlot, cabernet sauvignon, petit verdot (probably the best), and syrah (they call it shiraz). The pricier "Mater Matuta" (petit verdot–syrah) is eye-opening, considering the Lazio region's mostly sorry lineup of reds.

Casale-Falchini TOSCANA

Località Casale 40, 53037 San Gimignano (SI)
Tel./Fax: 0577941305/www.falchini.com
DOC(G)s: Vernaccia di San Gimignano; Chianti Colli Senesi

Whites here include "Vigna a Solatio," a light, crisp Vernaccia di San Gimignano, and "Abvinea Doni," pumped up (not necessarily for the better) with oak. More interesting are the reds, including "Campora" (cabernet) and "Paretaio" (sangiovese).

Casalfarneto MARCHE

Via Farneto 16, 60030 Serra de' Conti (AN)
Tel.: 0731889001/Fax: 0731889001/www.casalfarneto.it
DOC(G)s: Verdicchio dei Castelli di Jesi

A lesser-known producer of fresh and structured Verdicchio dei Castelli di Jesi. Try the "Gran Casale," a nice white that's free of the nutty, oxidative notes so common to verdicchio.

Casaloste TOSCANA

Via Montagliari 32, 50020 Panzano in Chianti (FI)
Tel.: 055852725
DOC(G)s: Chianti Classico
   Dark and spicy Chianti in the forceful Panzano style. The *riserva* can compete with wines twice its price. Try it with some lamb chops *alla griglia*.

★ Casanova di Neri TOSCANA

Frazione Torrenieri, 53024 Montalcino (SI)
Tel.: 0577834455/Fax: 0577346177
DOC(G)s: Brunello di Montalcino
   Giacomo Neri's "Tenuta Nuova" Brunello di Montalcino is a high-impact wine with silty tannins and toasty oak buttressing its great mass of fruit (it spends a total of 27 months in casks of various sizes). Even more massive is "Cerretalto," a cru wine from a southeast-facing site with 25-year-old vines (and all-barrique aging).

Casanuova delle Cerbaie TOSCANA

Podere Casanova delle Cerbaie 335, 53024 Montalcino (SI)
Tel.: 0577849284
DOC(G)s: Brunello di Montalcino
   A small, up-and-coming estate in Montalcino making serious Brunello. The style is lean, sinewy, and refined, with a whiff of vanilla from new oak.

Cascina Adelaide PIEMONTE

Via Aie Sottane 14, 12060 Barolo (CN)
Tel.: 0173560503/Fax: 0173560963
www.cascinaadelaide.com
DOC(G)s: Barbera d'Alba; Barolo; Dolcetto d'Alba; Langhe
   The Drocco family took over here in 2000 and, with the help of winemaker Sergio Molino, has made great strides in a short time. The Langhe Rosso (barbera-nebbiolo) has great aromatics and depth, the barbera and dolcetto wines are fruity and correct, and the Barolo is well balanced and softly contoured. Their first single-vineyard wine is "Cannubi."

Cascina Ballarin PIEMONTE

Frazione Annunziata 115, 12064 La Morra (CN)
Tel./Fax: 017350365/www.cascinaballarin.it
DOC(G)s: Barolo; Barbera d'Alba; Dolcetto d'Alba; Langhe
   Small but significant Barolo producer with holdings in both La Morra (Bricco Rocca) and Monforte d'Alba (Bussia). Their house style is more La Morra, however: plush and perfumy, with nice foresty notes.

Cascina Bongiovanni PIEMONTE

Via Alba-Barolo 4, 12060 Castiglione Falletto (CN)
Tel.: 0173262184
DOC(G)s: Barolo; Dolcetto d'Alba; Langhe
   Davide Mazzone's small estate is best known for the deep Barolo "Pernanno," a new-generation Barolo aged in barriques. His "straight" Barolo is a softly contoured wine that could be consumed young. He also makes good dolcetto and barbera wines. Fair prices.

Cascina Bruni PIEMONTE

Via Alba 6, 12050 Serralunga d'Alba (CN)
Tel./Fax: 0173613208/www.cascinabruni.it
DOC(G)s: Barolo
   The Veglio family makes old-fashioned Barolo
(fermentation in cement, aging in large Slavonian *botti*),
and there are four single-vineyard bottlings from the
Carpegna cru of Serralunga.

Cascina Ca' Rossa PIEMONTE

Località Case Sparse 56, 12043 Canale (CN)
Tel.: 017398348/Fax: 017398348
DOC(G)s: Barbera d'Alba; Roero
   Ca' Rossa is one of the best in Roero, with a delicious,
citrusy arneis ("Merica"); a supple and elegant nebbiolo
from a single vineyard called "Audinaggio"; a juicy
barbera ("Mulassa"); and a *frizzante* brachetto ("Birbét").

Cascina Castlèt PIEMONTE

Strada Castelletto 6, 14055 Costigliole d'Asti (AT)
Tel.: 0141966651/Fax: 0141961492
DOC(G)s: Barbera d'Asti; Barbera del Monferrato;
Monferrato; Moscato d'Asti
   Bright, light barberas with nice aromatics. Good pasta/
pizza wines. The Monferrato Rosso DOC "Policalpo" is a
more powerful blend of barbera and cabernet sauvignon.

Cascina Chicco PIEMONTE

Via Valenino 144, 12043 Canale (CN)
Tel.: 0173979069/Fax: 0173979069
www.cascinachicco.com
DOC(G)s: Barbera d'Alba; Langhe; Nebbiolo d'Alba; Roero
   Between the Roero "Valmaggiore" and the Nebbiolo
d'Alba "Mompissano" you can indulge your nebbiolo jones
without paying up for a Barolo or a Barbaresco. Barbera
"Bric Loira" is pretty luxurious as well.

Cascina Cucco PIEMONTE

Via Mazzini 10, 12050 Serralunga d'Alba (CN)
Tel.: 0173613003/www.cascinacucco.it
DOC(G)s: Barbera d'Alba; Barolo; Dolcetto d'Alba
   Consultant Beppe Caviola helps craft the wines here.
Top wines are two Barolos: "Vigna Cucco" and "Cerrati,"
both from Serralunga vineyards and both spending some
time in small French oak (the Cucco more so). Both are
sleek and modern, but with characteristic Serralunga bite.

Cascina degli Ulivi PIEMONTE

Strada Mazzola 14, 15067 Novi Ligure (AL)
Tel.: 0143744598/Fax: 01436756430
DOC(G)s: Gavi; Piemonte
   A small organic winery specializing in the cortese grape,
showcasing it in an herbal Gavi and in a more plumped-
up IGT version ("Montemarino").

Cascina Ebreo PIEMONTE

Località Ravera 3, 12060 Novello (CN)
Tel.: 0173744007/Fax: 0173744928
   "Segreto" is a blend of 85% barbera and 15% nebbiolo.
"Torbido!" is nebbiolo from Barolo, but it does not qualify
for the Barolo DOC designation because it is unfiltered
and contains too much dry extract (*torbido* means cloudy,
or murky). Decadent "super-Piedmontese" wines.

Cascina Giovinale PIEMONTE

Strada San Nicolao 102, 14049 Nizza Monferrato (AT)
Tel.: 0141793005

DOC(G)s: Barbera d'Asti; Moscato d'Asti

Nizza Monferrato is considered a prime area for great barbera, so much so that an official "Nizza" subzone was added to the Barbera d'Asti appellation. This producer is among those who use the designation, bottling several bold barberas along with the interesting "Trinum" (barbera-cabernet-dolcetto) and some bright and appealing Moscato d'Asti.

★ Cascina La Barbatella PIEMONTE

Strada Annunziata 55, 14049 Nizza Monferrato (AT)
Tel.: 0141701434

DOC(G)s: Barbera d'Asti; Monferrato Rosso

Why do some producers make "big" wine that is also elegant and focused, while others can only make wine that's big? Barbatella's enologist, Giuliano Noè, is one of the former. He shows a deft touch with the flagship "Sonvico" (named for owner Angelo Sonvico), a blend of barbera and cabernet sauvignon that is built for drinking now or in the future. Also worth trying is the white "Noé," a sauvignon-cortese blend with lots of yeasty richness from barrel fermentation.

Cascina Luisin PIEMONTE

Via Rabajà 23, 12050 Barbaresco (CN)
Tel.: 0173635154; 3286568583/Fax: 0173635154

DOC(G)s: Barbaresco; Barbera d'Alba; Dolcetto d'Alba

An excellent small producer of Barbaresco in a plush, berried style. Single-vineyard wines from Rabajà and Asili (in Barbaresco) and Sorì Paolin (near Basarin in Neive). Barbera d'Alba "Maggiur" is the more straightforward of two very good barberas; the other, "Asili," is a giant that spends nearly 2 years in barrique.

★ Cascina Morassino PIEMONTE

Via Ovello 32, 12050 Barbaresco (CN)
Tel.: 0173635149/Fax: 0173635149

DOC(G)s: Barbaresco; Barbera d'Alba; Dolcetto d'Alba; Langhe

A bargain in Barbaresco. Morassino's wine from the Ovello vineyard is drinkable young and priced right. A nebbiolo with the plush texture and bright aromatics of pinor noir, though not at all lacking in body. The Dolcetto d'Alba is dense and good.

Cascina Orsolina PIEMONTE

Via Caminata 28, 14036 Moncalvo (AT)
Tel.: 0141917277/Fax: 0141917277

DOC(G)s: Barbera d'Asti; Grignolino d'Asti; Monferrato; Piemonte

This small estate makes the inky Barbera d'Asti "Bricco dei Cappuccini" and the equally lush Monferrato Rosso "Sole" (barbera–merlot–pinot nero). Bright, fruity wines.

Cascina Roera PIEMONTE

Frazione Bionzo 32, 14055 Costigliole d'Asti (AT)
Tel.: 0141968437

DOC(G)s: Barbera d'Asti; Piemonte

A tiny upstart winery with a full yet aromatic white,

"Ciapin" (chardonnay-arneis-cortese), and a sweet and slick Barbera d'Asti called "Cardin."

Cascina Val del Prete PIEMONTE

Strada Santuario 2, 12040 Priocca (CN)
Tel.: 0173616534

DOC(G)s: Roero; Barbera d'Alba; Nebbiolo d'Alba

Another gem in the Roero DOC. The Roero Arneis "Luet," which is the top white, is partially barrel-fermented for a more luscious texture. On the red side, the Nebbiolo d'Alba "Vigna di Lino" is luscious, too (from 30-year-old vines on a south-facing vineyard). Also recommended are the Roero Rosso (nebbiolo also) and some big barberas.

Cascina Vano PIEMONTE

Via Rivetti 9, 12057 Neive (CN)
Tel.: 017367263; 0173677705

DOC(G)s: Barbaresco; Barbera d'Alba; Langhe

Vano's Barbera d'Alba "Carulot" is a great example of why people love barbera: it's a succulent, palate-coating red with chewy but soft tannins. It's a great wine to drink while you're waiting for the "Canova" Barbaresco to age. Great value from a tiny producer.

CASE BASSE DI SOLDERA TOSCANA

Località Case Basse, 53024 Montalcino (SI)
Tel.: 0233000928/Fax: 023271961/www.casebasse.it

DOC(G)s: Brunello di Montalcino

Gianfranco Soldera is an elusive figure, and his brawny Brunellos are the cult wines of Montalcino. His approach is rigorously, righteously all-natural: vineyard work is done by hand, and the wines are fermented in large oak with no temperature control and no added yeasts. Aging lasts a whopping 5 years in large Slavonian casks. Dense, earthy, evocative wines—what wine geeks call "wines of place"—are the result, and they're impenetrably tannic on release. Superexclusive and expensive.

Casisano Colombaio TOSCANA

Località Collina PD Colombaio 336, 53024 Montalcino (SI)
Tel.: 0577835540/Fax: 0577849087

DOC(G)s: Brunello di Montalcino

A good-sized (if lesser-known) Montalcino estate with Brunello in a tannic, brightly acidic style.

Casòn Hirschprunn ALTO ADIGE

Piazza Santa Geltrude 5, Magré/Margreid (BZ)
Tel.: 0471809590/Fax: 0471809591/www.lageder.com

A striking seventeenth-century estate purchased by Alois Lageder in 1991. There are four wines—two "first wines" and two "second wines," in the style of a Bordeaux château. The firsts are "Contest Bianco" (pinot grigio, chardonnay, and others, vinified as a field blend) and the lush "Casòn Rosso" (merlot-cabernet-lagrein). The seconds are "Etelle Bianco" and "Corolle Rosso" (the blends are similar, but these see less oak aging).

★ Castel de Paolis LAZIO

Via Val de Paolis, 00046 Grottaferrata (RM)
Tel.: 0694549457/Fax: 0694316025/www.casteldepaolis.it
DOC(G)s: Castelli Romani, Frascati

The Santarelli family transformed its estate from anonymous grape grower into a leading Lazio winery. "Vigna Adriana" defies traditional perceptions of Frascati with its tropical fruitiness and considerable heft (thanks in part to a touch of viognier). The sleek and spicy reds "I Quattro Mori" and "Campo Vecchio," both of which combine syrah, merlot, petit verdot, and cabernet sauvignon, are among the few serious reds in the Castelli Romani.

Castel di Salve PUGLIA

Frazione Depressa, Piazza Castello 8, 73030 Tricase (LE)
Tel.: 0833771012/www.casteldisalve.com
An ever-improving winery and a specialist in negroamaro. Try "Santi Medici" (spicy varietal negroamaro), or "Priante" (negroamaro-montepulciano). Superripe, immediately drinkable in the Puglian style.

CASTELGIOCONDO TOSCANA

Località Castelgiocondo, 53024 Montalcino (SI)
Tel.: 05527141/www.frescobaldi.it
DOC(G)s: Brunello di Montalcino
Large, beautiful Montalcino estate owned by Frescobaldi. The Brunello here has a deep, brooding personality under a sheen of French oak and a proven track record for aging (especially the *riserva*). Attracting even more attention than this now-legendary wine is "Lamaione," a giant merlot aged 2 years in barriques.

CASTELL'IN VILLA TOSCANA

Località Castell'in Villa, 53019 Castelnuovo Berardenga (SI)
Tel.: 0577359074
DOC(G)s: Chianti Classico
Proof that Chianti can age. Leonessa Coralia Pignatelli's Chianti is vineyard driven, emphasizing the smoky cherry flavors (and life-blood acidity) of sangiovese. The wines are sinewy, aromatic, often brickish in color. Older vintages can be found and should be tried. There's also "Santacroce" (sangiovese-cabernet), which has a firm, focused style designed for aging (24 months in barrique, then 3 more in bottle before release).

Castellani TOSCANA

Frazione Santa Lucia 1, 56025 Pontedera (TK)
Tel.: 0587292900/Fax: 0587292626/www.castelwine.com
DOC(G)s: Chianti; Chianti Classico
A huge and diversified firm controlling more than 2,500 acres in Tuscany, with estates scattered throughout: Poggio al Casone near Pisa (solid Chianti); Burchino, also near Pisa (best known for a nice sangiovese, "Genius Loci"); and Campomaggio in Chianti Classico (the *riserva* is great for the price). And the Castellani tentacles reach farther—there's bargain-priced montepulciano from Abruzzo and primitivo from Puglia in the vast "regional varietals" line. There is also an "artist series" of wines called "Solo Arte," which is notable mainly for its cool labels designed by an ever-changing group of artists.

★ Castellani, Michele & Figli VENETO

Via Granda 1–Valgatara, 37020 Marano di Valpolicella (VR)

€−
€€
Tel.: 0457701253/Fax: 0457702076

DOC(G)s: Valpolicella; Amarone della Valpolicella; Soave
   The concentrated "I Castei" Amarone is a highlight from this small producer, which also makes several supple Valpolicellas (try the *ripasso*-style "San Michele").

Castellare di Castellina TOSCANA

€€ Località Castellare, 53011 Castellina in Chianti (SI)
Tel.: 0577742903/Fax: 0577742814

 DOC(G)s: Chianti Classico
   Paolo Panerai's high-altitude vineyards near Castellina produce brightly aromatic sangiovese that is showcased in fine Chiantis. The flagship "I Sodi di San Niccolò," a sangiovese–malvasia nera blend loaded with woodsy, *frutti di bosco* flavors, still toes the classic line. There's a brooding nobility to it, and it's still the best Castellare wine despite the addition of cabernet and merlot to the lineup.

Castellari Bergaglio PIEMONTE

Frazione Rovereto 136, 15066 Gavi (AL)
Tel.: 0143644000/Fax: 0143644900

€ www.castellaribergaglio.it
DOC(G)s: Gavi; Gavi di Rovereto
   "Pilin" is Gavi on steroids: a partial drying of the grapes precedes fermentation in barriques, resulting in a viscous, creamy white. But ultimately, the "fresh" wines are more interesting. Go with the crisp Gavi "Fornaci" if you like some acidic tang; Gavi "Rovereto" has old-vine concentration but without the oak influence.

Castelli del Grevepesa TOSCANA

Frazione Mercatale Val di Pesa, Via Grevigiana 34, 50024 San Cascina in Val di Pesa (FI)
€€ Tel.: 055821911/www.castellidelgrevepesa.it
DOC(G)s: Chianti Classico
   "Gualdo al Luco," a rich sangiovese-cabernet blend, is a winner, and the Chianti Classico "Clemente VII" Riserva is an old-school Chianti that has stood the test of time.

Castellino

See Tenuta Castellino.

CASTELLO BANFI TOSCANA

 53024 Montalcino (SI)
Tel.: 0577840111/Fax: 0577840444
€− www.castellobanfi.com
€€€ DOC(G)s: Brunello di Montalcino; Sant'Antimo
   New York's Mariani family began acquiring land in Montalcino in 1978, when the area was sparsely populated; today, thanks in large part to the Marianis, Montalcino is Tuscany's most prestigious zone and Castello Banfi, centered on the eleventh-century Poggio alle Mura castle, is its best-known producer. With 2,400 acres of vineyards, Castello Banfi is perennially honored for its chocolate-rich Brunellos ("Poggio alle Mura" is the single-vineyard wine, "Poggio all'Oro" the *riserva*). Other stars include the sumptuous reds "Summus" (sangiovese-syrah-cabernet) and "Excelsus" (cabernet-merlot), as well as a spicy single-vineyard syrah called "Colvecchio." At the low end is "Centine" (sangiovese-cabernet-merlot) and "Col di Sasso" (sangiovese-cabernet). About 20 wines in total, all of them clean, ripe, and consistent.

Castello d'Albola TOSCANA

Località Pian d'Albola 31, 53017 Radda in Chianti (SI)
Tel.: 0577738019/www.albola.it

DOC(G)s: Chianti Classico

Consistent, affordable Chiantis and a decent super-Tuscan named "Acciaiolo" (60% sangiovese, 40% cabernet).

CASTELLO DEI RAMPOLLA TOSCANA

Via Case Sparse 22, 50020 Panzano in Chianti (FI)
Tel.: 055852001

DOC(G)s: Chianti Classico

Rampolla is still a farmhouse-style operation, with Luca and Maurizia DiNapoli at the helm. Starting with the muscular Chianti Classico and continuing on to "Sammarco" (90% cabernet, 10% sangiovese) and "Vigna d'Alceo" (85% cabernet sauvignon, 15% petit verdot; first vintage 1996), the wines have a Bordeaux-like "breed" that is easier to taste than to explain; they have not only plenty of power but also harmony and complexity that makes them sought-after collectibles.

★ Castello del Terriccio TOSCANA

Via Bagnoli 20, 56040 Castellina Marittima (PI)
Tel.: 050699709

Like many on the Tuscan coast, Terriccio favors "international" grapes. The estate, north of Bolgheri, gained fame with the cabernet-merlot blend "Lupicaia," a wine that tastes expensive—and is. Luckily, there are other wines that also taste expensive but aren't: "Tassinaia," a concentrated sangiovese-merlot-cabernet blend; "Con Vento," a powerful and aromatically precise sauvignon blanc; and "Rondinaia," a creamy chardonnay.

Castello della Paneretta TOSCANA

Strada della Paneretta 35, 50021 Barberino Val d'Elsa (FI)
Tel.: 0558059003/Fax: 0558059024
www.castellodellapaneretta.com
DOC(G)s: Chianti Classico

Nobody talks about canaiolo, but this longtime second banana to sangiovese is given particular attention at Paneretta. "Terrine" is a 50-50 blend of sangiovese and canaiolo that is somehow full-bodied and light-footed at the same time, with great aromatics. Ditto for the Chianti wines, headlined by "Torre a Destra."

Castello della Sala UMBRIA

Località Sala, 05016 Ficulle (TR)
Tel.: 076386051/www.antinori.it

DOC(G)s: Orvieto

The story at this picturesque winery, owned by Antinori, is not the local Orvieto but the heady "Cervaro della Sala," a chardonnay-grechetto blend with all the depth and mineral tang of a Chablis. The wine has great structure and a mineral edge from the tufaceous soils of the zone. There's also an excellent late-harvest wine, "Muffato della Sala," made from botrytis-affected sauvignon blanc, grechetto, traminer, and riesling. Orvieto Classico "Campograde" is good and affordable.

Castello delle Regine UMBRIA

Frazione Le Regine, Via di Castelluccio, 05022 Amelia (TR)
Tel.: 0744702005/www.castellodelleregine.com

The top wine is a varietal merlot with the kind of chocolaty intensity that excites the critics. "Princeps" (cabernet-sangiovese-merlot) also fits right into the juicy, new-generation Umbrian mold, as do the sangioveses "Divus" and "Podernovo."

CASTELLO DI AMA TOSCANA

Frazione Lecchi in Chianti, 53013 Gaiole in Chianti (SI)
Tel.: 0577746031/www.castellodiama.com

DOC(G)s: Chianti Classico

Firm, fine, and expensive Chianti Classico (in an earthy, aromatic "Burgundian" style) is the staple, while collectors hoard the "Vigneto L'Apparita," an elegant yet muscular merlot. Purchased in the 1970s by a consortium of four families, Castello di Ama is run by Lorenza Sebasti and her winemaker husband, Marco Pallanti, and is one of Chianti's most beautiful wineries. The top Chianti is the single-vineyard "Vigneto Bellavista." There's also an excellent sangiovese rosé.

Castello di Bossi TOSCANA ━●

Località Bossi in Chianti 28,
53019 Castelnuovo Berardenga (SI)
Tel.: 0577359330/Fax: 0577359048
www.castellodibossi.it
DOC(G)s: Chianti Classico

There is more excellent Chianti Classico available now than you could drink in a lifetime, and you can identify a good producer on the strength of its basic Chianti Classico; in Bossi's case, the wine is velvety and rich without losing the personality of sangiovese to over-extraction. Meanwhile, the "Berardo" Riserva ups the ante with more merlot in the blend and a year of barrique aging. "Corbaia" (sangiovese-cabernet) and "Girolamo" (old-vine merlot) are two sinful super-Tuscans.

Castello di Brolio

See Barone Ricasoli.

Castello di Buttrio

FRIULI–VENEZIA GIULIA

Via Morpurgo 9, 33042 Buttrio (UD)
Tel./Fax: 0432673015/www.marcofelluga.it

Part of the Marco Felluga empire; a renovated castle with vineyards in the hamlet of Buttrio. There is one white, "Ovestein," a stylish, full-bodied blend of tocai and ribolla gialla aged in barrique, and one red, "Marburg," a concentrated mix of refosco and the rare pignolo.

Castello di Cacchiano TOSCANA

Via Monti in Chianti, 53101 Monti in Chianti–Gaiole in Chianti (SI)
Tel.: 0577747018/Fax: 0577747157
DOC(G)s: Chianti Classico

A classic Chianti estate run by Giovanni Ricasoli, known for the dark and woodsy "Millennio."

Castello di Farnetella TOSCANA

Strada Siena-Bottolle, Km. 37, 53048 Sinalunga (SI)
Tel.: 0577355117

DOC(G)s: Chianti Colli Senesi

This estate run by Giuseppe Mazzocolin (of Fattoria di
Felsina) has an interesting lineup. "Poggio Granoni" is the
top wine—a blend of sangiovese, cabernet, merlot, and
syrah made in a tightly wound style and released in
magnums. Chianti Colli Senesi is a good starting point,
and they're also making some decent pinot noir. A fleshy
sauvignon blanc is the white of choice.

CASTELLO DI FONTERUTOL TOSCANA

Località Fonterutoli, 53011 Castellina in Chianti (SI)
Tel.: 057773571/Fax: 0577735757/www.fonterutoli.com

DOC(G)s: Chianti Classico

A celebrated estate—a town, actually—owned by the
Mazzei family, with velvety reds styled by Carlo Ferrini.
There are two Chianti Classicos, "Castello di Fonterutoli"
(the flagship wine) and "Fonterutoli" (less expensive). This
is Chianti in a bold international style, sleek and sweetly
fruity, impossible to resist. "Siepi" is a lip-smacking
sangiovese-merlot from a single vineyard, and the IGT
"Badiola" (sangiovese-merlot-cabernet) transcends its
bargain price.

Castello di Gabbiano TOSCANA

Località Gabbiano 22, 50024 Mercatale Val di Pesa (FI)
Tel.: 055821053/Fax: 0558218082/www.gabbiano.com

DOC(G)s: Chianti Classico

A twelfth-century estate now owned by the Beringer-
Blass conglomerate. Solid, traditional Chiantis (the *riserva*
is especially good) head the list, while the sangiovese-
merlot-cabernet "Alleanza" ("Alliance," in reference to the
collaboration of Gabbiano's Giancarlo Roman and
Beringer's Ed Sbragia) is a good buy.

Castello di Lispida VENETO

Via IV Novembre 4, 35043 Monselice-Padova (PD)
Tel.: 0429-780530/Fax: 0429-780530/www.lispida.com

From the same school of thought as Friulian iconoclast
Francesco Gravner, this estate makes modern whites
using ancient techniques. The wines ferment naturally on
their skins in open vats, without temperature control. Then
they are aged for long periods (including time spent in
terra-cotta amphorae) and bottled unfiltered. In the glass,
these wines are cloudy, with a cidery color, and, while
strange, they're not without appeal. "Terralba" (tocai–
ribolla gialla) is an example of the style—creamy yet
acidic, redolent of honey and herbs.

Castello di Luzzano LOMBARDIA

Frazione Luzzano, 27040 Rovescala (PV)
Tel.: 0523863277/www.castelloluzzano.it

DOC(G)s: Colli Piacentini; Oltrepò Pavese

Situated right on the border of Lombardia and Emilia-
Romagna, and producing very good wines from both
sides. The Colli Piacentini Gutturnio "Romeo" is a luscious
barbera-bonarda blend at a great price, and there's also a
smoky, spicy Oltrepò Pavese Bonarda.

Castello di Meleto TOSCANA 🍾

Località Castello di Meleto, 53013 Gaiole in Chianti (SI)
Tel.: 0577749217/Fax: 0577749762/www.castellomeleto.it
DOC(G)s: Chianti Classico

A good-sized producer (Vittorio Fiore consults) with
consistent, reasonably priced Chianti Classico and the
plummy sangiovese-merlot "Fiore."

Castello di Monastero TOSCANA 🍾

Località Monastero d'Ombrone 19,
53019 Castelnuovo Beradenga (SI)
Tel.: 0290960931/www.borgomonastero.com
DOC(G)s: Brunello di Montalcino; Chianti Classico;
Morellino di Scansano

Connected with the Borgo Monastero resort (a former
monastery) in the Chianti Classico zone. The broad range
of wines includes good Chiantis and the supple, plump
blend "Infinito" (60% sangiovese, 40% cabernet
sauvignon). Good pricing.

Castello di Neive PIEMONTE

Via Castelborgo 1, 12057 Neive (CN)
Tel.: 017367171/Fax: 0173677515
DOC(G)s: Barbaresco

Austere, aromatic Barbaresco from a winery located in
an ancient castle. The white arneis has a flinty, floral
profile, and there's also a light and fragrant dolcetto.

Castello di Nipozzano

See Frescobaldi.

Castello di Poppiano TOSCANA

Frazione Poppiano, Via di Fezzana 45, 50025
Montespertoli (FI)
Tel.: 05582315
DOC(G)s: Chianti Colli Fiorentini

This large and historic property is helping draw attention
to the vineyards just west of Florence. A deep, funky syrah
is the best-known wine, but the range is very broad, from
old-fashioned Chianti Colli Fiorentini to big, sappy reds like
"Tricorno" (sangiovese-merlot-cabernet).

Castello di Querceto TOSCANA 🍾

Via Dudda 61, 50020 Greve in Chianti (FI)
Tel.: 05585921/Fax: 0558592200
www.castellodiquerceto.it
DOC(G)s: Chianti Classico

Firm and traditionally styled Chiantis from high-altitude
vineyards in the hamlet of Dudda, above Greve in Chianti.
There are some good super-Tuscans, most notably
"Querciolaia" (sangiovese-cabernet). "Cignale" is a
luxurious cabernet-based red produced in collaboration
with wine importers Neil and Maria Empson.

Castello di Selvole TOSCANA 🍾

Frazione Vagliagli, Località
Selvole 1, 53019 Castelnuovo Berardegna (SI)
Tel.: 0577322662/www.selvole.com
DOC(G)s: Chianti Classico

An excellent producer in Castelnuovo Berardegna, the
southeastern edge of Chianti Classico. The Chianti

Classico Riserva is well built and aromatic; more flashy is
the barrique-aged "Barullo" (sangiovese-cabernet-merlot).

Castello di Spessa FRIULI–VENEZIA GIULIA
Via Spessa 1, 34070 Capriva del Friuli (GO)
Tel.: 0481639914/Fax: 0481630161
www.castellospessa.com
DOC(G)s: Collio
   Located in a beautiful castle in Capriva, this winery, like
its neighbor Schiopetto, makes clean, elegant whites and
a few reds. Go for the whites: a fragrant, minerally pinot
bianco is a specialty, and the tocai friulano is great.

Castello di Tassarolo PIEMONTE
Cascina Alborina 1, 15060 Tassarolo (AL)
Tel.: 0143342248
DOC(G)s: Gavi; Monferrato
   Marchese Paolo Spinola crafts all of his Gavis from
100% cortese. Try the juicy Gavi Tassarolo "S" (partially
barrel-fermented), the single-vineyard "Vignavecchia," or
the barriqued single-vineyard "Alborina." The white blend
"Ambrogio Spinola" (cortese-chardonnay-sauvignon-
sémillon) is also pretty good.

Castello di Verduno PIEMONTE
Via Umberto I 9, 12060 Verduno (CN)
Tel.: 0172470284/www.castellodiverduno.com
DOC(G)s: Barbaresco; Barolo; Barbera d'Alba; Dolcetto
d'Alba
   Owned by a branch of the Burlotto family and best
known for Barolos from the Massara and Monvigliero crus.
Traditional style, with aromas of cherry liqueur and wood
smoke. Ditto for the Barbarescos from the Rabajà and
Faset vineyards. Good values, and there's also a wine from
the spicy and unusual pelaverga grape.

Castello di Verrazzano TOSCANA
Località Verrazzano, 50022 Greve in Chianti (FI)
Tel.: 055854243/Fax: 055854241/www.verrazzano.com
DOC(G)s: Chianti Classico
   This seventh-century castle and estate was acquired by
the Cappellini family in 1953. Their benchmark Chianti
still has a rustic, wild edge. The pure sangiovese
"Sassello" shows the dark and brooding side of the grape.

Castello di Volpaia TOSCANA
Piazza della Cisterna 1, 53017 Radda in Chianti (SI)
Tel.: 0577738066/www.volpaia.com
DOC(G)s: Chianti Classico
   An actual village was bought outright by the Mascheroni
family in the sixties and transformed into a winery. Its
vineyards lay at some of Chianti Classico's highest altitudes, and the wines have an almost Burgundian character: angular, perfumed, earthy. Very good Vin Santo as well.

Castello Romitorio TOSCANA
Località Romitorio 279, 53024 Montalcino (SI)
Tel.: 0577847212/Fax: 0577847212
www.castelloromitorio.it
DOC(G)s: Brunello di Montalcino
   If you can't (or won't) pay up for the velvety Brunello di
Montalcino (a stout, modern style) then try "Romito del
Romitorio" (sangiovese-cabernet), which has genuine

class at a more reasonable price. Solid wines at the low end, too, like the fruity "Brio" (sangiovese) and Chianti Colli Senesi.

Castello Schwanburg ALTO ADIGE

Via Schwanburg 16, 39010 Nalles/Nals (BZ)
Tel.: 0471678622
DOC(G)s: Alto Adige

Modeling its wines on those of Bordeaux, Schwanburg is best known for a deep, peppery cabernet sauvignon. The pinot bianco "Pitzon" is weighty and nice.

 ### Castello Vicchiomaggio TOSCANA

Castello Vicchiomaggio, 50022 Greve In Chianti (FI)
Tel.: 055854079/Fax: 055853911/www.vicchiomaggio.it
DOC(G)s: Chianti Classico

Smooth and smoky Chianti, headlined by the "La Prima" Riserva. The sangiovese-cabernet blend "Ripa delle Mandorle" is an excellent value, while "Ripa delle More" is a delicious (and still affordable) pure sangiovese.

 ### ★ Castelluccio EMILIA-ROMAGNA

Via Tramonto 15, 47015 Modigliana (FC)
Tel.: 0546942486/Fax: 0546940383
www.ronchidicastelluccio.it
DOC(G)s: Sangiovese di Romagna

This winery, perched above Forlì, makes a case for sangiovese from Romagna. It starts with the smooth and fragrant "Le More" and "Ronco dei Ciliegi" bottlings and continues up to "Ronco delle Ginestre," a truly evocative expression of the grape. The reds are complemented by two potent and aromatic sauvignon blancs, "Lunaria" and "Ronco del Re." Partly owned by the Tuscan consultant Vittorio Fiore and managed by his son, Claudio.

Castelvecchio TOSCANA

Via Certaldese 30, 50026 San Casciano in Val di Pesa (FI)
Tel.: 0558248032/Fax: 0558248921/www.castelvecchio.it
DOC(G)s: Chianti Colli Fiorentini

"Il Brecciolino" is a sangiovese-cabernet-colorino blend of some note. The Vin Santo is good.

Castiglion del Bosco TOSCANA

Località Castiglion del Bosco, 53024 Montalcino (SI)
Tel.: 0577808348
DOC(G)s: Brunello di Montalcino

Big and bruising Brunello di Montalcino, now crafted with the help of consultant Riccardo Cotarella.

★ Cataldi Madonna ABRUZZO

Località Piano, 67025 Ofena (AQ)
Tel.: 0854911680
DOC(G)s: Montepulciano d'Abruzzo; Trebbiano d'Abruzzo

One of Abruzzo's top properties, located in the high plains near L'Aquila. The "Tonì" in particular makes a case for montepulciano as a "noble" variety—it is densely concentrated and well structured. "Malandrino" is a smooth and inky blend of montepulciano and cabernet; "Occhiorosso" showcases cabernet on its own. The rosé Cerasuolo drinks more like a light red, and the fleshy white Trebbiano d'Abruzzo is better than most.

Cavalchina (La Prendina) VENETO/LOMBARDIA

Località Cavalchina, 37066 Sommacampagna (VR)
Tel.: 04551602/www.cavalchina.com
DOC(G)s: Bardolino; Bianco di Custoza
 Garda-area estates owned by the Piona family.
Cavalchina is known for minerally Bianco di Custoza, while
La Prendina specializes in softly contoured Garda reds
such as Bardolino. Simple everyday wines.

Cavalier Bartolomeo PIEMONTE

Via Alba-Barolo 55, 12060 Castiglione Falletto (CN)
Tel./Fax: 017362866
DOC(G)s: Barolo; Dolcetto d'Alba; Langhe
 A tiny producer whose Barolo "Solanotto-Altinasso"
(from vineyards in Castiglione Falletto) is round and deep,
with a healthy dose of barrique aging.

★ Cavalleri LOMBARDIA

Via Provinciale 96, 25030 Erbusco (BS)
Tel.: 0307760217
DOC(G)s: Franciacorta; Terre di Franciacorta
 A top producer of Franciacorta sparklers, including the
excellent "Collezione Rosé" (about 85% chardonnay, 15%
pinot nero), and the blanc de blancs "Pas Dosé." Stands
alongside Bellavista and Ca' del Bosco as one of the best
and brightest in the region.

CAVALLOTTO (TENUTA BRICCO BOSCHIS) PIEMONTE

Via Alba Monforte Bricco Boschis, 12060 Castiglione
Falletto (CN)
Tel.: 017362814/Fax: 017362914/www.cavallotto.com
DOC(G)s: Barolo; Barbera d'Alba; Dolcetto d'Alba; Langhe
 These guys don't get the credit they deserve. You won't
see much Cavallotto Barolo in the auction market, and it's
not a trendy brand—it's just great, long-aging Barolo.
Cavallotto wines are all about finesse, bright acidity, and
aromas that jump out of the glass. The "Bricco Boschis"
vineyard is Cavallotto's home base, and the *riserva* "San
Giuseppe" is from a small site within that vineyard; Vignolo
is another vineyard from which they bottle a velvet-textured
riserva. The other wines (dolcetto, barbera, freisa) are fruity
and fine, but the Barolos are such great values, why not
shoot for the top?

Cavit TRENTINO

Via del Ponte 31, 38040 Trento (TN)
Tel.: 0461381758/Fax: 0461912700/www.cavit.it
DOC(G)s: Trento Brut; Trentino; Teroldego Rotaliano
 A giant consortium of cooperative wineries known for
pinot grigio and other varietal wines on a supermarket
scale. Lesser known but better regarded are their Trento
Brut sparklers, as is the line of wines called "Bottega
Vinaia," which includes more distinctive Trentino
specialties like the smoky red lagrein.

Cecchi TOSCANA

Località Casina dei Ponti 56, 53011 Castellina in Chianti (SI)
Tel.: 0577743024/www.cecchinet.it
DOC(G)s: Brunello di Montalcino; Chianti Classico;
Morellino di Scansano; Vernaccia di San Gimignano;
Sagrantino di Montefalco

Cecchi owns a range of Tuscan properties, including Villa Cerna in Chianti Classico, Valle delle Rose in Scansano, and Castello di Montauto in San Gimignano. Now there's the Tenuta Alzatura vineyard in Montefalco, Umbria, where the Sagrantino di Montefalco "Uno di Uno" is a dark-hued addition to the growing crop of wines there. The plush Val le delle Rose Morellino di Scansano has paved the way for other Maremma wines, while the soft-textured Chiantis from Villa Cerna remain good values.

Cecilia Beretta

See Pasqua.

Cennatoio TOSCANA

Via di San Leolino 37, 50020 Panzano (FI)
Tel.: 055852134/www.cennatoio.it
DOC(G)s: Chianti Classico

A lot of good wines from sangiovese, most of them in a fine floral style. The rustic "E" sangiovese is a good place to start before graduating to the dark and stormy "O'Leandro" Chianti Classico Riserva or the barrique-aged "Etrusco" (100% sangiovese). The broad range also includes "Mammolo" (70% merlot, 30% sangiovese) and "Arcibaldo" (50% sangiovese, 50% cabernet sauvignon).

Centolani TOSCANA

Località Strada Maremmana, Tenuta Friggiali, 53024 Montalcino (SI)
Tel.: 0577849314/Fax: 0577849454
DOC(G)s: Brunello di Montalcino

This estate includes the Tenuta Friggiali vineyard, from which Centolani bottles a powerful, hard-edged Brunello of the same name, and a property called Pietranera, also in Montalcino. The Pietranera is softer and plusher than the Friggiali, but the Friggiali Brunello is more widely distributed in the United States.

Ceraudo, Roberto CALABRIA

Località Marina di Strongoli,
88815 Crotone (CR)
Tel.: 0962865613/www.dattilo.it

On the Ionian coast, not far from Cirò, this little Calabrian property is one to keep an eye on. "Dattilo" is a plush, slightly rustic red based on gaglioppo, while the deeper "Petraro" combines gaglioppo with cabernet and monte-pulciano. "Imyr" is barrique-aged chardonnay, and it's one of very few Calabrian whites with some stuffing and style.

★ Cerbaiona TOSCANA

Località Cerbaiona, 53024 Montalcino (SI)
Tel.: 0577848660
DOC(G)s: Brunello di Montalcino

A luxurious Brunello di Montalcino that has become a favorite of critics and collectors. Dense and extracted but also exquisitely aromatic—a wine that combines power and elegance. The IGT rosso is a more affordable blend of sangiovese, cabernet, merlot, and syrah.

CERETTO PIEMONTE

Località San Cassiano 34, 12051 Alba (CN)
Tel.: 0173282582/www.ceretto.com

DOC(G)s: Barolo; Barbaresco; Langhe; Nebbiolo d'Alba; Barbera d'Alba; Dolcetto d'Alba

The Ceretto family owns seven estates around Alba, and they produce a wide array of wines, from the bright and fruity "Blangé" Arneis to the brawny Barolo/Barbaresco wines of their Bricco Rocche and Bricco Asili estates—see the listing for Bricco Rocche (Bricco Asili). One of the more interesting wines carrying the Ceretto brand name is the Langhe Rosso "Monsordo," a smooth and fragrant blend of cabernet, merlot, and nebbiolo.

Cesani, Vincenzo TOSCANA

Via Piazzetta 82/D, 53037 San Gimignano (SI)
Tel.: 0577955084
DOC(G)s: Vernaccia di San Gimignano; Chianti Colli Senesi

Located in a hamlet called Pancole, a subzone of San Gimignano known more for reds than the usual white vernaccia. The soft and succulent "Luenzo" (90% sangiovese, 10% colorino) is the top wine.

Cesari, Gerardo VENETO

Via Luigi Ciocca 35, 25027 Quinzano (BS)
Tel.: 0309925811/Fax: 0309923455/www.cesari-spa.it
DOC(G)s: Amarone della Valpolicella; Soave

A large producer of inexpensive Verona wines, including Soave and Valpolicella. The estate's Amarone "Il Bosco" is a good bargain, as is the "Mara" Valpolicella, which takes on some toffee-ish richness from the *ripasso* method.

Cesari, Umberto EMILIA-ROMAGNA

Via Stanzano 1120, 40050 Castel San Pietro Terme (BO)
Tel.: 051941896/Fax: 051944387/www.umbertocesari.it
DOC(G)s: Albana di Romagna; Sangiovese di Romagna; Trebbiano di Romagna

One of Emilia-Romagna's best-known (and biggest) wineries. The sweet Albana di Romagna "Colle del Re" is a good wine, but the real story is sangiovese—from fruity, inexpensive Sangiovese di Romagna DOC to deeper wines such as "Tauleto" (a reserve selection of sangiovese) and "Liano" (sangiovese-cabernet).

Cesconi TRENTINO

Via Marconi 39, 38015 Pressano di Lavis (TN)
Tel.: 0461240355/Fax: 0461243731
DOC(G)s: Trentino

Finely tuned varietal whites (especially the plump pinot grigio) and an exotic-tasting blend called "Olivar" (chardonnay–pinot bianco–pinot grigio). The top red is "Pivier" (cabernet-merlot), which is deep and tasty but with that vegetal edge so common to Alpine reds.

Ceuso SICILIA

Via Enea 18, 91011 Alcamo (TP)
Tel.: 0924507860/Fax: 0924510522/www.ceuso.it

An estate near Alcamo that was once a grower of white grapes for a local co-op, but grafted its vines over to reds and created a stir with the tiny-production "Vigna Custera" (nero d'avola–cabernet sauvignon–merlot). Today, "Custera" is the top-of-the-line bottling in a growing range that includes the 100% nero d'avola "Scurati" (great depth for the price) and "Fastaia" (70% nero d'avola with cabernet franc and merlot, sort of a Custera Junior).

Charrère, Constantino VALLE D'AOSTA

Les Moulins 28, 11010 Aymavilles (AO)
Tel.: 0165902135/www.lescretesvins.it
DOC(G)s: Valle d'Aosta

The second label of Les Crêtes proprietor Constantino Charrère, with a focus on light mountain reds from grapes like prëmetta, petit rouge, and fumin.

Chiappone PIEMONTE

Via San Michele 51, 14049 Nizza Monferrato (AT)
Tel./Fax: 0141721424/www.eredechiappone.com
DOC(G)s: Barbera d'Asti; Monferrato

"Ru" Barbera d'Asti is flashy and powerful but not cheap.

CHIARLO, MICHELE PIEMONTE

Strada Statale Nizza–Canelli, Km. 99, 14042 Calamandrana (AT)
Tel.: 0141769030/Fax: 0141769033/www.chiarlo.it
DOC(G)s: Barbera d'Asti; Barolo; Barbaresco; Gavi; Langhe; Monferrato; Moscato d'Asti

Michele Chiarlo started making wine in the 1950s, and since then he has built his firm into one of the largest in Piedmont, with 124 acres of estate-owned vineyards and another 148 under lease in both the Langhe and Monferrato hills. His vast selection includes the austere, elegant Barolo "Cerequio"; the plusher, easier-drinking Barolo "Tortoniano"; and the brightly acidic Barbaresco "Asili." Also noteworthy are Moscato d'Asti "Nivole" (one of the best wines of its type) and the rich, barrel-aged Barbera d'Asti "La Court." "Countacc!" (nebbiolo-barbera-cabernet) is a silken-textured newcomer to the portfolio.

Chionetti PIEMONTE

Frazione San Luigi 44, 12063 Dogliani (CN)
Tel.: 017371179/www.chionettiquinto.com
DOC(G)s: Dolcetto di Dogliani

Considered the leader among dolcetto specialists in Dogliani. The wines, particularly the single-vineyard "Briccolero," are dense and dark-toned, with coffee-ground tannins and a savory edge.

★ Ciabot Berton PIEMONTE

Località Santa Maria 1, 12064 La Morra (CN)
Tel./Fax: 017350217
DOC(G)s: Barolo; Barbera d'Alba; Dolcetto d'Alba

A boutique producer in La Morra with a base Barolo sourced from the Bricco San Biagio, Roggeri, and Rive vineyards. The cru wine is from Roggeri only. A bright, well-rounded style with lots of forward fruit.

★ CIACCI PICCOLOMINI D'ARAGONA TOSCANA

Frazione Castelnuovo Abate, 53020 Montalcino (SI)
Tel.: 0577835616/Fax: 0577835785
www.ciaccipiccolomini.com
DOC(G)s: Brunello di Montalcino; Sant'Antimo

Ciacci's Pianrosso vineyard is among the best in Montalcino. It produces a bold and fruit-driven Brunello that has the sweeter tannins typical of wines from the southern end of the Montalcino zone. Aging is in large Slavonian oak. More unabashedly oak-influenced and superextracted are "Ateo" (sangiovese-cabernet-merlot) and "Fabius" (syrah from the Sant'Antimo DOC).

Cieck PIEMONTE

Strada Bardesono, 10011 Agliè (TO)
Tel.: 0124330522/Fax: 0124429284/www.cieck.it
DOC(G)s: Caluso; Canavese; Erbaluce di Caluso
   Interesting northern Piedmontese wines. Start with the minerally Erbaluce Spumante Brut (a serious *Champenoise* sparkler) or the still white Erbaluce di Caluso, then move on to the spicy Canavese Rosso (a smoky, spicy blend of nebbiolo, barbera, neretto, and freisa).

Cigliuti PIEMONTE

Via Serraboella 17, 12057 Neive (CN)
Tel.: 0173677185/Fax: 0173677185
DOC(G)s: Barbaresco; Barbera d'Alba; Dolcetto d'Alba; Langhe
   A long-established (and tiny) estate in Neive known for its Barbaresco "Serraboella"—an austere and aromatic wine in the Neive style, one that needs some time in the cellar to show its best. There's also a good Barbera d'Alba.

Cignale

See Castello di Querceto.

★ Cima TOSCANA

Via del Fagiano 1, 54100 Massa (MA)
Tel./Fax: 0585831617/www.aziendagricolacima.it
DOC(G)s: Candia dei Colli Apuani
   Set in the coastal hills where Tuscany meets Liguria. Whites are based on the herbaceous vermentino (the Candia dei Colli Apuani DOC "Candia Alto" is a good buy), while reds incorporate sangiovese ("Anchigi"), merlot ("Montervo"), and the local red ("Romalbo" is a tangy blend of sangiovese with about 15% of a local oddity called massaretta).

Cinciole

See Le Cinciole.

Cinelli Colombini

See Donatella Cinelli Colombini.

Citra ABRUZZO

Contrada Cucullo, 66026 Ortona (CH)
Tel.: 0859031342/Fax: 0859031332/www.citra.it
DOC(G)s: Montepulciano d'Abruzzo; Trebbiano d'Abruzzo
   Inexpensive wines on a grand scale. Some (like the Montepulciano d'Abruzzo) are surprisingly good.

★ Clelia Romano CAMPANIA

Via Arianiello 47, 83030 Lapio (AV)
Tel.: 0825982184/Fax: 0825982198
DOC(G)s: Fiano di Avellino
   One of the more concentrated fianos available—because of well-selected fruit from prime vineyards in the Lapio subzone, not oak. There's a honeyed edge to the more classic notes of pine boughs and citrus. An aglianico-based red from vineyards near Taurasi is in development.

CLERICO PIEMONTE

Località Manzoni Cucchi 67, 12065 Monforte d'Alba (CN)
Tel./Fax: 017378171
DOC(G)s: Barolo; Langhe; Barbera d'Alba
   While you're waiting for the sexy and sought-after Barolos to age, drink the silky barbera ("Tre Vigne") and

dolcetto ("Visadi"). The south-facing Ginestra cru in Monforte is the source of the "Ciabot Mentin Ginestra" and "Pajana" Barolos, while the "Percristina" is from the Mosconi cru, just a few ticks south. These are powerful, modern Barolos with lots of black fruit extract. Explosive and expensive.

Cocci Grifoni MARCHE

Contrada Messieri 12, 63038 Ripatransone (AP)
Tel.: 073590143/www.tenutacoccigrifoni.it
DOC(G)s: Rosso Piceno; Falerio dei Colli Ascolani
  "Il Grifone" is deep and round, if a touch expensive; while the soft and juicy "Vigna Messieri" and "Le Torri" are solid values. There is also an exotically aromatic white from Falerio.

Coffele VENETO

Via Roma 5, 37038 Soave (VR)
Tel.: 0457680007/www.coffele.it
DOC(G)s: Soave
  The fresh and clean basic Soave Classico is a great buy, while "Alzari" is the fatter, oaked-up version. Good aromatics all around.

Cogno, Elvio PIEMONTE

Località Ravera 2, 12060 Novello (CN)
Tel.: 0173744006/Fax: 0173744921/www.elviocogno.com
DOC(G)s: Barolo; Barbera d'Alba; Dolcetto d'Alba; Langhe
  From the lesser-known village of Novello, home of the Ravera vineyard. Barolo "Ravera" is Cogno's best-known wine, with aromas of dried fruits, mushrooms, leather, and spice. Barolo "Vigna Elena" is from a plot within Ravera; it sees more time in wood and has a denser feel. "Montegrilli" is a bright barbera-nebbiolo blend.

COL D'ORCIA TOSCANA

Tenuta Col d'Orcia, 53020 San Angelo in Colle (SI)
Tel.: 0577808911/Fax: 0577844018
DOC(G)s: Brunello di Montalcino; Sant'Antimo
  Owned by Francesco Marone Cinzano, this state-of-the-art winery turns out dense yet accessible Brunello di Montalcino and, more recently, a powerfully structured cabernet sauvignon called "Olmaia." The fruity Rosso di Montalcino is a wine to snap up by the case. Maurizio Castelli consults.

Colla

See Poderi Colla.

Collalbrigo VENETO

Via Marsiglion 77, 31015 Conegliano (TV)
Tel.: 0438455229/Fax: 0438451013/www.collalbrigo.com
DOC(G)s: Prosecco di Conegliano
  A large maker of prosecco and one of the better names from the Conegliano DOC.

Colle dei Bardellini LIGURIA

Via Fontanarosa 12, 18100 Imperia (IM)
Tel.: 0183291370
DOC(G)s: Riviera Ligure di Ponente
  Top-flight Ligurian winery owned by Genovese restaura-teurs Pino and Luigi Sola. Both the vermentino and pigato

wines are excellent, particularly the "Vigna U Munte" Vermentino. Tangy whites with a taste of the sea.

★ Collelungo TOSCANA

Località Collelungo, 53011 Castellina in Chianti (SI)
Tel.: 0577740489/www.collelungo.com
DOC(G)s: Chianti Classico

Under the supervision of Alberto Antonini (formerly of Antinori), the estate makes serious Chianti. The basic Chianti Classico is round and smooth and the barrique-aged *riserva* is worthy of several years' cellaring.

Collemattoni TOSCANA

Località San Angelo in Colle, 53020 Montalcino (SI)
Tel.: 0577844009/Fax: 0577844127/www.collemattoni.it
DOC(G)s: Brunello di Montalcino

A tiny-production estate (about 20,000 bottles total) with a rich, fruit-driven Brunello di Montalcino. The wine is "modern" in its plushness, but the oak influence is moderated. The first vintage was 1988.

★ Colle Picchioni di Paola DiMauro LAZIO

Via Colle Picchioni 46, 00040 Frattocchie di Marino (RM)
Tel.: 0693546329/Fax: 0693548440/www.collepicchioni.it
DOC(G)s: Marino

Paola DiMauro, a legendary Roman restaurateur, got into winemaking as a hobby in the seventies, and now she is one of Lazio's most important vintners. Her small farm south of Rome, which she runs with her son, Armando, is known for minerally whites from the Marino DOC (similar to Frascati) as well as smooth red blends of cabernet sauvignon and merlot. The Bordeaux-style "Vigna del Vassallo," with its peppery/earthy cabernet franc notes, is perhaps the best red being made in Lazio today—and it's still affordable. Riccardo Cotarella consults.

Colle Santa Mustiola TOSCANA

Via delle Torri 86, 53043 Chiusi (SI)
Tel./Fax: 057863462/www.poggioaichiari.it

A small property southeast of Siena with one luscious wine, "Poggio ai Chiari," a silken sangiovese aged 20 months in barrique.

Colli di Catone LAZIO

Cantine Colli di Catone, Via Frascati 31–33, 00040 Monteporzio Catone (RM)
Tel.: 069449113/Fax: 069449222/www.collidicatone.it
DOC(G)s: Frascati

Good, clean Frascati DOC whites, along with a number of interesting whites from the malvasia del Lazio grape ("Colle Gaio" captures its orange-blossom aromas well). There's also the smooth Bordeaux blend "Dedo."

Collosorbo TOSCANA

Località Villa a Sesta 25, 53020 Montalcino (SI)
Tel./Fax: 0577835534
DOC(G)s: Brunello di Montalcino

Dark, chunky Brunello di Montalcino from the southern end of Montalcino. Great concentration of flavor, lots of black fruit tones, not too much oak (all large-cask aging). The Rosso di Montalcino has been praised as being bigger than some Brunellos. "Sorbus" (sangiovese-cabernet) is the barriqued "international" entry.

Colmello di Grotta FRIULI–VENEZIA GIULIA

Via Gorizia 133, 34070 Farra d'Isonzo (GO)
Tel; 0481888445/Fax: 0481888485/www.colmello.it
DOC(G)s: Collio; Friuli Isonzo
  A good source of varietal whites from chardonnay, tocai, sauvignon, and pinot grigio. Also notable is "Rondon," a blend of chardonnay, sauvignon, and pinot grigio.

Colosi SICILIA

Via Militare Ritiro 23, 98152 Messina (ME)
Tel.: 09053852/Fax: 09047553/www.cantinecolosi.it
DOC(G)s: Malvasia delle Lipari; Passito di Pantelleria
  Headquartered on the island of Salina and best known for sweet and citrusy Malvasia delle Lipari, this winery also buys grapes from other vineyards for some solid, bargain-priced dry wines. The chunky Sicilia Rosso, made from nero d'avola, is a delicious everyday red.

★ Còlpetrone UMBRIA

Via della Collina 4, 06035 Gualdo Cattaneo (PG)
Tel.: 0578767722/Fax: 0578768040
DOC(G)s: Montefalco
  Acquired in 1995 by the agricultural arm of SAI Insurance, which also owns the Fattoria del Cerro winery in Montepulciano. Còlpetrone makes deeply extracted, barrique-influenced reds. The Montefalco Rosso is bigger than some sagrantinos, and the sagrantino is a cocoa-textured giant.

Colsanto UMBRIA

Via Montarezza 33, 33048 Dolegnano (UD)
Tel.: 0432757173/www.livon.it
DOC(G)s: Montefalco
  A new estate owned by Friuli's Livón group. They came right out of the gate with a rich and coffee-scented Montefalco Rosso and have been planting (and replanting) vineyards.

COLTERENZIO ALTO ADIGE

Strada del Vino 8, 39050 Cornaiano/Girlan (BZ)
Tel.: 0471664246/Fax: 0471660633/www.colterenzio.com
DOC(G)s: Alto Adige–Südtirol
  Outstanding wines from top to bottom. Established in 1960 by a group of 28 growers, Colterenzio now sources grapes from more than 300 member-growers. Top picks from the huge selection include the pinot banco "Weisshaus," Chardonnay "Cornell," Sauvignon "Lafoa," and, on the red side, the Lagrein "Cornell" (in typical Alto Adige fashion there are three product lines, with Cornell being the top one here). Great pricing, for the most part.

Col Vetoraz VENETO

Via Tresiese 1, 31040 Valdobbiadene (TV)
Tel.: 0423975291
DOC(G)s: Prosecco di Valdobbiadene
  Fine prosecco wines at great prices.

Colli Irpini
See Montesole.

Consorzio Viticoltori Associati del Vulture

BASILICATA
Strada Statale 93, 85022 Barile (PZ)
Tel.: 097232253/www.conviv.com

€ DOC(G)s: Aglianico del Vulture

The Aglianico del Vulture wines "Vetusto" (labeled in a way that makes it looks like Vetusto is the winery name) and "Carpe Diem" are spicy, savory takes on the aglianico grape—classic southern reds at great prices.

★ Contadi Castaldi LOMBARDIA

Via Colzano 32, 25030 Adro (BS)
Tel.: 0307450126/Fax: 0307450322
www.contadicastaldi.it
DOC(G)s: Franciacorta; Terre di Franciacorta

This beautiful winery was acquired in 1991 by Vittorio Moretti (Bellavista) and his son-in-law, Martino DeRosa. Castaldi's Franciacorta Brut remains a great value, measuring up well to Champagne. The Brut Rosé may be the best wine, although the creamy Satén has gotten more press. On the still side, there's solid Terre di Franciacorta Rosso and Bianco, along with the flashier "Manca Pane" (chardonnay) and "Marco Nero" (cabernet sauvignon).

Conte Zandotti LAZIO

Via Vigne Colle Mattia 8, 00132 Rome (RM)
Tel.: 0620609000/www.cantinecontezandotti.it
€ DOC(G)s: Frascati

Top wines include the crisp Frascati "Cannellino" and a smooth-textured red blend called "La Petrosa."

CONTERNO, ALDO PIEMONTE

Località Bussia 48, 12065 Monforte d'Alba (CN)
Tel.: 017378150/www.poderialdoconterno.com

DOC(G)s: Barolo; Barbera d'Alba; Dolcetto d'Alba; Langhe

Aldo Conterno is the son of Giacomo Conterno and the brother of Giovanni Conterno, the late proprietor of the Giacomo Conterno estate. Aldo's winery sits on the Bussia Soprana vineyard in Monforte (source of the "base" Barolo), and he makes intense, sought-after single-vineyard wines from Vigna Colonello, Bricco Cicala, and Romirasco—all of which flank the Bussia site. There's also the *riserva* "Gran Bussia" (70% from Romirasco, the rest from Cicala and Colonnello), aged three years in Slavonian oak, two years in stainless steel, and a year in bottle before release. These are some of the most powerfully structured, long-lived Barolos there are; you really don't want to drink it young. For immediate gratification, try the "Printanie" Langhe Chardonnay (a clean and minerally style), the "Il Favot" Langhe Nebbiolo (as powerful as some Barlos), or the elegant "Quartetto" (nebbiolo-barbera-cabernet-merlot).

★ Conterno Fantino PIEMONTE

Via Ginestra 1, 12065 Monforte d'Alba (CN)
Tel.: 017378204/www.conternofantino.it
DOC(G)s: Barolo; Barbera d'Alba; Dolcetto d'Alba; Langhe

Founded in 1982 by Diego Conterno and Guido Fantino, this estate in Monforte produces sleek, supple Barolos aged in new wood. The "Vigna del Gris" and "Parussi" Barolos are a little easier going than the dense "Sorì Ginestra," but across the board, the wines are fruit driven and velvet smooth. The luscious Langhe Rosso "Mon'Pra" (nebbiolo-barbera-cabernet) is great to drink now, as are the dolcetto and barbera wines, and the honeyed Langhe Chardonnay is solid, too.

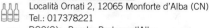

CONTERNO, GIACOMO PIEMONTE

Località Ornati 2, 12065 Monforte d'Alba (CN)
Tel.: 017378221

DOC(G)s: Barolo; Barbera d'Alba

The Francia vineyard, a west-facing site at the southern end of Serralunga d'Alba, is the source of Conterno's legendary "Cascina Francia" as well as the *riserva* "Monfortino." The winery, just outside the Monforte town center, is run by Roberto Conterno. He makes Barolo the old-fashioned way—long maceration on the skins during fermentation, large-cask aging—resulting in a wine that tastes as much of the earth as of fruit, one that is structured to age for decades. Good vintages from the sixties and seventies continue to shine; they are truly Italy's answer to great Burgundy. The tangy Barbera d'Alba is terrific to drink while you wait.

★ Conterno, Paolo PIEMONTE

Via Ginestra 34, 12065 Monforte d'Alba (CN)
Tel./Fax: 017378415/www.paoloconterno.com

DOC(G)s: Barolo; Barbera d'Alba; Dolcetto d'Alba; Langhe

The Barolo "Ginestra" is a *bomba* ("bomb," as in explosive). Its superripe nebbiolo fruit is framed in toasty oak, the tannins strong but sweet. Both the barbera and dolcetto also have a decadent, superripe quality.

Conti Contini

See Capezzana.

Conti Formentini Friuli–Venezia Giulia

Via Oslavia 5, 34070 San Floriano del Collio (GO)
Tel.: 0481884131

DOC(G)s: Collio

Formentini's large production includes both white and red varietals at good prices. "Tajut" Merlot has great concentration in a region where "thin and green" is still the norm.

Conti, Leone

See Leone Conti.

Conti Spalletti

See Folonari, Tenute Ambrogio e Giovanni.

Conti Zecca PUGLIA

Via Cesarea, 73045 Leverano (LE)
Tel.: 0832925613/www.contizecca.it

DOC(G)s: Salice Salentino

Good Salice Salentino and a superrich, darkly fruity cabernet-negroamaro blend, "Nero," that is one of the better Puglian reds to be found; unlike many, it's not just a fruit-bomb—there's some structure to it.

★ Contini, Attilio SARDEGNA

Via Genova 48/50, 09072 Cabras (OR)
Tel.: 0783290806

DOC(G)s: Vernaccia di Oristano; Cannonau di Sardegna; Vermentino di Sardegna

Contini's Vernaccia di Oristano wine bears a strong resemblance to Sherry. Though the vernaccia grape it's made from is indigenous to the area, the Spanish *solera*-style production method reflects Oristano's history as an alternative port to Spain's Sherry capital, Jerez. "Antico Gregori" is a multivintage blend reminiscent of a good Oloroso, but

★ RISING STAR   ⓐ VALUE   ⬧ AVAILABILITY   € PRICING

lately the more interesting story is the Contini dry wines: fragrant and succulent Cannonau di Sardegna, plush nieddera (a spicy local red), and the oddly herbaceous white "Karmis" (from the local vernaccia vinified dry).

Contratto, Giuseppe PIEMONTE

Via G. B. Giuliani 56, 14053 Canelli (AT)
Tel.: 0141823349/www.contratto.it
DOC(G)s: Asti; Barbera d'Asti; Barolo

A top producer of Asti Spumante, this historic Canelli cellar is owned by Antonella and Carlo Bocchino, who are better known for grappas. In addition to classic, semisweet Asti, the Contratto estate has focused more attention on dry sparklers ("De Miranda" is made in the Champagne method) and on rich reds from barbera ("Panta Rei" and the powerhouse "Solus Ad"). They also bottle a well-regarded Barolo from the Cerequio vineyard.

Coos, Dario FRIULI–VENEZIA GIULIA
Via Ramandolo, 33045 Nimis (UD)
Tel.: 0432790320/Fax: 0432797807
DOC(G)s: Colli Orientali del Friuli

Noteworthy for its production of the rare sweet white verduzzo—an intriguing mix of citrus, herb, and honey flavors from the tiny Ramandolo subzone, one of the newest DOCGs. Friuli's other famous sweet white, the creamy picolit, is also a specialty.

Coppo, Felice PIEMONTE
Cascina Coste 15, 15020 Mombello Monferrato (AL)
Tel.: 0142944503/Fax: 0142944503
DOC(G)s: Barbera del Monferrato

Rich and supple barbera and other reds from a small estate near Asti.

Coppo, Luigi e Figli PIEMONTE
Via Alba 68, 14053 Canelli (AT)
Tel.: 0141823146/www.coppo.it
DOC(G)s: Barbera d'Asti; Brachetto d'Acqui; Moscato d'Asti; Piemonte

Luxurious barbera wines. "Pomorosso" is densely fruity, with a sheen of new oak; the less expensive "Camp du Rouss" is brighter and lighter. The chardonnay "Monteriolo" is a great example of the good things being done with that grape in Piedmont. Excellent sparklers from brachetto and moscato as well.

Cordero di Montezemolo PIEMONTE

Via Annunziata 67/bis, 12064 La Morra (CN)
Tel.: 017350344/Fax: 0173509235
www.corderodimontezemolo.com
DOC(G)s: Barolo; Barbera d'Alba

Elegant, aromatic Barolos. The top wine is the "Vigna Enrico VI" (sourced from the Villero cru in Castiglione Falletto), while the excellent and affordable "house" Barolo comes from the Monfalletto vineyard (also known as Gattera) in La Morra. Crying out for some wild mushroom risotto.

Corino, Giovanni PIEMONTE
Frazione Annunziata 24, 12064 La Morra (CN)
Tel./Fax: 017350219
DOC(G)s: Barolo; Barbera d'Alba; Dolcetto d'Alba

A small La Morra estate known for lush and aromatic

Barolos from some of the top vineyards in La Morra, including Giachini, Rocche, and Arborina. The wines show a new-oak influence, though it is well integrated into the dense, fruity whole. There's a new cru, Roncaglie (another La Morra vineyard), and the supercharged "Vecchie Vigne" (a selection of fruit from various sites). Another star is the massive Barbera d'Alba from the Pozzo vineyard.

Cornarea PIEMONTE

Via Valentino 105, 12043 Canale (CN)
Tel.: 017365636/Fax: 0173979091
DOC(G)s: Roero
Solid, fairly fat arneis (also a sweet *passito* from the grape) and several nebbiolo-based reds.

Coroncino MARCHE

Contrada Coroncino, 7, 60039 Staffolo (AN)
Tel.: 0731779494
DOC(G)s: Verdicchio dei Castelli di Jesi
A verdicchio specialist with many distinct wines from the grape. The base-level "Staffilo" is green, piney, and grassy; "Il Coroncino" is made from a closer selection of grapes and is partially barrel-fermented, giving it an oilier, creamer feel on the palate.

★ Correggia, Matteo PIEMONTE

Case Sparse Gambinetto 124, 12043 Canale (CN)
Tel.: 0173978009/Fax: 0173978009
www.matteocorreggia.com
DOC(G)s: Barbera d'Alba; Nebbiolo d'Alba; Roero
Matteo Correggia was a rising star when he died in an accident a few years ago; his wife now oversees production of the still-excellent wines with the help of Giorgio Rivetti (of La Spinetta). The Roero Arneis is deeper than most, with great floral aromatics. There's also a rosy dry brachetto called "Anthos" and a number of bold barberas, but the star red is "Rocche d'Ampsej"—a nebbiolo that has helped put Roero on the map.

Corte Gardoni VENETO

Località Gardoni 5, 37067 Valeggio sul Mincio (VR)
Tel.: 0457950382
DOC(G)s: Bardolino; Bianco di Custoza
Corte Gardoni is among the better producers of the light red Bardolino. Their best is smooth and satisfying "La Fontane," and they make a good rosé *(chiaretto)* as well.

Corte Pavone TOSCANA

Località Corte Pavone, 53024 Montalcino (SI)
Tel.: 0577848110/Fax: 0577846442/www.loacker.net
DOC(G)s: Brunello di Montalcino; Rosso di Montalcino
A good, spicy, and affordable Brunello and a quite full-bodied Rosso di Montalcino.

Corte Rugolin VENETO

Località Rugolin 1–Valgatara, 37020 Marano di Valpolicella (VR)
Tel.: 0457702153/Fax: 0456831600
DOC(G)s: Valpolicella; Amarone della Valpolicella; Recioto della Valpolicella
The wines are solid across the board, with the *ripasso* Valpolicella meriting special mention. Pricing is reasonable.

Corte Sant'Alda VENETO

Via Capovilla 28, 37030 Mezzane di Sotto (VR)
Tel.: 0458880006/Fax: 0458880477/www.cortesantalda.it
DOC(G)s: Valpolicella; Amarone della Valpolicella; Recioto della Valpolicella

Perched on the eastern edge of the Valpolicella DOC, Marinella Camerani's high-altitude vineyards yield deeply concentrated fruit for her wines, especially the heady Amarone. The *ripasso* Valpolicella "Mithas" is velvety and rich, the "Ca' Flui" is a simple, fruity starting point.

Cortese, Giuseppe PIEMONTE

Via Rabajà 35, 12050 Barbaresco (CN)
Tel.: 0173635131

DOC(G)s: Barbaresco; Barbera d'Alba; Dolcetto d'Alba; Langhe

Inexpensive Barbaresco from the Rabajà cru is a highlight, but there's also the rich Barbera d'Alba "Morassina."

Corvo

See Duca di Salaparuta.

Cos SICILIA

Piazza del Popolo 34, 97019 Vittoria (RG)
Tel.: 0932864042

DOC(G)s: Cerasuolo di Vittoria

Cos makes one of best Cerasuolo di Vittoria DOC wines, with a style that really shows off the synergy between the darkly fruity nero d'avola and the raspberry-scented frappato. There are also two deep, dark, shiraz-like nero d'avola wines ("Scyri" and "Dedalo").

Costa, Teo PIEMONTE

Via San Salvario 1, 12050 Castellinaldo (CN)
Tel.: 0173213066/Fax: 0173214004/www.teocosta.it
DOC(G)s: Barbera d'Alba; Nebbiolo d'Alba; Roero

A small producer in Roero with a diverse lineup. Smooth and deeply fruity Barbera d'Alba is a specialty, as is the citrusy white Roero Arneis.

Costanti, Andrea TOSCANA

Colle al Matrichese, 53024 Montalcino (SI)
Tel.: 0577848195

DOC(G)s: Brunello di Montalcino

Big and bold Brunello di Montalcino is complemented by a consistently excellent Rosso di Montalcino, which is no wimp itself. "Vermiglio" is the super-Tuscan offering (sangiovese-merlot-cabernet).

Costanza Malfatti

See Malfatti, Costanza.

Costaripa LOMBARDIA

Via Cialdini 12, 25080 Moniga del Garda (BS)
Tel.: 0365502010

DOC(G)s: Garda; Lugana

Interesting Garda wines made by Mattia Vezzola, the enologist at Bellavista (and the owner here). Check out the funky "Le Mazane" (from the blueberry-scented marzemino grape) and the smooth Garda Rosso (incorporating groppello, a black and spicy local grape).

Cottanera SICILIA

Località Passo Pisciaro, Contrada Iannazzo Sp. 89, 95030
Castiglione di Sicilia (CT)

Tel.: 0942963601/www.cottanera.it

Cottanera's vineyards near Mount Etna produce a range
of piquant reds, starting with the well-priced "Barbazzale"
(from the local nerello mascalese) and "Fatagione"
(nerello–nero d'avola). From there, you move up to a
series of bigger reds from international varieties: "Sole di
Sesta" (a meaty syrah), "Ardenza" (the licorice-scented
mondeuse, aka refosco), "Nume" (cabernet sauvignon),
and "Grammonte" (merlot). High-impact wines.

Crognaletti MARCHE

Via San Lorenzo 6, 60036 Montecavrotto (AN)
Tel./Fax: 073189656

DOC(G)s: Verdicchio dei Castelli di Jesi; Rosso Piceno

Citrusy and substantial verdicchio (try the "Vigna delle
Oche"). The inky montepulciano "Solleone" is also worth
a try.

Cuomo, Marisa CAMPANIA

Via G. B. Lama 14, 84010 Furore (SA)
Tel.: 089830348/Fax: 0898304014

DOC(G)s: Costa d'Amalfi

A taste of the Amalfi coast. Marisa Cuomo's briny, citrusy
whites include the Ravello (a blend of falanghina and
biancolella) and the Furore Bianco "Fiorduva" (weird local
grapes). Chill well and serve with seafood salad.

Curto, Giovanbattista SICILIA

Via Galilei 4, 97014 Ispica (RG)
Tel./Fax: 0932950161/www.curto.it

Solid reds from nero d'avola. "Fontanelle" is the flagship
wine; the basic Rosso is a value pick.

Cusumano SICILIA

Strada Stale 113, 90047 Partinico (PA)
Tel.: 0918903456/www.cusumano.it

Diego and Alberto Cusumano created this brand by
assembling growers who had previously contributed
grapes to cooperatives. Two plump reds head the list:
"Noa" (nero d'avola with cabernet and merlot) and
"Sagana" (100% nero d'avola). Clean, well oaked, and
ready to drink.

D'Ambra Vini d'Ischia CAMPANIA (ISCHIA)

Via Mario d'Ambra 16, 80075 Forio (NA)
Tel.: 081907246/Fax: 081907210/www.dambravini.com

DOC(G)s: Ischia

The best-known producer on Ischia, with chalky whites
from the local biancolella and forastera, as well as an
Ischia Rosso, a spicy, herbaceous blend of guarnaccia
(grenache) and per'e palummo (piedirosso).

D'Angelo BASILICATA

Via Provinciale 8, 85028 Rionero in Vulture (PO)
Tel.: 0972721517

DOC(G)s: Aglianico del Vulture

Donato D'Angelo's wines are a little fierce, from the basic
Aglianico del Vulture DOC to the single-vineyard "Vigna
Caselle" and "Canneto" (also 100% aglianico, from the

estate's best old vines). "Serra delle Querce" (debuted in 1998) aims to soften the hard edges of aglianico with 30% merlot, but in general D'Angelo delivers the earthy, ashy flavors that aglianico purists crave.

D'Antiche Terre—Vega CAMPANIA
Strada Statale 7 bis, 83030 Manocalzati (AV)
Tel.: 0825675359/Fax: 0825675358
DOC(G)s: Greco di Tufo; Fiano di Avellino; Taurasi
   A large central Campanian producer with a rustic Taurasi and tangy whites from greco and fiano. The Taurasi is a solid wine with that forest-floor aglianico character.

Dal Fari FRIULI—VENEZIA GIULIA
Via Darnazzacco, 33043 Cividale del Friuli (UD)
Tel.: 0432731219/Fax: 0432706770
DOC(G)s: Colli Orientali del Friuli
   Consistently high-quality Friulian lineup of varietal whites and reds. A highlight is the faintly tropical "Bianco delle Grazie" (chardonnay-sauvignon-tocai-riesling).

Dal Forno, Romano
See Romano Dal Forno.

Dal Maso, Luigino VENETO
Via Selva 62, 36054 Montebello Vicentino (VI)
Tel.: 0444649104
DOC(G)s: Gambellara; Colli Berici
   One of the better producers of Gambellara DOC whites. Especially good are the sweet *recioto* versions. On the red side, the winery makes some Bordeaux-inspired wines from the up-and-coming Colli Berici DOC.

Damijan
See Podversic, Damijan.

Damilano PIEMONTE
Vicolo San Sebastiano 2, 12060 Barolo (CN)
Tel.: 017356265/Fax: 017356315/www.damilanog.co
DOC(G)s: Barolo; Barbera d'Alba
   Sleek, modern Barolos. Family holdings include pieces of the Liste and Cannubi vineyards, and the Barolo "Cannubi" is the top wine; it has a sweeter, rounder edge than "Liste," mainly due to more new-oak aging.

Danzante
See Frescobaldi.

Dattilo
See Ceraudo, Roberto.

De Angelis CAMPANIA
Via Marziale 14, 80067 Sorrento (NA)
Tel.: 0818781648/Fax: 081878382
DOC(G)s: Vesuvio
   Lacryma Christi ("Tears of Christ") sounds outdated, but a number of estates on Vesuvius are giving the Lacryma Christi designation some new style and substance. Both the Lacryma Christi Bianco (a minerally falanghina–coda di volpe blend) and Rosso (tart and spicy piedirosso) are excellent values. "Nero di Tasso" is a deeper, more luxurious aglianico aged in barrique.

DE BARTOLI (VECCHIO SAMPERI) SICILIA

Contrada Fornara 292, 91025 Marsala (TP)
Tel.: 0923962093/www.marcodebartoli.com
DOC(G)s: Marsala; Moscato di Pantelleria; Passito di
Pantelleria

Marsala has fallen out of fashion thanks to industrial
mass production, but Marco De Bartoli remains a small-
scale artisan, creating wines that are true to Marsala's
history as an alternative to Sherry. His wines—not fortified
but rather late-harvested to achieve their alcohol levels
naturally—are aged in varying types of cooperage
(chestnut, oak) to achieve their complex notes of dried
fruits, nuts, leather, orange peel . . . all the classic Sherry
flavors. "Ventennale" is made in the *solera* style, with an
average age of 20 years; it's a one-of-a-kind. Meanwhile,
De Bartoli's "Bukkarum" Passito di Pantelleria, from an
estate he owns on the remote satellite island of Pantelleria,
is one of the most sought-after dessert wines in Italy.

De Battè, Walter LIGURIA

Via Trancantu 25, 19017 Riomaggiore (SP)
Tel.: 0187920127
DOC(G)s: Cinque Terre

Unlike most of the light, herbal Cinque Terre whites
made from the local bosco grape, De Battè's is thick and
golden, although its Mediterranean tang still shows: it has
a wildflower honey kind of feel. And speaking of honey, De
Battè's sweet version of Cinque Terre, called Sciacchetrà, is
considered the gold standard; it's a sought-after cult wine.

★ DeConciliis CAMPANIA

Contrada Querce 1, 84060 Prignano Cilento (SA)
Tel.: 0974831090

In the hills above the ancient Greek city of Paestum,
free-spirited Bruno DeConciliis gives the classic local
varieties a new, coastal-climate feel. The white fiano is
plumper and more citrusy than its cousins from upland in
Avellino, and the reds, all from aglianico, slather some
sappy fruit extract over the classic aglianico notes of wood
smoke and tar. "Naima" (named for a John Coltrane song)
is the signature red, combining immediate drinkability with
savory complexity. "Donnaluna" is the value red, "Zero"
the big bruiser for the cellar.

Decugnano dei Barbi UMBRIA

Località Fossatello di Corbara 50, 05019 Orvieto (TR)
Tel.: 0763308255/www.decugnanodeibarbi.com
DOC(G)s: Orvieto Classico; Lago di Corbara

A good Orvieto winery. The barrel-fermented "IL" Orvieto
Classico Superiore is a step up from the clean and
straightforward base bottling. The smooth and easy-
drinking red version of "IL" combines montepulciano,
sangiovese, and canaiolo.

Dei TOSCANA

Via di Martiena 35, 53045 Montepulciano (SI)
Tel.: 0578716878/Fax: 0577758680/www.cantinedei.com
DOC(G)s: Vino Nobile di Montepulciano

A small estate with a luxurious, cleanly fruity Vino Nobile
di Montepulciano and the super-Tuscan "Sancta
Caterina," a blend of sangiovese, syrah, petit verdot, and

cabernet sauvignon. The wines have nice dark tones for a hearty Tuscan *ragù*.

Deltetto PIEMONTE

Corso Alba 43, 12043 Canale (CN)
Tel.: 0173979383/Fax: 017395710/www.deltetto.com
DOC(G)s: Barbera d'Alba; Langhe; Roero

A respected producer of mostly Roero DOC wines. The Roero Arneis "San Michele" shows off the bright floral aromatics of the grape, and the barrique-aged "Braja" (a deep and aromatic nebbiolo) is a highlight among the reds. Both are true steals.

Dessilani PIEMONTE

Via C. Battisti 21, 28073 Fara Novarese (NO)
Tel.: 0321829252/Fax: 0321829805
DOC(G)s: Fara; Gattinara; Ghemme

Nebbiolo wines of great character, without the eye-popping price tags of Barolo (or Burgundy!). This large estate makes wines from all of the major northern Piedmont appellations—Gattinara, Ghemme, Fara—and all are consistently excellent. Recent tastings show the Ghemme to be the most angular, perfumed, and delicate; Gattinara the earthiest and most powerful; and the Fara, especially the delicious "Caramino," the most forward and smooth textured.

Destefanis PIEMONTE

Via Mortizzo 8, 12050 Montelupo Albese (CN)
Tel.: 0173617189/Fax: 0173617189
www.marcodestefanis.com
DOC(G)s: Dolcetto d'Alba; Barbera d'Alba; Langhe; Nebbiolo d'Alba

The hand of consultant Beppe Caviola (who favors big extract and a dollop of barrique aging) can be felt in the rich reds made at this small estate. Thick and juicy barbera; ditto for dolcetto and nebbiolo.

Dettori, Tenute SARDEGNA

Località Badde Nigolosu, Strada Provinciale 29, Km. 10, 17036 Sennori (SS)
Tel.: 079514711/www.tenutedettori.it
DOC(G)s: Cannonau di Sardegna; Vermentino di Sardegna

A new boutique estate near Sassari in northern Sardinia. The reds from cannonau are undoubtedly lush, aromatic, structured—a step above the typically rustic wines from the grape, and the prices reflect that. The Vermentino di Gallura is a deep and expressive style, and it, too, is priced accordingly.

Dezi MARCHE

Contrada Fonte Maggio 14, 63029 Servigliano (AP)
Tel.: 0734710090
DOC(G)s: Rosso Piceno

"Solo" Sangiovese has gotten the hype, but it's awfully expensive; go with one of the well-priced montepulcianos. "Dezio" is juicy and straightforward, while "Regina del Bosco" (aged 15 months in barrique) has more bass notes.

Dezzani, F.lli PIEMONTE

Corso Pinin Giachino 140, 14023 Cocconato (AT)
Tel.: 0141907044/Fax: 0141907372/www.dezzani.it

€-
€€
DOC(G)s: Barbera d'Asti; Barolo; Gavi; Roero Arneis
   Dezzani has everything from Barolo/Barbaresco to Gavi. Barbera d'Asti is a specialty—try the pumped-up "Il Dragone" or the superrich "Plenum," a blend of 50% barbera and 50% sangiovese from Tuscany (the latter supplied by Dievole).

Di Lenardo FRIULI–VENEZIA GIULIA

Via Battisti 1, 33050 Gonars (UD)
Tel.: 0432928633/Fax: 0432923375
€   DOC(G)s: Friuli Grave

   Wines that hover around $10 but taste more expensive. Massimo Di Lenardo gives his viscous varietal whites odd names like "Woody" (for a toasty chardonnay) and "Toh!" (for a honeyed tocai friulano).

Dievole TOSCANA

Località Dievole, 53019 Castelnuovo Berardenga (SI)
Tel.: 0577322613; 0577322712/www.dievole.it
€-
€€
DOC(G)s: Chianti Classico

   Well-extracted Chiantis and super-Tuscans, but the black cherry fruit and savory edge of sangiovese still shows through. The voluptuous "Novecento" Chianti Classico Riserva is priced better than most wines of its class. "Broccato," a supple sangiovese, is also a good buy.

DiMajo Norante MOLISE

Contrada Ramitello 4, 86042 Campomarino (CB)
Tel.: 087557208/Fax: 087557379
www.dimajonorante.com
€-
€€
DOC(G)s: Biferno

   Molise's best-known producer. Alessio DiMajo makes a broad range of wines with the help of consultant Riccardo Cotarella. A smooth and tangy everyday red is the montepulciano-aglianico blend "Ramitello." His top-end red is the montepulciano-based "Don Luigi," which has a melted-chocolate feel. The most interesting white is the citrusy "Biblios" (falanghina-greco), and the moscato *passito* "Apianae" is a honeyed dessert wine.

DiMeo CAMPANIA

Contrada Coccovon 1, Salza Irpinia (AV)
Tel.: 0825981419/Fax: 0825986333
€-
€€
DOC(G)s: Fiano di Avellino; Greco di Tufo; Taurasi

   One of the classic Taurasi producers, making the wine in a fragrant, earthy, slightly rustic style. The fiano and falanghina whites are typically citrusy and clean.

★   ### DiPoli, Peter ALTO ADIGE

Via Villa 5-I, Egna (BZ)
Tel.: 0471813400/Fax: 0471813444
www.peterdipoli.com
€€   DOC(G)s: Alto Adige

   Although he's gotten lots of press for his reds "Fihl" and "Ygum" (nice Bordeaux blends combining cabernet and merlot, but not as awe-inspiring as everyone says), Peter DiPoli's real triumph is the Alto Adige Sauvignon "Voglar." Full-bodied, intensely aromatic sauvignon you could well drink with a cheese plate.

Di Prima, Gaspare SICILIA

Via G. Guasto 27, 92017 Sambuca di Sicilia (AG)
Tel.: 0925941201/Fax: 0925941279/www.diprimavini.it
Di Prima's "Villamaura" is a dense, ripe, and appealingly funky syrah.

DiPrisco CAMPANIA

Contrada Rotole 37, 83040 Fontanarosa (AV)
Tel./Fax: 0825475738
DOC(G)s: Taurasi; Greco di Tufo
Pasquale DiPrisco is setting his sights on great aglianico from the Taurasi area. Keep an eye out for powerful, angular Taurasi and other aglianicos (along with some whites) from this new-generation producer.

Distefano Grasso

See Grasso Casa Vinicola.

Dittajuti, Conte Leopardi MARCHE

Via Marina II 26, 60026 Numana (AN)
Tel.: 0717390116
DOC(G)s: Rosso Cònero
A small Rosso Cònero producer. The wines showcase montepulciano in all its inky, sweet glory. Great values.

Donatella Cinelli Colombini TOSCANA

Località Casato Prime Donne, 53024 Montalcino (SI)
Tel.: 0577849421/Fax: 0577662108
www.cinellicolombini.it
DOC(G)s: Brunello di Montalcino; Rosso di Montalcino
This estate includes two farms, Fattoria del Colle and Fattoria del Casato, both longtime Cinelli-Colombini family holdings that also include Fattoria dei Barbi. Donatella Cinelli Colombini does her own thing here, making sweet, softly contoured Brunellos, including one, "Prime Donne," that is an homage to women in wine. "Leone Rosso" is a soft and affordable sangiovese-merlot blend.

Donati, Marco TRENTINO

Via Cesare Battista 41, 38016 Mezzocorona (TN)
Tel.: 0461604141
DOC(G)s: Teroldego Rotaliano; Trentino
As the teroldego grape gets better known, so will Donati. "Bagolari" is suitably dark and funky, while "Sangue del Drago" turns up the intensity.

Donna Jolanda

See Meloni Vini.

Donnafugata SICILIA

Via S. Lipari 18, 91025 Marsala (TP)
Tel.: 0923724200/Fax: 0923722042/www.donnafugata.it
DOC(G)s: Contessa Entellina; Moscato di Pantelleria;
Passito di Pantelleria
The Rallo family turned away from Marsala back in the early eighties; today they make polished wines from Contessa Entellina, in southwest Sicily, and from Pantelleria. The massive "Mille e Una Notte" is a cult nero d'avola, but the stylishness of the wines even extends to simpler, cheaper bottling like the white "Anthìlia" (a fresh and aromatic inzolia-catarratto blend) and the supple and substantial reds "Sedàra" (nero d'avola) and "Tancredi"

(nero d'avola–cabernet). Passito di Pantelleria "Ben Ryè," with its intense flavors of dried figs, orange rind, and caramel, is one of Italy's best dessert wines.

Dorgali
See Cantina Sociale Dorgali.

Dorigati, F.lli TRENTINO
Via Dante 5, 38016 Mezzacorona (TN)
Tel.: 0461605313/www.dorigati.it
DOC(G)s: Teroldego Rotaliano; Trento Brut; Trentino
Renowned for a minerally Trento Brut sparkler called "Methius" (60% chardonnay, 40% pinot noir), although that wine doesn't typically make it stateside. Another specialty is the red teroldego, best expressed in the smoky, violet-hued "Diedri."

DORIGO FRIULI–VENEZIA GIULIA
Via del Pozzo 5, 33042 Buttrio (UD)
Tel.: 0432674268
DOC(G)s: Colli Orientali del Friuli
The most acclaimed red wine producer in Friuli, and no slouch with whites, either. Dorigo's Montsclapade vineyard in Buttrio is a well-situated, old-vine site that yields superb fruit for bold and barrique-aged reds: "Montsclapade" is a luscious Bordeaux blend named for the vineyard, but there's also a muscular pignolo; a tarry, succulent refosco; and, on the white side, a honeyed tocai friulano. There's also a rich single-vineyard sauvignon, "Ronc di Juri." Balancing out these big-impact wines are crisp, straightforward white varietals from, most notably, ribolla gialla. The rare picolit is also done well, and there's a good *Champenoise* sparkler from chardonnay.

Drei Donà (Tenuta La Palazza) EMILIA-ROMAGNA
Via del Tesoro 23, 47100 Forlì (FD)
Tel.: 0543769371/Fax: 0543765049
DOC(G)s: Sangiovese di Romagna
Big wines (reds mostly) meant to establish Romagna as serious wine territory. The luxurious (and quite expensive) "Magnificat" is a super-Tuscan-scale cabernet, and the "Pruno" Sangiovese di Romagna is similarly intense. The "Notturno" sangiovese is more affordable and very good. "Tornese" is a blown-up chardonnay.

Duca di Castelmonte
See Pellegrino.

Duca di Salaparuta (Corvo) SICILIA
la Nazionale, Strada Statale 113, 90014 Casteldaccia (PA)
Tel.: 091945201/www.vinicorvo.it
Illva Saronno (the large spirits company) now owns this historic winery, which had been run by the Sicilian regional government. Giuseppe Alliata, the Duke of Salaparuta, named his vineyard Corvo ("crow" in Italian) when he first established the winery in 1824. Both Corvo and Duca di Salaparuta have been somewhat moribund, but Saronno's infusion of new blood has brought new style: "Duca Enrico," the classic nero d'avola, is still going strong, but it's now flanked by richer, more modern reds like "Triskelè" (nero d'avola–cabernet aged in barrique) and "Megara" (frappato-syrah). "Colomba Platina"

remains a refreshing blend of inzolia and grecanico. The Corvo-branded stuff is cheap and simple.

Due Portine
See Gorelli, Giuseppe.

EINAUDI, LUIGI PIEMONTE
Borgata Gombe 31, 12063 Dogliani (CN)
Tel.: 017370191
DOC(G)s: Barolo; Dolcetto di Dogliani; Langhe
  Luigi Einaudi was the first president of the Italian Republic, and his namesake estate in Dogliani is run by his granddaughter, Paola. More than a dozen wines are produced, including the superconcentrated Langhe Rosso "Luigi Einaudi" (nebbiolo-barbera-cabernet-merlot). Dolcetto di Dogliani is a specialty (go for the luscious, violet-scented "Vigna Tecc"), and there are two elegant Barolos: the silky "nei Cannubi" (from the famed Barolo site) and "Costa Grimaldi" (a round and fruity style from the lesser-known Via Nuova cru in Barolo).

Elisabetta TOSCANA
Azienda Agricola
Brunetti, Via Tronto 10–14, 57023 Cecina (LI)
Tel.: 0586661096/Fax: 0586662308 www.agrihotel-elisabetta.com
  The Brunetti family's property near Bolgheri makes a quirky white that speaks to Luigi Brunetti's Campanian roots: the ripe and sunny "Le Marze" is 50% chardonnay with greco and fiano. "Le Marze Rosso" is a light Bordeaux blend, and the bright "Aulo" is sangiovese with canaiolo and cabernet; "Brunetti" is the big super-Tuscan (sangiovese-merlot-cabernet aged in barrique).

Elorina SICILIA
Via Minghetti 80, 96019 Rosolini (SR)
Tel.: 0931857068
DOC(G)s: Eloro
  Nero d'avola wines from the virtually unknown Eloro DOC in southeastern Sicily. Solid varietal nero d'avola with a dark, dense feel, while the brighter, more aromatic "Eloro Pachino" has a similar blend (and feel) to Cerasuolo di Vittoria. Also the very rare Moscato di Noto dessert nectar.

★ Ercole Velenosi MARCHE
Via dei Biancospini 11, 63100 Ascoli Piceno (AP)
Tel.: 0736341218/www.velenosivini.com
DOC(G)s: Rosso Piceno; Falerio dei Colli Ascolani
  The strangely appealing Falerio dei Colli Ascolani "Vigna Solaria" (whose exotic aromas rival gewürztraminer's) is something different, but the real story here is reds: the easygoing Rosso Piceno "Brecciarolo" and its toasty, chocolate-tinged big brother "Roggio del Filare" are very good, and now there's "Ludi," a supercharged blend of montepulciano, cabernet, and merlot.

Eredi Virginia Ferrero
See Ferrero, Eredi Virginia.

Ermacora, Dario e Luciano FRIULI–VENEZIA GIULIA
Località Ipplis, Via Solzaredo 9, 33040 Premariacco (UD)
Tel.: 0432716250/www.ermacora.it

DOC(G)s: Colli Orientali del Friuli
Substantial whites, especially the pinots bianco and grigio, as well as the rarer sweet picolit.

Eubea di Famiglia Sasso BASILICATA
Via Roma 209, 85028 Rionero in Vulture (PZ)
Tel.: 0972723574
DOC(G)s: Aglianico del Vulture
Francesco Sasso sold the Sasso brand in 1995 (it's still a known Basilicata commodity) to focus on this smaller Eubea estate he's developed in Rionero with his daughter. He is widely known for his skill with aglianico in Basilicata. The top-end "Covo dei Briganti" is loaded with black-fruit intensity and structured to age.

Falchini
See Casale-Falchini.

★ Falesco LAZIO
Zona Artigianale Guardie, 01027 Montefiascone (VT)
Tel.: 0761825669
DOC(G)s: Est! Est!! Est!!! di Montefiascone
A boutique Lazio winery owned by über-consultant Riccardo Cotarella, bottling wines from both Lazio and Umbria. The juicy and consistent "Vitiano" (merlot-cabernet-sangiovese, from Umbria) is a value sensation, while "Montiano" (merlot from Lazio) is built to rival Bordeaux. Smoky syrah (Lazio) and the cabernet–cabernet franc "Marciliano" (sourced from Umbria and loaded with peppery cabernet franc savor) round out an impressive portfolio.

Fanti (La Palazzetta) TOSCANA
Borgo di Sotto 25, 53020 Montalcino (SI)
Tel.: 0577835631
DOC(G)s: Brunello di Montalcino
Flavio Fanti is a hands-on grower-producer whose elegant Brunellos (and Rossos) are consistently good, with a nice balance of ripe fruit and more savory earth tones. Firmly structured and classic in their styling.

Fanti (San Filippo) TOSCANA
Via Borgo di Mezzo 15, 53020 Castelnuovo dell'Abate Montalcino (SI)
Tel.: 0577835628/Fax: 0577835523
DOC(G)s: Brunello di Montalcino; Sant'Antimo
A boutique producer in Castelnuovo dell'Abate, where the south-facing vineyards yield more rounded, fruit-driven Brunello. Filippo Fanti's limited-production Brunellos are deep and concentrated but not overoaked. A nice value is the spicy Sant'Antimo Rosso (100% sangiovese).

Fantinel FRIULI–VENEZIA GIULIA
Via Cussignacco 80, 33040 Pradamano (UD)
Tel.: 0432670444/Fax: 0432670864/www.fantinel.com
DOC(G)s: Colli Orientali del Friuli; Collio; Friuli Grave
A large producer with a clean, consistent lineup. Top wines come from the "Sant'Helena" range, and include pinot bianco, pinot grigio, sauvignon, and chardonnay.

Fantino, Alessandro e Gían Natale PIEMONTE

Via G. Silvano 18, 12065 Monforte d'Alba (CN)

Tel.: 017378253

DOC(G)s: Barolo; Barbera d'Alba

"Vigna dei Dardi" Barolo, named for a cru in Monforte d'Alba, is one of the great buys in Barolo. It's refined and complex, with a "Burgundian" profile. The Fantinos also make tangy barbera and an unusual nebbiolo *passito,* wherein nebbiolo grapes are dried before pressing to create a sweet red balanced with plenty of spice.

Farina, Remo VENETO

Via Fontana 8, 37020 Pedemonte (VR)

Tel.: 0457701349/Fax: 0456800137/www.farinawines.com

DOC(G)s: Amarone della Valpolicella; Valpolicella

Nice value in Amarone made in a more moderated, spicy style. The Valpolicella Classico "Montecorna" is also smooth and complex.

Farina, Stefano PIEMONTE

Via Case Sparse 77, 50020 Panzano in Chianti (FI)

Tel.: 055852153/Fax: 031629988

DOC(G)s: Barbaresco; Barolo; Barbera d'Alba; others

The Farina family owns estates in Piedmont and Tuscany (Le Bocce), and here they're known for value-priced Barolo and Barbaresco along with some fruity barberas and the chunky Langhe Rosso "Brumaio" (nebbiolo-barbera). The smooth and fragrant Barbarescos have gotten the most acclaim.

Farnese ABRUZZO

Via dei Bastioni 2, 66026 Ortona (CH)

Tel.: 0859067388/Fax: 0859067389

www.farnese-vini.com

DOC(G)s: Montepulciano d'Abruzzo; Trebbiano d'Abruzzo

Bargain wines. Montepulciano d'Abruzzo "Opis" is the richest, most structured red in the lineup.

Fassati TOSCANA

Via di Graccianello 3/A, 53040 Montepulciano (SI)

Tel.: 0578708708/www.fazibattaglia.it

DOC(G)s: Vino Nobile di Montepulciano

A large estate in Montepulciano owned by the Marche region's Fazi-Battaglia winery. Pleasant, fruity Vino Nobile at an affordable price.

Fattoi-Capanna TOSCANA

Località Santa Restituta, Podere Capanna 101, 53024 Montalcino (SI)

Tel.: 0577848613

DOC(G)s: Brunello di Montalcino

A tiny Montalcino estate with a good track record for age-worthy Brunellos with old-school elegance, rusticity, and subtlety (there are still some large chestnut-wood casks kicking around there). Break out the wild boar *ragù.*

Fattoria Cusona

See Guicciardini Strozzi.

Fattoria dei Barbi TOSCANA

Località Podernovi 170, 53024 Montalcino (SI)

Tel.: 0577841111/Fax: 0577841112/

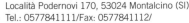

www.fattoriadeibarbi.it

DOC(G)s: Brunello di Montalcino; Rosso di Montalcino

A historic Montalcino house, traditionally known for burly, austere Brunellos (in recent years the style has softened somewhat, but they're still wines to age). At the lower end, Barbi offers great value with the dark and luscious "Brusco dei Barbi" (mostly sangiovese) and "Rosso dei Barbi" (all sangiovese). The estate, run by the Colombini-Cinelli family, also has a plush Morellino di Scansano.

Fattoria del Buonamico TOSCANA

Via di Montecarlo 43, 55015 Montecarlo (LU)

Tel.: 058322038/Fax: 0583229528/www.buonamico.it

DOC(G)s: Montecarlo

Spicy syrah and a lush cabernet-merlot blend, both of them labeled "Il Fortino." There's also a fleshy pinot bianco, "Vasario," and a red blend called "Cercatola," a mix of cabernet, sangiovese, and syrah.

Fattoria del Casato

See Donatella Cinelli Colombini.

Fattoria del Cerro TOSCANA

Via Grazianella 5, 53040 Montepulciano (SI)

Tel.: 0578767722/Fax: 0578768040/www.saiagricola.it

DOC(G)s: Vino Nobile di Montepulciano

Owned by the agribusiness arm of SAI insurance. The Vino Nobile "Antica Chiusina" embodies the high-impact house style, with its weighty extract and healthy dose of oak. Other reds include the sappy "Poggio Golo" merlot.

FATTORIA DI FELSINA TOSCANA

Strada Chiantigiana, Strada Statale 484, 53019 Castelnuovo Berardegna (SI)

Tel.: 0577355117/Fax: 0577355651

DOC(G)s: Chianti Classico

Finely tuned Chianti Classico is the specialty of Giuseppe Mazzocolin's estate, which also produces "Fontoalloro," a varietal sangiovese structured for aging. Rather than go for the big, oaky fruit-bomb, Felsina opts for refinement, aromatics, and balance. The single-vineyard "Vigneto Rancia" Chianti Classico Riserva is a superb wine—a Chianti for cellaring.

Fattoria di Montechiari TOSCANA

Via Montechiari 27, 55015 Montecarlo (LU)

Tel.: 058322189/Fax: 058322189

DOC(G)s: Montecarlo

Montechiari joins the likes of Wandanna, Fubbiano, and Buonamico in crafting international-style reds near Lucca. Montechiari's stylish varietals include cabernet sauvignon, chardonnay, and pinot nero (called "Nero").

Fattoria di Palazzo Vecchio

See Palazzo Vecchio.

Fattoria di Petroio TOSCANA

Via di Mocenni 7, 53010 Castelnuovo Berardenga (SI)

Tel.: 0577328045/Fax: 0577328153

DOC(G)s: Chianti Classico

Very plush, powerful Chianti wines from the Lenzi family. The product line is pure and simple: Chianti Classico and Chianti Classico Riserva.

Fattoria La Braccesca
See La Braccesca.

Fattoria La Ripa TOSCANA 🔑

Frazione San Donato in Poggio, 50020 Tavarnelle Val di Pesa (FI)

Tel.: 0558072948/Fax: 0558072121/www.laripa.it

DOC(G)s: Chianti Classico

Solid Chianti Classico, particularly the *riserva*. "Santa Brigida" (80% sangiovese, 20% cabernet) is full-bodied and toasty.

Fattoria La Lecciaia
See La Lecciaia.

Fattoria Laila MARCHE

Via San Filippo sul Cesano, 61040 Mondavio (PS)

Tel.: 0721979353/Fax: 0721979353

DOC(G)s: Verdicchio dei Castelli di Jesi; Rosso Piceno

Laila's clean, aromatic verdicchio is a terrific buy, as is the juicy Rosso Piceno. A little higher-end is "Lailum Rosso," a palate-coating montepulciano that spends 16 months in barrique. There's a late-harvested, barrel-fermented "Lailum" verdicchio as well.

Fattoria Le Corti
See Le Corti–Corsini.

Fattoria Le Fonti TOSCANA

Località San Giorgio, 53036 Poggibonsi (SI)

Tel./Fax: 0577935690

DOC(G)s: Chianti Classico

Located at the southwestern edge of Chianti Classico in Poggibonsi, this producer showcases sangiovese rather than turning to cabernet or merlot (the more traditional canaiolo grape still plays backup). "Vito Arturo" is an excellent varietal sangiovese with a nice balance of woodsiness and ripe fruit.

Fattoria Le Fonti TOSCANA

Via Le Fonti, 50020 Panzano in Chianti (FI)

Tel.: 055852194/Fax: 055852517/www.fattorialefonti.it

DOC(G)s: Chianti Classico

Limited-production Chianti and a sangiovese-cabernet blend called "Fontissimo." The wines are high-toned, perfumed, and angular.

★ Fattoria Le Pupille TOSCANA

Località Pereta, 58050 Magliano in Toscana (GR)

Tel.: 0564505129/Fax: 0564505153

www.elisabettageppetti.com

DOC(G)s: Morellino di Scansano

Stefano Rizzi and Elisabetta Geppetti run this elite Maremma estate (with consultation from Christian Le Sommer of Château Lafite). Everything from the soft and juicy Morellino di Scansano (a perennial value) to the collector's item "Saffredi" (cabernet-merlot-alicante) is sleek and impressive. "Poggio Valente" is a sexy single-vineyard Morellino, always enticingly drinkable in its youth. For dessert, there's the exotic late-harvest wine "Solalto," from gewürztraminer, sauvignon, and sémillon. A new addition is a plush value red called "Micante," from an offshoot project called Solo Maremma.

Fattoria Le Sorgenti TOSCANA

Via di Docciola 8, 50012 Bagno a Ripoli (FI)
Tel.: 055696004/Fax: 055696921
www.fattorialesorgenti.com
DOC(G)s: Chianti Colli Fiorentini

Sorgenti's Chianti is smooth and affordable, and the cabernet-merlot blend "Scirus" has Bordeaux-esque depth and class. "Sghiras" is a well-made chardonnay-sauvignon blend that sees a touch (about 20%) of barrel fermentation.

★ Fattoria Le Terrazze MARCHE

Via Musone 4, 60026 Numana (AN)
Tel.: 0717390352/Fax: 0717391285
DOC(G)s: Rosso Cònero

Antonio Terni's sleek and sophisticated "Sassi Neri" Rosso Cònero makes a strong case for montepulciano as a "noble" variety, while the chunky "Chaos" (montepulciano-syrah-merlot) is a decadent pleasure. The "basic" Rosso Cònero is anything but basic—a fantastic by-the-case wine. Chardonnay "Le Cave" is less exciting, but the reds have helped put the Marche on the map.

Fattoria Montecchio TOSCANA

Via Montecchio 4, 50020 Tavarnelle Val di Pesa (FI)
Tel.: 0558072907/www.fattoriamontecchio.it
DOC(G)s: Chianti Classico

Good Chiantis and the super-Tuscan "Pietracupa" (60% sangiovese, 40% cabernet).

Fattoria Montellori TOSCANA

Via Pistoiese 1, 50054 Fucecchio (FI)
Tel.: 0571260641
DOC(G)s: Chianti

"Il Moro," a sangiovese–malvasia nera blend, has depth and character at a reasonable price. Then you can jump up (in heft and price) to "Castelrapiti" (sangiovese with cabernet) and "Salamartano" (cabernet-merlot).

Fattoria Nittardi TOSCANA

Località Nittardi 76, 53011 Castellina in Chianti (SI)
Tel.: 0577740269/Fax: 0577741080
DOC(G)s: Chianti Classico

There's an awful lot of good Chianti out there; here's another with nice, rosy sangiovese aromatics and significant depth.

Fattoria Paradiso EMILIA-ROMAGNA

Via Palmeggiana 285, 47032 Bertinoro (FC)
Tel.: 0543445044/Fax: 0543444224
www.fattoriaparadiso.com
DOC(G)s: Sangiovese di Romagna; Albana di Romagna

The Pezzi family makes Albana di Romagna Passito "Gradisca," an apricot-scented dessert nectar that is among the best of its type. Typical of a Bologna-area producer, the focus is on sangiovese for reds. "Vigna delle Lepri" is well concentrated, with smoky aromatics. Another notable red is "Barbarossa," from a rare native grape of the same name.

Fattoria San Francesco CALABRIA
Strada Statale 106, 88813 Cirò (KR)
Tel.: 096232228/www.fattoriasanfrancesco.it
DOC(G)s: Cirò
A newish property owned by Francesco Siciliani, whose
family owns the Caparra & Siciliani winery, also in Cirò.
"Ronco dei Quattroventi" and "Donna Madda" Ciròs have
clean flavors and textures reminiscent of pinot noir. Great
additions to the Calabrian wine scene.

Fattoria San Giuliano PIEMONTE
Via Circonvallazione 14, 12057 Neive (CN)
Tel./Fax: 017367364
DOC(G)s: Barbaresco; Dolcetto d'Alba; Barbera d'Alba;
Moscato d'Asti
Look for this classically styled Barbaresco: perfumed,
smoky, elegant, high-acid. A great food wine at a fair price.

Fattoria San Lorenzo
See Crognaletti.

Fattoria Uccelliera TOSCANA
Via Pontita 26, 56043 Fauglia (PI)
Tel.: 050662747/www.uccelliera.it
DOC(G)s: Chianti
With the help of consultant Stefano Chioccioli, this small
property near Pisa has a richly satisfying red in
"Castellaccio" (sangiovese-cabernet-syrah).

Fattoria Uccelliera
See also Uccelliera.

Fattoria Zerbina EMILIA-ROMAGNA
Via Vicchio 11, 48010 Marzeno di Faenza (RA)
Tel.: 054640022/Fax: 054640275/www.zerbina.com
DOC(G)s: Albana di Romagna; Sangiovese di Romagna;
Trebbiano di Romagna
Zerbina makes one of the best Albana di Romagna
sweeties—the honeyed "Scacco Matto"—and some of the
most serious reds in Bologna. "Marzieno" Ravenna Rosso
is a blackberry-scented blend of sangiovese and cabernet,
a well-structured rival to many pricier super-Tuscans.

Fazi-Battaglia MARCHE
Via Roma 117, 60032 Castelpiano (AN)
Tel.: 06844311/Fax: 0684431300/www.fazibattaglia.it
DOC(G)s: Rosso Cònero; Verdicchio dei Castelli di Jesi
Years ago, this huge winery packaged its Verdicchio dei
Castelli di Jesi in fish- and amphora-shaped bottles. That's
not fashionable anymore, but Fazi-Battaglia still has some
solid whites to choose from, like "Le Moie," a bright and
aromatic selection, and "Riserva San Sisto," which is
plumped up with oak. Among the reds, the Rosso Cònero
"Passo San Lupo" is decent.

Fedrizzi, Cipriano TRENTINO
Via 4 Novembre 1, 38017 Mezzolombardo (TN)
Tel.: 0461602328
DOC(G)s: Teroldego Rotaliano; Trentino
Tiny production, but if you see the Teroldego Rotaliano,
grab it: it's one of the better examples of this tarry, funky
variety. Great savory red for a big steak or a braise.

Felline PUGLIA

Via N. Donadio 20, 74024 Manduria (TA)
Tel.: 0999711660
€ DOC(G)s: Primitivo di Manduria
This winery's silky Primitivo di Manduria is one of the better examples to be found, while the IGT "Alberello" lends the dark-hued heft of negroamaro (50% of the blend) to the jammy fruit of primitivo.

FELLUGA, LIVIO FRIULI–VENEZIA GIULIA

Via Risorgimento 1, 3070 Brazzano Cormons (GO)
Tel.: 048160203/Fax: 0481630126/www.liviofelluga.it
€€ DOC(G)s: Colli Orientali del Friuli
Pioneering Friulian estate that set the standards for great Italian white wine, from the textbook tocai friulano (a wonderfully aromatic, minerally white) to "Terre Alte," a silken blend of tocai, pinot bianco, and sauvignon. Lately, there's been more acclaim for the reds, which are sourced from the Rosazzo area: the elegant "Sossò" merlot proves that a wine doesn't have to be huge to be good, while the dense refosco is one of the best interpretations of that grape. Finally, there's the excellent sweet picolit.

FELLUGA, MARCO FRIULI–VENEZIA GIULIA

Via Gorizia 121, 34072 Gradisco d'Isonzo (GO)
Tel.: 048199164/Fax: 0481960270/www.marcofelluga.it
€ DOC(G)s: Collio
Making wines of this quality (high), on this scale (large), is an accomplishment that is underappreciated in our world of 500-case cult wines. Felluga's pinot grigio, tocai friulano, and sauvignon all have depth and class—and can still be had for under $20. "Molamatta," from tocai, ribolla gialla, and pinot bianco, and "Carantan," a red blend, are "super-Friulians" that only taste expensive.

Felsina

See Fattoria di Felsina.

Ferrando, Luigi PIEMONTE

Via Torino 599/A, 10015 Ivrea (TO)
Tel.: 0125641176/www.ferrandovini.it
€- DOC(G)s: Canavese; Carema; Erbaluce di Caluso
€€ When you're tired of fat and fruity and want complexity and classic structure (i.e., acid), try this northern Piedmontese house. Flinty, floral whites from erbaluce are a start (there's an excellent *Champenoise* sparkler from erbaluce, too), and then the nebbiolos: smoky, leathery reds from the Carema DOC that bring Burgundy to mind. Don't miss the sweet erbaluce *passito*, "Solativo."

FERRARI TRENTINO

Via Ponte di Ravina, 15, 38040 Trento (TN)
Tel.: 0461972311/Fax: 0461913008/www.cantineferrari.it
€- DOC(G)s: Trento Brut
€€ The Lunelli family makes some of Italy's best sparklers, all in the Champagne method. The vintage-dated "Giulio Ferrari" (all chardonnay) has the minerally structure of a good Champagne at a terrific price. The rosé also rivals Champagne at just over $20 a bottle.

Ferraris, Roberto PIEMONTE

Frazione Dogliani 33, 14041 Agliano Terme (AT)
Tel.: 0141954234
DOC(G)s: Barbera d'Asti
  Big, rich barberas are the specialty of this little producer, which gets a hand from La Barbatella enologist Giuliano Noè. The pumped-up "La Cricca" Barbera d'Asti gets the big scores, but the finer, more fruit-driven "Nobbio" (aged in stainless steel) is the one to look for.

Ferrero, Eredi Virginia PIEMONTE

Località San Rocco 71, Serralunga d'Alba (CN)
Tel.: 0173613283
DOC(G)s: Barolo
  Structure, savor, and ethereal aromatics from a historic property in Serralunga. The Barolo is sourced from the San Rocco cru and has the kind of Burgundian personality that makes Barolo-heads swoon.

Ferrucci, Stefano EMILIA-ROMAGNA

Via Casolana 3045/2, 48014 Castel Bolognese (RA)
Tel.: 0546651068/www.stefanoferrucci.it
DOC(G)s: Albana di Romagna; Sangiovese di Romagna
  High-end wines from Romagna, including the Albana di Romagna Passito "Domus Aurea" and the late-harvest "Vino da Uve Stramature," from malvasia left to hang until midwinter. On the dry side, the "Domus Caia" Sangiovese di Romagna is chocolate-rich and ready to drink on release.

Feudi di San Giuliano SICILIA

Contrada da Mazzaporro Duchessa, 90030 Contessa Entellina (PA)
Tel.: 0923952148
DOC(G)s: Contessa Entellina
  "Vento di Mayo" (chardonnay-catarratto-inzolia) is substantial and fresh—among the few Sicilian whites you'd want to drink more than once. Good values in nero d'avola and cabernet.

FEUDI DI SAN GREGORIO CAMPANIA

Contrada Cerza Grossa, 83050 Sorbo Serpico (AV)
Tel.: 0825986611/Fax: 0825986230/www.feudi.it
DOC(G)s: Fiano di Avellino; Greco di Tufo; Taurasi; Sannio
  Dynamic winery in Campania with an ever-expanding production. Classic local wines such as the spicy yet supple Taurasi ("Selve di Luoti" is exceptional) and a citrusy white Fiano di Avellino anchor a high-impact selection. The white "Campanaro," from slightly late-harvested fiano and greco, has a honeyed, off-dry feel (try it with cheese), while "Pàtrimo," a merlot with the density of motor oil, is the critics' darling. Most exciting is the massive aglianico "Serpico," which showcases the feral intensity of the grape.

Feudo Monaci PUGLIA

Contrada Monaci, 73015 Salice Salentino (LE)
Tel.: 0831665700/www.giv.it
DOC(G)s: Salice Salentino
  Puglian quaffers headlined by a nice Salice Salentino.

Feudo Principi di Butera SICILIA

Contrada Diliella, 93011 Butera (CL)
Tel.: 0934347726

A new and expansive Sicilian estate owned by the giant wine firm Zonin. Go for the nero d'avola "Deliella." There are also plush, clean reds from cabernet sauvignon ("San Rocco") and merlot ("Calat").

Fiegl FRIULI–VENEZIA GIULIA

Località Lenzuolo Bianco 1, 34170 Goriza (GO)
Tel.: 048131072/Fax: 0481547103/www.fieglvini.com
DOC(G)s: Collio

Located in Oslavia, steps from the border with Slovenia, this small producer offers great value in classic Friulian varietals such as pinot grigio, tocai friulano, and sauvignon. Weighty, well-made whites at reasonable prices.

Filiputti, Walter FRIULI–VENEZIA GIULIA

Piazza Abbazia 15, 33044 Manzano in Rosazzo (UD)
Tel.: 0432759429/Fax: 0432759887
DOC(G)s: Colli Orientali del Friuli

Winemaker Walter Filiputti lives in the historic Abbazia di Rosazzo and crafts wines from its vineyards. The rare red pignolo, which had its storied revival here, is a specialty, as is picolit ("Monasterium" is sumptuous dessert wine). More mainstream are the spicy red "Broili di Filip" (refosco-merlot) and some whites, headlined by the creamy and exotically fragrant "Poesis" (chardonnay-tocai-picolit).

Filomusi Guelfi ABRUZZO

Via Filomusi Guelfi 11, 65028 Tocco Casauria (PE)
Tel.: 085986906/Fax: 08598353
DOC(G)s: Montepulciano d'Abruzzo

Soft and richly fruity Montepulciano d'Abruzzo and deep rosé Cerasuolo. Warm, lush, and affordable.

★ Firriato SICILIA

Via Trapani 4, 91027 Paceco (TP)
Tel.: 0923882755/Fax: 0923883266/www.firriato.it
DOC(G)s: Alcamo; Etna

The high-end reds "Camelot" (cabernet sauvignon and merlot) and "Harmonium" (nero d'avola) are critical faves, while the dark and substantial "Chiaramonte" nero d'avola is an excellent value. The diverse and international production includes several white blends incorporating chardonnay.

Florio SICILIA

Via Vincenzo Florio 1, 91025 Marsala (TP)
Tel.: 0923781111/www.cantineflorio.com
DOC(G)s: Marsala

A large and historic Marsala house now owned by the Illva Saronno spirits company. Offers mostly cheap cooking wines, but if you happen across the Vergine "Baglio Oro" (a dry style, aged 5-plus years), check it out as an alternative to fine Sherry.

Folonari, Tenute Ambrogio e Giovanni

Via de' Bardi, 28, 50125 Firenze (FI)
Tel.: 055200281/www.tenutefolonari.com

DOC(G)s: Chianti Classico; Chianti Rúfina; Vino Nobile di Montapulciano

This firm was created in 2000 after the Folonari family (of Ruffino fame) split up its holdings. Father-son team Ambrogio and Giovanni Folonari now control the 800-acre Nozzole estate in Greve (producer of classic Chiantis and the powerful cabernet "Il Pareto"), as well as two other properties in Chianti Classico from which they craft "Cabreo La Pietra" (a juicy varietal chardonnay) and the luscious "Cabreo Il Borgo" (70% sangiovese, 30% cabernet sauvignon). There's also Gracciano Svetoni in Montepulciano (offering smooth and affordable Vino Nobile) and Spaletti in Chianti Rúfina.

Fontaleoni TOSCANA

Località Santa Maria 39, 53037 San Gimignano (SI)
Tel./Fax: 0577950193

DOC(G)s: Chianti Colli Senesi; Vernaccia di San Gimignano

Fresh and spicy vernaccia, including the partially barrel-fermented "Vigna Casanuova." There's also Chianti Colli Senesi and a barrel-aged sangiovese-merlot blend called "La Cerreta."

Fontana Candida LAZIO

Via Fontana Candida 11, 00040 MontePorzio Catone (RM)
Tel.: 069420066/www.fontanacandida.com

DOC(G)s: Frascati

Best known for lemony Frascati wines, which at the high end (try "Santa Teresa") are pretty appealing. Simple varietal wines (sourced from the Veneto) and Orvieto (from Umbria) as well. Priced for party consumption.

Fontana, Graziano TRENTINO

Via Case Sparse 9, 38010 Faedo (TN)
Tel.: 0461650400

DOC(G)s: Trentino

Perched in the hills of Faedo, Graziano Fontana makes superaromatic, varietally true whites from sauvignon, traminer, chardonnay, and müller-thurgau (a specialty). The sauvignon and müller are both exceptional, and the pricing is fantastic.

Fontana, Livia PIEMONTE

Via Pugnane 12, 12060 Castiglione Falletto (CN)
Tel.: 017362844/Fax: 017362967

DOC(G)s: Barbera d'Alba; Barolo; Dolcetto d'Alba; Langhe

Lesser-known but solid producer of Barolo, including one from the Villero cru in Castiglione Falletto. Fragrant, fine, and well priced—a description that suits the barberas and dolcettos as well.

Fontanabianca PIEMONTE

Frazione Bordini, 12057 Neive (CN)
Tel./Fax: 017367195

DOC(G)s: Barbaresco; Barbera d'Alba; Dolcetto d'Alba; Langhe

Small Piemontese house with good wine at great prices. The limited-production Barbaresco "Sori Burdin" is the top bottling; smooth and classically styled.

Fontanafredda PIEMONTE

Via Alba 15, 12050 Serralunga d'Alba (CN)
Tel.: 0173613161/Fax: 0173613451/www.fontanafredda.it
DOC(G)s: Barolo; Barbaresco; Barbera d'Alba; Nebbiolo
d'Alba

This landmark estate was founded in the late 1800s by
Emanuele Guerreri, son of King Victor Emmanuel II. Best
known for the dense and long-aging "Vigna La Rosa"
(from the home vineyard in Serralunga), Fontanafredda is
one of the largest producers of Barolo, along with a broad
array of other Piedmontese wines ranging from Asti
Spumante to Gavi. The Barbera d'Alba "Papagena" and
the Langhe Rosso "Eremo" (barbera-nebbiolo) are new-
style offerings from this old-school house.

Fontanavecchia CAMPANIA

Via Fontanavecchia, 82030 Torrecuso (BN)
Tel.: 0824876275
DOC(G)s: Aglianico del Taburno; Taburno Falanghina

Black and beautiful aglianico from Benevento, with all of
the tar and tobacco scents typical of the area. "Cataratte"
is a little bigger than the basic Aglianico del Taburno.
Spicy whites from falanghina as well.

Fonterutoli

See Castello di Fonterutoli.

FONTODI TOSCANA ▬▬●

Via San Leolino 89, 50020 Panzano in Chianti (FI)
Tel.: 055852005/Fax: 055852537/www.fontodi.com
DOC(G)s: Chianti Classico

The Manetti family acquired this estate in 1968. It is one
of Chianti's most striking wineries, overlooking the sun-
splashed bowl of vineyards in Panzano known as the
conca d'oro. The basic Chianti Classico drinks like a
Burgundy, while the massive *riserva* "Vigna del Sorbo,"
with a touch of cabernet and 18 months' aging in barrique,
rivals Brunello in intensity. "Flaccianello della Pieve"
remains one of the deeper, darker expressions of varietal
sangiovese, and the wines from the "Case Via" line—
syrah and pinot noir—are some of the better examples of
those varieties being made in Italy.

★ Foradori TRENTINO

Via Damiano Chiesa 1, 38017 Mezzolombardo (TN)
Tel.: 0461601046/Fax: 0461603447
www.elisabettaforadori.com
DOC(G)s: Teroldego Rotaliano

From the rock-strewn soils of Mezzolombardo, young
Elisabetta Foradori crafts one of Italy's most elegant and
interesting Alpine reds, "Granato," made from the typically
hard-edged teroldego grape. The base-level Teroldego
Rotaliano is excellent, too, and remains a great value. And
while "Granato" remains the flagship, newer reds like
"Karanar" (cabernet–syrah–petit verdot) and "Ailanpa"
(all syrah) speak to this region's potential for big reds. In
fact, there's only one white made here, the aromatic
"Myrto" (sauvignon–incrocio manzoni–pinot bianco).

Forlini Cappelini LIGURIA

Località Manarola, Via Riccobaldi 45, 19010
Riomaggiore (SP)

Tel.: 0187920496
DOC(G)s: Cinque Terre
  A producer of artisanal briny, fresh-flavored Cinque Terre whites. Unique but not cheap.

Fornaser, Paolo
See Monte Faustino.

FORTETO DELLA LUJA PIEMONTE
Regione Bricco Casa Rosso 4, 14050 Loazzolo (AT)
Tel.: 0141831596
DOC(G)s: Loazzolo; Monferrato; Piemonte
  Giancarlo Scaglione makes some of Italy's best sweet wines at his farmstead winery near Canelli. Tops is his Loazzolo DOC "Piasa Rischei," a late-harvest moscato that rivals Sauternes in its honeyed, smoky complexity. The delicate, berry-scented brachetto "Pian di Sogni" is another gem, and the Moscato d'Asti "Piasa San Maurizio" is exceptional. On the still side, the red blend "Le Grive" (barbera–pinot noir) is a plush and fragrant treat.

Fossacolle, Podere TOSCANA
Località Tavernelle 7, 53024 Montalcino (SI)
Tel./Fax: 0577816013
DOC(G)s: Brunello di Montalcino
  Sergio Marchetti launched this small Montalcino estate in the early eighties. The Brunello has big fruit and a touch of new oak, but overall it is a smoky, spicy style of wine.

★ Fossi, Enrico TOSCANA
Via degli Arrighi 4, 50058 Signa (FI)
Tel.: 0558732174/Fax: 0558792512
  Enrico Fossi plants whatever he likes—including gamay, pinot noir, riesling, and the full array of Bordeaux varieties. His style is over-the-top, favoring almost obscene extraction and lots of oak. He makes more than a dozen wines, including juicy monsters from malbec and syrah. There's also a cabernet, "Sassoforte," and a merlot, "Portico" (both spend 22 months in barrique), and similarly pumped-up whites from chardonnay ("Primo-preso") and Sauvignon ("Conteso").

Frascole TOSCANA
Via di Frascole 27, 50062 Dicomano (FI)
Tel.: 0558386340
DOC(G)s: Chianti Rúfina
  Still more great-value red wine from the Rúfina region. Buy it by the case for a great picnic and barbecue red.

FRESCOBALDI, MARCHESE DE TOSCANA
 Via San Spirito, 11, 50125 Firenze (FI)
 Tel.: 05527141/www.frescobaldi.it
DOC(G)s: Brunello di Montalcino; Chianti; Chianti Rúfina; Pomino
  Frescobaldi is a noble name with a centuries-old wine-making history. Today, the family operates nine estates covering more than 1,800 acres, headlined by Castelgiocondo in Montalcino (acquired in 1989; see separate listing) and Castello di Nipozzano in Rúfina. Nipozzano's excellent range includes the awesome-value Chianti Rúfina Riserva and its powerful sibling, "Montesodi,"

along with the cabernet-based "Mormoreto." Frescobaldi also partners with California's Robert Mondavi in the Luce della Vite vineyard, based out of Castelgiocondo in Montalcino (see listing). Danzante is a value-priced line of varietals (sourced from various regions) also produced by the Mondavi-Frescobaldi partnership.

Fucci, Elena BASILICATA

Località Contrada Solagna del Titolo, 85022 Barile (PZ)
Tel.: 0972770736
DOC(G)s: Aglianico del Vulture
  Originally purchased by the Fucci family in the early seventies, the estate turned out its first vintage in 2000. They're going for an inky, fruit-driven style of aglianico, aging "Titolo" for a year in barrique. Dense stuff.

★ Fuligni TOSCANA

Via San Saloni 33, 53024 Montalcino (SI)
Tel.: 0577848039/Fax: 0577848710
DOC(G)s: Brunello di Montalcino; Rosso di Montalcino
  Aromatic, fruit-driven Brunello aged partly in large Slavonian casks and partly in French oak *tonneaux;* the style is well rounded and plush. The super-Tuscan "SJ" combines sangiovese grosso with merlot.

Funtanin PIEMONTE

Via Torino 191, 12043 Canale (CN)
Tel.: 0173979488/Fax: 0173979488/www.funtanin.com
DOC(G)s: Barbera d'Alba; Langhe; Roero
  More good wine from unsung Roero. Start with the citrusy "Pierin di Soc" Roero Arneis, then move to the big reds: "Ciabot Pierin" is a lush Barbera d'Alba; "Bricco Barbisa" is a softly contoured red based on nebbiolo.

Gabbas, Giuseppe SARDEGNA

Via Tieste 65, 08100 Nuoro (NU)
Tel.: 078431351/Fax: 078431351
DOC(G)s: Cannonau di Sardegna
  Gabbas wines are all based on cannonau (also known as grenache), the specialty of his hometown of Nuoro. The aromatic "Lillovè" Cannonau di Sardegna DOC is the purest expression of the variety, while "Dule" and "Arbeskia" plump it up with cabernet and other grapes.

Gabutti di Franco Boasso

See Boasso.

Gagliardo, Gianni PIEMONTE

Frazione Santa Maria, 12064 La Morra (CN)
Tel.: 017350829/www.gagliardo.it
DOC(G)s: Barolo; Barbera d'Alba; Dolcetto d'Alba; Langhe
  Solid Piedmontese lineup. The top Barolo, "Le Preve," is a blend of fruit from La Morra and Castiglione Falletto vineyards. Also savory whites from the rare favorita grape.

Gagliole TOSCANA

Località 42, 53011 Castellina in Chianti (SI)
Tel.: 0577740369/Fax: 0577740875/www.gagliole.com
  A boutique estate in Chianti Classico. The "Rosso" is a luxurious blend of sangiovese with a touch of cabernet; "Bianco" is a tropically fruity, barrique-aged blend of trebbiano and chardonnay. "Pecchia" is an intense old-vine sangiovese.

Gaierhof TRENTINO

Via IV Novembre 51, 38030 Roverè della Luna (TN)
Tel.: 0461658514/www.gaierhof.com
DOC(G)s: Trentino

Pleasant varietal wines (mostly whites) from a large estate in Trentino, which also owns Maso Poli (see separate listing). Gaierhof's "Settecento" line is the stuff to look for.

GAJA PIEMONTE

Via Torino 36, 12050 Barbaresco (CN)
Tel.: 0173635158
DOC(G)s: Barbaresco; Langhe

The gold standard of Italian wine. Eagle-eyed Angelo Gaja has been an outspoken innovator since he took over his family estate in the 1960s. He is credited with the "modernization" of Barbaresco, having been one of the first in Piedmont to embrace controlled-temperature fermentation (to reduce oxidation) and small-oak aging (to stabilize color and preserve fruit). The power, elegance, and, above all, longevity of Gaja Barbaresco is practically unrivaled in Italy; his wines from great older vintages like '64 and '71 remain vibrant and clean, and, needless to say, more recent years have followed suit. Intensely perfumed Barbaresco is Gaja's signature, although he has removed the Barbaresco designation from his stellar single-vineyard wines, "Sorì San Lorenzo," "Sorì Tildìn," and "Costa Russi," all of which are now labeled Langhe Nebbiolo. He claimed that he made the change because people were ignoring his "base" Barbaresco bottling in favor of these "cru" wines, but it is notable that the single-vineyard wines now include small percentages of barbera, which is not allowed under the Barbaresco DOCG. Whatever the case, they're superb, as is the rest of the Gaja range, which includes the intensely powerful Langhe Nebbiolo "Sperss" (once a Barolo DOCG wine, it is sourced from a single vineyard in Serralunga); two rich chardonnays ("Gaia & Rey" and "Rossj Bass"); the overlooked cabernet "Darmagi" (from a vineyard planted in 1978); and several barberas, dolcettos, and blends. Gaja also owns estates in Tuscany's Montalcino (Pieve di Santa Restituta) and Bolgheri (Ca' Marcanda) (see separate listings). Everything he makes is luxurious and priced accordingly.

★ Galardi (Terra di Lavoro) CAMPANIA

Frazione San Carlo, 81030 Sessa Aurunca (CE)
Tel.: 0823925003

"Terra di Lavoro" is a Campanian cult wine (first vintage 1994) with an annual production of about 1,000 cases. The blend is 80% aglianico and 20% piedirosso, and while consultant Riccardo Cotarella extracts lots of fruit sweetness, there's also a dark-edged aglianico ferocity that lends this wine a complexity and ageability not often found in the general run of syrupy-sweet cult wine.

Galli e Brocatelli UMBRIA

Via degli Olmi, 06083 Bastia Umbria (PG)
Tel.: 0758001501/Fax: 0758000935
DOC(G)s: Montefalco; Torgiano

Long-established (if lesser-known) name in Umbria with an earthy, sangiovese-based Torgiano Rosso (one of the

few wines in that DOC besides Lungarotti) and some rustic
reds from nearby Montefalco.

Gancia PIEMONTE

Corso Libertà 66, 14053 Canelli (AT)
Tel.: 0141830245/Fax: 0141830204/www.gancia.it
DOC(G)s: Asti; Barolo; others

One of the giant vermouth and *spumante* houses in
Piedmont (Carlo Gancia is considered the first to vinify
moscato in the Champagne method, effectively creating
Asti Spumante in the 1860s). The product range includes
many sparklers and *aperitivi*, and the firm owns other
winemaking concerns throughout Italy. Asti Spumante is a
specialty, but there are also bargain-priced Barolo,
Barbaresco, and other still wines.

Garofoli MARCHE

Via Arno 9, 60025 Loreto (AN)
Tel.: 0717820162; 0717820163/Fax: 0717821437
www.garofolivini.it
DOC(G)s: Verdicchio dei Castelli di Jesi; Rosso Cònero

A historic Marche winery specializing in verdicchio. The
one to go for is the citrusy and substantial Verdicchio dei
Castelli di Jesi "Podium." There's also some juicy, fairly
weighty Rosso Cònero on the red side.

Gastaldi PIEMONTE

Via Albesani 20, 12057 Neive (CN)
Tel.: 0173677400
DOC(G)s: Barbaresco; Dolcetto d'Alba; Langhe

This small estate in Barbaresco has an excellent
reputation for big, round Barbaresco, as well as two
Langhe Rosso wines that rival it in intensity.

Gatti, Piero PIEMONTE

Località Moncucco 28, 12058 San Stefano Belbo (CN)
Tel./Fax: 0141840918
DOC(G)s: Langhe; Piemonte

The late Piero Gatti specialized in Piedmont's fun grapes:
moscato, brachetto, and freisa. Gatti's bright and fruity
moscato *frizzante* is one of the best there is, as is the
sweet and rosy brachetto; on the dry side, there's a
fragrant red blend called "Verbeia" (barbera-freisa).

Gattinara, Sergio PIEMONTE

Piazza Mons Francese 1, 13045 Gattinara (VC)
Tel.: 0163832704/Fax: 0163826631
www.gattinarasergio.it
DOC(G)s: Erbaluce di Caluso; Gattinara

Sergio Gattinara, a former banker, couldn't stay away
from his namesake town and wine. He produces Gattinara
in a perfumed, classic style.

Geografico TOSCANA

Via Mulinaccio 10, 53013 Gaiole in Chianti (SI)
Tel.: 0577749489/Fax: 0577749223
DOC(G)s: Chianti Classico; Vino Nobile di Montepulciano;
Brunello di Montalcino; others

A large co-op with bottlings from all the key Tuscan
appellations, many of them nice values. Chianti Classico
"Montegiachi" is one, as is the Chianti Colli Senesi "Torri."

Geppetti, Elisabetta

See Fattoria Le Pupille.

★ Germano, Ettore PIEMONTE

Località Cerretta 1, 12050 Serralunga d'Alba
Tel.: 0173613528/Fax: 0173613593
www.germanoettore.com
DOC(G)s: Barolo; Barbera d'Alba; Dolcetto d'Alba; Langhe
Massive, modern Barolos and other stylish wines from
young Sergio Germano. The Barbera d'Alba "Vigna della
Madre" is dense and silky, as is the Langhe Rosso "Balàu,"
a blend of barbera, dolcetto, and merlot. The Barolos are
deep and delicious: "Prapò" (larger cask aging) and
"Cerretta" (24 months in barrique) are loaded with the
dark coffee/cocoa notes typical of Serralunga wines.

Ghisolfi, Attilio PIEMONTE

Regione Bussia 27, 12065 Monforte d'Alba (CN)
Tel.: 017378345/Fax: 017378345
DOC(G)s: Barolo; Barbera d'Alba; Dolcetto d'Alba; Langhe
"Alta Bussia" Langhe Rosso is a barbera-nebbiolo blend
that showcases the rich fruit of the former and the
perfume of the latter. Good varietal barbera and dolcetto,
and a solid Barolo, "Visette," from a cru in Monforte.

Giacobazzi EMILIA-ROMAGNA

Via Provinciale Ovest 57, 41015 Nonantola (MO)
Tel.: 059540711/Fax: 059549030/www.giacobazzi.it
DOC(G)s: Lambrusco di Sorbara; Lambrusco Grasparossa
The glory days of Lambrusco are long past, but if you were
to come across one of the DOC-specified dry styles (either
the Grasparossa or the Sorbara), it'd be well worth trying.

GIACOSA, BRUNO PIEMONTE

Via XX Settembre 52, 12057 Neive (CN)
Tel.: 017367027/www.brunogiacosa.it
DOC(G)s: Barbaresco; Barolo; Dolcetto d'Alba; Roero
Some of the longest-lived wines in the Langhe. Giacosa's
cellars are in Neive, in the Barbaresco DOCG, but holdings extend into Barolo. Wines from marquee vineyards in
both areas: from Neive come intense Barbarescos from
the Gallina and Santo Stefano crus (the "red label" "Santo
Stefano" Riserva is released in select years), while the
Falletto vineyard, in Serralunga, is the source of Barolo,
barbera, and dolcetto (also check out the pretty dolcetto
from the Basarin vineyard in Neive). There's also a silken
Barbaresco from the Asili cru in Barbaresco, and, last but
not least, a great Roero Arneis, an aromatic white that is
always clean and consistent. Giacosa is a traditionalist,
producing fragrant yet austere wines aged for long periods
in large casks before release. Buy and hold!

Giacosa, Carlo PIEMONTE

Via Ovello 8, 12050 Barbaresco (CN)
Tel.: 0173635166
DOC(G)s: Barbaresco; Barbera d'Alba; Dolcetto d'Alba
The Barbaresco-based Giacosas have vineyards in
most of the commune's top crus, and their affordable
wines include the meaty "Montefico" and "Narin."

Giacosa F.lli PIEMONTE

Via XX Settembre 64, 12057 Neive (CN)
Tel.: 017367013/Fax: 017367662/www.giacosa.it
DOC(G)s: Barbaresco; Barolo; Barbera d'Alba; Langhe
  Another Giacosa winery, probably the lesser-known of
the three in the States. *Négociant* producer (meaning that
grapes are purchased from contract growers) with
Barbaresco from the Rio Sordo cru and a powerful Barolo
from Bussia. "Maria Gioana" is a good barrique-aged
barbera and "Vigna Mandorlo" is a cru nebbiolo from a
vineyard in Castiglione Falletto.

GINI VENETO

Via G. Matteotti 42, 37032 Monteforte d'Alpone (VR)
Tel.: 0457611908/Fax: 0456101610
DOC(G)s: Soave
  Brothers Sandro and Claudio Gini have a newly
renovated winery and prime vineyards in the Soave
Classico, from which they craft some of the area's (and
therefore Italy's) best whites. The single-vineyard Soave
"La Frosca" is a garganega with true class, with a creamy
touch of oak framing its juicy fruit flavors. The barrique-
aged, old-vine Soave "Selvarenza" has an almost tropical
fruit intensity. The pinot noir "Campo alle More," from a
high-altitude vineyard on the fringes of the Soave zone, is
one of the few Italian pinot noirs you'll want to drink again.

Giuncheo

See Tenuta Giuncheo.

Gojer, Franz ALTO ADIGE

Frazione Santa Maddalena, Via Rivellone 1, 39100
Bolzano/Bozen (BZ)
Tel.: 0471978775/www.gojer.it
DOC(G)s: Alto Adige
  An artisan who produces some of the best lagrein in the
Alto Adige, loaded with dark, coffee-ground intensity. A
light, tart red Santa Maddalena (St. Magdalener) is made
from another local red grape, schiava.

Gorelli, Giuseppe (Due Portine) TOSCANA

Via Cialdini 51/53, 53024 Montalcino (SI)
Tel.: 0577848098
DOC(G)s: Brunello di Montalcino
  Boutique Brunellos from Giancarlo Gorelli with lots of
fruit depth and sweet, soft tannins. The last vintage was
1998, as the estate was merged with that of Giancarlo's
son, Giuseppe, who named the new operation Le
Potazzine after a prized vineyard (see the separate listing).

Gracciano Svetoni

See Folonari, Tenute Ambrogio e Giovanni.

Gradis'ciutta FRIULI–VENEZIA GIULIA

Località Giasbana 10, 34070 San Floriano del Collio (GO)
Tel.: 0481390237
DOC(G)s: Collio
  Owned by the Princic family. Nice varietal values—tocai
and pinot grigio especially—with a Collio pedigree.
"Bianco del Bratinis" is a fresh, unoaked blend of tocai,
sauvignon, pinot grigio, and chardonnay. "Del Tuzz" is a
more tropically fruity, barrel-fermented mix of chardonnay,
tocai, pinot grigio, and malvasia.

Graf Enzenberg (Tenuta Manincor) ALTO ADIGE

San Giuseppe al Lago 4, 39052 Caldaro/Kaltern (BZ)
Tel.: 0471960230/Fax: 0471960204/www.manincor.com
DOC(G)s: Alto Adige×/Südtirole Terlaner

Count Michael Goëss-Enzenberg began bottling at his
Tenuta Manincor estate in 1996. Check out the fresh and
exotic moscato giallo or the "Mason" pinot noir, one of the
better Italian pinots around. "Cuvée Sophie" is a fat,
honeyed blend of chardonnay, viognier, and sauvignon,
while "Lieben Aich" is an intense single-vineyard
sauvignon fermented naturally in large wood casks.

Grasso Casa Vinicola SICILIA

Via Albero 5, 98057 Milazzo (ME)
Tel.: 0909281082/Fax: 0909224001
DOC(G)s: Faro

One of the few producers of Faro DOC rosso (an earthy,
spicy red based on the nerello mascalese grape).

GRASSO, ELIO PIEMONTE

Località Ginestra 40, 12065 Monforte d'Alba (CN)
Tel.: 017378491/Fax: 0173789907
DOC(G)s: Barolo; Barbera d'Alba; Dolcetto d'Alba; Langhe

The Gavarini vineyard, just north of Ginestra in Monforte
d'Alba, is home to this excellent Barolo vintner, which
bottles two potent wines from the site: "Runcot" and
"Gavarini Vigna Chiniera." From the Ginestra cru, meanwhile, comes "Ginestra Case Matè," which is no less
intense but more plush, immediately drinkable, and
affordable. Great dolcetto and barbera, too.

GRASSO, SILVIO PIEMONTE

Frazione Annunziata 112, 12064 La Morra (CN)
Tel.: 017350322/Fax: 017350322
DOC(G)s: Barolo; Barbera d'Alba; Dolcetto d'Alba

Sleek, modern, yet brightly acidic Barolo from the
Luciani and Ciabot Manzoni crus in La Morra. Luciani is
"classic La Morra," aromatic and soft, while Ciabot
Manzoni is a little denser and deeper (though there's no
barrique aging on either wine). Also a plump and fruity
barbera, "Fontanile," among other well-made wines.

GRATTAMACCO TOSCANA

Podere Grattamacco, 57022 Castagneto Carducci (LI)
Tel.: 0564990496/Fax: 0564990498
www.grattamacco.com
DOC(G)s: Bolgheri

Legendary Bolgheri winery. Longtime owner Piermario
Meletti Cavallari recently sold a controlling interest to
Swiss pharmaceutical entrepreneur Claudio Tipa. Maurizio
Castelli still crafts the wines, headlined by the sangiovese-
cabernet blend "Grattamacco Rosso," consistently one of
the most elegant super-Tuscans around. The Bianco is a
crisp, herbaceous coastal white from vermentino.

GRAVNER FRIULI–VENEZIA GIULIA

Via Lenzuolo Bianco 9, 34170 Oslavia (GO)
Tel.: 0481130882/www.gravner.it
DOC(G)s: Collio

Josko Gravner is an iconoclastic producer who has led
several winemaking revolutions in Friuli–Venezia Giulia.
The first was in the eighties, when he moved away from

the popular style of clean, cold-fermented whites aged only in steel and employed fermentation and aging in French oak barriques. He's since taken it a step further, with a minimal-intervention approach in which the wines (whites and reds) are fermented in open-topped wood casks without temperature control, aged for exceptionally long periods in wood, and bottled unfiltered. The whites, such as "Breg" (chardonnay–sauvignon–pinot grigio–riesling), have a cloudy, cidery appearance and lots of extract, checked by amazingly racy acidity. Ditto for the ribolla gialla. These are unusual whites with a complex mix of yeasty, woody, deeply fruity flavors. The reds are powerful and lean, with a real Bordeaux sensibility.

Greppone Mazzi TOSCANA

Località Greppone, 53024 Montalcino (SI)
Tel.: 05583605

DOC(G)s: Brunello di Montalcino
  Montalcino estate owned by Ruffino. Aromatic, value-priced Brunello with nice depth.

Grimaldi, Giacomo PIEMONTE

Via Luigi Einaudi 8, 12060 Barolo (CN)
Tel.: 017335256

DOC(G)s: Barolo; Barbera d'Alba; Dolcetto d'Alba; Nebbiolo d'Alba
  Tiny-production Barolo from Le Coste, the smallest vineyard in the village of Barolo. Dense and dark-hued, with a pronounced new-oak influence. Juicy, toasty barbera and dolcetto as well.

Grotta del Sole CAMPANIA

Via Spinelli 2, 80010 Quarto (NA)
Tel.: 0818762566/www.grottadelsole.it

DOC(G)s: Asprinio d'Aversa; Campi Flegrei; Fiano di Avellino; Greco di Tufo
  Naples-area winery with a decent, inexpensive range, including Lacryma Christi, both white and red. A fragrant and minerally Greco di Tufo is probably their best wine.

Gruppo Italiano Vini (GIV) VENETO

Villa Belvedere, 37010 Calmasino (VR)
Tel.: 0456269600/Fax: 0457235772/www.giv.it
  A Verona-based firm whose portfolio of producers includes Nino Negri (Lombardia), Santi (Veneto), Lamberti (Veneto), Conti Formentini (Friuli–Venezia Giulia), Folonari (Toscano), Melini (Toscana), Machiavelli (Toscana), Bigi (Umbria), Fontana Candida (Lazio), Tenute Rapitalà (Sicilia), and Terre degli Svevi (Basilicata). GIV is the largest wine company in Italy, producing more than 60 million bottles a year.

Guado al Tasso

See Antinori; Tenuta Guado al Tasso.

Gualdo del Re TOSCANA

Località Notri 77, 57028 Suvereto (LI)
Tel.: 0565829888/Fax: 0565829361

DOC(G)s: Val di Cornia
  Suvereto is an up-and-coming zone on Tuscany's south coast, and this is one of the local producers to keep an eye on. "Rennero" (merlot–pinot nero) and "Federico Primo" (cabernet sauvignon) are both pretty, lush reds,

while the Val di Cornia Suvereto DOC (a smoky, slightly rustic red based on sangiovese) is a solid value.

Guicciardini Strozzi (Fattoria Cusona)
TOSCANA

Località Cusona 5, 53037 San Gimignano (SI)
Tel.: 0577950028/Fax: 0577950260
www.guicciardinistrozzi.it
DOC(G)s: Chianti; Vernaccia di San Gimignano
  The local white vernaccia is a specialty ("Perlato" adds some flesh to its typically lean, minerally frame), although it's taken a backseat to rich reds like "Millani" (sangiovese-cabernet-merlot) and the tarry, toasty "Sódole" (sangiovese).

Gulfi SICILIA

Contrada Passo Guastella, 97012 Chiaramonte Gulfi (RG)
Tel.: 0932921654/Fax: 0932921728/www.gulfi.it
  Located in southeastern Sicily, birthplace of nero d'avola. "Rossoibleo" and "Neroibleo" are deep, fruity values, but the goal here is site-specificity: the pumped-up (and pricier) "Nerobufaleffi" is from a cru in the village of Noto, while "Neromaccari," which is weightier still, comes from a site in Pachino. While the Gulfi wines are big, they are not just fruit-bombs: they have nice aromatics and good balance.

Haas, Franz ALTO ADIGE

Via Villa 6, 39040 Montagna/Montan (BZ)
Tel.: 0471812280/www.franz-haas.it
DOC(G)s: Alto Adige
  One of the bigger estates in the Alto Adige. A wide range of wines, highlighted by the varietal wines of the "Schweizer" line: gewürztraminer, pinot nero, and especially the rare sweet red from the moscato rosa grape. There's also a value line labeled "Kris," including a clean pinot grigio and a ripe-and-ready merlot.

★ Hastae PIEMONTE

Frazione Quartino 6, 14042 Calamandrana (AT)
Tel.: 0141769146
DOC(G)s: Barbera d'Asti
  A collaboration of six producers—Braida, Chiarlo, Coppo, Prunotto, Vietti, and the Berta Distillery—with the stated goal of exalting Asti and its barbera grape. "Quorum" is sourced from vineyards owned by the various collaborators. It's a massive, inky barbera that's beloved by the critics.

Hauner, Carlo SICILIA

Via Umberto 1, 98050 Santa Marina, Isola Salina (ME)
Tel.: 0909843141/Fax: 090922655
DOC(G)s: Malvasia delle Lipari; Cerasuolo di Vittoria
  The late Carlo Hauner settled on the island of Salina in the early seventies, and became its most famous producer of malvasia sweet wines. His estate is known for two excellent Malvasia delle Lipari DOC wines (one a natural late-harvest wine, the other a dried-grape *passito*). Along with the sweeties are some pleasant dry wines, including the tropical Salina Bianco (inzolia-catarratto) and the spicy Salina Rosso (nero d'avola–nerello).

★ Hilberg-Pasquero PIEMONTE

Via Bricco Gatti 16, 12040 Priocca (CN)
Tel.: 0173616197
DOC(G)s: Barbera d'Alba; Nebbiolo d'Alba

Juicy, clean wines brimming with extract and bright aromas. Barbera is a specialty (check out the beefy Superiore), but there's also an exceptionally plush Nebbiolo d'Alba; a dark-hued nebbiolo-barbera blend called "Pedrocha"; and an exotically aromatic blend of brachetto and barbera called "Vareij."

HOFSTÄTTER ALTO ADIGE

Piazza Municipio 5, 39040 Termeno/Tramin (BZ)
Tel.: 0471860161/Fax: 0471860789/www.hofstatter.com
DOC(G)s: Alto Adige

A top Alto Adige winery, with some of the region's most distinctive single-vineyard wines: there's the head-spinning "Kolbenhof" gewürztraminer, the creamy "Yngram" pinot bianco, the smoky "Sant'Urbano" pinot nero, and the savory "Steinraffler" lagrein.

I Baldazzini

See La Vis.

I Balzini TOSCANA

Località Pastine 19, 50021 Barberino Val d'Elsa (FI)
Tel.: 0556580484

Friuli's Walter Filiputti helps craft the two reds made at Vincenzo D'Isanto's estate just outside Chianti Classico; the wines are syrupy-slick sangiovese-cabernet blends, with "Black Label" being the more intense of the two.

I Campetti TOSCANA

Via della Collacchia 2, 58027 Roccastrada (GR)
Tel.: 0564579663
DOC(G)s: Monteregio di Massa Marittima

On the southern Tuscan coast, this interesting winery makes a spicy viognier ("Almabruna") as well as an aromatic malvasia ("L'Accesa"). On the red side, the bargain-priced "Castruccio" is a tangy blend of sangiovese and ciliegiolo.

I Girasoli di Sant'Andrea UMBRIA

Frazione Collevalenza, 06059 Todi (PG)
Tel.: 075887122

Well-priced reds based on sangiovese. "Ca' Andrea" is the simpler, steel-aged red (sangiovese with canaiolo and montepulciano), while "Muda" (sangiovese-montepulciano-merlot) is richer.

I Giusti e Zanza TOSCANA

Via dei Puntoni 9, 56043 Fauglia (PI)
Tel.: 058544354/www.igiustiezanza.it

Flashy reds from vineyards near Pisa. The fruity "Belcore" combines sangiovese and merlot; "Dulcamara," a winner with the critics, is a Bordeaux-style blend of 70% cabernet sauvignon and 30% cabernet franc and merlot.

I Paglieri (Roagna) PIEMONTE

Via Rabajà 8, 12050 Barbaresco (CN)
Tel.: 0173635109
DOC(G)s: Barbaresco; Barolo; Langhe

A family winery known for Barbarescos from the Pajé

vineyard. "Crichët Pajé" is the top wine, with a denser structure and more oak influence than the more feminine "Pajé." The Roagna family also bottles a Barolo, "La Rocca e La Pira," from the Rocche and Pira vineyards in Castiglione Falletto; it's a dark, smoky Barolo.

Icardi PIEMONTE

Via Balbi 30, 12053 Castiglione Tinella (CN)
Tel.: 0141855159/Fax: 0141855159
DOC(G)s: Barolo; Barbera d'Alba; Langhe; Monferrato
A wide range of wines from a large producer, including the fleshy, fruit-driven Barolo "Parej" and several juicy barberas (try the "Surì di Mù"). Similarly ripe, rich, and ready to go is the Monferrato Rosso "Bricco del Sole" (barbera-nebbiolos).

★ Il Borro TOSCANA

Frazione San Giustino Valdarino, Località Il Borro 1, 52020 Loro Ciuffenna (AR)
Tel.: 055977053/www.ilborro.it
Once a village unto itself, this noble *tenuta* was purchased in the early nineties by the Ferragamo family (of fashion fame), who refurbished the buildings and vineyards. The estate red, Il Borro, is a cult favorite—a jet-black fruit-bomb fashioned from merlot, cabernet, petit verdot, and syrah. Styled to drink young.

Il Carpino FRIULI–VENEZIA GIULIA

Località Sovenza 14/1, 34070 San Floriano del Collio (GO)
Tel.: 0481884097/www.ilcarpino.com
DOC(G)s: Collio
The well-traveled consultant Roberto Cipresso lends some style (and a good dose of oak) to the range of varietal wines made here. Wines such as the tocai and sauvignon have that typically Fruilian mix of precise aromatics, tangy minerality, and balance of fruit extract and acidity.

Il Colle TOSCANA

Località Il Colle 102B, 53024 Montalcino (SI)
Tel./Fax: 0577848295
DOC(G)s: Brunello di Montalcino; Rosso di Montalcino
A small estate producing about 30,000 bottles of classi-cally styled Brunello each year. Good aromatics and balance, with medium weight.

Il Colombaio di Cencio TOSCANA

Località Cornia, 53013 Gaiole in Chianti (SI)
Tel.: 0577747178
DOC(G)s: Chianti Classico
Chianti Classico "I Massi" rivals many super-Tuscans in heft (and price), and "Il Futuro" (sangiovese-cabernet-merlot) has earned incredible ratings from the critics. Rich, luxurious reds.

Il Faggeto TOSCANA

Frazione San Albino, Località Fontelellera, 53040 Montepulciano (SI)
Tel.: 0577940600
DOC(G)s: Vino Nobile di Montepulciano
Plummy, plush Vino Nobile from a single vineyard called "Pietra del Diavolo" is the wine to get. Nice price for a substantial sangiovese with chocolaty oak tones.

Il Feuduccio ABRUZZO

Via Feuduccio 1/A, 66036 Orsogna (CH)
Tel./Fax: 0871891646
DOC(G)s: Montepulciano d'Abruzzo

Fairly new player on the ever-improving Abruzzo wine scene, with a trio of clean, luxurious montepulcianos. The lineup starts with the great-value "Il Feuduccio," then moves to the partially barrique-aged "Ursonia" (probably the best buy of the three), then to the superrich "Margae" (a little overblown).

Il Grillesino TOSCANA

Borgo degli Albizi 14, 50123 Firenze (FI)
Tel.: 055243101
DOC(G)s: Morellino di Scansano

Fruity Morellino di Scansano and a fat morellino-cabernet blend called "Ceccante."

Il Marroneto TOSCANA

Località Madonna delle Grazie, 53024 Montalcino (SI)
Tel.: 0577849382/Fax: 0577846075
DOC(G)s: Brunello di Montalcino

Tiny production (about 5,000 bottles a year) of Brunello di Montaleino in a more woodsy, earthy, "traditional" style.

Il Palagione TOSCANA ▬▬●

Via per Castel San Gimignano, 53037 San Gimignano (SI)
Tel.: 0577953134

Up-and-coming producer with an intense, citrusy vernaccia, "Hydra," along with the richer white "Enif" (trebbiano-malvasia). The peppery red "Antajr" (sangiovese-cabernet-merlot) is a pleasant, medium-bodied choice.

Il Palazzino TOSCANA

Località il Palazzino, 53013 Gaiole in Chianti (SI)
Tel.: 0577747008
DOC(G)s: Chianti Classico

Critically acclaimed Chianti wines from high-altitude vineyards in Gaiole. The lineup starts with the unoaked "Argenina" (nice rustic aromas) and climbs to the culty "Grosso Sanese," which has a healthy dose of new French oak but lots of rich fruit to carry it.

Il Paradiso

See Poderi del Paradiso.

Il Poggiolino TOSCANA

Via Chiantigiana 42, 50020 Sambuca Val di Pesa (FI)
Tel.: 0558071635/Fax: 0558071635
www.ilpoggiolino.com
DOC(G)s: Chianti Classico

Consistently good Chianti Classicos and a varietal sangiovese called "Le Balze." Aromatic and savory expressions of sangiovese at great prices.

Il Poggiolo TOSCANA

Località Poggiolo 259, 53024 Montalcino (SI)
Tel.: 0577848412/Fax: 3483411848
www.ilpoggiolomontalcino.com
DOC(G)s: Brunello di Montalcino; Rosso di Montalcino

A range of solid Montalcino wines, including two powerful single-vineyard Brunellos: "Sassello" (aged in barrique) and "Beato" (aged in 500-liter *tonneaux*). Simpler wines include the pleasant sangiovese "Sasso Nero" and "Bottaccio" (sangiovese-cabernet).

Il Poggione TOSCANA

Frazione San Angelo in Colle, 53020 Montalcino (SI)
Tel.: 0577844029/Fax: 0577844165
DOC(G)s: Brunello di Montalcino

A historic winery in Montalcino known for fine, long-aging Brunello. The late Piero Talenti was the longtime winemaker here, and now his protégé, Fabrizio Bindocci, continues to craft the wines in a tight, traditional style. A great introduction to classic Brunello. "San Leopoldo" (sangiovese–cabernet sauvignon–cabernet franc) gets the super-Tuscan barrique treatment.

Il Puntone TOSCANA

DOC(G)s: Morellino di Scansano

Owned by the Baroncini firm, this small estate released its first wines in 1997. Supple, sweetly fruity Morellino di Scansano at a by-the-case price.

Il Roncal FRIULI–VENEZIA GIULIA

Località Montebello, Via Fornailis 100, 33043 Cividale del Friuli (UD)
Tel.: 0432716156/Fax: 0432730138/www.ilroncal.it
DOC(G)s: Colli Orientali del Friuli

Well worth a try are the floral and minerally tocai and the semisweet verduzzo; on the red side, the pignolo and refosco are relatively light but appealing takes on these tangy, spicy traditional grapes. "Ploe di Stelis" is a creamy white blend of chardonnay, sauvignon, and riesling.

Il Tesoro

See Terrabianca.

Il Vescovino TOSCANA

Via XX Luglio 39, 50020 Panzano in Chianti (FI)
Tel.: 055852907/Fax: 055852907/www.vescovino.it
DOC(G)s: Chianti Classico

Gamy Chianti Classico and a super-Tuscan called "Merlotto" (sangiovese–cabernet sauvignon), which has a black, spicy edge and medium weight.

Il Vignale Cappelletti PIEMONTE

Via Gavi 130, 15067 Novi Ligure (AL)
Tel.: 014372715/www.ilvignale.it
DOC(G)s: Gavi; Monferrato Rosso

Crisp, floral Gavis (particularly the "Vigne Alte") for aperitifs or a good bowl of pesto pasta. Also the plush red "Rosso di Mali" (cabernet–pinot noir blend).

Illuminati ABRUZZO

Contrada San Biagio, 18, 64010 Controguerra (TE)
Tel.: 0861808008/Fax: 0861810004/www.illuminativini.it
DOC(G)s: Controguerra; Montepulciano d'Abruzzo; Trebbiano d'Abruzzo

Located in the northeastern corner of Abruzzo (a top *terroir* for montepulciano), the Illuminati family makes some of the region's best reds. Rather than go for fruit-bombs, they make montepulcianos of surprising elegance. The single-vineyard "Zanna" has great depth, fragrance, and longevity. "Lumen" is an inkier style from montepul-

ciano and cabernet. Also some gutsy whites combining
the local trebbiano with chardonnay

Inama VENETO
Via 4 Novembre 1, 37047 San Bonifacio (VR)
Tel.: 0456104343/www.inamaaziendaagricola.it
DOC(G)s: Soave; Colli Berici
   Stefano Inama's calling card is rich, barrel-fermented
Soaves, including the single-vineyard "Foscarino" and
"Vigneto du Lot" bottlings (the latter has an overripe,
almost sweet edge that suggests some late-harvested or
dried fruit in the mix). From the nearby Colli Berici, Inama
also produces a first-rate cabernet sauvignon,
"Bradisismo."

Incontri TOSCANA
Località Fossoni 38, 57028 Suvereto (LI)
Tel.: 0565829401
DOC(G)s: Val di Cornia
   You may see this estate listed as "Martelli & Busdraghi,"
in reference to the families who own it. From vineyards in
up-and-coming Val di Cornia, they craft an intense, herb-
scented vermentino and a number of savory reds.
"Lagobruno" (sangiovese-merlot) is the top red.

Ioppa PIEMONTE
Via O. Trinchieri 12, 28078 Romagnano Sesia (NO)
Tel./Fax: 0163833079
DOC(G)s: Colline Novaresi; Ghemme
   If you crave the complex aromas of nebbiolo but don't
want to shell out for Barolo or Barbaresco, try this
northern Piedmont gem. Giorgio and Giampaolo Ioppa
make a fragrant, softly contoured Ghemme DOCG (80%
nebbiolo, 20% vespolina). There are also nice varietal
wines from both vespolina and nebbiolo.

Ippolito 1845 CALABRIA
Via Tirone 118, 88811 Cirò Marina (CR)
Tel.: 096231106/www.ippolito1845.it
DOC(G)s: Cirò
   One of the few Ciròs you'll see aside from Librandi's (see
separate listing). The wines are light and rustic, but recent
press has noted improvements.

ISOLE E OLENA TOSCANA
Località Isole 1, 50021 Barberino Val d'Elsa (FI)
Tel.: 0558072767/Fax: 0558072236
DOC(G)s: Chianti Classico
   Starting with a consistently good Chianti Classico that
shows off the pinot noir–ish side of sangiovese and
moving up to "Cepparello," which takes sangiovese in a
darker, denser direction, Paolo DeMarchi's wines are what
wine geeks call "vineyard-driven"— varietally true and
laced with the savor of the earth. "Cepparello" is a brawny,
hard-edged sangiovese for aging, while the "Collezione De
Marchi" wines—from cabernet sauvignon and, more
notably, syrah—are also big but more luxurious in texture.
Last but not least is one of the best Vin Santos in Tuscany.

Iuli, Fabrizio PIEMONTE
Via Centrale 9, 15020 Cerrina (AL)
Tel.: 014294123/Fax: 0142943894

DOC(G)s: Monferrato

A small estate of recent foundation with some mammoth, chocolate-rich barbera-based wines, most notably "Barabba." Like many new-generation Monferrato vintners, Iuli goes for an ultraconcentrated style.

JERMANN VINNAIOLI FRIULI–VENEZIA GIULIA

Via Ronco del Fortino 17, 34070 Farra d'Isonzo (GO)
Tel.: 0481888080/www.jermannvinnaioli.it

Silvio Jermann's whites have long set standards for varietal correctness, cleanliness, and character, and for the most part—aside from the toasty "Dreams" chardonnay—his use of oak is moderated. In fact, the legendary "Vintage Tunina" (chardonnay-sauvignon-malvasia-picolit) is fermented and aged only in stainless steel—it gets its tropical fruit intensity solely from superripe fruit. "Capo Martino" (pinot bianco–malvasia–tocai) is a little creamier from barrel fermentation. "Vinnae" is ribolla gialla as it should be (i.e., clean and fresh), and the other varietal whites are ever-reliable. The reds, with the exception of the excellent pignolo "Pignacolusse," are fairly light and less exciting.

★ Kante, Edi FRIULI–VENEZIA GIULIA

Località Prepotto 3, 34011 Duino Aurisina (TS)
Tel.: 040200761
DOC(G)s: Carso

Edi Kante's subterranean winery digs down into the limestone of the Carso, and his excellent whites capture that minerality in a bottle. The vitovska (a rare local variety) has the grip and punch of an Austrian grüner, while the sauvignon (among the best in Friuli) has both aromatic intensity and fruity depth. The weightiest white is the malvasia istriana, with its orange-blossom fruit and hints of vanilla from barrel fermentation.

Keber, Edi FRIULI–VENEZIA GIULIA

Via Zegla 15, 34071 Cormons (GO)
Tel.: 048161184/Fax: 048161184
DOC(G)s: Collio

A pain in the neck to find, but the elegant and deeply aromatic tocai friulano in particular is worth the search. Excellent artisanal whites across the board, along with an above-average merlot.

Keber, Renato FRIULI–VENEZIA GIULIA

Località Zegla 15, 34071 Cormons (GO)
Tel.: 0481639844/Fax: 048161196
DOC(G)s: Collio

Another Keber, also tiny and tough to find, also worth the search. Pinot grigio in the appropriately fleshy Friulian style (as opposed to the watery mass-produced stuff most people think of as pinot grigio) and equally good tocai and chardonnay (look for the "Grici" line).

Kris

See Haas, Franz.

★ Kuen Hof (Peter Plieger) ALTO ADIGE

Weinbergstrasse 66, 39042 Bressanone/Brixen (BZ)
Tel.: 0472832672
DOC(G)s: Alto Adige; Valle Isarco/Südtirol Eisacktaler

A cult favorite with a range of aromatic whites from the

northern reaches of Alto Adige. Peter Pliger's high-altitude vineyards near Bressanone are planted to veltliner, gewürztraminer, sylvaner, and riesling, and his wines are bright, mineral-rich expressions of these grapes. Focused aromas and firm acidity, with an underlying power.

La Badiola
See Tenuta La Badiola.

La Barbatella
See Cascina La Barbatella.

La Biancara VENETO
Contrà Biancara 14, 36053 Gambellara (VI)
Tel./Fax: 0444444244
DOC(G)s: Gambellara

Angiolino Maule's unusual "Pico" is made from garganega and is fermented with wild yeasts. Bottled unfiltered, it is cloudy and creamy, with a citrusy, clovey flavor and a strong backbone of acidity. Maule's Gambellara Recioto (dried-grape sweet wine) has Sauternes-like richness.

La Boatina FRIULI–VENEZIA GIULIA
Via Corona 62, 34071 Cormons (GO)
Tel.: 048160445/Fax: 0481630161/www.boatina.com
DOC(G)s: Collio

Well-regarded, well-priced varietal whites from sauvignon, pinot grigio, ribolla, tocai. The red "Picol Maggiore" (merlot–cabernet sauvignon–cabernet franc) has that green-bell-pepper edge typical of Friulian reds, but it's not without appeal. Same for the varietal reds.

La Braccesca TOSCANA
Frazione Gracciano–Strada Statale 326, 15, 53040 Montepulciano (SI)
Tel.: 0578724252
DOC(G)s: Vino Nobile di Montepulciano

The Montepulciano estate of Antinori, with a smooth and stylish Vino Nobile as well as a soft and succulent merlot.

★ La Brancaia TOSCANA
Località Poppi 42, 53017 Radda in Chianti (SI)
Tel.: 0577742007/Fax: 0577742010/www.brancaia.com
DOC(G)s: Chianti Classico

Swiss advertising executive Bruno Widmer first came to Chianti in 1981, and the grapes from his vineyards in Castellina were vinified by the Mazzei family of Castello di Fonterutoli until 1996. Now Bruno's daughter, Barbara (with consultant Carlo Ferrini), makes the concentrated, velvet-textured Brancaia wines at a sparkling new winery. The range is simple: there's the dense, sweetly fruity Chianti Classico and the even thicker "Il Blu," a blend of 55% sangiovese, 40% merlot, and 5% cabernet. Also check out the reds from the Widmers' Maremma estate, Poggio al Sasso, now called Brancaia in Maremma.

La Busattina TOSCANA
Frazione San Martino sul Fiora, 58014 Manciano (GR)
Tel.: 0564607823
DOC(G)s: Rosso Sovana

A tiny organic winery in southern Tuscany. Try the "Terre Eteree" (sangiovese-ciliegiolo) as well as the more powerful varietal ciliegiolo, which has a nice combination of red cherry fruit, rosy perfume, and earthy heft.

La Ca' Nova PIEMONTE
Via Casa Nuova 1, 12050 Barbaresco (CN)
Tel./Fax: 0173635123
DOC(G)s: Barbaresco; Dolcetto d'Alba; Barbera d'Alba
  Smoky and finely structured traditional Barbarescos from several different crus, including "Bric Mentina" (part of the Montefico vineyard in the village of Barbaresco).

La Cadalora TRENTINO
Via Trento 44, 38060 Santa Margherita di Ala (TN)
Tel.: 0464696443/Fax: 0464696540
DOC(G)s: Trentino
  Pinot grigio with character, and it won't break the bank. Also a spicy red from the rare casetta grape.

La Calonica TOSCANA
Via della Stella 27, 53040 Valiano di Montepulciano (SI)
Tel.: 0578724119/Fax: 0578724119/www. lacalonica.com
DOC(G)s: Vino Nobile di Montepulciano; Cortona
  Full-bodied Vino Nobile with good sangiovese character. Super-Tuscans include the barrique-aged "Signorelli" (merlot) and "Girifalco" (sangiovese from nearby Cortona, fattened up with cabernet and merlot).

La Cappuccina VENETO
Via San Brizio 125, 37030
Monteforte d'Alpone (VR)
Tel.: 0456175036/Fax: 0456175755/www.lacappuccina.it
DOC(G)s: Soave; Recioto di Soave
  An acclaimed Soave producer making solid, inexpensive wines. "San Brizio" has a vanilla sheen from barrique aging, while "Fontego" adds some chardonnay to the mix. "Arzimo" is an excellent sweet *passito*. "Campo Buri" is a peppery, fairly light cabernet franc.

★ La Carraia UMBRIA
Località Tordimonte 56, 05018 Orvieto (TR)
Tel.: 0763304013/Fax: 0763304048/www.lacarraia.it
DOC(G)s: Orvieto Classico
  "Fobiano," a mix of 70% merlot and 30% cabernet, is a succulent "super-Umbrian" that goes toe-to-toe with its Tuscan cousins. This estate is part owned by consultant Riccardo Cotarella, who also makes several Orvieto whites (go for the round and fruity "Poggio Calvelli," a single-vineyard wine that is barrel-fermented for added depth).

★ La Castellada FRIULI–VENEZIA GIULIA
Frazione Oslavia 1, 34170 Gorizia (GO)
Tel.: 048133670/Fax: 048133670
DOC(G)s: Collio
  Nicolò and Giorgio Bensa achieve real depth and complexity in their wines, which are made in tiny quantities at their farmhouse winery. "Bianco della Castellada" (tocai–pinot grigio–sauvignon) is creamy, concentrated, and a touch smoky from its fermentation in French barriques, but there's citrusy acidity and appley fruit to balance it. The ribolla gialla follows suit. "Rosso della Castellada" (a Bordeaux blend) is deep and elegant, but the whites are the stars.

La Cerbaiola

See Salvioni.

La Ciarliana TOSCANA

Frazione Gracciano, Via Ciarliana 31, 53040
Montelpuciano (SI)
Tel.: 0578758423/Fax: 03355652718
DOC(G)s: Vino Nobile di Montepulciano
Smooth and smoky sangiovese flavors in a medium-bodied Vino Nobile.

La Colombina TOSCANA

Località La Colombina, Frazione Castelnuovo dell'Abate,
53020 Montalcino (SI)
Tel.: 0577849399/Fax: 0577846666
DOC(G)s: Brunello di Montalcino
The Caselli family traditionally sold their grapes from
their vineyards in Castelnuovo dell'Abate, but in 1997 they
began releasing wines under their own label. Rich and
powerful wines with lots of up-front fruit.

La Contea PIEMONTE

Vicolo Asilo 13, 12057 Neive (CN)
Tel.: 0173677585/Fax: 017367367/www.la-contea.it
DOC(G)s: Barbaresco; Barbera d'Alba; Dolcetto d'Alba;
Nebbiolo d'Alba; Moscato d'Asti
La Contea, in the village of Neive, is one of the most
famous restaurants in the Langhe (opened in 1971). La
Contea's winery was originally created in 1992 to produce
wines for the restaurant, but it now exports a wide range of
wines from estate vineyards throughout Alba and Roero.
The Barbaresco Riserva "Ripa Sorita" is a tight, aromatic
wine sourced from crus such as Starderi and Gallina. Nice
dolcetto, barbera, and moscato as well.

La Corte PUGLIA

Via Trepuzzi, 73051 Novoli (LE)
Tel.: 0559707594/Fax: 0559707597/www.renideo.com
Owned by a Tuscan firm called Renídeo, this Lecce-area
winery came on the scene a few years ago with serious
reds from negroamaro and primitivo grapes. The varietal
wines are plenty good, deep and structured, or you could
step up the intensity with "Ré," a barrique-aged
negroamaro-primitivo blend. Great additions to the often
overhyped Puglian wine scene.

La Crotta de Vignerons VALLE D'AOSTA

Piazza Roncas 2, 11023 Chambave (AO)
Tel.: 016646670
DOC(G)s: Valle d'Aosta
The dry Chambave Muscat, with its exotic moscato
perfume, is definitely worth a try, as is the sweet *passito*
version. The pinot noir rosé is less exciting.

La Distesa MARCHE

Via Romita 28, 60034 Cupramontana (AN)
Tel.: 0731781230/www.ladistesa.it
DOC(G)s: Verdicchio dei Castelli di Jesi
A small estate specializing in wines from verdicchio.
"Terre Silvate" is the fresher, tangier wine, while "Gli
Eremi" is a reserve selection with the more tropically fruity
notes of ultraripe verdicchio grapes.

La Fiorita TOSCANA

Piagga della Porta 3, 53024 Montalcino (SI)
Tel.: 0577835657

DOC(G)s: Brunello di Montalcino

Consultant Roberto Cipresso is a partner in this growing
Montalcino winery, which now produces about 20,000
bottles a year of sweetly fruity, oak-influenced Brunello.

La Fiorita–Lamborghini

See Lamborghini.

La Fornace TOSCANA

53024 Montalcino (SI)
Tel.: 0577848465/www.agricola-lafornace.it

DOC(G)s: Brunello di Montalcino; Rosso di Montalcino

Smooth, sweet, sexy Brunello with enough extract to
allow for drinking young, though it should be a great short-
term ager. A tiny production (about 15,000 bottles) from
young upstart Fabio Giannetti. The fleshy Rosso di
Montalcino is a lot of wine for the money.

La Gerla TOSCANA

Località La Gerla, 53024 Montalcino (SI)
Tel.: 0577848599/Fax: 0577849465

DOC(G)s: Brunello di Montalcino; Rosso di Montalcino

Fairly traditional Brunellos with muscular tannins and
lots of earthy, smoky edges to the black cherry fruit. Buy
and hold. A touch pricey.

La Ghersa PIEMONTE

Via San Giuseppe 19, 14050 Moasca (AT)
Tel.: 0141856012/www.laghersa.it

DOC(G)s: Barbera d'Asti; Monferrato; Moscato d'Asti

Old-vine barbera wine from the subzone of Nizza.
Monferrato is the big story here, as expressed in the
superslick Barbera "Vignassa" selection (purportedly from
90-year-old vines). The rich and spicy Monferrato Rosso
"Piagè" (barbera-merlot-syrah) and the ripe, almost
tropically fruity "Sivoy" Bianco (cortese-chardonnay-
sauvignon) are well priced and interesting.

La Giustiniana PIEMONTE

Frazione Rovereto 5, 15066 Gavi (AL)
Tel.: 0143682132

DOC(G)s: Gavi; Asti; Brachetto d'Acqui

A premier Gavi producer (check out the floral and fine
"Lugarara"). There's a barrel-fermented cortese called
"Just Bianco" and a fat and fruity Monferrato Rosso, but
Gavi is the way to go.

La Lastra TOSCANA

Via R. De Grada 9, 53037 San Gimignano (SI)
Tel.: 0577941781/Fax: 0577236423/www.lalastra.it

DOC(G)s: Vernaccia di San Gimignano; Chianti Colli
Senesi

An emerging name in San Gimignano, with a series of
fresh, fruit-driven Vernaccia di San Gimignano whites and
a pretty good red, "Rovaio" (cabernet-merlot-sangiovese).

La Lecciaia TOSCANA

Podere Vallafrico, 53024 Montalcino (SI)
Tel./Fax: 0577849287

DOC(G)s: Brunello di Montalcino; Rosso di Montalcino
Well-regarded Brunello wine made in a traditional (woodsy, earthy, smoky) style.

La Lumia, Barone SICILIA

Contrada Pozzillo, 92027 Licata (AG)
Tel.: 0922770057/Fax: 0922891709

Rustic nero d'avola (at least in comparison to the plush shiraz-style giants coming out of Sicily these days) from a long-established estate near Agrigento. "Don Toto" is the top selection (a little expensive), but there are some values, including the fragrant "Cadetto" (also nero d'avola).

La Macolina EMILIA-ROMAGNA

Via Pieve San Andrea 2, Montecatone di Imola (BO)
Tel.: 051940234/Fax: 051944387
DOC(G)s: Sangiovese di Romagna

Bright and spicy sangiovese-based wines from the hills southeast of Bologna. "Museum" is a softly contoured blend of sangiovese and merlot. Nice values.

La Madonnina TOSCANA

Via Palaia 39, 50027 Greve in Chianti (FI)
Tel.: 055858003
DOC(G)s: Toscana; Chianti Classico

Acquired in the early seventies by the Triacca family of Lombardia, this historic Chianti estate makes the deep and spicy "Riserva La Madonnina." Chianti "Vigna La Palaia" is a flashy show wine, dosed with 15% cabernet and aged in new barriques. "Bello Stento" is a consistently great value, a smooth and aromatic red.

La Magia TOSCANA

Località Montalcino, 53024 Montalcino (SI)
Tel.: 0577835667
DOC(G)s: Brunello di Montalcino; Rosso di Montalcino

Past tastings have always shown these Brunellos to be rustic and earthy (and maybe a bit too funky), but now that consultant Roberto Cipresso is on board, expect a cleaner, plusher profile.

★ La Massa TOSCANA

Via Case Sparse 9, 50020 Panzano (FI)
Tel.: 055852722
DOC(G)s: Chianti Classico

"Giorgio Primo" is one of the most luxurious Chianti Classicos you'll ever taste; in fact, it blows away many celebrated super-Tuscans. Though dosed with merlot and a good amount of oak, the black cherry fruit of sangiovese (sourced from the famed Conca d'Oro vineyards in the village of Panzano) still shows through. There's also a new, less expensive red blend combining merlot, sangiovese, and cabernet.

★ La Monacesca MARCHE

Contrada Monacesca, 62024 Matelica (MC)
Tel.: 0733812602/www.monacesca.it
DOC(G)s: Verdicchio di Matelica

Monacesca's verdicchio has steely minerality and great freshness at a great price. The excellent "Mirum" is the top selection, from 100% verdicchio aged for 2 years in tank and bottle before release. The red "Camerte" is a powerful, stylish blend of sangiovese grosso and merlot.

La Montecchia VENETO

Frazione Feriole, Via Montecchia 16, 35030
Selvazzano Dentro (PD)
Tel.: 049637294/www.lamontecchia.it
DOC(G)s: Colli Euganei
   The Colli Euganei DOC, near Padova in central Veneto, has a growing number of good Bordeaux-style reds. If you like the leafy, peppery, aromatic side of cabernet, check out the varietal cabernet franc "Godimondo" or the blend "Capodilista" (merlot-cabernet-raboso).

La Morandina PIEMONTE

Località Morandina 11, 12053 Castiglione Tinella (CN)
Tel.: 0141855261
DOC(G)s: Barbera d'Asti; Langhe; Moscato d'Asti
   The bright, effervescent Moscato d'Asti gets high marks, and there are also powerful wines from the barbera grape, notably the chunky Barbera d'Asti "Varmat," a single-vineyard wine aged 18 months in barrique.

L'Olivella LAZIO

Via di Colle Pisano 1, 00044 Frascati (RM)
Tel.: 069424527/www.racemo.it
DOC(G)s: Frascati
   An up-and-comer in the hills south of Rome, with a better-than-average Frascati ("Racemo") and some excellent reds—"Racemo Rosso" (a tangy blend of sangiovese and the spicy local cesanese) and "Concerto" (a fruitier, more aromatic blend of cesanese and syrah).

La Palazzetta

See Fanti (La Palazzetta).

La Palazzola UMBRIA

Località Vascigliano, 05039 Stroncone (TR)
Tel.: 0744607735
   "Rubino," a blend of cabernet and merlot, is designed to stand up to the super-Tuscans. It does. The varietal merlot wine is also dense, sweet, chocolaty, decadent. Riccardo Cotarella consults.

La Parrina TOSCANA

Località Albinia, 58010 Orbetelo (GR)
Tel.: 0564862636/Fax: 0564862626
DOC(G)s: Ansonica Costa dell'Argentario; Parrina
   On the extreme south coast of Tuscany, this is one of the few producers of Ansonica Costa dell'Argentario (a clean, simple white made from the ansonica grape, aka inzolia). "Muraccio" (sangiovese-cabernet-merlot blend) is sweetly fruity, with some tangy notes of Mediterranean scrub. The fat-bottomed red "Radaia" is the show wine, from 100% merlot.

La Poderina TOSCANA

Località Poderina, Castelnuovo dell'Abate, 53020 Montalcino (SI)
Tel./Fax: 0577835737
DOC(G)s: Brunello di Montalcino; Moscadello di Montalcino

Dark, coffee-scented Brunello with bitter chocolate tannins. Accessible young, yet powerful—a decent value, too. The Rosso di Montalcino is similarly clean and flashy, and the sweet Moscadello di Montalcino has the unctuous, peaches-and-cream flavors typical of the grape.

La Prendina
See Cavalchina.

La Quadratura del Cerchio MULTIPLE REGIONS
Via dell'Olmo 24/28, 53024 Castelnuovo dell'Abate (SI)
Tel.: 0577835511/Fax: 0577835521

The name of the winery means "squaring the circle." The principal wine—a rich multiregional red blend, including, in recent vintages, teroldego from Trentino, montepulciano from Abruzzo, and carmenère from Veneto —is renamed as a new "Viaggio" (voyage) each year, as in "Terzo [third] Viaggio," "Quarto [fourth] Viaggio," etc. There's also "Pigreco," a juicy varietal montepulciano.

La Rampa di Fugnano TOSCANA
Località Fugnano 55, 53037 San Gimignano (SI)
Tel.: 057791655/www.rampadifugnano.it
DOC(G)s: Vernaccia di San Gimignano; Chianti Colli Senesi

"Bombereto" sangiovese is a smooth, medium-bodied super-Tuscan, while "Alata" is an above-average Vernaccia di San Gimignano with some substantial citrus depth. "Privato" vernaccia is more intense, and there's also an interesting viognier ("Vi Ogni é"). "Gisèle" merlot is fat and fruity, with a touch of chocolaty oak.

La Rasina TOSCANA
Località La Rasina, 53024 Montalcino (SI)
Tel./Fax: 0577848536
DOC(G)s: Brunello di Montalcino; Rosso di Montalcino

This small Montalcino estate (35,000 bottles) delivers round and fruity Brunello at a reasonable price. Wines are aged in large casks and tend toward the softer, more perfumed end of the Brunello spectrum.

La Roncaia FRIULI–VENEZIA GIULIA
Frazione Cergneu, Via Verdi 26, 33045 Nimis (UD)
Tel.: 0432790280/www.laroncaia.com
DOC(G)s: Colli Orientali del Friuli; Ramandolo

Owned by Fantinel, with consultation from enologist Tibor Gal (the original winemaker at the Ornellaia winery in Tuscany). Specialties include sweet nectars from the verduzzo and picolit grapes. "Eclisse" is a bright blend of sauvignon blanc and picolit; "Il Fusco" is a spicy red from refosco, cabernet franc, merlot, and tazzelenghe; the denser "Gheppio" is a merlot, cabernet, and refosco blend.

La Sala TOSCANA
Via Sorripa 34, 50026 San Casciano Val di Pesa (FI)
Tel.: 055828111/www.lasala.it
DOC(G)s: Chianti Classico

Elegant sangiovese wines, and affordable. Laura Baronti's basic Chianti Classico is a perennial value, and the powerful *riserva* is a bargain, too (relatively speaking). "Campo all'Albero" is 50% sangiovese and 50% cabernet, and it, too, delivers great power for the price.

La Scolca PIEMONTE

Villa Scolca, 15066 Gavi (AL)
Tel.: 0143682176/Fax: 0143682197/www.scolca.it
DOC(G)s: Gavi

An Italian classic, this winery has been the standard-bearer of the Gavi DOCG for generations. La Scolca's "Etichetta Nera" Gavi di Gavi (known here as the "black label") is consistently bright, minerally, and clean. There are also some Champagne-style sparklers from cortese.

La Serena TOSCANA

Località Podere Rasa 1 133, 53024 Montalcino (SI)
Tel.: 0577848659
DOC(G)s: Brunello di Montalcino

A good small producer of Brunello di Montalcino wine in an elegant, fruit-driven style. Fairly accessible young, with sweet tannins and bright aromatics.

La Spinetta PIEMONTE

Via Annunziata 17, 14054 Castagnole Lanze (AT)
Tel.: 0141877396/Fax: 0141877566
DOC(G)s: Barbaresco; Barbera d'Asti; Langhe; Moscato d'Asti; Monferrato Rosso

Rock-star winemaker Giorgio Rivetti does everything big: his Barbarescos, from the Gallina and Starderi crus in the commune of Neive as well as the Valeirano cru in Treiso, are gigantic, barrique-aged bruisers with sappy extract to spare. The Gallina cru wine, from a south-facing vineyard, is probably the most immediately accessible of the three, while the Starderi has some sharper edges; the Valeirano wine falls somewhere in the middle. Rivetti's barberas are also huge, as is the Monferrato Rosso "Pin" (nebbiolo-barbera-cabernet). The barrel-fermented whites from chardonnay and sauvignon are—you guessed it—intense. Great Moscato d'Asti as well. Very fashionable, sexy wines, so be prepared to spend. (Look also for Rivetti's new Tuscan sangiovese, "Sezzana," and a new Barolo, "Campé," from vineyards in Grinzane Cavour.)

La Spinona PIEMONTE

Via Secondine 22, 12050 Barbaresco (CN)
Tel.: 0173635169/Fax: 0173635276
DOC(G)s: Barbaresco; Barbera d'Alba; Dolcetto d'Alba; Langhe

Warm, smoky Barbaresco from the Faset cru in Barbaresco, with plush tannins and classic woodsy nebbiolo aromas at a very attractive price. Also a similarly traditional Barolo from a vineyard in Novello, "Sorì Gepin" (first vintage 1996). Solid varietals from dolcetto, barbera, and chardonnay as well.

La Stoppa EMILIA-ROMAGNA

Località Ancarano, 29029 Rivergaro (PC)
Tel.: 0523958159/Fax: 0523951141
DOC(G)s: Colli Piacentini

A tart, spicy red called "Macchiona" (barbera-croatina) and the savory "Stoppa" cabernet top the lineup of this winery near Piucienza, in western Emilia-Romagna. Also an excellent *passito*-style wine from malvasia grapes, "Vigna del Volta," with great orange blossom aromas.

La Tenaglia PIEMONTE

Via Santuario di Crea 6, 15020 Serralunga di Crea (CN)
Tel.: 0142940252/www.latenaglia.com

DOC(G)s: Barbera d'Asti; Grignolino del Monferrato
Casalese; Monferrato; Piemonte

A rare (and good) varietal syrah from Monferrato,
"Paradiso," is among the deeply fruity reds made here.
Barbera wine is the main event, starting with the bright,
unoaked "Bricco Crea" bottling and moving to the thick-
textured "Emozioni." Also a chardonnay with the crisp
acidity and minerality of Chablis. Attilio Pagli consults.

★ La Togata (Tenuta Carlina) TOSCANA

Località Tavernelle, 53024 Montalcino (SI)
Tel.: 0668803000/Fax: 0668134047/www.latogata.com
DOC(G)s: Brunello di Montalcino

Small-production Brunello wines that have earned
considerable critical praise in recent vintages: deep, dark,
sweet tannins and fleshy black fruit. Aging is done in a
combination of small and large casks, lending a moderated note of vanilla/chocolate. Good price-to-value ratio.

La Tosa EMILIA-ROMAGNA

Località La Tosa, 29020 Vigolzone (PC)
Tel.: 0523870727

DOC(G)s: Colli Piacentini

Stylish, well-concentrated wines, especially the tangy
"Vignamorello" Gutturnio (from a blend of barbera and
croatina grapes) and the "Luna Selvatica" cabernet
sauvignon, a serious wine for the money. The sauvignon
blanc is citrusy and intense.

La Valentina ABRUZZO

Via Colle Cesi 10, 65010 Spoltore (PE)
Tel.: 0854478158/www.fattorialavalentina.it

DOC(G)s: Montepulciano d'Abruzzo; Trebbiano d'Abruzzo

Plump, immediately drinkable, affordable wines. The
basic montepulciano wine is simple and soft, but the ante
is upped with the barrique-aged "Binomio," made in
collaboration with Soave's Stefano Inama. "Spelt" is
another more serious, single-vineyard montepulciano.

La Viarte FRIULI–VENEZIA GIULIA

Via Novacuzzo 50, 33040 Prepotto (UD)
Tel.: 0432759458/Fax: 0432753354/www.laviarte.it
DOC(G)s: Colli Orientali del Friuli

The pinots (bianco and grigio) are the stars of the clean
and correct lineup of whites, which includes tocai, ribolla,
sauvignon, and the sweet white "Sìum" (a blend of
verduzzo and picolit). Reds include the spicy natives
tazzelenghe, refosco, and schioppettino.

La Vis TRENTINO

Via del Carmine 7, 38015 Lavis (TN)
Tel.: 0461246325/www.la-vis.com
DOC(G)s: Trentino

A large co-op. The basic La Vis varietal wines (pinot
grigio, chardonnay, merlot, etc.) have more class than
you'd expect for the price, but there are many other
distinct product lines to explore: "Ritratti" is a varietal
range considered a step up from the La Vis line; the
"Sornì" range, named for a geographic subzone of the

Trentino DOC, includes a bright and creamy Bianco (nosiola–chardonnay–pinot bianco) and a meaty Rosso (teroldego-lagrein); and "Linea Masi" is a selection of single-vineyard wines such as the fat and funky "I Baldazzini" Lagrein and the exotically fragrant, brightly acidic "Maso Roncador" müller-thurgau.

Lageder ALTO ADIGE

Via dei Conti 9, 39040 Magré/Margreid (BZ)
Tel.: 0471809500/Fax: 0471809550/www.lageder.com
DOC(G)s: Alto Adige

The premier estate in the Alto Adige, with a futuristic winery cut into a hillside in the village of Magré. The product line is huge, with consistent quality from bottom to top. The "Classic Wines" range includes a fresh, minerally chardonnay and an appley pinot grigio. The "Single Vineyards" line boasts weightier selections of pinot grigio ("Benefizium"), pinot bianco (the creamy "Haberlehof"), and lagrein (the tarry "Lindenburg"). Then there's the "Single Estate" line, with its powerful chardonnay, "Lowengang"; a deep and smoky pinot noir, "Krafuss"; and the peppery, Bordeaux-inspired "Cor Römigberg" cabernet. See also Casòn Hirschprunn.

Laila

See Fattoria Laila.

★ Lamborghini UMBRIA

Località Soderi 1, 06064 Panicale (PG)
Tel.: 0758350029/www.lamborghinionline.it
DOC(G)s: Colli del Trasimeno

Yes, *that* Lamborghini. Located near Lake Trasimeno, the winery (there's an *agriturismo* and golfing club as well) is known for the cultish "Campoleone," a sangiovese-merlot blend. It's got depth and class that's worth paying up for. Its cheaper sibling, "Trescone," is a smooth and appealing mix of sangiovese, ciliegiolo, and merlot.

Lamole di Lamole TOSCANA

Località Vistarenni, 53013 Gaiole in Chianti (SI)
Tel.: 0577738186/Fax: 0577738549
DOC(G)s: Chianti Classico

Owned by Santa Margherita. Several solid Chianti Classicos, headlined by the *riserva* "Campolungo."

★ Lanari MARCHE

Via Zara 21/A, 60029 Varano (AN)
Tel.: 0712861343/Fax: 0712861343
DOC(G)s: Rosso Cònero

"Fibbio" may be the best Rosso Cònero on the market, loaded with rich black fruit and silty, sweet tannins. A great expression of the montepulciano grape. The base-level Rosso Cònero has plenty of depth in its own right.

Lanciola TOSCANA

Via Imprunetana 210, 50023 Impruneta (FI)
Tel.: 055208324
DOC(G)s: Chianti Colli Fiorentini; Chianti Classico

Headquartered just outside Florence and known for "Terricci," a peppery, slightly funky blend of sangiovese, cabernet sauvignon, and cabernet franc.

Landi, Luciano MARCHE

Via Gavigliano 16, 60030 Belvedere Ostrense (AN)
Tel.: 073162353/www.aziendalandi.it
DOC(G)s: Lacrima di Morro d'Alba

A specialist in the Marche's rare lacrima grape, which has a purple, gamay-like fruitiness. Landi's DOC Lacrima di Morro d'Alba is inky and soft, and his sappy *passito* from the grape is an interesting dessert-wine choice.

Laurentina MARCHE

Via San Pietro 19/A, 60036 Montecarotto (AN)
Tel.: 073189435
DOC(G)s: Rosso Piceno; Verdicchio dei Castelli di Jesi

Citrusy verdicchio and a substantial Rosso Piceno.

Le Boncie TOSCANA

Località San Felice, Strada delle Boncie 5, 53019 Castelnuovo Berardenga (SI)
Tel.: 0577359383
DOC(G)s: Chianti Classico

Giovanna Morganti's Chianti Classico "Le Trame" is woodsy, earthy, and aromatic—more about elegance than power. A classic Chianti Classico that speaks of its place.

Le Botti di Antistene SICILIA

Viale Leonardo Sciascia 36, 92100 Agrigento (AG)
Tel.: 0934939007/Fax: 0934939000
www.lebottiantistene.it

More rich and funky nero d'avola from Sicily. "Symposio" is the simpler, more affordable choice, while the "Rosso delle Noce" pumps up the volume.

Le Calcinaie TOSCANA

Località Santa Lucia 36, 53037 San Gimignano (SI)
Tel.: 0577942121
DOC(G)s: Vernaccia di San Gimignano; Chianti

"Vigna ai Sassi" is one of the best vernaccias around, with good ripeness, weight, and aroma. A step up from the mostly light whites coming out of San Gimignano.

Le Calvane TOSCANA

Via Castiglioni 1/5, 50020 Montespertoli (FI)
Tel.: 0571671073
DOC(G)s: Chianti Colli Fiorentini

"Borro del Boscone" is a velvety cabernet sauvignon with some real class. "Il Trecione" is a substantial Chianti with great aromas and an attractive price. There's also a well-made Vin Santo, "Zípolo d'Oro," which has a moderated sweetness and a Sherry-like character.

Le Caniette MARCHE

Contrada Canali 23, 63038 Ripatransone (AP)
Tel.: 07359200/www.lecaniette.it
DOC(G)s: Rosso Piceno

Rosso Piceno varies widely in style because of the variable blending formula of the DOC. Le Caniette uses a good dose of merlot along with 60% sangiovese in its softly textured "Morellone" Rosso Piceno, while the pricier, inkier "Nero di Vite" is montepulciano driven.

Le Chiuse TOSCANA

Località Pullera 228, 53024 Montalcino (SI)
Tel.: 0577848595/Fax: 055597052/www.lechiuse.com
DOC(G)s: Brunello di Montalcino

A modern but moderated style of Brunello. Good weight, sweet tannins, and a savory sangiovese edge that shows through the sheen of oak. Pricing is very fair.

Le Chiuse di Sotto

See Brunelli, Gianni.

Le Cinciole TOSCANA

Case Sparse 83, 50020 Panzano in Chianti (FI)
Tel.: 055852636/Fax: 0558560307
DOC(G)s: Chianti Classico

A small estate in the village of Panzano. The Chiantis here are bright and elegant, with emphasis on the rosy, spicy aromatics of sangiovese and an almost Burgundian feel. The basic Chianti Classico is floral and fine, while the *riserva* "Petresco" (100% sangiovese) is more powerful.

Le Corti–Corsini TOSCANA ▄▄▄▄●

Via San Piero di Sotto 1, 50026 San Casciano
Val di Pesa (FI)
Tel.: 055820123/www.principecorsini.com
DOC(G)s: Chianti Classico

Sleek and substantial Chianti Classicos that all get a sweetening touch of French oak.

★ Le Due Terre FRIULI–VENEZIA GIULIA

Via Roma 68/B, 33040 Prepotto (UD)
Tel.: 0432713189
DOC(G)s: Colli Orientali del Friuli

Interesting artisanal wines. "Sacrisassi Rosso," a refosco-schioppettino blend, is both unique and luxurious, while "Sacrisassi Bianco" (tocai-ribolla-sauvignon) has an almost late-harvest viscosity and lots of tropical notes on the nose. "Implicito" is a rare dry version of picolit with good heft and pretty white-flower aromas.

Le Filigare TOSCANA ▄▄▄▄●

Via Sicelle, 50020 Barberino Val d'Elsa (FI)
Tel.: 0558072796
DOC(G)s: Chianti Classico

A great track record for elegant Chianti Classico, as well as the consistently good (and still affordable) super-Tuscan "Le Rocce" (65% sangiovese, 35% cabernet sauvignon).

Le Fonti

See Fattoria Le Fonti.

Le Fracce LOMBARDIA

Via Castel del Lupo 5, 27045 Casteggio (PV)
Tel.: 038382526/Fax: 0383804151/www.le-fracce.it
DOC(G)s: Oltrepò Pavese

Considered one of the better producers in Oltrepò, with a spicy bonarda in the old-fashioned *frizzante* style ("La Rubiosa"). A more serious still red is the tart and spicy "Garboso" (barbera–croatina–pinot nero), and, on the white side, try the bone-dry riesling renano.

Le Fraghe VENETO

Località Colombara
3, 37010 Cavaion Veronese (VR)
Tel.: 0457236832
DOC(G)s: Bardolino; Valdadige
  Nice values from the Lake Garda area, including one of
the top Bardolinos (a pleasant light red) and a fragrant,
clean varietal from garganega called "Camporengo."

★ Le Gode di Ripaccioli TOSCANA

Località Le Gode 343, 53024 Montalcino (SI)
Tel.: 0577848547/Fax: 0577847089
DOC(G)s: Brunello di Montalcino
  A small estate of recent foundation (the first harvest was
1995). Deep yet finely structured Brunello that's built for
long aging. An aromatic, spicy style with great sangiovese
character. Expensive.

★ Le Macchiole TOSCANA

Via Bolgherese 189, 57020 Bolgheri (LI)
Tel.: 0565766092
DOC(G)s: Bolgheri
  One of the Bolgheri DOC's high-end boutique wineries,
with a supercharged super-Tuscan lineup headed by the
explosive, barrique-aged "Paleo" (cabernet sauvignon–
cabernet franc), filled with Bordeaux-like depth and savor.
The same goes for the tiny-quantity "Messorio" merlot,
with an intensity (and price) to rival Ornellaia's "Masseto."
Then there's "Scrio," perhaps the ultimate expression of
syrah in Italy (and also priced accordingly). Luscious,
luxurious wines.

Le Macioche TOSCANA

Località Palazzina, Strada Provinciale 55 di Sant'Antimo,
Km. 4, 85, 53024 Montalcino (SI)
Tel.: 0577849168
DOC(G)s: Brunello di Montalcino
  Bright, round, fruit-driven Brunello di Montalcino, with
an emphasis on sangiovese aromatics—the hallmark of
consultant enologist Maurizio Castelli. Plenty of body and
personality and no barrique. Tiny production.

Le Mandorlae

See Baroncini.

Le Murelle

See Terre del Sillabo.

★ Le Potazzine (Gorelli) TOSCANA

Via Cialdini 51/53, 53024 Montalcino (SI)
Tel.: 0577848098
DOC(G)s: Brunello di Montalcino; Rosso di Montalcino
  Giuseppe Gorelli of Due Portine heads this new boutique
estate, which is already a critical (and cult) favorite. Sinful,
superconcentrated Brunello di Montalcino in eyedropper
quantities, but the Rosso di Montalcino (a bruiser that
spends some time in barrique) is more than satisfying.

Le Presi TOSCANA

Via Costa della Porta, Frazione Castelnuovo dell'Abate,
53020 Montalcino (SI)
Tel./Fax: 0577835541
DOC(G)s: Brunello di Montalcino

Angular, aromatic Brunello di Montalcino. A dark, woodsy style from a lesser-known producer. Good pricing.

Le Pupille
See Fattoria Le Pupille.

Le Ragose VENETO
Via Molino Turri 30, 37024 Negrar (VR)
Tel.: 0457501740

DOC(G)s: Valpolicella; Amarone della Valpolicella; Recioto della Valpolicella; Garda

With some of the highest-elevation vineyards in Valpolicella Classico and a production philosophy that favors long aging in large oak barrels (and bottle) before release, Le Ragose's Amarone has a spicy, leathery edge and a moderated sweetness, distinguishing it from the multitude of fruit-bomb Amarones on the market. The medium-bodied Valpolicellas are smoky and spicy—great values from a long-established family estate.

Le Salette VENETO
Via Pio Brugnoli 11/C, 37022 Fumane (VR)
Tel.: 0457701027

DOC(G)s: Valpolicella; Amarone della Valpolicella; Recioto della Valpolicella

Amarone "La Marega" is some sexy stuff, as is the more expensive "Pergole Vece," which has a nice balance of sweetness and savor. Great sweet Recioto della Valpolicella, also called "Pergole Vece." Slick and serious Valpolicellas in multiple incarnations, including "I Progni" (a *ripasso* style) and "Ca' Carnocchio" (made without dried fruit, but spends nearly 2 years in barrique).

Le Solive TOSCANA 🍷
Località San Benedetto 11/D, 53037 San Gimignano (SI)
Tel.: 0577944840/Fax: 0577945670/www.lesolive.com

DOC(G)s: Vernaccia di San Gimignano

A pleasant, citrusy vernaccia called "Vigna Aprico," and a savory sangiovese called "Connubio." Good pricing.

Le Sorgenti
See Fattoria Le Sorgenti.

Le Terrazze
See Fattoria Le Terrazze.

Le Trame
See Le Boncie.

Le Velette UMBRIA
Località Le Velette 23, 05019 Orvieto (TR)
Tel.: 076329090

DOC(G)s: Orvieto Classico

Go for the basic Orvieto for a great picnic white (avoid the "Velico" bottling, which sees some wood and isn't necessarily better for it). The reds are nice value finds and include the sangiovese-cabernet blend "Calanco."

LE VIGNE DI ZAMÒ FRIULI–VENEZIA GIULIA
Via Abate Corrado 4, 33044 Manzano (UD)
Tel.: 0432759693/Fax: 0432759884

www.levignedizamo.com

DOC(G)s: Colli Orientali del Friuli

From vineyards in the village of Rosazzo, plus key sites elsewhere in the Colli Orientali DOC, proprietor Pierluigi Zamò's winemaking team of Emilio Del Medico and consultant Franco Bernabei craft luxurious wines. Try the richly concentrated tocai friuliano and its big brother, the luscious "Vigne Cinquant'Anni." The top red is a varietal merlot, although the Zamò classic "Ronco dei Roseti" (a savory, Bordeaux-style blend of cabernet, cabernet franc, and merlot) remains among the better Friulian reds. The Zamò family was one of the saviors of pignolo (older vintages of its tightly wound Abbazia di Rosazzo Pignolo can still be found, and they now make pignolo from sites outside of Rosazzo). Precise varietal whites and the creamy blend "Ronco delle Acacie" (tocai–chardonnay–pinot bianco) are also superb and fairly priced.

★ Leone Conti EMILIA-ROMAGNA

Via Pozzo 6, Tenuta Santa Lucia, Faenza (RA)
Tel.: 0546642149/Fax: 0546642222/www.leoneconti.it
DOC(G)s: Albana di Romagna; Sangiovese di Romagna; Colli di Faenza

Top producer of Sangiovese di Romagna, with multiple versions: the basic Sangiovese di Romagna DOC is about pure fruit unadorned by oak; "Le Betulle" is deeper and denser; and "Contiriserva" is a knockout, incorporating about 10% cabernet. The syrah-based "Rosso Nero" is also worth checking out. Serious Romagnan reds.

Leone de Castris PUGLIA

Via Senatore de Castris 50, 73015 Salice Salentino (LE)
Tel.: 0832731112/Fax: 0832731114
DOC(G)s: Salice Salentino

A pioneering privately owned winery in southern Puglia, specializing in Salice Salentino wine. "Donna Lisa" and "Majana" are the versions to look for—lots of soft, warm, berry fruit. "Five Roses," one of Italy's historic brands, is a nice rosé from negroamaro and malvasia nera.

Leopardi Dittajuti

See Dittajuti, Conte Leopardi.

Lequio, Ugo PIEMONTE

Via del Molino 10, 12057 Neive (CN)
Tel.: 0173677224
DOC(G)s: Barbaresco; Barbera d'Alba; Dolcetto d'Alba; Langhe

A tiny producer of a smooth, aromatic, traditionally styled Barbaresco from the Gallina cru in the village of Neive. Also solid varietal wines from barbera and dolcetto.

Les Crêtes VALLE D'AOSTA

Località Villetos 50, 11010 Aymavilles (AO)
Tel.: 0165902274/www.lescretesvins.it
DOC(G)s: Valle d'Aosta

The standard-bearer of Valle d'Aosta wines. Constantino Charrère is best known for chardonnays that are some of Italy's best answers to Chablis. There's the partially barrel-fermented "Cuvée Frissonière" and the full-bore "Cuvée Bois," both of which offer a delicious combination of fruity depth, acidity, and minerality. From there, the portfolio extends to Valle d'Aosta specialty varieties like the steely white petite arvine and the plush red fumin. The peppery,

Rhône-like "Coteau Latour" (syrah) is also a treat.

LIBRANDI CALABRIA

Strada Statale 106, Contrada San Gennaro, 88811 Ciro
Marina (CR)
Tel.: 096231518/Fax: 0962370542/www.librandi.it
DOC(G)s: Cirò

The premier winery in Calabria. Librandi's Cirò wines define the style: plush and berried, with plenty of acidity and a touch of earthy funk. "Gravello" pairs the native gaglioppo with cabernet sauvignon, while the deeply spicy "Magno Megonio" showcases the ancient magliocco grape. Also unique is the sweet "Le Passule," from another ancient grape, mantonico. It's an unctuous mix of honey, nut, and apricot flavors.

Lilliano TOSCANA ▬▬●

Località Lilliano, 53011 Castellina in Chianti (SI)
Tel.: 0577743070/Fax: 0577743036/www.lilliano.com
DOC(G)s: Chianti Classico

Lillano's offerings include classy Chianti, a smoky, sangiovese-driven *riserva*, and an evocative super-Tuscan called "Anagallis" (sangiovese-merlot-colorino). "Vignacatena" is a darkly fruity barrique-aged merlot.

★ Lis Neris FRIULI–VENEZIA GIULIA

Via Gavinana 5, 34070 San Lorenzo Isontino (GO)
Tel.: 048180105/Fax: 0481809592/www.lisneris.it
DOC(G)s: Friuli Isonzo

Some of the best whites in Friuli, with the characteristic richness of the Isonzo DOC. Alvaro Pecorari arranges his range in three tiers: varietal wines vinified solely in stainless steel; vineyard-designated wines with a portion of barrel-fermented wine (the fleshy "Gris" Pinot Grigio and the intense "Picól" Sauvignon); and 100% barrel-fermented, single-vineyard wines (the luscious Sauvignon "Dom Picól," and the superfat Chardonnay "Sant'Jurosa"). "Lis" (pinot grigio–chardonnay–sauvignon), combines creamy richness with bright aromatics. The reds are solid, if a little less interesting.

LISINI TOSCANA

Via San Angelo in Colle, 53020 Montalcino (SI)
Tel.: 0577844040/Fax: 0577844219/www.lisini.com
DOC(G)s: Brunello di Montalcino; Rosso di Montalcino

One of Montalcino's long-established leaders (the first wines were released in the late 1960s). This is Brunello that, like all great wines, is full of delicious contradictions: it is concentrated yet elegant, muscular yet refined. The single-vineyard "Ugolaia," meanwhile, is bona fide nobility in the world of Italian wine.

★ Livernano TOSCANA ▬▬●

Località Livernano, 53017 Radda in Chianti (SI)
Tel.: 0577738353/www.livernano.it

Slick wines from a perch above Radda in Chianti Classico. Although there is a fat, superfruity white, "Anima" (chardonnay-sauvignon), you'll want to save up for the reds. "Livernano" is a luscious sangiovese-merlot-cabernet blend—sweetly fruity, densely colored, velvet textured. "Puro Sangue," entirely from sangiovese grapes, has the same sappy extract as "Livermano," but the aromatics are bright and lively.

 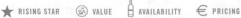

★ Livón FRIULI–VENEZIA GIULIA

Via Montarezza 33, 33048 San Giovanni al Natisone (UD)
Tel.: 0432757173/Fax: 0432757690/www.livon.it
DOC(G)s: Collio; Colli Orientali del Friuli

An ever-growing, ever-improving estate with an acclaimed lineup headlined by "Braide Alte," an oily and aromatic blend of chardonnay, sauvignon, picolit, and moscato giallo grapes. In general, Livón whites are superripe and often barrel-fermented, evidenced by the creamy "Braide Mate" Chardonnay and the "Valbuins" Sauvignon. There are some deep, funky reds, too, including "Tiareblù" (merlot-cabernet) and "Riul" Refosco. Livón also owns the Friulian estates Villa Chiopris (inexpensive Grave DOC varietals) and Tenuta RoncAlto in the Collio DOC, where they make ribolla gialla and cabernet sauvignon.

Loacker (Tenuta Schwarhof) ALTO ADIGE

Santa Giustina 3, 39100 Bolzano (BO)
Tel.: 0471365125/Fax: 0471365313/www.loacker.net
DOC(G)s: Alto Adige

The Loacker family (also famous for biscotti) make the typically broad range of Alto Adige varietal wines (more than a dozen in all, each with a funky name). Highlights include the barrel-fermented chardonnay "Ateyon," the spicy gewürztraminer "Atagis," the citrusy sauvignon blanc "Tasnim," and the silky pinot grigio "Isargus." There is a range of spicy Alpine reds as well.

Lodola Nuova (Tenimenti Ruffino) TOSCANA

Frazione Valiano, Via Lodola 1, 53045 Montepulciano (SI)
Tel.: 0578734032/www.ruffino.it
DOC(G)s: Vino Nobile di Montepulciano

Reliable, soft-textured Montepulciano wines. Good black cherry sangiovese fruit, reliable from vintage to vintage, and reasonably priced.

Lohsa

See Poliziano.

Loi, Alberto SARDEGNA

Strada Statale 125, 08040 Cardedu (NU)
Tel.: 070240866; 078275807
DOC(G)s: Cannonau di Sardegna

Plush, earthy reds from the Barbagia region around the central Sardinian village of Nuoro. The "Alberto Loi Riserva" is excellent, expressive cannonau, and the winery offers other interesting red blends, such as "Tuvara," a deep blend of cannonau, bovale, and muristellu.

Lonardi VENETO

Via delle Poste 2, 37020 Marano di Valpolicella (VR)
Tel.: 0457755154/www.lonardivini.it
DOC(G)s: Valpolicella; Amarone della Valpolicella

Restaurateur/winemaker Giuseppe Lonardi makes round, rich, stylish Amarone; full-bodied Valpolicella (go for the richer Superiore); and some heady, sweet Recioto della Valpolicella. "Privilegia" is a unique, Amarone-like mix of cabernet franc and semidried corvina.

Longariva TRENTINO

Via R. Zandonai 6, 38068 Rovereto (TN)
Tel.: 0464437200/www.longariva.it
DOC(G)s: Trentino

A tiny estate known for a copper-colored pinot grigio called "Graminé." Across the board, the wines (whites in particular) are varietally sound and powerful.

Loredan Gasparini

See Venegazzù.

Luce delle Vite TOSCANA

Località Castelgiocondo, 53024 Montalcino (SI)
Tel.: 0577848492

The Montalcino-based joint venture of the Frescobaldi winery and California's Robert Mondavi winery. The slick "Luce" (a 50-50 blend of merlot and sangiovese) is hard to resist drinking immediately, loaded as it is with sweet extract and chocolaty oak. "Lucente" (more sangiovese in the blend, less oak influence) is bright and smooth, and an excellent value.

Lucignano

See Fattoria di Lucignano.

Lunelli TRENTINO

Frazione Ravina, Via Ponte di Ravina 15, 38040 Trento (TN)
Tel.: 0461972311/www.cantineferrari.it
DOC(G)s: Trentino

The still-wine side of the Lunelli family operation, famous for its Ferrari sparklers (see separate listing). You'll find surprising values here, including "Terre di Pietra," an unusually appealing blend of cabernets sauvignon and franc, merlot, lagrein, and teroldego.

LUNGAROTTI UMBRIA

Via M. Angeloni 16, 06089 Torgiano (PG)
Tel.: 075988661/Fax: 075986650/www.lungarotti.it
DOC(G)s: Torgiano

The late Giorgio Lungarotti was an Umbrian pioneer, and his legend lives on at an estate that includes a luxury country hotel, wine and olive oil museums, more than 20 different wines, and a variety of specialty foods. The flagship wines are the Rubesco Riserva "Vigna Montic- chio," a sangiovese-canaiolo blend aged a year in barrel and 5 years in bottle before release, and "San Giorgio," a sangiovese-cabernet with a similar aging regimen. These are earthy, aromatic, finely textured reds with a track record for long aging. The line also includes great-value wines like the smooth and earthy "Rubesco" as well as several fragrant varietal whites and good Vin Santo.

Machiavelli TOSCANA

Località Sant'Andrea in Percussina, 50023 San Casciano Val Di Pesa (FI)
Tel.: 055828471/www.giv.it
DOC(G)s: Chianti Classico

One of the better wineries owned by Gruppo Italiano Vini (GIV). Chianti Classico "Vigna di Fontalle Riserva" gets high marks, as does "Ser Niccolò Solatio del Tani," a deep and fruity Tuscan cabernet.

MACULAN VENETO

Via Castelletto 3, 36042 Breganze (VI)
Tel.: 0445873733/Fax: 0455300149
DOC(G)s: Breganze

With more than a dozen wines, including some of Italy's best dessert nectars, Fausto Maculan is one of Veneto's stars. He's a master of *passito* (drying grapes before fermentation), and his sweet trio of "Acininobili" (vespaiolo-tocai-garganega), "Torcolato" (same blend), and "Dindarello" (moscato) have all been compared to great Sauternes. On the dry side, the lineup is slick and varied, starting with the creamy, great-value "Pinot & Toi" (pinots bianco and grigio, tocai, chardonnay) and the smooth and savory Bordeaux blend "Brentino." The top reds are the densely concentrated merlot "Crosara" and the voluptuous "Fratta" (cabernet-merlot). Both have an undeniably luxurious sheen and prices to match.

Madonia, Giovanna EMILIA-ROMAGNA

Via de' Cappuccini 130, 47032 Bertinoro (FC)
Tel.: 0543444361; 0543445085
DOC(G)s: Sangiovese di Romagna; Albana di Romagna Passito

Considered one of the best producers of sangiovese in Romagna, as exemplified by the consistently good "Ombroso," which has great ripeness and a velvety texture. For dessert, there's the rich Albana di Romagna Passito "Remoto," loaded with sweet apricot fruit.

Maffini, Luigi CAMPANIA

Località Cenito, 84071 San Marco di Castellabate (SA)
Tel.: 0974966345

Along with neighbor Bruno DeConciliis, Maffini has drawn attention to the Cilento region of southern Campania. "Kràtos," a wine made from fiano, has a citrusy weight not often found in the spicier fianos of Avellino, and his tangy reds from aglianico and piedirosso are well worth trying. The top-end "Cenito" is dense and smoky—try it when you're looking for something serious but different.

Malacari MARCHE

Via Enrico Malacaro 6, 60020 Offagna (AN)
Tel.: 0717207606
DOC(G)s: Rosso Cònero

A lesser-known but very good Rosso Cònero producer. "Grigiano" is an exceptionally smooth and stylish version that shows off the berried intensity of ripe montepulciano.

Malfatti, Costanza TOSCANA

Località San Andrea-Pod. 351, 58051 Magliano in Toscana (GR)
Tel.: 0564592535
DOC(G)s: Morellino di Scansano

Young, up-and-coming estate with a smooth and juicy Morellino di Scansano called "Colle di Lupo." A winery to watch in southern Tuscany.

★ Malvirà PIEMONTE

Località Canova, Case Sparse 144, 12043 Canale (CN)
Tel.: 0173978145/www.malvira.com

DOC(G)s: Roero

If you want wine from elegant, fragrant nebbiolo at sub-Barolo pricing, check out this tiny winery's Roero DOC "Trinità." Malvira's Roero Arneis "Saglietto" is partially fermented in oak, but the toast doesn't overwhelm the citrusy, floral character of the grape. Great finds.

Mancinelli, Stefano MARCHE

Via Roma 62, 60030 Morro d'Alba (AN)
Tel.: 073163021
DOC(G)s: Lacrima di Morro d'Alba; Rosso Piceno; Verdicchio dei Castelli di Jesi

A specialty is the soft, grapy Lacrima di Morro d'Alba (an Italian take on cru Beaujolais), but they also make several whites from verdicchio.

Mancini, Piero SARDEGNA

Località Cala Saccaia, 07026 Olbia (SS)
Tel.: 078950717
DOC(G)s: Cannonau di Sardegna; Vermentino di Gallura

The Gallura region of northeastern Sardinia is considered the premier area for weighty, aromatic vermentino wines. Check out Mancini's great-value version with pasta topped with *bottarga* (mullet roe) or any tangy seafood dish.

Manincor

See Graf Enzenberg.

Mantellassi TOSCANA

Località Banditaccia 26, 58051 Magliano in Toscana (GR)
Tel.: 0564592037/Fax: 0564592127/www.fatt-mantellassi.it
DOC(G)s: Morellino di Scansano

Solid, serviceable Morellino di Scansano in several incarnations (go for "Le Sentinelle"). Also try the plush and Mediterranean-inflected "Querciolaia," made from alicante (grenache).

★ Manzone, Giovanni PIEMONTE

Via Castelletto 9, 12065 Monforte d'Alba (CN)
Tel.: 017378114
DOC(G)s: Barolo; Barbera d'Alba; Dolcetto d'Alba; Langhe

An approachable, fruit-driven style of Barolo. Giovanni Manzone's best wines come from a tiny, west-facing cru called Gramolere, not far from the Santo Stefano vineyard in the village of Monforte (the "Bricat Gramolere" bottling comes from a tiny plot on the crest of the hill). His Barolos are plush and perfumed, with only a small percentage of new oak used for aging, and the tannins are always well integrated. Similarly clean, softly contoured wines from dolcetto and barbera.

MARCARINI PIEMONTE

Piazza Martiri 2, 12064 La Morra (CN)
Tel.: 017350222/www.marcarini.it
DOC(G)s: Barolo; Barbera d'Alba; Dolcetto d'Alba; Langhe

Marcarini's classic Barolos still epitomize the style traditionally associated with the village of La Morra: supple, perfumed, berried . . . all in all, more gentle and brightly aromatic than the darker-toned wines from the Serralunga or Monforte villages. Marcarini's elegant Barolos are sourced from two of La Morra's classic vineyards, Brunate and La Serra (with the Brunate wine considered the more austere of the two). Older vintages—thanks to a strong backbone of acidity—are well worth seeking out.

Marchesi Alfieri PIEMONTE

Piazza Alfieri 32, 14010 San Martino Alfieri (AT)
Tel.: 0141976288/Fax: 0141976288
www.marchesialfieri.it
DOC(G)s: Barbera d'Asti; Monferrato; Piemonte

A historic Baroque castle in which the San Germano family makes a range of good reds, especially from barbera. The single-vineyard "Alfiera" Barbera d'Asti is a consistent critical favorite, and the pinot noir "San Germano" is fairly weighty and varietally correct.

Marchesi de' Frescobaldi

See Frescobaldi.

MARCHESI DI BAROLO PIEMONTE

Via Alba 12, 12060 Barolo (CN)
Tel.: 0173564400/Fax: 0173564444
www.marchesibarolo.com
DOC(G)s: Barolo; Barbera d'Alba; Dolcetto d'Alba; Moscato d'Asti

Considered the birthplace of Barolo, which is said to have been first made here by the noble Falletti family in the nineteenth century. Marchesi di Barolo owns pieces of most of the great vineyards in the village of Barolo, including the majority of Cannubi, from which it bottles one of its better single-vineyard wines (there's also the more austere Sarmassa). Here's a great introduction to the smoky, leathery, earthy flavors of classic Barolo, and there's lots of old-vintage wine in the market, much of it very good. A full range of non-Barolo Piedmontese wines is offered, but stick with the Barolos.

MARCHESI DI GRÉSY PIEMONTE

Via Rabaja 43, 12050 Barbaresco (CN)
Tel.: 0173635222/1/Fax: 0173635187
www.marchesidigresy.com
DOC(G)s: Barbaresco; Dolcetto d'Alba; Moscato d'Asti

Marchesi di Grésy's home base is in Barbaresco, in a broad bowl of vineyards surrounded by the Asili and Rabajà vineyards. The genteel proprietor Alberto di Grésy makes tense, smoky, muscular Barbaresco—some of the most Barolo-like in the appellation, in fact—from several sites within his Martinenga vineyard. The starting point is the perfumed and brightly acidic "Martinenga," while "Gaiun" (from a site facing west toward Asili) and "Camp Gros" (from a site facing east toward Rabajà) have a heavier oak influence and denser tannic structures. Give them time. Complementing this trio of great Barbarescos is some good Langhe Chardonnay, a chunky barbera-cabernet blend called "Virtus," and a tart, typical dolcetto.

Marchesi Pancrazi (Tenuta di Bagnolo) TOSCANA

Via Montalese 156, 50045 Montemurlo (PO)
Tel.: 0574652439/www.pancrazi.it

Vittorio Pancrazi's fifteenth-century estate west of Florence specializes in pinot noir, which is said to have been planted here by accident in the mid-1970s. "Villa di Bagnolo" is soft, fragrant, and pleasant, and the pinot noir–gamay blend "San Donato" is an easy-drinking value red—if a little atypical for Tuscany. Most interesting is the dark-toned "Casaglia," a barrique-aged red from the little-used colorino grape.

Marchetti MARCHE

Via di Pontelungo 166, 60131 Ancona (AN)
Tel.: 071897386/www.marchettiwines.it
DOC(G)s: Rosso Cònero; Verdicchio dei Castelli di Jesi
Check out the "Villa Bonomi" Rosso Cònero from this small producer, if you can find it; there's also a clean and fragrant verdicchio.

Marega FRIULI–VENEZIA GIULIA

Località Valerisce 4, 34070 San Floriano del Collio (GO)
Tel.: 0481884058/Fax: 0481884057
DOC(G)s: Collio
Good Collio varietal whites, especially round, ripe, and fragrant tocai and pinot bianco, and an interesting chardonnay-riesling blend, "Holbar Bianco," which is aged in acacia-wood barrels. "Holbar Rosso" is a savory, oak-aged mix of merlot and cabernet franc.

Marenco PIEMONTE

Piazza V. Emanuele 10, 15019 Strevi (AL)
Tel.: 0144363133/Fax: 0144364108
www.marencovini.com
DOC(G)s: Brachetto d'Acqui; Barbera d'Asti; Dolcetto d'Acqui; Moscato d'Asti
Nice sweet Piedmontese specialties from brachetto ("Pineto") and moscato ("Scrapona"), along with a fat, barrique-aged barbera, "Ciresa," and a similarly oak-kissed dolcetto, "Marchesa."

Marengo, Giacomo TOSCANA ⚬━●

Frazione Capraia, Località Palazzuolo, 52048 Monte San Savino (AR)
Tel.: 0575847083/www.marengo.it
DOC(G)s: Chianti
A nice find in the hills between Siena and Arezzo, with several well-priced reds that showcase the brambly black cherry fruit of sangiovese. The "La Commenda" Chianti has some serious black-fruit depth, and the super-Tuscan "Stroncoli" (80% cabernet, 20% sangiovese) is a big wine without the correspondingly big price tag.

Marengo, Marco PIEMONTE

Via XX Settembre 32, 12064 La Morra (CN)
Tel./Fax: 017350127
DOC(G)s: Barolo; Dolcetto d'Alba
Another Barolo producer in La Morra whose wines exemplify some of the classic characteristics of the area: bright red-fruit aromas of raspberry and cherry, a hint of rose petal, plush tannins . . . but in this case a healthy dose of French oak that takes some time to integrate. In 1997 Marengo's Brunate bottling was joined by the similarly plush "Bricco le Viole," from the tiny cru in the village of Barolo.

★ Marion VENETO

Via Borgo 1, 37036 San Martino Buon Albergo (VR)
Tel.: 0458740021/www.marionvini.it
DOC(G)s: Valpolicella
The Valpolicella made at Stefano and Nicoletta

Campedelli's small estate has a great combination of spicy savor and a hint of toffeeish sweetness, while the smoky, peppery cabernet has similar heft. The teroldego is funky and interesting but has a way to go, but no doubt the new Amarone will be a smash. Big reds and still priced well.

Marotti Campi MARCHE

Località Sant'Amico 14, 60030 Morro d'Alba (AN)
Tel.: 0731618027/Fax: 0731618846/www.marotticampi.it
DOC(G)s: Lacrima di Morro d'Alba; Verdicchio dei Castelli di Jesi

Marotti Campi offers "Rubico," a plump red from the Marche's lacrima grape, but the real story here is the white verdicchio wine. Check out the "Luzano," the unoaked version, for a nice blast of citrusy freshness.

Marramiero ABRUZZO

Contrada da Sant'Andrea 1, 65010 Rosciano (PE)
Tel.: 0858505766
DOC(G)s: Montepulciano d'Abruzzo; Trebbiano d'Abruzzo

Montepulciano will be the next red wine sensation in Italy, once producers like Marramiero (and Cataldi Madonna, Illuminati, and Masciarelli) get some more airtime on wine lists. From coastal vineyards near Pescara, Marramiero has gotten the most notice for its densely packed "Inferi" Montepulciano d'Abruzzo.

Martelli & Busdraghi

See Incontri.

Martilde LOMBARDIA

Frazione Croce 4/A1, 27040 Rovescala (PV)
Tel.: 0385756280/www.martilde.it
DOC(G)s: Oltrepò Pavese

The best-known wine is "Zaffo," a dark and spicy red from bonarda (a grape also known as croatina). The entire lineup is interesting and includes a bigger, barrique-aged bonarda called "Il Ghiro Rosso d'Inverno" and "Martuffo del Glicine," a crisp, earthy pinot noir.

★ Martinetti, Franco PIEMONTE

Corso F. Turati 14, 10128 Torino (TO)
Tel.: 0118395937/Fax: 0118106598
DOC(G)s: Colli Tortonesi; Barbera d'Asti; Gavi; Monferrato

Franco Martinetti doesn't have his own winery, but rather vinifies and ages wines in a variety of different cellars, and bottles them under his name. His powerful, modern reds are headlined by the Monferrato Rosso "Sul Bric" (barbera-cabernet), which has the underlying structure to age but a mulberry-toffee sweetness that makes it hard to resist young. The barrique-aged "Montruc" is one of a growing number of massive barberas, while the "Bric dei Banditi" bottling is in a fruitier, higher-acid style. The Barolo "Marasco" is an intense wine, buttressed with lots of barrique.

MASCARELLO, BARTOLO PIEMONTE

Via Roma 15, 12060 Barolo (CN)
Tel.: 017356125
DOC(G)s: Barolo; Barbera d'Alba; Dolcetto d'Alba

Bartolo Mascarello, assisted now for many years by his daughter, Maria Teresa, is a mythic figure in Barolo. His exceptionally long-lived wines are staunchly traditional, redolent of earth and tar and tobacco, framed with firm acidity and steely tannins. There are no "cru" wines, just a single Barolo sourced from a variety of sites, and in general this is not a wine to drink young: like a great Grand Cru Burgundy (to which it is usually compared), it evolves beautifully over time (older vintages like '82 and '85 are still babies). While you're waiting, drink the meaty dolcetto or the tangy barbera, both of which share the rough-hewn appeal of the Barolo.

Mascarello, Giuseppe e Figlio PIEMONTE

Strada del Grosso 1, 12060 Castiglione Falletto (CN)
Tel.: 0173792126/Fax: 0173792124
www.mascarello1881.com
DOC(G)s: Barolo; Barbera d'Alba; Dolcetto d'Alba; Langhe

More old-school Barolo from a family named Mascarello, this one with a century of history. The wines are aromatic, high-toned, even pinot noir–ish in style. The best-known wine is the Barolo "Monprivato," loaded with rosy aromas and red cherry fruit, while the "Villero" and "Santo Stefano" bottlings are a little more austere. Aging is only in large cask, and in general the wines are finely structured, without a lot of excess extract. There are a number of jammy, traditionally styled barberas (lots of tomatoey acidity) and an exotically fragrant wine from freisa, "Toetto," among the other wines in the line.

★ Masciarelli ABRUZZO

Via Gamberale 1, 66010 San Martino sulla Marrucina (CH)
Tel.: 087185241/Fax: 087185330/www.masciarelli.it
DOC(G)s: Montepulciano d'Abruzzo; Trebbiano d'Abruzzo

With the exception of the pricey, single-vineyard "Villa Gemma," which ranks as one of the most intense Montepulciano d'Abruzzo wines, this estate is all about terrific values. The basic Montepulciano d'Abruzzo is a great by-the-case red, and so, for that matter, is the higher-level "Marina Cvetic" bottling. The lush "Marina Cvetic" Trebbiano d'Abruzzo has more guts than most and is also a bargain.

MASI VENETO

Via Monteleone, 37020 Garganago di San Ambrogio di Valpolicella (VR)
Tel.: 0456832511/Fax: 0456832536/www.masi.it
DOC(G)s: Bardolino; Valpolicella; Amarone della Valpolicella; Soave; others

The premier estate in Verona and one of the first producers (along with Bolla) to commercialize Amarone. The firm controls hundreds of acres throughout Valpoli-cella, while also managing the vineyards (and marketing the wines) of the Serègo Alighieri estate, still owned by descendants of Dante. Masi's line includes some two dozen wines, from tartly fruity Bardolino and Valpolicella bargains to massive single-vineyard Amarones such as "Mazzano" and "Campolongo di Torbe." Especially interesting are the various "super-Veronese" wines: check out the toffee-scented "Brolo di Campofiorin," a corvina-rondinella blend in which partially dried grapes are used during fermentation, or "Toar," a superripe "fresh" red (i.e., no dried fruit used) meant to showcase the potential of the local varieties. The Serègo Alighieri Valpolicella and

Amarone ("Vaio Armaron") are superripe and slick, and the Serègo Alighieri Bianco (garganega-sauvignon) is creamy and fleshy.

Maso Poli TRENTINO
Via 4 Novembre 51, Rovere della Luna (TN)
Tel.: 0461658514/Fax: 0461658587/www.masopoli.com
DOC(G)s: Trentino; Sornì
Crisp, high-altitude whites, including pinot grigio, are a specialty. "Costa Erta," a barrique-aged blend of chardonnay and sauvignon, is a fatter, creamier white.

Maso Roncador
See La Vis.

Massa Vecchia TOSCANA
Podere Fornace 11, 58024 Massa Marittima (GR)
Tel.: 0566904144
DOC(G)s: Monteregio di Massa Marittima
An unusual lineup of wines from the south Tuscan coast. "Ariento" is vermentino fermented in open-topped chestnut casks, and its rather weird melding of oxidative nuttiness, citrusy acidity, and herbal aromas is definitely unique (leave it for the wine geeks). Better are the plush "Fonte di Pietrarsa" (cabernet-merlot) and the "Terziere" alicante, as well as the late-harvest aleatico "Il Matto delle Giunchae," which makes a light alternative to Port.

Masseria Monaci PUGLIA
Località Tenuta Monaci, 73043 Copertino (LE)
Tel.: 0832947512/www.masseriamonaci.com
DOC(G)s: Copertino
"Santa Brigida," from chardonnay and sauvignon, is one of the few whites from Puglia you'd drink again, while the red lineup includes some great values: try the Copertino DOC "Eloquenzia" or "Simpotica" (negroamaro–montepulciano–malvasia nera) for lots of superripe berry fruit. "Le Braci" is a more structured old-vine negroamaro.

Massolino (Vigna Rionda) PIEMONTE
Piazza Cappellano 8, 12050 Serralunga d'Alba (CN)
Tel.: 0173613138
DOC(G)s: Barolo; Barbera d'Alba; Dolcetto d'Alba; Langhe
Classic Barolo. The famed Vigna Rionda vineyard in Serralunga d'Alba is the home base and the source of the winery's powerful, angular *riserva*. The Massolino family has been at it since the late 1800s, with several different Barolos that personify the dark, smoky, tannic Serralunga style. The only nods to modern trends are the partially barrel-fermented, barrique-aged "Vigna Parafada" Barolo, and the juiced-up Barbera d'Alba "Gisep."

Mastino
See Villa Girardi.

MASTROBERARDINO CAMPANIA
Via Manfredi 75/81, 83042 Atripalda (AV)
Tel.: 0825614111/Fax: 0825614231/www.mastro.it
DOC(G)s: Fiano di Avellino; Greco di Tufo; Taurasi; Vesuvio
This winery put Campanian wines on the map decades ago. The recent breakup of the Mastroberardino holdings (this branch got the brand name, the other got the family vineyards and established the Terredora winery) left this

historic house in need of new vineyard sources, and recent tastings have been less than exciting. The legendary Taurasi "Radici" is still intense (older vintages continue to show well), and winemaker Piero Mastroberardino is bringing some new energy to the lineup. The red "Naturalis Historia" is a rustic blend of aglianico and piedirosso. Classic varietal whites from fiano, greco, and falanghina are all flinty and correct. There's still Lacryma Christi, white and red, both of which have their rustic, simple appeal.

MASTROJANNI TOSCANA

Podere Loreto San Pio, 53020 Castelnuovo Abate (SI)
Tel.: 0577835681/Fax: 0577835505
www.mastrojanni.com
DOC(G)s: Brunello di Montalcino; Rosso di Montalcino
    Elegant Brunellos that place a premium on aromatics. There is a single-vineyard wine, "Schiena d'Asino," and a *riserva*, but the basic Brunello is a perennial great value—it's known for terrific balance, firm structure, well-moderated oak, and consistency from vintage to vintage. Ditto for the excellent Rosso di Montalcino.

Masùt da Rive FRIULI–VENEZIA GIULIA

Via Manzoni 82, 34070 Mariano del Friuli (GO)
Tel.: 048169200/www.masutdarive.com
DOC(G)s: Friuli Isonzo
    The Isonzo DOC is a source of especially weighty whites, as well as some of the better reds in Friuli. This producer's well-priced lineup (5 whites, 5 reds) includes good, ripe sauvignon, tocai, and chardonnay (try the "Maurus"), along with a decent selection of reds highlighted by a fleshy pinot noir.

Mazzi, Roberto VENETO

Località San Peretto, Via Crosetta 8, 37024 Negrar (VR)
Tel.: 0457502072/Fax: 0458266150/www.robertomazzi.it
DOC(G)s: Valpolicella Classico; Amarone della Valpolicella Classico
    A light, fresh style of Valpolicella with soft tannins and a pinot noir–ish feel. The cru "Poiega" is juiced up with a brief *appassimento* (grape drying) and more wood, but it also toes a gentle line. The Amarone is done in a brightly aromatic style, with a relatively short aging period in French oak (2 years) for a fruity, up-front profile.

Mecella, Enzo MARCHE

Via Dante 112, 60044 Fabriano (AN)
Tel.: 073221680
DOC(G)s: Rosso Cònero; Verdicchio di Matelica
    Mecella was one of the first to bring international attention to Rosso Cònero, and he still does it well, extracting plenty of depth from the smooth and fruity montepulciano grape. Overall, he makes a wide variety of whites and reds from outsourced grapes. Check out the crisp Verdicchio di Matelica "Pagliano" in addition to the always good (and always affordable) Rosso Cònero.

Medici, Ermete & Figli EMILIA-ROMAGNA

Via I. Newton 13/a, 42040 Reggio Emilia (RE)
Tel.: 0522942135/Fax: 0522941641/www.medici.it

€-
€€ DOC(G)s: Reggiano

Frizzante ("semisparkling") is the word here, whether it's the tart and refreshing dry lambrusco wine "Concerto" (a great aperitif with some hunks of Parmigiano) or the aromatic dry malvasia "Daphne."

Melini TOSCANA

Località Gaggiano, 53036 Poggibonsi (SI)
Tel.: 0577998511/www.giv.it
DOC(G)s: Chianti Classico; Vernaccia di San Gimignano; Vino Nobile di Montepulciano

The line ranges from straw-flask supermarket wine to single-vineyard gems like "La Selvanella," an elegant, long-aging Chianti Classico. There are pumped-up New World reds like "Bonorli" (merlot), but woodsy Chianti is a trademark (even the barrique-aged "Massovecchio" Chianti has a rustic feel). Light whites from Orvieto and San Gimignano add to the value-priced selection.

Meloni Vini SARDEGNA

Via A. Gallus 79, 09047 Selargius (CA)
Tel.: 070852822/Fax: 070840311/www.meloni-vini.com
DOC(G)s: Cannonau di Sardegna; Monica di Sardegna; Moscato di Cagliari; Vermentino di Sardegna

The vermentino "Astice" is a tangy white for seafood; the red Monica di Sardegna has a soft but spicy feel, with lots of tangy Mediterranean aromas. Also try the rare Moscato di Cagliari "Donna Jolanda," which has an unctuous texture and a nose of dried apricots and citrus.

Merk FRIULI–VENEZIA GIULIA

Casa Geretto, Via Triestina 12, 30029 Santo Stinto di Livenza (VE)
Tel.: 0421460253/Fax: 0421314546/www.geretto.it
DOC(G)s: Friuli Aquileia

Solid varietal lineup including tocai, pinot bianco, and a number of reds. Refosco "Vigne Vecchie" is a highlight.

Meroi FRIULI–VENEZIA GIULIA

Via Stretta del Parco 7, 33042 Buttrio (UD)
Tel.: 0432674025
DOC(G)s: Colli Orientali del Friuli

Mentored by Enzo Pontoni of Miani, Paolo Meroi makes substantial wines. "Blanc di Buri" (pinot grigio–chardonnay–malvasia) is tropically fruity and creamy, and the tocai friulano has good, oily weight. "Ros di Buri" (merlot-cabernet-refosco) is a smoky, peppery red.

Methius

See Dorigati.

MezzaCorona TRENTINO

Via del Teroldego 1, 38016 Mezzocorona (TN)
Tel.: 0461605163/www.mezzacorona.it
DOC(G)s: Trento Brut; Trentino; Teroldego Rotaliano

A giant Trentino co-op known for sparklers, particularly its Rotari brand. These are inexpensive and pretty good, as are the still wines from pinot grigio, chardonnay, cabernet, and merlot, along with local wines such as the tarry teroldego and the blueberry-scented marzemino. In addition to the huge MezzaCorona line, the company, Gruppo MezzaCorona, produces wine all over Italy—the newest addition is the Feudo Arancio winery in Sicily (supercheap varietals, most notably nero d'avola and syrah). Other holdings include Tolloy (Alto Adige), Castello di Querceto (Chianti Classico, Tuscany), Nannetti (Montalcino, Tuscany), and Righetti (Veneto).

★ Miani FRIULI–VENEZIA GIULIA
Via Peruzzi 10, 33042 Buttrio (UD)
Tel.: 0432674327
DOC(G)s: Colli Orientali del Friuli

A tiny cult winery run by Enzo Pontoni, whose minuscule production is headlined by a tocai friulano that's thick as honey, exotically aromatic, and framed with toasty oak. The sauvignon blanc is similarly intense, coating the palate with extract and filling the head with intense aromas of wildflowers, citrus, and herbs. The merlot is dense and decadent, with structure and savor to rival Right Bank Bordeaux. "Calvari," the rarest of all, is a dense and decadent refosco loaded with black fruit and dark spice (Pontoni promises more refosco in the future). Superexpensive, but they deliver.

Micante
See Fattoria Le Pupille.

Miceli SICILIA
Via Denti di Piraino 9, 90142 Palermo (PA)
Tel.: 0916396111/www.midmicelli.it
DOC(G)s: Alcamo; Passito di Pantelleria

The late Ignazio Miceli was a force in promoting Sicilian wines abroad, and his firm still operates wineries in Sciacca (near Palermo) and Pantelleria. The sweet styles of Pantelleria are a specialty. Try the *frizzante* moscato "Garighe" (a Sicilian answer to Moscato d'Asti) and the unctuous Passito di Pantelleria "Tanit."

Midolini FRIULI–VENEZIA GIULIA
Via Udine 40, 33044 Manzano (UD)
Tel.: 0432754555/www.midolini.com
DOC(G)s: Colli Orientali del Friuli

Well-priced varietals with a Friulian pedigree, which is to say they are clean, varietally correct, and pretty sleek for the price. Try the tocai and refosco.

Mionetto VENETO
Via Colderove 2, 311049 Valdobbiadene (TV)
Tel.: 04239707/Fax: 390423975766/www.mionetto.it
DOC(G)s: Prosecco di Valdobbiadene

Masters of prosecco (and prosecco packaging). The product line is huge and bubbly, with the top-end wines coming from the "MO" line—check out the structured "Sergio" or the bright and refined "Cartizze," which carries the Prosecco di Valdobbiadene DOC designation. The *frizzante*-style "Il," finished with a bottle cap instead of a cork, is a fun aperitif. Great-value sparklers and *frizzanti* all around, and some simple still wines.

Mocali TOSCANA
Località Mocali, 53024 Montalcino (SI)
Tel.: 0577849485
DOC(G)s: Brunello di Montalcino; Rosso di Montalcino

Softly contoured Brunello and Rosso with perceptible new-oak notes and a round, fruity texture.

Moccagatta PIEMONTE

Via Rabajà 24, 12050 Barbaresco (CN)
Tel.: 0173635152/Fax: 0173635279
DOC(G)s: Barbaresco; Barbera d'Alba; Dolcetto d'Alba; Langhe

Franco and Sergio Minuto make round, luxurious Barbarescos. They are the sole bottlers from the Cole vineyard, an extension of the more famous Montestefano cru; "Vigneto Cole," aged in barrique, has cocoa-rich depth but an enticing approachability in its youth. The Basarin cru in the commune of Neive is used for angular Barbaresco and a rich Barbera d'Alba, while the velvety "Bric Balin" Barbaresco (sourced from a piece of Barbaresco's Moccagatta cru, appropriately enough) is the top wine. Everything is sleek and modern, including a noteworthy chardonnay.

Moio, Michele CAMPANIA

Viale Regina Margherita 6, 81034 Mondragone (CE)
Tel.: 0823978017
DOC(G)s: Falerno del Massico

Most people don't associate primitivo with Campania, but here on the north coast of Campania the grape has deep roots. Moio's primitivos have lots of dark black fruit and firmer tannins than the Puglian versions. There are also some flinty white wines from falanghina.

Molettieri, Salvatore CAMPANIA

Contrada Musanni 19/B, 83040 Montemarano (AV)
Tel.: 082763424/Fax: 082763722
DOC(G)s: Taurasi

Powerful aglianico from a fast-rising producer. The Taurasi "Vigna Cinque Querce" combines great extraction with all of the angular, tobacco-tinged aromatics you expect from aglianico. Easily one of the best Taurasis available. The Irpinia Aglianico, also called "Cinque Querce," is the little brother, but there's nothing little about it.

Molino, Mauro PIEMONTE

Borgata Gancia 11, 12064 La Morra (CN)
Tel.: 017350814
DOC(G)s: Barolo; Barbera d'Alba; Dolcetto d'Alba; Langhe

Warm and gentle La Morra Barolo, starting with the well-priced base bottling and moving up to the single-vineyard "Vigna Gancia" and "Vigna Conca" (as in Conca dell'Annunziata) bottlings. There's a plush, bright, fruit-forward feel to these wines, and the style carries through to the barberas, dolcettos, and the very appealing "Acanzio" (barbera-nebbiolo-cabernet).

Monchiero, F.lli PIEMONTE

Via Alba Monforte 58, 12060 Castiglione Falletto (CN)
Tel./Fax: 017362820/www.monchierovini.it
DOC(G)s: Barolo; Barbera d'Alba; Dolcetto d'Alba; Langhe

Small-production Barolo from holdings in Castiglione Falletto, including "Le Rocche," which is contiguous with Ceretto's famous Bricco Rocche vineyard (see separate listing). An earthy, leathery, more traditional style and good pricing.

Monfalleto (Cordero di Montezemolo)

See Cordero di Montezemolo.

Monrubio UMBRIA

Località Le Prese 22, 05010 Monterubaglio (TR)
Tel./Fax: 0763626064

DOC(G)s: Orvieto

Orvieto-area cooperative that boasts Riccardo Cotarella as enologist. "Palaia" is a very good bargain, a deep and polished blend of merlot, pinot noir, and cabernet.

Monsanto TOSCANA

Via Monsanto 8, 50021 Barberino Val d'Elsa (FI)
Tel.: 0558059000/www.castellodimonsanto.it

DOC(G)s: Chianti Classico

Earthy, aromatic, high-toned Chianti from an eighteenth-century estate owned by the Bianchi family since 1961. The Riserva "Il Poggio" is noteworthy (older vintages still drink well and can be found in the market), while the super-Tuscans "Tinscvil" (sangiovese-cabernet) and "Nemo" (all cabernet) are solid and well priced.

Monte Antico LOMBARDIA

Via Mosé Bianchi 41, 20149 Milano (MI)
Tel.: 0248010101/Fax: 0248008036/www.empson.com

An IGT sangiovese created by importer Neil Empson and wine consultant Franco Bernabei, sourced from select vineyards throughout Tuscany and vinified at the Santa Lucia winery in Pisa (see listing). Smoky, supple, and extremely well priced.

Monte Faustino VENETO

Via Bure Alto 1, 37029 San Pietro in Cariano (VR)
Tel./Fax: 0457701651/www.fornaser.com

DOC(G)s: Valpolicella Classico; Amarone della Valpolicella

A firm, vinous style of Amarone built for long aging. More aromatic and lean as opposed to fat and sweet. Valpolicella "La Traversagna" is done in a *ripasso* style, giving it a hint of toffee sweetness and added weight.

Monte Pugliano CAMPANIA

Via San Vito, 84090 Montecorvino Pugliano (SA)
Tel.: 3283412515

A Salerno-area winery with a superripe aglianico called "Castellaccio," made with the help of neighbor Bruno DeConciliis. The ashy smoke of aglianico is there, but it also has some black currant sweetness.

Monte Rossa LOMBARDIA

Frazione Bornato, Via Luca Marenzio 14, 25040 Cazzago San Martino (BS)
Tel.: 030725066/Fax: 0307254614/www.monterossa.com

DOC(G)s: Franciacorta

One of the best producers in Franciacorta. "Cabochon," which includes barrel-fermented base wine (the blend is 70% chardonnay and 30% pinot nero), is a deep wine that belongs on a table with food; the Satén (chardonnay–pinot bianco) is creamy and delicate.

★ Monte Schiavo MARCHE

Frazione Monteschiavo, Via Vivaio, 60030 Maiolati Spontini (AN)
Tel.: 0731700385/Fax: 0731700297

€–
€€
DOC(G)s: Rosso Piceno; Rosso Cònero; Verdicchio dei Castelli di Jesi

The "Adeodato" bottling is a rich, chocolaty take on Rosso Còero, and headlines the very good lineup of wines made here. "Esio" (montepulciano-cabernet) is good, too, and reasonably priced. There are a number of clean and fragrant verdicchios and a supercheap Rosso Piceno, "Sassaiolo," that makes an excellent, juicy house pour.

Monte Tondo VENETO

Via San Lorenzo 89, 37038 Soave (VR)
Tel.: 0457680347/www.montetondo.it
€–
€€
DOC(G)s: Soave Classico

The single-vineyard "Casette Foscarin" Soave Classico is worth a search and "Mito" is no slouch, either. Both are aromatic, structured, well-concentrated Soave wines.

Montecalvi TOSCANA

Via Citille 85, 50022 Greve in Chianti (FI)
Tel.: 0558544665
€€
Deep, structured, old-vine sangiovese from the Chianti Classico, although it doesn't carry the appellation. The wine (which includes some cabernet, merlot, and syrah) has a track record of critical acclaim and a fair price.

Montecchio

See Fattoria Montecchio.

Montechiari

See Fattoria di Montechiari.

Montecucco TOSCANA

Località Montecucco, 58044 Cinigiano (GR)
Tel.: 0564999029
€–
€€
DOC(G)s: Montecucco

Montecucco is a town near Grosseto that lends its name to a DOC and, in this case, to a wine estate. The sangiovese-based "Le Coste" is a soft, simple south Tuscan red, as is the red blend "Passionaia."

Montegrossi

See Rocca di Montegrossi.

Montellori

See Fattoria Montellori.

Montepeloso TOSCANA

Località Montepeloso 82, 57028 Suvereto (LI)
Tel.: 0565828180
€€–
€€€
DOC(G)s: Val di Cornia

The explosive, sangiovese-based "Nardo" is undeniably good, as is the "Gabbro" cabernet sauvignon, but you'll pay handsomely to taste these inky coastal Tuscan reds.

Montepò

See Biondi-Santi.

Montesole CAMPANIA

Serra di Montefusco, 83038 Montefusco (AV)
Tel.: 0825963972/Fax: 0825963970/www.colliirpini.com
€
DOC(G)s: Fiano di Avellino; Greco di Tufo; Sannio; Taurasi

Classic Campanian wines (rustic, spicy) from all the local varieties, including one of the better Greco di Tufo whites available. "Sussurro" is an interesting greco-fiano blend, and the Sannio Falanghina is bright and chalky. The Taurasi is dark, brooding, tannic.

MONTEVERTINE TOSCANA

Località Montevertine, 53017 Radda in Chianti (SI)
Tel.: 0577738009/www.montevertine.it

In this era of fruit-bomb super-Tuscans, not everyone quite appreciates "Le Pergole Torte," this estate's flagship wine. A varietal sangiovese from Radda (as famous for its labels as its taste), it has always been positioned as a Grand Cru Burgundy as grown in Chianti Classico. This comparison may be a little extreme, but "Pergole" is all about the rosy, smoky aromas of sangiovese, with a tightly wound structure that needs lots of time to resolve. The other Montevertine reds are based on sangiovese and canaiolo, aged only in large Slavonian oak, all redolent of earth and smoke. The white "M" (trebbiano-malvasia) has some nice aromas and good weight, but it's the superperfumed, Burgundian reds you want to look for.

★ Montevetrano CAMPANIA

Via Montevetrano 3, 84099 San Cipriano Piacentino (SA)
Tel.: 089882285

Silvia Imparato's onetime hobby estate was a media favorite right out of the gate, giving the tiny-production wine a mystique that quickly elevated its price. Montevetrano is an explosive, darkly fruity red from vineyards near Salerno, and the style has fleshed out (and sweetened up) since the first vintages in the early nineties: today the blend is said to be 60% cabernet, 30% merlot, and 10% aglianico, though it's hard to believe that older vintages ('94, '95) didn't contain more aglianico. Whereas those older wines are smokier and more fiercely tannic, the younger versions are juicier and approachable in their youth.

★ Monti, Antonio e Elio ABRUZZO

Contrada Pignotto 62, 64010 Controguerra (TE)
Tel.: 086189042
DOC(G)s: Montepulciano d'Abruzzo

Check out the single-vineyard "Pignotto," an unctuous and dark-robed montepulciano that isn't just superripe but muscular and, for montepulciano, elegant.

Monti, Paolo PIEMONTE

Località San Sebastiano 39, 12065 Monforte d'Alba (CN)
Tel.: 017378391/www.paolomonti.com
DOC(G)s: Barolo; Barbera d'Alba; Langhe

Pier Paolo Monti has been known for massive, superripe barberas and the chocolaty Langhe Rosso "Dossi Rossi" (merlot-cabernet-nebbiolo). He has recently added Barolos from Monforte, and there's also an interesting white "L'Aura" (barrel-fermented chardonnay with about 30% riesling). Showy, sleek, sweetly fruity wines.

Montori, Camilo ABRUZZO

Contrada Piane Tronto 80, 64010 Controguerra (TE)
Tel.: 0861809900/Fax: 0861809912
DOC(G)s: Controguerra; Montepulciano d'Abruzzo; Trebbiano d'Abruzzo

More good Montepulciano d'Abruzzo from the area around Controguerra. "Fonte Cupa" is an elegant style (it's sourced from the prized Colline Teramane subzone), not a

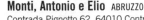

huge wine but one with a silky-smooth feel. "Leneo Moro" (montepulciano-cabernet) is darker and chunkier.

Morgante SICILIA

Contrada Racalmare, 92020 Grotte (AG)
Tel./Fax: 0922945579/www.morgante-vini.it

Longtime contract growers for local co-ops, the Morgante family began making their own wines in 1994. With the help of consultant Riccardo Cotarella, they craft two excellent nero d'avola wines: "Don Antonio" has the depth and funk of an Australian shiraz, and the basic nero d'avola is a wine to buy by the case (or three) to have around the house. Juicy and delicious.

Morgassi Superiore PIEMONTE

Via Case Sparse Sermoria, 15066 Gavi (AL)
Tel.: 0143642007/Fax: 0143645607
www.morgassisuperiore.it
DOC(G)s: Gavi

Better-than-average Gavi di Gavi and some stylish, deeply fruity reds from syrah ("Tamino") and cabernet-barbera ("Sarastro"). Also interesting is a fat, oily barrel-fermented viognier called "Cherubino."

Mori, Giacomo TOSCANA

Piazza Pertini 8, 53043 San Casciano dei Bagni (SI)
Tel.: 0578227005/Fax: 057821661
DOC(G)s: Chianti

An excellent house pour. Giacomo Mori began estate-bottling in the nineties, and he makes fragrant, smooth, pretty serious Chianti for around $20. "Castelrotto" has some nice black berry fruit and a sheen of toasty oak, but the basic Chianti will more than suffice.

Moris Farms TOSCANA

Località Cura Nuova, 58024 Massa Marittima (GR)
Tel.: 0566919135/Fax: 0566919380/www.morisfarms.it
DOC(G)s: Morellino di Scansano; Monteregio di Massa Marittima

One of the first producers of good Morellino di Scansano, which introduced wine drinkers to the softer, juicier flavors of warm-climate sangionese. The basic bottling is light and juicy; the *riserva* has more stuffing. The real gem is "Avvoltore," one of the better south Tuscan blends (a luscious mix of sangiovese, cabernet sauvignon, and syrah).

Mormoraia TOSCANA

Località Sant'Andrea 15, 53037 San Gimignano (SI)
Tel.: 0577940096/www.mormoraia.it
DOC(G)s: Vernaccia di San Gimignano

Clean, fragrant vernaccia and a barrel-fermented chardonnay-vernaccia blend, "Ostria Grigia." The rich "Neitea" (sangiovese-cabernet) and "Mytilus" (sangiovese-merlot-syrah) are among the better new-generation San Gimignano reds, with good heft and silky tannins.

Moroder MARCHE

Via Montacuto 112, 60062 Ancona (AN)
Tel.: 071898232/www.moroder-vini.it
DOC(G)s: Rosso Cònero

Smooth, silky montepulciano from one of the big names in the Rosso Cònero DOC. "Dorico," made from a selection of Alessandro Moroder's best fruit, is usually held back before release: rather than being a fruit-bomb, it has an elegance and spicy savor not typically associated with montepulciano.

Moschioni FRIULI–VENEZIA GIULIA

Località Gagliano, Via Doria 30, 33043 Cividale del Friuli (UD)

Tel.: 0432730210

DOC(G)s: Colli Orientali del Friuli

Some of the most intense, ageworthy reds made in Friuli, and they'll cost you: the rare pignolo (a dark, brooding giant) is the one to lock up first, while the tarry, violet-scented refosco is a little more affordable (and immediately drinkable). There's also excellent wine from schioppettino (appropriately spicy and smoky) and the Bordeaux blend "Celtico." Lots of muscle and color.

Mottura, Sergio LAZIO

Località Poggio della Costa 1, 01020 Civitella d'Agliano (VT)

Tel.: 0761914533/www.motturasergio.it

DOC(G)s: Orvieto

On the Lazio-Umbria border near Viterbo, this organic winery makes clean and fresh Orvieto, as well as a semi-sweet Orvieto *amabile* and a more honeyed late-harvest white, "Muffo," from grechetto and procanico, which shows off some botrytis notes. The clean and spicy "Poggio della Costa" grechetto shows that variety's citrusy appeal.

★ Movia SLOVENIA

Ceglo 18, 5212 Dobrovo, Slovenia

Tel.: 386053959510/Fax: 3860539511

DOC(G)s: Brda (Collio)

Honorary Italian Ales Kristancic (whose Slovenian winery is steps from the Italian border and whose vineyards stretch into the Italian Collio DOC) makes a wide range of unique wines. The winery has been family run since 1820. Kristancic's whites are not unlike those made across the border by the Gravner winery, in that they are aged on the lees in oak for long periods before bottling, lending them a yeasty, oxidative quality. Try the blends especially: the bright yet creamy "Veliko Bianco" (ribolla, chardonnay, sauvignon, pinot grigio) and the old-vine "Turno" (pinots grigio, bianco, and noir, the last vinified as white). The red pinot nero is plush and quite good, and the late-harvest "Izbrani Plodovi," made in select years, boasts a whiff of botrytis.

Murana SICILIA

Contrada Khamma 276, 91017 Pantelleria (TP)

Tel./Fax: 0923915231

DOC(G)s: Moscato di Pantelleria; Passito di Pantelleria

Excellent Pantelleria wines. The Moscato di Pantelleria "Turbé" is dried for shorter periods than the more unctuous Passito di Pantelleria bottlings "Khamma" and "Martingana," which also spend some time in oak.

Muri-Gries, Cantina Convento ALTO ADIGE

Piazza Gries 21, 39100 Bolzano (BZ)

Tel.: 0471282287/Fax: 0471273448/www.muri-gries.com

DOC(G)s: Alto Adige

Located in a monastery, this winery is known for dark-hued lagrein from vineyards near Bolzano. Chunky, savory reds loaded with notes of tar, blackberry, and bitter chocolate. Totally unique and, in the case of the "Abtei Muri Riserva," pretty serious Alpine reds. A nice spicy lagrein *rosato* (*kretzer* in German) is also worth a try.

Musella VENETO

Località Monte del Drago, 37036 San Martino Buon Albergo (VR)

Tel.: 045973385/Fax: 0458956287/www.musella.it

DOC(G)s: Amarone della Valpolicella; Valpolicella

Luxurious, extracted Amarone that wraps its intensity in a velvety package, from an up-and-coming Veronese winery in a beautiful setting.

Musso, Walter PIEMONTE

Via Domizio Cavazza 5, 12050 Barbaresco (CN)

Tel.: 0173635129/Fax: 0173635914

DOC(G)s: Barbaresco; Barbera d'Alba; Dolcetto d'Alba; Langhe

These deep, spicy, yet softly contoured Barbarescos— from the Rio Sordo and Pora crus—are fantastic buys. The soft and juicy Langhe Chardonnay is also good.

Mustilli CAMPANIA

Via dei Firoi 20, 82019 Sant'Agata dei Goti (BN)

Tel.: 823717433/www.mustilli.com

DOC(G)s: Sant'Agata dei Goti

An improving line of wines from a small town west of Benevento, in northern Campania. "Conte Artus," a tobacco-scented blend of piedirosso and aglianico grapes, has nice concentration for the price, and there are a number of other wines from either piedirosso or aglianico.

Nada, Ada

See Ada Nada.

Nada Fiorenzo PIEMONTE

Località Rombone, Via Ausario 12/C, 12050 Treiso (CN)

Tel.: 0173638254/www.nada.it

DOC(G)s: Barbaresco; Dolcetto d'Alba; Langhe

Barbaresco "Rombone," from a southwest-facing cru in Treiso, has considerable heft and a touch of vanilla-chocolate sweetness from oak, but in general the Nada style captures all the great savor, spice, and edge of nebbiolo. "Seifile" is rounder, a nebbiolo-barbera blend with plenty of juicy fruit for immediate drinking.

Napolini UMBRIA

Località Gallo 71, Frazione Turrita, 06036 Montefalco (PG)

Tel.: 0742379362/Fax: 0742371119/www.napolini.it

DOC(G)s: Montefalco; Colli Martani

A nice value in Montefalco: the sagrantino here has a plush and perfumed character, while being bright and spicy instead of big and black like some sagrantinos. The white grechetto wine is a citrusy value.

NEGRI, NINO LOMBARDIA

Via Ghibellini 3, 23030 Chiuro (SO)

Tel.: 0342485211/Fax: 0342482235/www.giv.it

DOC(G)s: Valtellina

One of the oldest wineries in Italy, founded in 1897 by innkeeper Nino Negri. Run for the last thirty years by Casimiro Maule, Negri is the Valtellina DOC's star. For an exceptionally aromatic take on the nebbiolo grape, try Negri's incredibly well-priced bottlings from the "crus" of Valtellina: Sassella "La Tense," Grumello "Sassorosso," and Inferno "Mazér." Aromas of Earl Grey tea, dried cherry, and pipe tobacco waft up out of the glass while the tannin/acidity of nebbiolo grab hold of the palate and don't let go. The dried-grape *sfursat* wine, called "5 Stelle," is, of course, denser and faintly sweet, but the mélange of exotic perfumes is still there (*sfursat* wines are made using dried grapes, like Amarone, and tend to hint at sweetness while being technically dry). Very cool stuff.

Negro, Angelo & Figli PIEMONTE

Frazione Sant'Ana 1, 12040 Monteu Roero (CN)
Tel.: 017390252/www.negroangelo.it
DOC(G)s: Barbera d'Alba; Roero
    Good Roero whites and reds. "Sodisfà" is the top Roero nebbiolo, with plenty of density and aroma, and the "Bric Bertù" Barbera d'Alba gets the French oak treatment for added sweetness. The single-vineyard "Perdaudin" is a bigger-than-average version of Roero Arneis.

Nervi PIEMONTE

Corso Vercelli 117, 13045 Gattinara (VC)
Tel./Fax: 0163833228
DOC(G)s: Gattinara
    A historic property dating back to the turn of the nineteenth century, which was purchased from the Nervi family in 1991 by Germano Boccicolone. The Gattinara made here rivals Barolo in intensity and longevity. The single-vineyard "Vigneto Molsino" has all of the nebbiolo hallmarks: leather, tobacco, wintry spice, firm acidity. It's a wine with a proven track record for long aging. And it's still affordable.

Nicodemi, Bruno ABRUZZO

Contrada da Veniglio, 64024 Notaresco (TE)
Tel.: 085895493
DOC(G)s: Montepulciano d'Abruzzo, Trebbiano d'Abruzzo
    Nicodemi's Trebbiano d'Abruzzo Riserva "Bacco" is one of the better wines of its type, an aromatic and substantial white for the money. The montepulcianos are smooth and supple, if on the lighter side.

Nicolis VENETO

Via Villa Girardi 29, 37029 San Pietro in Cariano (VR)
Tel.: 0457701261/Fax: 0456800551/www.vininicolis.com
DOC(G)s: Amarone della Valpolicella; Valpolicella
    Excellent small producer of Veronese reds. The pruny "Seccal" Valpolicella has nice weight from the inclusion of withered fruit, and the corvina-cabernet "Testal" also incorporates some dried fruit to achieve its supple texture. With the Amarone, it is worth it to trade up to the single-vineyard "Ambrosan," which is considerably rounder and more powerful than the perfumed base bottling.

Niedrist, Ignaz ALTO ADIGE

Via Ronco 5, 39050 Cornaiano/Girlan (BZ)
Tel./Fax: 0471664494
DOC(G)s: Alto Adige
    An admired artisan producer known for nervous, super-aromatic whites from riesling, sauvignon, and pinot

bianco. The lagrein "Berger-Gei" is a meaty red with a lot of character for the price.

Nino Franco VENETO

Via Garibaldi 147, 31049 Valdobbiadene (TV)
Tel.: 0423972051/www.ninofranco.it
DOC(G)s: Prosecco di Valdobbiadene

Primo Franco's wines are more structured, aromatic, and finely tuned than the general mass of prosecco in the Veneto. "Rustico" and "Primo Franco" proseccos both transcend the category.

Nottola TOSCANA

Località Nottola, Strada Statale 326, 15, 53045 Montepulciano (SI)
Tel.: 0578707060/Fax: 0577684711
DOC(G)s: Vino Nobile di Montepulciano; Rosso di Montepulciano

An estate created when Antinori sold off a chunk of its La Braccesca vineyard to the Giomarelli family. With Riccardo Cotarella consulting, they've created a slick, chunky, oak-influenced style of Vino Nobile di Montepulciano.

Nozzole TOSCANA

Passo dei Pecorai, 50022 Greve in Chianti (FI)
Tel.: 055200281/Fax: 0552002823
DOC(G)s: Chianti Classico

Woodsy, high-acid Chianti from a property once controlled by the Ruffino winery and now run by Ambrogio and Alberto Folonari. "Il Pareto" is a finely structured super-Tuscan cabernet.

Oasi degli Angeli MARCHE

Contrada Sant'Egidio 50, 63012 Cupra Marittima (AP)
Tel.: 0735778569

A boutique estate on the south coast of the Marche, known for the black and viscous "Kurni," an explosive montepulciano produced in eyedropper quantities.

Oberto, Andrea PIEMONTE

Via G. Marconi 25, 12064 La Morra (CN)
Tel./Fax: 0173509262
DOC(G)s: Barolo; Barbera d'Alba; Dolcetto d'Alba; Langhe

Tiny production from vineyards in La Morra and Barolo, including the potent, densely packed Barolo "Rocche." The monolithic Barbera d'Alba "Giada" is another find. Intense wines.

Ocone CAMPANIA

Via del Monte, 82030 Ponte (BN)
Tel.: 0824874040/www.oconevini.it
DOC(G)s: Sannio; Solopaca; Taburno

Ocone has been a mainstay of winemaking in the village of Benevento, in northern Campania. The flinty falanghina is a good starting point; next go for the reds, from aglianico and piedirosso. The basic Aglianico del Taburno DOC has the tobacco-tinged savor typical of the zone. "Diomede" is a richer style of aglianico; "Calidonio" is a smoky, meaty combination of aglianico and piedirosso.

Oddero, F.lli PIEMONTE

Borgata Tetti–Santa Maria, 28, 12064 La Morra (CN)
Tel.: 017350618/Fax: 0173509377

www.odderofratelli.com

DOC(G)s: Barolo; Barbaresco; Dolcetto d'Alba; Langhe

A larger producer of tightly compacted Barolo, from a series of cru sites in Serralunga (the dark and stormy "Vigna Rionda"), Castiglione Falletto (the gentler "Rocche" and "Rocche Rivera"), and Monforte (the deep and generous "Mondoca di Bussia"). Elegant wines with lots of earthy, Burgundian notes.

Oddero, Massimo PIEMONTE

Via San Sebastiano 1, 12055 Diano d'Alba (CN)
Tel.: 017369169

DOC(G)s: Barolo; Barbaresco; Diano d'Alba; Gavi

Wedged between Barolo and Barbaresco in Diano d'Alba, this small property makes both Barolo and Barbaresco along with the local dolcetto (try the cru "Sorba"). A well-priced treat is the lush barbera-nebbiolo blend "Rosso del Notaio." The barrique-aged barbera "Carbea" is a rich and affordable red for a big steak dinner.

Odoardi CALABRIA

Contrada Campodorato, 88047 Nocera Terinese (CZ)
Tel.: 096891159/Fax: 098428503

DOC(G)s: Scavigna; Savuto

An up-and-comer in Calabria with spectacular coastal vineyards near the town of Cosenza. Using the little-known DOCs Savuto and Scavigna, they bottle funky yet polished red blends featuring grapes such as aglianico, magliocco, and greco nero. The luscious "Vigna Garrone" (aglianico-cabernet-merlot) is the top red, but the cheaper Savuto Rosso (from a wild mix of odd local grapes) has great depth.

Olim Bauda PIEMONTE

Strada Prata 22, 14045 Incisa Scapaccino (AT)
Tel.: 014174266

DOC(G)s: Barbera d'Asti; Piemonte

The basic Barbera d'Asti is juicy and refreshing (no oak), while the Superiore is more pumped up (almost 2 years in barrique).

Orlandi Contucci Ponno ABRUZZO

Località Piana Ulivi 1, 64026 Roseto degli Abruzzi (TE)
Tel.: 0858944049

DOC(G)s: Montepulciano d'Abruzzo; Trebbiano d'Abruzzo

Marina Orlandi Contucci has brought this estate a long way in a few vintages, with elegant, deeply concentrated Montepulciano d'Abruzzo (go for the great-value "Regia Specula") complemented by the deeper "Liburnio" (montepulciano-cabernet-sangiovese).

Ormanni TOSCANA

Località Ormanni 1, 53036 Poggibonsi (SI)
Tel.: 0577937212/Fax: 0557936640

DOC(G)s: Chianti Classico

Here's a good Chianti find: the *riserva* in particular has great smoky depth and rich extract, and the "Julius" (sangiovese-merlot) is a dense super-Tuscan at a still-approachable price.

ORNELLAIA TOSCANA

Via Bolgherese 191, 57020 Bolgheri (LI)
Tel.: 056571811/www.ornellaia.it

DOC(G)s: Bolgheri

Founded by Lodovico Antinori (brother of Antinori's Piero) in the early 1980s and now owned by the Frescobaldi–Robert Mondavi partnership. The wines here were designed to rival great red Bordeaux (famed agronomist André Tchelistcheff planted the original vineyards), and "Ornellaia" (65% cabernet, 30% merlot, 5% cabernet franc) has lived up to expectations. "Masseto," a merlot, is the best example of the variety in Italy: dense, structured, with an deep mineral savor. These are collector wines and are priced accordingly. The new Ornellaia "second" wine, "Le Serre Nuove" (debuted with the 2000 vintage), is a voluptuous (and relatively affordable) introduction to the house style. "Le Volte" (cabernet-merlot-sangiovese) is a smooth and spicy entry-level red.

Orsolani PIEMONTE

Via Michele Chiesa 12, 10090 San Giorgio Canavese (TO)
Tel.: 012432386/Fax: 0124450342/www.orsolani.it
DOC(G)s: Erbaluce di Caluso; Caluso Passito

Floral, mineral-rich whites from erbaluce are the specialty (check out the laser-sharp "Vignot S. Antonio"). Orsolani also turns this racy white into a structured sparkler and an unctuous-yet-refreshing sweet wine, "Sulé." High-strung whites with nice "cut" for cheeses.

Ottavi

See AnticoTerrenOttavi.

★ Pacenti, Siro TOSCANA

Località Pelagrilli 1, 53024 Montalcino (SI)
Tel.: 0577848662
DOC(G)s: Brunello di Montalcino; Rosso di Montalcino

Giancarlo Pacenti's small production is best described as opulent: you get the rich extract, the rich new oak, all the bells and whistles . . . and it works. Irresistible Brunello that's worth the price, and a Rosso di Montalcino that is consistently one of the biggest and best of its type.

Paitin PIEMONTE

Via Serraboella 20, 12057 Neive (CN)
Tel.: 017367343/Fax: 0173677732
DOC(G)s: Barbaresco; Barbera d'Alba; Dolcetto d'Alba; Langhe

Named for one of the great crus of the Barbaresco zone. "Sorì Paitin" Barbaresco is at once muscular and brightly aromatic, and the "Vecchie Vigne," from 40- to 50-year-old vines on the site, goes a little deeper without losing the trademark Barbaresco perfume. These wines find that rare balance of power and elegance. Solid barbera, dolcetto, and a very concentrated Roero Arneis.

Pala SARDEGNA

Via Verdi 7, 09040 Serdiana (CA)
Tel.: 070740284
DOC(G)s: Cannonau di Sardegna; Vermentino di Sardegna

Stylish wines from the Cagliari area. The vermentino "Crabilis" is distinctively herbaceous, the cannonau smooth and smoky, and the "S'Arai"—from cannonau, carignano, and bovale—sappy and thoroughly satisfying.

Palagetto TOSCANA 🍷●
Via Monteoliveto 46, 53037 San Gimignano (SI)
Tel.: 0577943090/Fax: 0577942098
DOC(G)s: Brunello di Montalcino; Chianti Colli Senesi;
Vernaccia di San Gimignano
  The crisp whites from vernaccia are inexpensive and
solid, and there's a supple super-Tuscan called "Sotto-
bosco" (sangiovese-cabernet-merlot) that has nice class
for the price. The Brunello has a well-rounded texture
plumped up with French oak, as does the sweeter
sangiovese-merlot blend "Solleone."

★ Palari SICILIA
Contrada Barna, 98135 S. Stefano Briga (ME)
Tel.: 090630194
DOC(G)s: Faro
  Salvatore Geraci's old vines near Messina yield wines
that combine superripe Mediterranean warmth with firm
structure and a deep undercurrent of smoke (maybe it's
all that Etna ash). Palari's Faro DOC Rosso, a meaty blend
of a multitude of local varieties, including the Etna greats
nerello mascalese and cappuccio, has been compared to
Châteauneuf-du-Pape. The Faro has become a sought-
after cult wine, while "Rosso del Soprano," a second
selection of the same grapes given a gentler oak treatment, has a warm, spicy, Rhône-ish charm.

Palazzacci TOSCANA
  Small estate in Scansano owned by Tuscany's Baroncini
wine firm (see separate listing). Superripe Maremma
wines with berried aromas, particularly the "Maraia"
(sangiovese-ciliegiolo). The "Sexo" (sangiovese-syrah) is a
little deeper, but overall these wines are more about soft-
textured fruitiness than big extract or oak.

Palazzo Vecchio, Fattoria di TOSCANA
Via Terrarossa 5, 53040 Montepulciano (SI)
Tel.: 0578724170/Fax: 0248009704/www.vinonobile.it
DOC(G)s: Vino Nobile di Montepulciano
  A nice find: a luxurious Vino Nobile, with lots of deep
black cherry fruit and a vanillin sheen from French oak, at
an affordable price. "Rosso dell'Abate Chiarini" is a
similarly supple sangiovese-merlot blend.

★ Palazzone UMBRIA 🍷●
Località Rocca Ripesena 68, 05019 Orvieto (TR)
Tel.: 0763344921/Fax: 0763344921/www.palazzone.com
DOC(G)s: Orvieto Classico
  The single-vineyard Orvieto Classico "Terre Vineate" has
some nice flesh on its minerally bones. A delicious white
at a by-the-case price. "Campo del Guardiano" Orvieto is
a deeper Superiore selection released a year after
"Vineate." On the red side is the chunky "Armaleo," a
barrique-aged blend of cabernets sauvignon and franc.
The sweet "Muffa Nobile," a late-harvested, botrytis-
affected sauvignon, should not be missed.

Palladino PIEMONTE
Piazza Cappellano 9, 12050 Serralunga d'Alba (CN)
Tel.: 0173613108/Fax: 0173613448

€-
€€
DOC(G)s: Barolo; Barbaresco; Barbera d'Alba; Dolcetto d'Alba; Gavi

"Vigna Brolio" Barolo, from a tiny cru in Serralunga, is tops in this broad Piedmont lineup. Classic Serralunga wine with lots of dark spice and powerful tannins.

Palombo, Giovanni LAZIO

Corso Munanzio Planco, 03042 Latina (VT)
Tel.: 0776610200/Fax: 0776610639

€-
€€
DOC(G)s: Atina

Riffs on the classic Bordeaux blend—the lighter, spicier "Rosso delle Chiaie" and the more substantial "Colle delle Torre"—and two good varietal cabernets, the better of which is "Duca Cantelmi." These reds have a discernible mint–green pepper quality, but it's wrapped in enough black currant fruit that it seems more an expression of varietal character than underripeness. The white "Somiglio" (sauvignon-semillon) has a great mix of aromatic intensity and fruity weight. An interesting Lazio producer.

Panizzi, Giovanni TOSCANA

Località Racciano 34, 53037 San Gimignano (SI)
Tel.: 0577941576

€
DOC(G)s: Vernaccia di San Gimignano; Chianti

Light, herbaceous vernaccia pushed to a riper, fruitier level. The *riserva* bottling, which has gotten a fair amount of press, is one of the richer vernaccias around.

★ Parusso, Armando PIEMONTE

Località Bussia 55, 12065 Monforte d'Alba (CN)
Tel.: 017378267/Fax: 0173787276/www.parusso.com

€€
DOC(G)s: Barolo; Barbera d'Alba; Dolcetto d'Alba; Langhe

Unabashedly New World Barolos—ample fruit and chocolaty richness from barrique aging and lots of up-front power. They're sourced from pieces of Monforte's Bussia cru as well as the Mariondino cru in Castiglione Falletto. There are subtle differences among the wines based on their aging/oak regimens—"Piccole Vigne," from both vineyards, gets the least new oak and is considered the most approachable of the group, while "Mariondino," which sees 80% new wood and comes solely from that west-facing site, is more austere—but they're all as juicy and polished as Barolo comes. "Bricco Rovella" (nebbiolo-barbera-cabernet) is also luscious, as are the barbera and dolcetto varietals.

Pasqua VENETO

Via Belviglieri 30, 37131 Verona (VR)
Tel.: 0458402111/Fax: 0458402121/www.pasqua.it

€-
€€
DOC(G)s: Soave; Valpolicella; Amarone della Valpolicella

This huge firm near Verona pumps out 16 million bottles (or more) a year. Decent and reasonably priced Amarone wines under the Cecilia Beretta and Villa Borghetti labels; also worth trying is "Sagromoso" Valpolicella.

Paternoster BASILICATA

Via Nazionale 23, 85022 Barile (PZ)
Tel.: 0972770224/Fax: 0972770658

€-
€€
DOC(G)s: Aglianico del Vulture

Headquartered in Barile, at the foot of Monte Vulture, Paternoster is a landmark. Its Aglianico del Vulture wine is one of the archetypes—rosy, tarry, tannic, a red that speaks of its high-altitude vineyards and volcanic soils. The rarer "Rotondo" (a single-vineyard Aglianico, debuted in 1997) and "Don Anselmo" (the best selections of Aglianico) are powerful reds that merit some aging.

Pecchenino, F.lli PIEMONTE
Borgata Valdiberti 59, 12063 Dogliani (CN)
Tel.: 017370686/Fax: 0173721868/www.pecchenino.it
DOC(G)s: Dolcetto di Dogliani; Langhe
Voluptuous wines from Dogliani. "Sirì d'Jermu" is black and viscous, with the bitter chocolate tannins of Dogliani dolcetto. "Bricco Botti" is even more jacked-up. Also try the sultry Langhe Rosso "La Castella," a rich but balanced blend of barbera, nebbiolo, and cabernet.

Pecorari, Pierpaolo FRIULI–VENEZIA GIULIA
Via Tommaseo, 36/C, 34070 San Lorenzo Isontino (GO)
Tel.: 0481808775/www.pierpaolopecorari.it
The large production of mostly whites is very good for the price—tocai, sauvignon, pinot grigio, and pinot bianco are all distinctive and substantial.

Pelissero PIEMONTE
Borgata Ferrere 19, 12050 Treiso (CN)
Tel.: 0173638430/Fax: 0173638431/www.pelissero.com
DOC(G)s: Barbaresco; Barbera d'Alba; Dolcetto d'Alba; Langhe
The barrique-aged "Vanotù" Barbaresco is dark, brooding, complex. "Vanotù" is Piedmontese dialect for Giovanni, the name of Giorgio Pelissero's grandfather—the original owner of the Pelissero family vineyard, an extension of the Basarin cru. The Barbaresco *annata* has good savor and balance, and along with a solid supporting cast of barbera, dolcetto, etc., there's the lush Langhe Rosso "Long Now," made from non-Barbaresco nebbiolo and barbera.

Pellegrino SICILIA
Via del Fante 39, 91025 Marsala (TP)
Tel.: 0923719911/Fax: 0923953542/
www.carlopellegrino.it
DOC(G)s: Alcamo; Marsala; Moscato di Pantelleria; Passito di Pantelleria
Sadly, we haven't seen any of the Sherry-style *vergine* Marsalas from this large Marsala house in this market, just the basic "dry" and "sweet." There's also Moscato di Pantelleria and the richer Passito di Pantelleria, both of which are good dessert values.

Pepe, Emidio ABRUZZO
Via Chiesi 10, 64010 Torano Nuovo (TE)
Tel./Fax: 0861856493/www.montepulcianodabruzzo.it
DOC(G)s: Montepulciano d'Abruzzo; Trebbiano d'Abruzzo
When these wines are on, they are like good older Burgundies, though there is considerable bottle-to-bottle variation. The Pepe family remains committed to organic farming, hand-picking and foot-crushing grapes, minimal-intervention vinification, and long bottle aging (there are stocks in the cellar dating back to 1964, and there's plenty of vintage wine in the market). They regularly decant and rebottle wines, the effect being a sort of controlled oxidation, but in tasting the wines you'll often find the oxidative balsamic notes overpowering the rosy, spicy fruit.

Then again, maybe those just *seem* like flaws because no other wines taste quite like these. There's a big cult following who appear to "get" the Pepe style, so maybe it's just a question of more practice.

Perrone, Elio PIEMONTE

Strada San Martino 3/bis, 12053 Castiglione Tinella (CN)
Tel.: 0141855803

DOC(G)s: Moscato d'Asti; Barbera d'Asti

Bright and fruity *frizzante*-style wines. The Moscato d'Asti "Clarté" is consistently good (a lot of moscato just tastes like sugar water; this stuff is wine), and "Bigaró" is a rosy, peachy blend of moscato and brachetto. There are several deeply fruity barberas as well.

Pertimali

See Sassetti, Angelo/Sassetti, Livio.

Pertinace, Vignaioli Elvio PIEMONTE

Località Pertinace 2, 12050 Treiso (CN)
Tel.: 0173442238

DOC(G)s: Barbaresco; Barbera d'Asti; Dolcetto d'Alba; Langhe

A co-op with a large output by Piedmontese standards (about 16,000 cases a year). The majority is fairly earthy, fragrant, traditionally styled Barbaresco, including three crus, all from Treiso: "Castellizzano," "Marcarini," and "Nervo." "Nervo," from a south-facing slope, is probably the deepest and smokiest of the group, but overall these wines are about finesse. The Langhe Rosso, called simply "Pertinace" (nebbiolo-barbera-cabernet), has a nice mix of perfumy nebbiolo aromas and fruity depth.

Pervini PUGLIA

Via Santo Stasi Primo, 74024 Manduria (TA)
Tel.: 0999711660/Fax: 0999711530
www.accademiadeiracemi.it

DOC(G)s: Primitivo di Manduria

Puglian co-op run by Gregorio and Fabrizio Perrucchi, who use it as the base for Accademia dei Racemi, a consortium that markets the wines of smaller Puglian estates. Pervini makes plush and savory Primitivo di Manduria wines, particularly "Archidamo." Also try the tarry "Bizantino," a blend of primitivo and negroamaro.

Petilia CAMPANIA

Contrada Pincera, 83011 Altavilla Irpinia (AV)
Tel.: 0825991409/Fax: 0825991696

DOC(G)s: Fiano di Avellino; Greco di Tufo; Taurasi

All the classic Irpinia (i.e., inland Campania) varietals. The whites from greco and fiano are chalky, racy, and simple; the red Taurasi is old-school aglianico—lean and leathery, with savory aromatics. Good values.

Petra TOSCANA

Località San Lorenzo Alto 131, 57028 Suvereto (LI)
Tel.: 0565845308/Fax: 0565845180

DOC(G)s: Val di Cornia

Plush sangiovese-based reds from a coastal Tuscan estate owned by the Franciacorta region's Bellavista winery. The wines are a little rustic at this point, but with that kind of capital behind them, they're worth keeping an eye on.

Petriolo
See Villa Petriolo.

★ Petrolo TOSCANA ⚷—•
Località Galatrona, Frazione Mercatale Valdarno, 52020
Montevarchi (AR)
Tel.: 0559911322/www.petrolo.it
  Proprietor Luca Sanjust's opaque, syrupy merlot,
"Galatrona," is designed to compete with the best from
Tuscany, and it's getting there: it's an oil-slick of black fruit
and dark spice, temptingly drinkable on release. The
smooth and concentrated "Torrione" sangiovese is a nice
alternative should you decide to wait.

Petrucco FRIULI–VENEZIA GIULIA
Via Morpurgo 12, 33042 Buttrio (UD)
Tel.: 0432674387
DOC(G)s: Colli Orientali del Friuli
  Clean varietal whites are the specialty here (none are
fermented or aged in wood). Check out the chardonnay
(for a rare, minerally taste of that grape without wood), the
tocai friulano (for even more minerality), and the ribolla
gialla (racy and floral, as it should be). The reds, also
unwooded, are bright and simple.

Piaggia TOSCANA
Via Cegoli 47, 59016 Poggio a Caiano (PO)
Tel.: 055870541
DOC(G)s: Carmignano
  Mauro Vannucci's tiny estate (about 12 acres) is sort of a
Bordeaux château in Carmignano. There's a "first wine"—
the powerful, critically praised Carmignano Riserva—and
a "second" wine, also from sangiovese, cabernet, and
merlot, with plenty of richness in its own right.

Pian delle Vigne TOSCANA
Località Pian delle Vigne, 53024 Montalcino (SI)
Tel.: 0577816066/www.antinori.it
DOC(G)s: Brunello di Montalcino
  A Montalcino estate acquired in 1993 by Antinori. The
first vintage, 1995, debuted in 2000, and with each new
release the wine gains layers of extract and intensity. Fat
and juicy Brunello with dark chocolate tannins.

Pian dell'Orino TOSCANA
Località Pian dell'Orino 189, 53024 Montalcino (SI)
Tel.: 3355250115
DOC(G)s: Brunello di Montalcino; Rosso di Montalcino
  Another good, small estate in Montalcino, toeing that line
between traditional and modern (i.e., the new oak
influence and extract is moderated, but the smoky black
cherry fruit is clean and forward). Good pure sangiovese
flavors and aromatics, medium weight, and fair pricing.

Piancornello TOSCANA
Podere Piancornello, 53020 Montalcino (SI)
Tel./Fax: 0577844105
DOC(G)s: Brunello di Montalcino
  Piancornello debuted in 1990, although the Piere family
had been growing grapes in Montalcino generations
before. The Brunello is bold, round, and deeply colorful,
with lots of ripe black fruit. The varietal sangiovese

"Poggio dei Lecci" is light and affordable, while the Rosso di Montalcino, aged a year in barrique, is pretty robust.

Picollo, Ernesto PIEMONTE

Frazione Rovereto 60, 15066 Gavi (AL)
Tel./Fax: 0143682175
DOC(G)s: Gavi
   Tart, minerally, inexpensive Gavi wines. "Rughé" has a little more weight.

Pierazzuoli, Enrico TOSCANA

Via Valicarda 35, 50056 Capraia e Limite (PO)
Tel.: 057190078/www.enricopierazzuoli.com
DOC(G)s: Carmignano; Chianti Montalbano
   Carmignano is to Tuscany what Roero is to Piedmont—an unsung appellation with good wines that is overshadowed by its more famous neighbor. A good-value alternative to Chianti Classico Riserva is Pierazzuoli's darkly elegant "Le Farnete" Carmignano Riserva. The more rustic "Gioveto" combines sangiovese with syrah and merlot.

Pieri, Agostina TOSCANA

Località San Angelo Scalo, Località Piancornello, 53024 Montalcino (SI)
Tel.: 0577375785/Fax: 0577844163
DOC(G)s: Brunello di Montalcino; Rosso di Montalcino
   Rich and ripe Brunello and Rosso di Montalcino with some sweet notes from oak. Deep and serious.

PIEROPAN, LEONILDO VENETO

Via Camuzzoni 3, 37038 Soave (VR)
Tel.: 0456190171/www.pieropan.it
DOC(G)s: Soave; Recioto di Soave
   Pieropan's Soave Classico is always reliable, with its fleshy texture, firm minerality, and, most notably, uplifted aromas that most producers can't coax out of Soave's garganega grape. The single-vineyard "La Rocca," one of the best whites in Italy, spends a year in oak, lending a creamy sheen to the fragrant, superripe package. The word *focused* is thrown around a lot in the wine world, but Pieropan's wines are examples of what "focused" is supposed to mean—precise, balanced, clean. The excellent sweet wines, such as the Recioto di Soave "Le Colombare," are unctuous yet balanced by bright acidity.

Pietra Porzia LAZIO

Via di Pietraporzia 60, 00044 Frascati (RM)
Tel.: 069464392/Fax: 069464361
DOC(G)s: Frascati
   Frascati "Regillo" is a clean, fruity, inexpensive choice.

Pietrafitta TOSCANA

Località Cortennano, 53037 San Gimignano (SI)
Tel.: 0577943200/www.pietrafitta.com
DOC(G)s: Vernaccia di San Gimignano; Chianti Colli Senesi; Vin Santo
   Inexpensive Vernaccia di San Gimignano in a typically crisp and herbal style (the "Vigna Borghetto" has a little more stuffing) and light, plush reds.

Pietratorcia CAMPANIA (ISCHIA)

Frazione Cuotto, Via Provenciale Panza 267, 80075
Forio (NA)
Tel.: 081908206/Fax: 081907232
DOC(G)s: Ischia

Credit is due to Pietratorcia for making a go of
winemaking out on Ischia and for using funky grapes like
guarnaccia (Ischia's name for grenache) and the white
biancolella. "Scheria Rosso" is a little too dirty and funky
at its price point, though it does have good Mediterranean
underbrushy flavors. The basic Ischia Bianco ("Chignole")
and Ischia Rosso ("Ianno Piro") are the way to go, but be
sure to get them next to some food.

★ Pieve di Santa Restituta TOSCANA

53024 Montalcino (SI)
Tel.: 0577848610/Fax: 0577849309
DOC(G)s: Brunello di Montalcino

More Angelo Gaja? He acquired this 40-acre Montalcino
property in 1994 and immediately put his indelible stamp
on the Brunello di Montalcino. Gaja has a knack for
creating dense, tightly coiled wines that attack the palate
in a slow, steady crescendo—rather than just let it all hang
out right away. There are two Brunellos: "Rennina,"
sourced from three noncontiguous vineyards, and the
power-packed "Sugarille," from the vineyard on which the
pieve (church) of Santa Restituta sits. Both spend a year
in barrique, a year in large barrel, and 2 years in bottle
before release, and both display a certain freshness
despite their considerable power.

Pighin, F.lli FRIULI–VENEZIA GIULIA

Viale Grado 1, 33050 Pavia di Udine (UD)
Tel.: 0432675444/Fax: 0432675999/www.pighin.com
DOC(G)s: Friuli Grave; Collio

A large estate with holdings in both the Grave and Collio
DOCs. Clean, aromatic, straightforward varietal wines at
bargain prices. The Collio DOC pinot grigio is a step up.

PIO CESARE PIEMONTE

Via C. Balbo 6, 12051 Alba (CN)
Tel.: 0173440386/Fax: 0173363680/www.piocesare.it
DOC(G)s: Barolo; Barbaresco; Langhe; Nebbiolo d'Alba;
Barbera d'Alba; Dolcetto d'Alba

Founded in 1881, the estate is run by fourth-generation
proprietor Pio Boffa, who oversees more than 100 acres of
choice vineyards throughout Barolo and Barbaresco. One
of these holdings is Ornato, a south-facing cru in
Serralunga and the source of a massive, brooding Barolo;
another is Il Bricco, in the village of Treiso, which is the
source of a velvety Barbaresco and the chardonnay
"Piodilei." Overall Boffa has some 14 different wines,
headlined by his basic Barolo (which actually sees a lot of
French oak during its aging process) and including flashy
wines such as "Fides," a powerfully built Barbera d'Alba.

Piovene Porto Godi, Conte Alessandro VENETO

Via Villa 14, 36020 Villaga (VI)
Tel./Fax: 0444885142
DOC(G)s: Colli Berici

Good and inexpensive cabernet sauvignon and sauvignon

blanc from the Colli Berici DOC, an up-and-coming appellation between Verona and Vicenza. The sauvignon blanc "Fostine" is assertively aromatic, and while the cabernets are not entirely free of that green Veneto edge, there's some good concentration.

Pira PIEMONTE

Borgata Valdiberti 69, 12063 Dogliani (CN)
Tel.: 017378538
DOC(G)s: Barbera d'Alba; Dolcetto d'Alba; Dolcetto di Dogliani; Langhe; Piemonte

A Dolcetto specialist right on the fringe of Dogliani, with vineyard holdings there and in nearby Monforte. The Dolcetto di Dogliani "Bricco dei Botti" is superripe and intense, with just a short passage in barrique; the "Vigna Landes" is big and ripe, too, but a little gentler. The wines from barbera are also dense, particularly the Barbera "Briccobotti," which incorporates some dried fruit.

★ Pira, Luigi PIEMONTE

Via XX Settembre 9, 12050 Serralunga d'Alba (CN)
Tel./Fax: 0173613106
DOC(G)s: Barolo; Dolcetto d'Alba

Another Pira, this one in the Serralunga area. These Piras only started bottling their own wines in 1996, but they've come a long way fast, with three explosive cru Barolos: "Marenca" (considered the gentlest, "Margheria" (a little harder-edged), and "Vigna Rionda" (aged 100% in new oak and as black as night). Interestingly, the "base" Barolo is aged only in large oak *botti* and has a more rosy, leathery, classic style, whereas the crus have varying degrees of vanilla-chocolate slathered over the darker-toned mineral flavors of the Serralunga soil. Either way, you can't go wrong. Even the dolcetto is huge.

Pira & Figli (Chiara Boschis) PIEMONTE

Via Vitorio Veneto 1, 12060 Barolo (CN)
Tel.: 017356247
DOC(G)s: Barolo

A historic estate brought back to prominence by the Boschis family, owners of the Borgogno winery, who acquired it in 1990. In contrast to the more traditional wines of Borgogno, the current Pira wines are fruit-forward and pumped up with new oak. The Barolo "Cannubi" is a sought-after wine. There's also flashy dolcetto and barbera, should the Barolo prove elusive (very little is made).

★ Planeta SICILIA

Contrada Dispensa, 92013 Menfi/Sambuca di Sicilia (AG)
Tel.: 092580009/www.planeta.it
DOC(G)s: Cerasuolo di Vittoria

This dynamic Sicilian estate creates new wines so fast it's hard to keep up. Young Francesca and Alessio Planeta, with enologist Carlo Corino, have assembled vineyard holdings all over the island and make voluptuous reds with New World flair. "Santa Cecilia," a dark, meaty red from nero d'avola, is the sentimental favorite, but it's been overshadowed by syrah, merlot, and the sumptuous "Burdese" cabernet. Planeta chardonnay has a tropically fruity intensity reminiscent of the stuff from California, while "Alastro" lends the fat chardonnay some slimming acidity via the local grecanico grape. Value wines include the tangy new Cerasuolo di Vittoria and the always-reliable "La Segreta" wines (a clean, fleshy white from grecanico-chardonnay and a juicy, soft red from nero d'avola).

Plozner FRIULI–VENEZIA GIULIA

Via delle Prese 19, 33097 Barbeano di Spilimbergo (PN)
Tel.: 04272902/Fax: 042750509/www.plozner.it
DOC(G)s: Friuli Grave
Pinot grigio, tocai friulano, sauvignon, chardonnay, merlot . . . all incredibly cheap but surprisingly good. Party wine you might actually remember the next day.

Podere Le Boncie
See Le Boncie.

Podere Capaccia TOSCANA
Località Capaccia, 53017 Radda in Chianti (SI)
Tel.: 0577738385/Fax: 0574582426
DOC(G)s: Chianti Classico
"Querciagrande," a dark and deeply fruity sangiovese, remains a pretty good buy in the pricey world of super-Tuscans. The Capaccia Chiantis have good depth and sangiovese character.

Podere Poggio Scalette TOSCANA
Via Barbiano 7, 50022 Greve in Chianti (FI)
Tel.: 0558546108/Fax: 0558547960
Tuscan enologist Vittorio Fiore acquired this property in the early nineties, mainly because of a small plot called "Il Carbonaione" ("coal pit") containing sangiovese planted just after World War I. "Il Carbonaione" wine is coal-black and loaded with notes of black currant, tobacco, and tar—a super-Tuscan sangiovese that's among the region's best. Hard to get and pricey.

Podere San Luigi
See San Luigi.

Podere Sopra La Ripa
See Sopra La Ripa.

Poderi Alasia PIEMONTE
Via Albera 19, 14040 Castel Boglione (AT)
Tel.: 0141763111/Fax: 0141762433
Here are some flashy "super-Piedmont" wines, including the almost honeyed "Sorilaria" arneis and a similarly intense sauvignon blanc called "Camillona." Pretty good pricing, considering the heft. Ditto for the soft and fruity reds, which include a decent pinot noir called "ReNero."

Poderi Colla PIEMONTE
Frazione San Rocco Seno d'Elvio 82, 12051 Alba (CN)
Tel.: 0173290148/www.podericolla.it
DOC(G)s: Barolo; Barbaresco; Langhe; Nebbiolo d'Alba; Dolcetto d'Alba; Barbera d'Alba
A large-production estate with holdings throughout the Langhe, including part of the Dardi vineyard in Monforte d'Alba (the source of Colla's dark and tarry Barolo) and the Tenuta Roncaglia vineyard, set on the Roncaglie cru in Barbaresco. The wines have a classically earthy and finely structured feel, a characteristic that shows in the plump Dolcetto d'Alba "Pian Balbo" and the funky (and rare) red blend, "Bricco del Drago" (dolcetto-nebbiolo).

Poderi dal Nespoli EMILIA-ROMAGNA

Località Nespoli, Villa Rossi 50, 47012 Civitella di Romagna (FC)

Tel.: 0543989637/www.poderidalnespoli.com

DOC(G)s: Sangiovese di Romagna

"Borgo dei Guidi" (sangiovese, cabernet, and a touch of the local raboso, aged in barrique for a year) is pretty substantial, as is the "Il Nespoli" sangiovese.

Poderi del Paradiso TOSCANA

Località Strada 21, San Gimignano (SI)

Tel./Fax: 0577941500

DOC(G)s: Vernaccia di San Gimignano; Chianti Colli Senesi

Here's another San Gimignano winery at which the reds, not the usual vernaccia, are the story: from a rocky vineyard in one of the hottest parts of the zone comes "Saxa Calida," a blend of cabernet and merlot as viscous and sweet as chocolate syrup. Also worth a look is the "extreme" (their word) sangiovese called "Paterno/Eterno II." These reds typify the sappy, "international" style.

Poderi San Savino

See San Savino.

★ Podversic, Damijan FRIULI–VENEZIA GIULIA

Via Brigata Pavia 61, 34170 Gorizia (G)

Tel.: 048178217

DOC(G)s: Collio

An up-and-coming young producer whose Collio Bianco (chardonnay-malvasia-tocai) finds a nice balance of fruit, mineral, and oak. It's a serious white with some of that trademark Friulian oiliness. His rich Collio Rosso is a big Bordeaux blend, with good heft and class.

★ Poggerino TOSCANA

Località Poggerino, 3017 Radda in Chianti (SI)

Tel.: 0577738958/www.poggerino.com

DOC(G)s: Chianti Classico

Another up-and-coming young producer. Piero Lanza's tiny estate is just across the street from the Montevertine winery in Radda. His Chiantis bring out the dark side of sangiovese: black cherry, black currant, smoke, tar . . . and yet they're supple and bright. The basic Chianti Classico is a great buy, and the lush and smoky Riserva "Bugialla" would make a great short-term ager.

Poggio a Poppiano TOSCANA

Via di Poppiano 19, 50025 Montespertoli (FI)

Tel.: 055213084/Fax: 055295132/www.poggiopoppiano.it

Here are some relatively affordable finds in the ever-expanding super-Tuscan universe: the easy-drinking "Calamita" (70% sangiovese, 30% merlot) is a good start, then move on to the more luxurious "Flocco" (50% cabernet, 30% merlot, 15% sangiovese, 5% cabernet franc).

Poggio ai Chiari

See Colle Santa Mustiola.

Poggio al Casone

See Castellani.

Poggio al Sasso

See La Brancaia.

Poggio al Sole TOSCANA

Strada Rignana, 50028 Tavarnelle Val di Pesa (FI)
Tel.: 0558071850

DOC(G)s: Chianti Classico

Good Chianti Classico, especially the deep, elegant "Casasilia" Riserva, along with a meaty varietal syrah and a sweetly intense cabernet-merlot blend called "Seraselva."

Poggio Antico TOSCANA

Località Poggio Antico, 53024 Montalcino (SI)
Tel.: 0577848044/Fax: 0577848563

DOC(G)s: Brunello di Montalcino; Rosso di Montalcino

The Gloder family purchased this property in 1984 and quickly turned it into one of Montalcino's premier estates. Poggio Antico's Brunello has good weight and ripeness but a nice bass note of mulchy funk. "Altero" is designed to be a more fruity, "forward" Brunello, (spending only 2 of its required 4 years' aging in wood, as opposed to the flagship Brunello's 3).

Poggio Argentiera TOSCANA

Località Banditella di Alberese, Strada Statale 1, 54, 58010 Grosseto (GR)
Tel.: 0564405099/www.poggioargentiera.com

DOC(G)s: Morellino di Scansano

"CapaTosta" is considered one of the premier reds of the south Tuscan coast, loaded with sweetly ripe fruit and ready to roll immediately (that's what the kids are into these days). The cheaper "BellaMarsilia" is plush and tangy—a house pour.

Poggio Bertaio UMBRIA

Frazione Casamaggiore, Località Frattavecchia 29, 06061 Castiglione del Lago (PG)
Tel.: 075956921/Fax: 075956791

Newish wines (they debuted in 1998) from a small estate near Perugia. The lush sangiovese "Cimbolo" spends 18 months in barrique; "Crovello" is a 50-50 merlot-cabernet blend, plummy and rich and a touch expensive.

Poggio Castellare

See Baroncini.

Poggio di Sotto TOSCANA

Località Poggio di Sopra 222, 53020 Montalcino (SI)
Tel.: 0577835502

DOC(G)s: Brunello di Montalcino; Rosso di Montalcino

Wines in a resolutely traditional style of Brunello, with a leaner frame than what is fashionable today. The hook with this wine is the woodsy aroma, evocative of the thickly forested hills around Montalcino, and the almost-Burgundian texture (think of other finely tuned sangioveses like Montevertine or Soldera).

Poggio Gagliardo TOSCANA

Località Poggio Gagliardo, 56040 Montescudaio (PI)
Tel.: 0586630775/www.poggiogagliardo.com

DOC(G)s: Montescudaio

Funky reds from Montescudaio, just north of the village of Bolgheri on the Tuscan coast. Check out the delicious "Gobbo" (sangiovese-merlot-cabernet), which has some nice black berry fruit and a silky-smooth texture. Also interesting is "Rovo" (sangiovese, colorino, malvasia nera, ciliegiolo), which has a brighter, spicier feel.

Poggio Pollino EMILIA-ROMAGNA

Via Monte Meldola 2/T, 40026 Imola (BO)
Tel.: 0522942135
DOC(G)s: Sangiovese di Romagna

"Campo Rosso" and "Vigna di Cambro" are two more new-generation sangioveses from Romagna, with lots of berry fruit concentration—in all, a rounder, plumper take on the grape than what you might be used to in Tuscany.

Poggio Salvi TOSCANA

Località Poggio Salvi 251, 53018 Sovicille (SI)
Tel.: 0577349045/Fax: 057745237/www.poggiosalvi.it
DOC(G)s: Chianti Colli Senesi

Located a little southwest of Siena, Poggio Salvi is best known for a smooth, savory, and deeply fruity Chianti Colli Senesi that transcends its price category. The top wine is "Campo del Bosco," produced only in select years (100% sangiovese grosso aged a year in *tonneaux*). Not to be confused with the Villa Poggio Salvi winery of Montalcino (see listing for Biondi-Santi).

Poggio San Polo TOSCANA

Località Podere San Polo 161, 53024 Montalcino (SI)
Tel.: 0577835522
DOC(G)s: Brunello di Montalcino; Rosso di Montalcino

Small but growing estate with a plush and modern Brunello, as well as the super-Tuscan "Mezzopane" (80% sangiovese, 20% cabernet), which has a palate-coating richness that's hard to resist. The all-sangiovese "Rubio" is a great value.

Poggio Scalette

See Podere Poggio Scalette.

POJER & SANDRI TRENTINO

Località Molini, 38010 Faedo (TN)
Tel.: 0461650342/Fax: 0461651100/www.pojeresandri.it
DOC(G)s: Trentino

Perched in the heights of Faedo, this winery/distillery produces varietally precise whites, crisp sparklers, delicate reds, and aromatic grappas. Whites are the calling card, particularly the minerally müller-thurgau "Vigna Palai" and the nosiola, which grabs the palate by the lapels with its green-apple acidity. The late-harvest "Essenzia," from a mix of local grapes, is a fantastic dessert wine. The reds are light, a little vegetal, but not without appeal: try the softly contoured pinot nero.

Polencic, Ferdinano e Aldo FRIULI–VENEZIA GIULIA

Località Plessiva 13, 34071 Cormons (GO)
Tel.: 048161027
DOC(G)s: Collio

Serious, weighty Collio whites—pinot grigio, sauvignon, and tocai friulano all have a depth rarely found in Italian varietals elsewhere on the peninsula.

POLIZIANO TOSCANA

Via Fontago 11, 53045 Montepulciano (SI)
Tel.: 0578738171/Fax: 0578738752
DOC(G)s: Vino Nobile di Montepulciano; Morellino di Scansano

Originally a producer of cheap Chianti Colli Senesi until Federico Carletti took over in 1980, acquiring prime vineyards and building a space-age cellar. Poliziano is now known for massive Vino Nobile di Montepulciano, crafted by consultant Carlo Ferrini. "Asinone" Vino Nobile is coal-black, at once sweetly fruity and savory from its ferrous tannins, while the Bordeaux blend "Le Stanze" is just plain decadent. Ferrini and Carletti lend a luxurious sheen to every wine made here, not to mention those of Lohsa, Carletti's expansive new estate in the Maremma, where the slick new Morellino di Scansano, a deeply fruity red with a new-oak sheen, is already among the best.

Porro, Bruno PIEMONTE

Borgata Valdiberti 24, 12063 Dogliani (CN)
Tel./Fax: 017370371
DOC(G)s: Dolcetto di Dogliani; Langhe; Piemonte
More of that fat and funky Dogliani dolcetto at a good price: try the Dolcetto di Dogliani "Vigne Ribote," a nice meaty style for food.

Prà, Graziano VENETO

Via della Fontana 31, 37032 Monteforte d'Alpone (VR)
Tel.: 0457612125
DOC(G)s: Soave Classico; Recioto di Soave
"Monte Grande" Soave Classico, fermented and aged in large barrels, has depth that transcends its price category—great pear/apple fruit with just a hint of yeasty creaminess from the barrel fermentation makes it sort of the middle child in the Prà range. The basic Soave Classico Superiore is fruity and fresh while the "Colle S. Antonio," which incorporates some late-harvested fruit, is over the top, even tropical in tone.

Pratesi TOSCANA

Loc Seano, Via Rizzelli 10, 59011 Carmignano (PO)
Tel.: 0558706400/Fax: 0558953531
DOC(G)s: Carmignano
Pratesi goes for super-Tuscan depth in its powerful Carmignano, and the cassis scents of cabernet are definitely in evidence. Simpler and suppler is the sangiovese "Lococco."

Pravis TRENTINO

Località Biolche di Castel Madruzzo, 38076 Lasino (TN)
Tel.: 0461564305
DOC(G)s: Trentino
A large estate with value-priced wines from the exotically aromatic nosiola and müller-thurgau grapes, as well as a variety of reds, including the rare rebo, syrah, and cabernet sauvignon.

Primosic FRIULI–VENEZIA GIULIA

Località Madonnina di Oslavia 3, 34070 Oslavia (GO)
Tel.: 0481535153/Fax: 0481536705/www.primosic.com
DOC(G)s: Collio
Collio is the place to be for precise and powerful whites. This artisan producer has an elegant pinot grigio and a richly textured super-white called "Klin" (chardonnay-sauvignon-ribolla). The varietal whites with the "Gmajne" designation (the appley ribolla and floral sauvignon especially) are superb.

Princic, Alessandro FRIULI–VENEZIA GIULIA

Località Plessiva 12, 34071 Cormons (GO)
Tel.: 048160655
DOC(G)s: Collio

Doro Princic was a pioneer of Friulian winemaking, and his estate continues a tradition of crafting stylish whites. Fresh, fruity, and floral tocai friulano, aromatic malvasia, and fleshy pinot grigio.

Principiano, Ferdinando PIEMONTE

Via Alba 19, 12065 Monforte d'Alba (CN)
Tel.: 0173787158
DOC(G)s: Barolo; Barbera d'Alba; Dolcetto d'Alba

Softly textured but deeply flavorful Barolos from the Boscareto cru in the village of Serralunga and Le Coste in Monforte d'Alba. Young Ferdinando Prinicipiano is fanatical about reducing yields to deepen concentration, and the wines are fermented and aged in barrique. The silky Barbera d'Alba "La Romualda" harnesses the power of old-vine fruit from the Pian Romualdo vineyard.

PRODUTTORI DEL BARBARESCO PIEMONTE

Via Torino 52, 12050 Barbaresco (CN)
Tel.: 0173635139/Fax: 0173635130
www.produttoridelbarbaresco.com
DOC(G)s: Barbaresco; Langhe

A landmark cooperative founded in 1958, sourcing grapes from a growers' association first assembled in 1894. This underappreciated winery serves for many as an introduction to Barbaresco and offers a panorama of the DOCG with a whopping nine single-vineyard wines: Asili, Moccagatta, Montefico, Montestefano, Ovello, Pajé, Pora, Rabajà, and Rio Sordo. Although the characteristics of these wines are too myriad to delve into here, it's safe to say that all are made in a more traditional style, with ample tannins, acid, and lots of leathery, earthy tones. These wines are proven agers, they're affordable, and they're findable—all welcome traits in the rarefied world of Piedmont wine.

Produttori Nebbiolo di Carema PIEMONTE

Via Nazionale 32, 10010 Carema (TO)
Tel.: 0125811160
DOC(G)s: Carema

This cooperative winery is one of the few sources of Carema DOC wine, with its delicate, earthy, high-altitude nebbiolo flavors. The basic Carema di Carema, a great value, wraps the saddle leather and dried cherry flavors of nebbiolo in a more delicate package—a really pinot noir–ish take on the variety. Check out the Carema di Carema "Selezione" for less earth tones and more plush fruit.

Progetto DiVino BASILICATA

Via Nazionale 76, 75100 Matera (MT)
Tel.: 0835262851/Fax: 0835259549

Up-and-coming Basilicata winery with a rich aglianico-merlot blend, "San Biagio," which combines the smoky edge of the former with the plummy sweetness of the latter.

Promessa

See A-Mano.

Provenza LOMBARDIA

Via dei Colli Storici, 25015 Desenzano del Garda (BS)
Tel.: 0309910006
DOC(G)s: Garda; Lugana

One of the better Garda-area producers, with several nice Lugana whites (stick with the fresh "Ca' Maiol" over the barriqued "Ca' Molin") and a chunky, aromatic, toffee-rich Rosso, also called "Ca' Maiol," that combines the local varieties groppello, barbera, marzemino, and others. Also a spicy Garda Chiaretto (rosé) from a similar mix.

Prunotto PIEMONTE

Regione San Cassiano 4/G, 12051 Alba (CN)
Tel.: 0173280017/Fax: 0173281167/www.prunotto.it
DOC(G)s: Barolo; Barbaresco; Barbera d'Alba; Dolcetto d'Alba; Nebbiolo d'Alba

Historic *cantina* first established by Alfredo Prunotto in 1923 and purchased by Tuscany's Antinori in 1989. Prunotto was originally a cooperative, acquiring fruit from contract growers, but in more recent times Antinori has acquired a variety of different vineyards, including a chunk of Bussia in Monforte, from which they craft a dark-hued Barolo with a luxurious sheen (the other cru wine, Cannubi, is similiar). Also notable are the heady, richly oaked barberas, one from Alba ("Pian Romualdo") and one from Asti ("Costamiòle"). In all, a reliable and broad lineup, with some excellent values.

Puiatti, Giovanni FRIULI–VENEZIA GIULIA

Via Aquileia 30, 34070 Capriva del Friuli (GO)
Tel.: 0481809922/www.puiatti.com
DOC(G)s: Collio

Their slogan is "Save a tree, drink Puiatti," so if you like fresh, unoaked wines, this is the place for you. There are a variety of different product lines and overall output is huge (from both estate-owned and brought-in grapes), so prices are generally fair. The unique "Oltre" is made from pinot noir vinified as a white wine, though you're more likely to find the crisp, clean, more classic whites: pinot grigio, chardonnay, sauvignon, and tocai.

Punset PIEMONTE

Frazione Moretta 5, 12057 Neive (CN)
Tel.: 017367072/www.punset.com
DOC(G)s: Barbaresco; Barbera d'Alba; Dolcetto d'Alba; Langhe

Excellent value in Barbaresco, whether it's the basic bottling or the single-vineyard "Campo Quadro," which takes on a more lush tone from aging in French oak. An under-the-radar producer with one of the area's few female winemakers, Marina Marcarino.

Pupillo SICILIA

Contrada da Targia, 96100 Siracusa (SR)
Tel.: 0931494029
DOC(G)s: Moscato di Siracusa

A producer of the extremely rare Moscato di Siracusa dessert nectar, and noteworthy because of it.

Quadratura del Cerchio

See La Quadratura del Cerchio.

QUERCIABELLA TOSCANA

Via Barbiano 17, 50022 Greve in Chianti (FI)
Tel.: 0272002256/www.querciabella.com
DOC(G)s: Chianti Classico

Perched high above Greve in Chianti, this beautiful estate, owned by the Castiglioni family, is one of Chianti Classico's best. The wines, made by soft-spoken enologist Guido de Santi, are full and ripe but elegant, the products of high-altitude vineyards and a winemaking philosophy that emphasizes balance. Querciabella Chianti Classico is a deliciously smoky, savory take on sangiovese, while the firmly structured "Camartina" combines sangiovese with cabernet sauvignon. The "Batàr" Chardonnay is a rich and buttery nod to current white wine fashion, and the excellent Vin Santo "Orlando" has a richness and complexity matched by few others. An ultramodern winery where everything is done well.

Querciavalle TOSCANA

Azienda Agricola Losi, Querciavalle Pontignanello, 53010 Vagliagli (SI)
Tel./Fax: 0577356842
DOC(G)s: Chianti Classico

The Losi family estate still produces, among other wines, a Chianti Classico in the all-but-forgotten *governo* style, wherein some unfermented juice from dried grapes is added to the young wine just after it finishes its alcoholic fermentation. This creates a fruity, slightly fizzy, almost Beaujolais nouveau–like feel. There are some other rustic but more familiar-tasting reds, including the sangiovese-canaiolo blend "Armonia" and a decent Vin Santo.

QUINTARELLI, GIUSEPPE VENETO

Via Cerè 1, 37024 Negrar (VR)
Tel.: 0457500016
DOC(G)s: Valpolicella; Amarone della Valpolicella; Recioto della Valpolicella

Giuseppe Quintarelli is an elder statesman in the Valpolicella zone, and a mythic figure among winemakers and consumers alike. His wines, most notably his Amarone, are unadorned expressions of old-vine fruit from high-altitude vineyards outside Negrar. Fermented and aged primarily in large oak casks, Quintarelli Amarone is weighty and intensely aromatic, but ultimately it's a wine of great balance and refinement.

Radikon FRIULI–VENEZIA GIULIA

Località Tre Buchi 4, 34170 Oslavia (GO)
Tel./Fax: 048132804
DOC(G)s: Collio

Stanko Radikon is an artisan-producer whose tiny winery sits near Italy's border with Slovenia. His white lineup includes a powerfully built ribolla gialla, its rich appley fruit carried on a raft of bright acidity, while his white blend "Oslavje" (chardonnay, ribolla gialla, tocai friulano, sauvignon) also boasts incredible richness and structure. Radikon, like his neighbor Gravner, favors a highly oxidized style of white wine with a golden hue and an almost cidery character. His are unique whites that have the tannic intensity of some reds. On the red side, Radikon's barrique-aged merlot is a cult wine to rival the merlot-based reds of Bordeaux.

Raimondi (Villa Monteleone) VENETO

Frazione Gargagnago, Via Monteleone 12, 37020 Sant'Ambrogio di Valpolicella (VR)
Tel.: 0456800533/Fax: 0457704974
DOC(G)s: Amarone della Valpolicella Classico; Valpolicella Classico

A well-regarded producer of Amarone in a silky, approachable style, with a touch of rusticity. Although the "Villa Monteleone" Amarone has sweetness and weight, it is a more vinous, acidic style in comparison to a lot of the fruit-bomb Amarones on the market. Nice finesse and aromatics in the Valpolicellas, too.

Rainoldi LOMBARDIA

Via Stelvio 128, 23030 Chiuro (SO)
Tel.: 0342482225/Fax: 0342483775/www.rainoldi.com
DOC(G)s: Valtellina; Valtellina Superiore; Valtellina Sforsato

A small family winery that creates some of the most evocative wines in the Valtellina, be they more "traditional" reds aged in large Slovenian oak *botti* or more modern, fruit-forward wines aged in barrique. Either way, what you get is an entirely new and intriguing take on the nebbiolo grape, its aromatics lifted to new heights in sub-Alpine vineyards. Try some of Rainoldi's more traditional *riserve,* such as the Sassella Riserva and Inferno Riserva, for superfine nebbiolo with scents of everything from dried cherries to mushrooms to Earl Grey tea. For a bigger wine, trade up to the barrique-aged Sfursat "Fruttaio Ca' Rizzieri," which offers the plush extract of a dried-grape wine while retaining the ethereal aromas of nebbiolo.

Rascioni & Cecconello TOSCANA

Località Poggio Sugherino, 58010 Fonteblanda (GR)
Tel./Fax: 0564885642

A small estate on the south Tuscan coast noteworthy for a varietal wine from the local ciliegiolo grape called "Poggio Ciliegio." Lots of wild berry fruit flavors and aromas; a nice red to drink with a slight chill in the summertime, maybe alongside a grilled pizza or a cool *panzanella* salad.

RATTI, RENATO PIEMONTE

Frazione Annunziata 7, 12064 La Morra (CN)
Tel.: 017350185/www.renatoratti.com
DOC(G)s: Barolo; Barbera d'Alba; Dolcetto d'Alba; Monferrato; Nebbiolo d'Alba

The late Renato Ratti was considered the father of modern Barolo. In the 1960s, it was Ratti who concluded that most Barolo was too tannic and too oxidized because of what he felt were overly long maceration periods and overly long aging periods in old and dirty wood barrels. Ratti helped revolutionize Barolo by introducing controlled-temperature fermentations in stainless steel, shortening maceration times, and aging the wines for less time before release. Today Ratti's son Pietro runs the winery, which is situated near the historic Abbey of Annunziata in the village of La Morra. There are three different Barolo bottlings, starting with the base "Marcenasco" and continuing to the cru wines "Rocche" and "Conca," all of them sourced from various pieces of the Rocche dell'Ammunziata vineyard in La Morra. The Ratti take on Barolo is bright and berried, with underlying notes of smoke and cedar, and it is crisp acidity, more so than hard tannin, that gives Ratti wines terrific longevity. The Barolos are all excellent values, as is the pinot noir–ish "Ochetti" Nebbiolo. "Villa Pattono" is a dark, plush blend from vineyards in Monferrato.

Redi TOSCANA

Via di Collazzi 5, 53045 Montepulciano (SI)
Tel.: 0578716092; 0578716093/www.cantinadelredi.com
DOC(G)s: Vino Nobile di Montepulciano; Vin Santo
   Redi is a brand name given to the top wines of the Vecchia Cantina, a Montepulciano cooperative with hundreds of member-growers (Francesco Redi is the Tuscan poet who wrote "Bacchus in Tuscany"). The top Vino Nobile is the brawny and succulent "Briarero," and there's also a good Vin Santo.

Regaleali

See Tasca d'Almerita.

Revello PIEMONTE

Frazione Annunziata 103, 12064 La Morra (CN)
Tel.: 017350276/Fax: 017350139/www.revellofratelli.com
DOC(G)s: Barolo; Barbera d'Alba; Dolcetto d'Alba
   Enzo and Carlo Revello released their first Barolos in the early 1990s and quickly became known for silky, finely tuned wines that speak of their roots in the village of La Morra. The Revellos bottle wines from many top La Morra vineyards, including Giachini, Rocche, and Gattera, and their house style favors heady, perfumy aromatics and soft tannic contours. There's a vanilla sweetness imparted by aging in small oak barriques, but the wood effects are pretty well modulated. Another noteworthy wine is the densely concentrated "Ciabot del Re" Barbera d'Alba.

Riecine TOSCANA

Località Riecine, 53013 Gaiole in Chianti (SI)
Tel.: 0577749098/Fax: 0577744935/www.riecine.com
DOC(G)s: Chianti Classico
   American Gary Barmann owns this small Gaiole estate, where longtime winemaker and sangiovese fanatic Sean O'Callaghan crafts polished, velvet-smooth Chiantis that really showcase the black cherry aromatics of the sangiovese grape. Riecine is all about sangiovese, in fact, boasting that its Chiantis are 100% pure expressions of the variety. The super-Tuscan "La Gioia," also 10% sangiovese, goes for more chocolaty richness than the fine and fragrant Chiantis.

Righetti

See MezzaCorona.

Rinaldi, Giuseppe PIEMONTE

Via Monforte 3, 12060 Barolo (CN)
Tel.: 017356156
DOC(G)s: Barolo; Barbera d'Alba
   One of Barolo's classics, with wines from the well-known Brunate and Cannubi vineyards. If you like a more

classically styled Barolo, a wine with some of the more earthy, leathery, spicy aromatics of the nebbiolo grape, then these wines are for you. Rinaldi also produces a rich yet rustic Barbera d'Alba, among other wines.

Rinaldi, Francesco PIEMONTE

Via U. Sacco 4, 12051 Alba (CN)
Tel.: 0173440484/Fax: 0173449378
DOC(G)s: Barolo; Barbera d'Alba

Here is a great introduction to old-school Barolo, and a reasonably priced one at that. This reliable house makes smooth and brightly fragrant Barolos from the well-known Brunate and Cannubi crus in the village of Barolo. A tight, spicy, rosy style of Barolo, and further proof that acidity is as valuable as tannin in lending longevity to a wine.

Rio Grande UMBRIA

Località Montecchie, 05028 Penna in Teverina (TR)
Tel.: 0744993102/www.aziendaagricolariogrande.com

The Pastore family acquired this small property in the Terni area of Umbria back in 1988. There are some nice value finds in the Rio Grande lineup, particularly on the red side: the Bordeaux blend "Casa Pastore" has some nice heft for the price, with a peppery cabernet sauvignon edge, while the merlot-cabernet-sangiovese blend "Poggio Muralto" is a plush and super-cheap everyday sipper.

Riseccoli TOSCANA

Via Convertoie 9, 50022 Greve in Chianti (FI)
Tel.: 055853598/www.riseccoli.it
DOC(G)s: Chianti Classico

Enologist Giorgio Marone crafts rich, oak-influenced Chiantis that contain more than a dollop of cabernet and merlot. Unabashedly modern wines, but hard to resist. The super-Tuscan "Saeculum" (60% sangiovese–30% cabernet–10% merlot) is a dense and flashy red aged in French oak, the kind of Tuscan powerhouse you want alongside a juicy Florentine steak.

Ritratti

See La Vis.

RIVERA PUGLIA

Strada Statale 98, Km. 19.800, 70031 Andria (BA)
Tel.: 0883569501/Fax: 0883569575/www.rivera.it
DOC(G)s: Castel del Monte

One of Puglia's top estates, characteristically large (producing about 1.5 million bottles a year). It's known for a dark and spicy red called "Il Falcone," a Castel del Monte DOC wine combining uva di troia (70%) and montepulciano (30%). The estate does just about everything well, including primitivo (the chocolaty "Triusco") and aglianico (the ripe yet tangy "Cappellaccio"). A new addition to the lineup is the 100% uvadi troia "Puer Apuliae," loaded with deep bitter chocolate intensity. This is a first-class southern Italian winery.

Roagna

See I Paglieri.

Rocca, Albino PIEMONTE

Via Rabajà 15, 12050 Barbaresco (CN)
Tel.: 0173635145/Fax: 0173635145

DOC(G)s: Barbaresco; Barbera d'Alba; Dolcetto d'Alba; Langhe

Angelo Rocca makes massive Barbarescos in the modern style—superextracted through the use of a roto-fermenter, aged in barrique, and as such, dense and exceptionally weighty on the palate. The "Vigneto Brich Ronchi," a single-vineyard selection, rivals most Barolos in intensity. His barberas and dolcettos are powerhouses in their own right, loaded with rich fruit and chocolaty oak. Give these wines time to age and you'll be rewarded.

★ Rocca, Bruno PIEMONTE

Località Rabajà 29, 12050 Barbaresco (CN)
Tel./Fax: 0173635112
DOC(G)s: Barbaresco; Barbera d'Alba; Dolcetto d'Alba; Langhe

Just down the street from Albino Rocca (no relation), this estate is known for powerful Barbaresco from the Rabajà and Coparossa vineyard sites. Difficult to find, these are sleek and very potent Barbarescos for long-term cellaring.

Rocca Bernarda FRIULI–VENEZIA GIULIA

Via Rocca Bernarda 27, 33040 Premariacco (UD)
Tel./Fax: 0432716273/www.roccabernarda.com
DOC(G)s: Colli Orientali del Friuli

A good and diverse production that includes one of the best picolits available (if you can find it). Firm and fruity dry whites are solid across the board, from tocai to chardonnay to pinot grigio.

Rocca delle Macie TOSCANA

Località Le Macie 45, 53011 Castellina in Chianti (SI)
Tel.: 05777321/Fax: 0577743150
www.roccadellemacie.com
DOC(G)s: Chianti Classico; Morellino di Scansano; Orvieto; Vernaccia di San Gimignano; Vino Nobile di Montepulciano

One of the larger private estates in the Chianti Classico zone, although the Zingarelli family's reach extends south into the Maremma (their Campomaccione estate produces a soft and sweetly fruity Morellino di Scansano) and into neighboring Umbria (a light and simple Orvieto). Best known among the Rocco delle Macie wines are the Chiantis, which are soft, friendly, and easy to find. The Chianti Classico Riserva is a reliable value, while at the higher end, the super-Tuscans "Roccato" (sangiovese-cabernet) and "Ser Gioveto" (sangiovese) can compete with wines twice their price.

Rocca di Castagnoli TOSCANA

Località Castagnoli, 53013 Gaiole in Chianti (SI)
Tel.: 0577731004/Fax: 0577731050
www.roccadicastagnoli.com
DOC(G)s: Chianti Classico

Though not easy to find, the Chiantis from this estate are well regarded, particularly the Riserva "Poggio à Frati." Generally, the Chiantis toe a spicier, more sangrovese-driven line while the super-Tuscans, like the cabernet-based "Buriano" and the merlot-based "Le Pratola," are chunkier and more oak-influenced.

Rocca di Fabbri UMBRIA

06036 Fabbri di Montefalco (PG)
Tel.: 0742399379/Fax: 0742399199
DOC(G)s: Montefalco Rosso; Sagrantino di Montefalco;
Colli Martani

Good reds from the Montefalco DOC, and a "super-Umbrian" wine called "Faroaldo," a rich and savory blend of sagrantino and cabernet sauvignon. The Sagrantino di Montefalco is dark, spicy, and tannic, but ultimately clean rather than rustic. A solid, lesser-known producer.

Rocca di Montegrossi TOSCANA

San Marcellino Località Monti in Chianti, 53013 Gaiole in Chianti (SI)
Tel.: 0577747977/Fax: 0577747836
DOC(G)s: Chianti Classico; Vin Santo

Run by Marco Ricasoli, the estate's small, carefully crafted production includes a traditionally styled Chianti Classico and a luscious sangiovese-based super-Tuscan called "Geremia." Ricasoli is passionate about the "traditional" Chainti varieties, and has the majority of the estate planted to sangiovese and canaiolo. Rounding out the list is a rich Vin Santo, which is aged for 5 years in 13-gallon casks before release, lending it great intensity.

Roccaducale

See Spoletoducale.

Rocche Costamagna PIEMONTE

Via V. Emanuele 8, 12064 La Morra (CN)
Tel.: 0173509225/Fax: 0173509283
www.rocchecostamagna.it
DOC(G)s: Barolo; Barbera d'Alba; Dolcetto d'Alba

One of a number of Barolo producers sourcing grapes from the Rocche dell 'Annunziata vineyard in La Morra. The Costamagna "Rocche" is an austere and brightly perfumed style, and is well priced. There's also a tangy barbera from the Rocche cru.

ROCCHE DEI MANZONI PIEMONTE

Località Manzoni Soprani 3, 12065 Monforte d'Alba (CN)
Tel.: 017378421/Fax: 0173787161
DOC(G)s: Barolo; Barbera d'Alba; Langhe

Proprietor Valentino Migliorini is one of Barolo's "modernists," and one of its biggest personalities. His wines are deeply extracted and aged in barrique, but for all their richness they hold on to their nebbiolo personality. The top cru wine is the Barolo "Cappella di Santo Stefano," but the more widely available "Vigna Big" and "Vigna d'la Roul" (the most delicate of the three) are more than acceptable substitutes. Migliorini also makes several luscious, generously oaked red blends, among them "Bricco Manzoni" (80% nebbiolo, 20% barbera), "Varo" (80% barbera, 20% nebbiolo), and "Quatr Nas" (nebbiolo, cabernet, merlot, pinot noir). His "Pinonero" pinot noir is also slick, and his *méthode Champenoise* sparkler "Brut Zero" (all chardonnay, made from barrel-fermented base wine) is one of Italy's better bubblies.

★ Roccolo Grassi VENETO

Via San Giovanni di Dio 19, 37030 Mezzane di Sotto (VR)
Tel.: 0458880089

DOC(G)s: Amarone della Valpolicella; Valpolicella

Young Marco Sartori changed the brand name of his family's estate to Roccolo Grassi, the name of his prized vineyard near Mezzane di Sotto, at the eastern end of the Valpolicella DOC. Sartori has helped make a name for "Valpolicella Est," the series of valleys just east of the Valpolicella Classico. Sartori's Roccolo Grassi Amarone is a voluptuous wine, but it carries its weight well—there's no excess alcohol heat or cloying sweetness. Another gem is the Valpolicella, which incorporates a small amount of Amarone to lend it a silken texture and added heft.

Rodano TOSCANA

Località Rodano 84, 53011 Castellina in Chianti (SI)
Tel.: 0577743107

DOC(G)s: Chianti Classico

Deep, smoky, woodsy Chianti Classico at fair prices (the one to seek out is the "Vincosta" Riserva). There's a chocolaty, dark-hued intensity to just about everything this winery makes, particularly its super-Tuscans, "Monna Claudia" (sangiovese-cabernet) and "Lazzicante" (merlot).

Rodaro, Paolo FRIULI–VENEZIA GIULIA

Via Cormons 8, 33040 Cividale del Friuli (UD)
Tel.: 0432716066

DOC(G)s: Collio

For clean, pure expressions of Friuli's prized white varieties, check out Paolo Rodaro: his pinot grigio is minerally and fleshy, his sauvignon bright and laser sharp, and his white-blend "Ronc" (pinot bianco–chardonnay–tocai) a rich yet refreshing departure from a world of oak-bomb white (it's aged only in steel and bottle).

★ Roddolo, Flavio PIEMONTE

Località Sant' Anna 5, 12065 Monforte d'Alba (CN)
Tel.: 017378535

DOC(G)s: Barolo; Barbera d'Alba; Dolcetto d'Alba; Nebbiolo d'Alba

Roddolo's wines are rich and are made in tiny quantities. Although the best wine is the well-concentrated "Ravera" Barolo, the most talked-about bottling is the "Bricco Appiani" carbernet sauvignon. Everything made here has depth and style, and prices reflect that.

Romano, Clelia

See Clelia Romano.

★ Romano Dal Forno VENETO

Località Lodoletta 4, 37030 Illasi (VR)
Tel.: 0457834923

DOC(G)s: Valpolicella; Amarone della Valpolicella; Recioto della Valpolicella

The most sought-after (and expensive) Amarone in the market. Romano Dal Forno takes the idea of dense vineyard spacing to the extreme, claiming to plant 11,000 vines per hectare—each of which produces a minuscule amount of superconcentrated grapes. In the cellar, Dal Forno ages his Valpolicellas, Amarones, and Reciotos in barriques, lending them even greater concentration. The Dal Forno Amarone is one step shy of Port, the Recioto one of Italy's most intense dessert wines. The "regular" Valpolicella (which includes some Amarone blended in) is

as rich as most producers' Amarone wines. These are
tightly allocated wines that have a devoted cult following,
truly over-the-top in their styling.

Ronchi PIEMONTE

Via Rabajà 4, 12050 Barbaresco (CN)
Tel./Fax: 0173635156
DOC(G)s: Barbaresco; Barbera d'Alba; Dolcetto d'Alba;
Langhe

Young proprietor Giancarlo Rocca sources grapes from
his parcel of the Ronchi cru, which has been made famous
by his cousin Angelo Rocca of the Albino Rocca winery.
Unlike the Albino Rocca wines, however, the Ronchi
Barbarescos are more traditional in style—aged in large
casks, with spicier, earthier scents and sharper angles. If
you can find this stuff, grab it: it's good and well priced.

Ronchi di Cialla FRIULI-VENEZIA GIULIA

Cialla di Prepotto, 33040 Udine
Tel.: 0432731679/Fax: 0432709806
DOC(G)s: Colli Orientali del Friuli

A specialist in the distinctive "native" vines of Friuli–
Venezia Giulia, including the spicy reds refosco and
schioppettino and the fragrant whites verduzzo and picolit.
The Rapuzzi family, which planted its vineyards back in
the early 1970s, has remained committed to traditional,
minimal-intervention winemaking, typically holding wines
for long periods in cask and bottle before releasing them.
Older vintages of both refosco and schioppettino can be
found in this market, and they're interesting—the funky
old refoscos are a little reminiscent of older Barolos, while
the schioppettinos have a spicy, herbal, Rhône-like
character. The verduzzo and picolit are vinified in an
amabile (semisweet) style, lending them a versatility at the
table that their sweeter contemporaries don't have. In all,
a rustic and very particular lineup.

Ronchi di Manzano FRIULI–VENEZIA GIULIA

Via Orsaria 42, 33044 Manzano (UD)
Tel.: 0432740718/Fax: 0432754378
www.ronchidimanzano.com
DOC(G)s: Colli Orientali del Friuli

Proprietor Roberta Borghese favors bold wines, as
evidenced by her chunky, ink-black reds and her heady,
often tropically fruity whites. Her "Ronc di Subule" Merlot
is like liquid chocolate in good vintages, as is the
cabernet-merlot blend "Le Zuccule." Check out the tarry,
well-rounded refosco as well. Like the reds, the whites see
time in barrique, lending even the basic tocai friulano a
creamy viscosity. The sweet picolit is fat and honeyed, a
relatively affordable wine for sipping after dinner.

Ronco dei Pini FRIULI–VENEZIA GIULIA

Via Ronchi 93, 33040 Prepotto (UD)
Tel.: 0432713239/www.roncodeipini.com
DOC(G)s: Colli Orientali del Friuli

Steel-fermented and aged whites from many of the usual
Friuli suspects, including pinot bianco, pinot grigio, and
tocai friulano. Minerally and straightforward. On the red
side, there's the peppery local stuff like schioppettino and
refosco, as well as a deeper Bordeaux blend.

Ronco dei Tassi FRIULI–VENEZIA GIULIA

Località Monte 38, 34071 Cormons (GO)
Tel.: 048160155/Fax: 0481629549/www.roncodeitassi.it
DOC(G)s: Collio

There's something special about the white wines of the Collio DOC, and the wines of Ronco dei Tassi have it: a rare mixture of weighty extract, aromatic intensity, and mineral crispness. Try the tocai in particular, and the lightly oaked white blend called "Fosarin" (tocai–malvasia–pinot bianco). On the red side, the merlot-based blend "Cjarandon" has a leafy, spicy edge.

Ronco del Gelso FRIULI–VENEZIA GIULIA

Via Isonzo 117, 34071 Cormons (GO)
Tel.: 048161310/Fax: 0481634667
DOC(G)s: Friuli Isonzo

Giorgio Badin's whites are full-bodied and expressive, examples of the greater heights of concentration that are possible in the Isonzo DOC's slightly warmer climate. The rich pinot grigio "Sot Lis Rivis" is a far cry from the watery pinot grigios that are held up as the industry standard, and the rest of Badin's varietal whites follow suit: there's a plump and peachy tocai, a fleshy sauvignon, and a spicy riesling, among others.

Ronco del Gnemiz FRIULI–VENEZIA GIULIA

Via Ronchi 5, 33048 San Giovanni al Natisone (UD)
Tel.: 0432756238/Fax: 0432936297
DOC(G)s: Colli Orientali del Friuli

There's a tightly coiled intensity to the wines of this estate that lends them a long life: even several years from the vintage the varietal whites have brisk acidity and good, minerally freshness. Try the excellent, chalky tocai first, then the plumper yet firmly acidic chardonnay (a good, clean, varietally true take on the grape). The "Rosso del Gnemiz" (a Bordeaux blend with a touch of schioppettino) has gotten a lot better in recent vintages, with some nice dark fruit flavors and a powerful tannic structure.

Ronco delle Betulle FRIULI–VENEZIA GIULIA

Via Abate Colonna 24, 33034 Manzano (UD)
Tel./Fax: 0432740547
DOC(G)s: Colli Orientali del Friuli

A small estate with prime vineyards in Rosazzo. There's a delicious, minerally tocai, full-bodied pinot bianco, and one of the brightest and most floral sauvignons to be found in Friuli–Venezia Giulia. Rosazzo is considered to be Friuli's key subzone for reds, though the "Narciso Rosso" (cabernet-merlot) doesn't make an especially strong case for that opinion.

Ronco Vieri FRIULI–VENEZIA GIULIA

Località Ramandolo, 33045 Nimus (UD)
Tel.: 0432904726/Fax: 043286437
DOC(G)s: Colli Orientali del Friuli; Ramandolo

A specialist in the Friulian nectars picolit and verduzzo.

Roncùs FRIULI–VENEZIA GIULIA

Via Mazzini 26, 34070 Capriva del Friuli (GO)
Tel.: 0481809349
DOC(G)s: Collio

Winemaker Marco Perco crafts a stylish range of wines,

particularly whites: most notable in recent vintages have been the pinot bianco and the tocai friulano, both of which have a depth of flavor derived not from oak but from ultra-ripeness. The cabernet-merlot blend "Val di Miez" is one of a growing number of substantial Friulian reds, offering nice color, density, and a velvety texture.

Rosa del Golfo PUGLIA

Via Garibaldi 56, 73011 Alezio (LE)
Tel.: 0833281045/www.rosadelgolfo.com
DOC(G)s: Salice Salentino

A small estate in southern Puglia specializing in spicy, deep, unusually expressive rosés from blends of negroamaro and malvasia nera grapes. The solid lineup of reds includes the superripe Primitiro del Salento, and the negroamaro-based "Portulano." The top-of-the-line offering is called "Quarantule" and combines negroamaro, aglianico, primitivo, and malvasia nera.

Rosso, Gigi PIEMONTE

Strada Alba-Barabolo, 12060 Castiglione Falletto (CN)
Tel.: 0173262369/Fax: 017326224/www.gigirosso.com
DOC(G)s: Barolo; Barbaresco; Barbera d'Alba; Dolcetto d'Alba; Gavi; Roero Arneis

One of the larger houses in the Barolo zone. The top Barolo is "Arione," from a vineyard in Serralunga, and it is made in a leathery, angular, classical style. Similarly classic in style is the crisp Barbera d'Alba "Racca-Giovino," which is aged only in steel and bottle. There's also a light and fragrant Bararesco and delicate, clean whites from Roero and Gavi. All are very reasonably priced.

Rotari

See MezzaCorona.

RUFFINO TOSCANA

Via Aretina 42/44, 50065 Pontassieve (FI)
Tel.: 05583605/Fax: 0558313677/www.ruffino.it
DOC(G)s: Chianti Classico; Brunello di Montalcino; others

One of the best-known Italian wine brands in America, thanks to the popularity of its two "Riserva Ovcale" Chianti Classicos: the basic "Riserva Ovcale," a consistently smooth and smoky red, and the longer-aged "Ovcale Oro," known affectionately in the United States as "Gold Label." Acquired by the Folonari family of Brescia in 1913, Ruffino has long used a combination of estate-owned vineyards and purchased grapes to produce a vast array of wines. In all, there are nine Ruffino properties with more than 1,200 acres of vineyards. The Chianti wines are the best known, whether they carry the Ruffino or Santedame labels, but there is also a solid and well-priced Brunello di Montalcino (from the firm's Il Greppone Mazzi estate), a supple Vino Nobile (Lodola Nuova), and other wines.

Ruggeri VENETO

Via Prà Fontana, 31049 Valdobbiadene (TV)
Tel.: 04239092/Fax: 0423973304/www.ruggeri.it
DOC(G)s: Prosecco di Valdobbiadene

Round and tasty proseccos, perfect for aperitifs, with all the peachy softness of the prosecco grape on display. The extra dry "Giall'Oro" is one to seek out, a fine and balanced sparkler.

Ruggeri Corsini PIEMONTE

Località Bussia Corsini 106, 12065 Monforte d'Alba (CN)
Tel.: 017378625

DOC(G)s: Barbera d'Alba; Barolo; Dolcetto d'Alba; Langhe Nebbiolo

The best-known wine from this small estate is its rich and velvety Barbera d'Alba "Armvjan." It is a big wine, though not as over-the-top as many of today's barrique-aged barberas. The estate also produces a deep and balanced Barolo from vineyard holdings in Monforte d'Alba.

Russiz Superiore FRIULI–VENEZIA GIULIA

Via Russiz 7, 34070 Capriva del Friuli (GO)
Tel.: 048199164; 048180328/www.marcofelluga.com

DOC(G)s: Collio

Part of the Marco Felluga family's group of holdings, and an extremely reliable producer, particularly whites. The best-regarded wine from this estate is the fragrant, mineral-rich tocai friulano, and there are a number of other excellent varietal whites to choose from. The red blend "Riserva degli Orzoni" (a spicy/savory blend of cabernets sauvignon and franc) and the straight cabernet franc are both unique reds, comparable to some of the cabernet franc–based reds of France's Loire valley.

Saladini Pilastri MARCHE

Via Saladini 5, 63030 Spinetoli (AP)
Tel.: 0736899534

DOC(G)s: Rosso Piceno; Falerio dei Colli Ascolani

Fleshy and fruity Rosso Piceno (most notably the "Conte Saladino") and a spicy red blend, "Pregio del Conte," which combines aglianico and montepulciano, are the wines to look for from this good-value Marche winery.

Salcheto TOSCANA

Via di Villa Bianca 15, 53045 Montepulciano (SI)
Tel.: 0578799031/www.salcheto.it

DOC(G)s: Chianti Colli Senesi; Vino Nobile di Montepulciano

Undoubtedly one of the top producers of Vino Nobile di Montepulciano, the small Salcheto estate has gotten lots of press for its dense and luxurious "Salco," a wine made from a specific clone of sangiovese, harvested superripe, and aged primarily in barrique. It's a rich (and expensive) wine, to be sure, but the real gem is the "basic" Vino Nobile, an always-consistent wine with a smooth texture and the distinctive smoke-and-cherry aromatics of sangiovese.

Salviano

See Tenuta di Salviano.

Salvioni (La Cerbaiola) TOSCANA

Piazza Cavour 19, 53024 Montalcino (SI)
Tel./Fax: 0577848499

DOC(G)s: Brunello di Montalcino

Since the mid-1980s, Giclio Salvioni has produced tiny quantities of his cocoa-rich Brunello di Montalcino, a perennial critics' darling and a wine sought after by collectors. This is one of those wines you read a lot about but don't necessarily see, because those collectors, along with a few lucky restaurants, take most of what little there is. If you see it on a list and feel like splurging, you won't be disappointed: this is a wine of great density, with a deep black color and a richness imparted by ripeness, not wood (the wine is aged only in large Slovenian casks). A powerhouse Brunello that's built to age.

San Biagio MARCHE

Via San Biagio 32, 62024 Matelica (MC)
Tel.: 073783997/Fax: 073784002
DOC(G)s: Verdicchio di Matelica
   The crisply acidic, minerally white Verdicchia di Matelica is the specialty of this small estate, which is assisted by famed consultant Riccardo Cotarella. The winery also makes a couple of spicy red blends.

★ San Fabiano Calcinaia TOSCANA ━●

Località Cellole, 53011 Castellina in Chianti (SI)
Tel.: 0577979232/www.sanfabianocalcinaia.com
DOC(G)s: Chianti Classico
   Here is a producer of Chianti Classico in a lush, polished, oak-kissed style, which was perfected by the consulting winemaker Carlo Ferrini. Try the Chianti Classico Riserva "Cellole" and you'll see just how far Chianti has come since the days of the straw flask: it's as dark as chocolate and just as rich. The red blend "Cerviolo" (sangiovese-cabernet-merlot) is deeper still, with sappy fruit, sandy tannins, and penetrating aromas. These wines have gotten a lot of press, but their prices remain relatively accessible.

SAN FELICE TOSCANA ━●

Località San Felice, 53019 Castelnuovo Berardegna (SI)
Tel.: 05773991/www.agricolasanfelice.it
DOC(G)s: Chianti Classico
   A classic choice in Chianti, and one of the best-situated wineries in the Chianti Classico zone (it is the heart of a small hamlet, or *borgo,* near Castelnuovo Berardenga that houses a sumptuous Relais & Châteaux resort called Borgo San Felice). The Chianti Classico "Il Grigio" and the single-vineyard Chianto Classico "Poggio Rosso" are well-known wines, both of them still capturing the rustic, aromatic side of sangiovese. "Vigorello" is a 60–40 blend of sangiovese and cabernet aged in French oak barriques, and while it is decidedly flashier than the Chiantis, it shares their smoky, smoldering edge. See also the listing for San Felice's Montalcino estate, Campogiovanni.

San Fereolo PIEMONTE

77 Borgata Valdiba 59, 12063 Dogliani (CN)
Tel.: 0173742075
DOC(G)s: Dolcetto di Dogliani; Langhe Rosso
   More black and burly dolcetto from Dogliani. San Fereolo's version is loaded with ripe fruit and a fair amount of coffee-ground tannin, while the barbera "Brumaio" is bigger still. These are thick-textured, sweetly fruity reds that need *osso buco* or an oxtail *ragù* to rein them in.

San Giusto a Rentennano TOSCANA

Località San Giusto a Rentennano, 53013 Gaiole in Chianti (SI)
Tel.: 0577747121
DOC(G)s: Chianti Classico
   Housed in a ninth-century fortress, this small estate

makes sleek and structured Chianti Classico and the varietal sangiovese "Percarlo," one of the few super-Tuscans that favor aroma and bright acidity over extract. Another eye-opener is the single-vineyard Chianti Classico "Baroncole," aged 18 months in second-pass barrique. Head-spinning Vin Santo, too.

San Leonardo
See Tenuta San Leonardo.

San Leonino
See Tenimenti Angelini.

San Lorenzo-Crognaletti
See Crognaletti.

San Luigi TOSCANA
Via dell'Arsenale 16, 57025 Piombino (LI)
Tel.: 0565220578/Fax: 056530380
This small winery in Piombino has received considerable acclaim for its thick-textured "Fidenzio," a cabernet sauvignon spiced with a touch of cabernet franc.

San Michele Appiano (St. Michael Eppan)
See Cantina Produttori San Michele–Appiano/St. Michael Eppan.

San Nicolò a Pisignano TOSCANA
Via Pisignano 36, 50026 San Casciano Val di Pesa (FI)
Tel.: 055828834/www.marcofelluga.it
A new estate in the Chianti area owned by the Marco Felluga estate of Friuli (see separate listing). The sleek "Sorripa" combines sangiovese with cabernet and merlot. A substantial super-Tuscan at a reasonable price.

San Patrignano EMILIA-ROMAGNA
Località San Patrignano, Via San Patrignano 53, 47852 Coriano (RN)
Tel.: 0541362362/Fax: 0541756764
www.sanpatrignano.org
DOC(G)s: Sangiovese di Romagna
Based not far from Rimini, this winery is staffed by residents of a rehabilitation community called San Patrignano, and in recent years the wines have received well-deserved accolades. Rich reds are the specialty, headlined by the chunky, chocolaty Sangiovese di Romagna "Avi." A little more affordable but no less flashy is the Bordeaux blend "Montepirolo," which has a thick, velvety texture and a savory edge.

★ San Romano PIEMONTE
Borgata Giachelli 8, 12063 Dogliani (CN)
Tel.: 017376289/www.sanromano.com
DOC(G)s: Dolcetto di Dogliani
San Romano is one of the Dogliani's many dolcetto specialists, making a number of extremely full-bodied wines from the grape. The top gun is the powerful "Vigna del Pilone," which is undoubtedly rich but not overblown. In all there are several dolcettos that climb the ladder in price, and they're all smooth and full of ripe fruit flavor.

San Savino MARCHE
Località San Savino, C. da Santa Maria in Carro 13, 63038 Ripatransone (AP)

Tel.: 073590107

DOC(G)s: Rosso Piceno; Offida

Soft and supple reds from sangiovese, montepulciano, and combinations of both, as is the custom in the Rosso Piceno DOC. The Rosso Piceno DOC wines are big and plump, but the headliners are a rich yet unoaked montepulciano ("Ver Sacrum") and a heavily oaked sangiovese ("Fedus"). These fat-bottomed reds are complemented by more traditional wines like the white "Ciprea," from the high-acid pecorino grape.

San Vincenti TOSCANA

Località San Vincenti, Podere di Stignano 27, 53013 Gaiole in Chianti (SI)

Tel.: 0577734047

DOC(G)s: Chianti Classico

A tiny estate that has attracted considerable critical attention for its powerfully structured Chianti Classico, particularly the *riserva*.

Sandri, Giovanni PIEMONTE

Località Perno 13, 12065 Monforte d'Alba (CN)

Tel.: 017378126/Fax: 0173787337/www.cascinadisa.com

DOC(G)s: Barolo; Barbera d'Alba; Dolcetto d'Alba; Langhe Nebbiolo

A historic property called Cascino Disa serves as the base for this tradition-minded estate, which produces a classic style of Barolo: high-acid, spicy, smoky, earthy. The other varietal wines (dolcetto, barbera) are similarly tangy and a touch rustic.

SANDRONE, LUCIANO PIEMONTE

Via Pugnane 4, 12060 Barolo (CN)

Tel.: 0173560023; 0173560024/

www.sandroneluciano.com

DOC(G)s: Barolo; Barbera d'Alba; Dolcetto d'Alba; Nebbiolo d'Alba

Luciano Sandrone worked at the historic Marchesi di Barolo winery before acquiring a tiny plot of land outside the village of Barolo in 1977. Since then, the Sandrone winery has become a Barolo boutique, with a small production of rich, handcrafted, supersleek Barolos and other wines. Sandrone could be called a modernist in that he opts for shorter macerations, shorter aging, and at least some new wood for his wines (although he, like Enrico Scavino, has come to prefer larger 500-liter *tonneaux* over 225-liter barriques). This is Barolo at its most luxurious, especially the top cru "Cannubi Boschis," from a choice plot just above the famed Cannubi vineyard. Also outstanding are his violet-scented Dolcetto d'Alba and a soft, accessible Nebbiolo d'Alba called "Valmaggiore." Drink these lower-priced options as you allow the Barolos to age, which they will, and gracefully.

Sant'Elena FRIULI–VENEZIA GIULIA

Via Gasparini 1, 34072 Gradisco d'Isonzo (GO)

Tel.: 048192388

DOC(G)s: Friuli Isonzo

A small estate acquired in 1997 by the New York–based wine importer Dominic Nocerino. With the help of consultant Franco Bernabei, Nocerino produces a well-priced lineup that expresses the fuller-figured style of Isonzo DOC wines. A round and creamy pinot grigio headlines the whites, and there are some spicy, smoky reds from cabernet sauvignon and merlot.

Santa Anastasia
See Abbazia Santa Anastasia.

Santa Barbara MARCHE
Borgo Mazzini 35, 60010 Barbara (AN)
Tel.: 0719674249/www.vinisantabarbara.it
DOC(G)s: Verdicchio dei Castelli di Jesi; Rosso Piceno
   Fresh and fragrant verdicchio is a specialty at Stefano Antonucci's estate (the citrusy "Le Vaglie" is more appealing than the oaked-up "Stefano Antonucci" selection), but there are a number of good and reasonably priced reds, starting with a smooth and simple Rosso Piceno. The Marche Rosso "Stefano Antonucci" is a juicy blend of equal parts cabernet sauvignon and merlot.

Santa Lucia PUGLIA
Strada San Vittore 1, 70033 Corato (BA)
Tel.: 0818721168; 0817642888/www.vinisantalucia.com
DOC(G)s: Castel del Monte
   Castel del Monte is the most interesting DOC wine in Puglia, and Santa Lucia makes some of the best. The Castel del Monte Riserva is dark and spicy, thanks to a dash of malbec along with the traditional uva di troia and montepulciano. Santa Lucia is also one of the few producers of rare sweet red Aleatico, which combines superripe cherry kirsch flavors with a hint of cinnamon spice.

Santa Maddalena (St. Magdalener)
See Cantina Produttori Santa Maddalena/St. Magdalener.

Santa Margherita VENETO
Via Ita Marzotto 8, 30025 Fossato di Portogruaro (VE)
Tel.: 0421246268/Fax: 0421246417
www.santamargherita.com
DOC(G)s: Alto Adige; Valdadige; Lison-Pramaggiore
   One of Italy's largest wine firms, and the one that turned pinot grigio into a brand. Although the production at this estate includes a variety of whites and reds (carrying various Veneto, Trentino, and Alto Adige DOC designations), the wine that defines it is its clean, minerally, and always consistent pinot grigio, of which more than 5 million bottles a year are now produced.

Santa Maria La Palma
See Cantina Sociale Santa Maria La Palma.

Santadi
See Cantina Sociale di Santadi.

Santavenere (Casa Vinicola Triacca) TOSCANA
Via Nazionale 21, 23030 Tirano (SO)
Tel.: 0342-701352/Fax: 0342704673/www.triacca.com
DOC(G)s: Vino Nobile di Montepulciano
   A one-wine estate in Montepulciano acquired in 1990 by the Triacca family of Valtellina. Vineyards span 82 acres, with plans for more plantings and an expanded cellar at this writing. Good smoky sangiovese aromatics.

Santi VENETO

Via Ungheria, 33, 37031 Illasi (VR)
Tel.: 0456520077

DOC(G)s: Valpolicella; Amarone della Valpolicella; Soave

Part of the Gruppo Italiano Vini (GIV) conglomerate, this is a well-regarded Valpolicella estate making solid Valpolicellas and Amarones. The Amarone "Proemio" is a luxurious wine that can stand up to some of the bigger names, while the Valpolicellas are simpler and less expensive wines for more casual occasions.

Saracco, Paolo PIEMONTE

Via Circonvallazione 6, 12053 Castiglione Tinella (CN)
Tel.: 0141855113/Fax: 0141855360

DOC(G)s: Moscato d'Asti; Langhe Chardonnay

A leading producer of Moscato d'Asti, Paolo Saracco also has a deft touch with dry whites. So before moving on to dessert, check out his Langhe Chardonnay "Bianch del Luv." It is a well-structured, minerally chardonnay without the ponderous oakiness.

Sardus Pater SARDEGNA

Via Rinascita 46, 09017 Sant' Antioco (CA)
Tel.: 0781800274/www.cantinesarduspater.com

DOC(G)s: Carignano del Sulcis

Yet another cooperative winery in southwestern Sardegna, with a well-priced, well-made lineup of wines. The savory, spicy blend of vermentino and nuraghus, called "Albus," is a unique white to pair with seafood dishes, while the red lineup is focused on ripe and supple wines from the carignano grape. Check out the red blend "Sulky" (carignano-syrah-cabernet), which offers a funky, fruity concentration for the money.

★ Sartarelli MARCHE

Via Coste del Molino 24, 60030 Poggio San Marcello (AN)
Tel.: 073189732/Fax: 0731889902

DOC(G)s: Verdicchio dei Castelli di Jesi

This estate is considered one of the top producers of the citrusy white Verdicchio dei Castelli di Jesi. Its three wines are arranged in ascending order of richness: the basic DOC bottling is limy and bright, the "Tralivio" is a little fuller and fruitier (the result of a closer selection in the vineyard), and the "Balciana" has an almost tropical fruit quality, thanks to a small percentage of late-harvested fruit. Recent tastings of "Balciana" show it to be quite fat and waxy, almost viognier-like in its richness.

Sartori VENETO

Via Casette 2, 37024 Negrar (VR)
Tel.: 0456028011/www.sartorinet.com

DOC(G)s: Soave; Valpolicella; Amarone della Valpolicella

With roots in the Valpolicella zone going back more than 100 years, this large firm continues to turn out value-priced Veneto wines at a clip of about 10 million bottles per year. Among the offerings are a host of inexpensive varietal wines, along with more serious stuff like the Amarone "Corte Bra."

Sassetti, Angelo TOSCANA

53024 Montalcino (SI)
Tel./Fax: 0577848748

DOC(G)s: Brunello di Montalcino; Rosso di Montalcino
  Angelo shares the estate name "Pertimali" with his
estranged brother Livio, but not the family vineyards, which
is not to say that Angelo Sassetti Brunellos aren't good:
they have depth, structure, and fruity aromatics, without
intrusive wood notes. A deep yet fairly accessible style.

★ Sassetti, Livio TOSCANA

Località Pertimali 329, 53024 Montalcino (SI)
Tel./Fax: 0577848721

DOC(G)s: Brunello di Montalcino; Rosso di Montalcino
  Pertimali, the name of a cottage on the Montosoli
vineyard in Montalcino and the estate name of the Sassetti
family, has been deemphasized on Livio Sassetti's labels
since he and his brother Angelo parted ways. Sourced
from that Montosoli cru, Livio's wines have the edge in
intensity and critical acclaim. Aging is all in large casks
and the style is deep and smoldering, with coffee-ground
tannins and penetrating aromas. A serious, elegant
Brunello.

Sasso, Francesco

See Eubea di Famiglia Sasso.

Sassotondo TOSCANA

Località Pian di Conati 52, 58010 Sovano (GR)
Tel.: 0564614218

DOC(G)s: Bianco di Pitigliano
  The pet grape here is ciliegiolo, found sporadically in the
Tuscan Maremma and a handful of other regions and
showcased in Sassotondo's "San Lorenzo" bottling.
There's a bright, berried, slightly spicy quality to the wine,
and yet it has good depth. "Sassotondo Rosso" is
essentially a lighter version of the "San Lorenzo."

Satta, Michele TOSCANA

Località Casone Ugolino 23, 57020 Castagneto
Carducci (LI)
Tel.: 0565763894/Fax: 0565773041
DOC(G)s: Bolgheri
  Artisan producer whose "Piastraia" (cabernet-merlot-
sangiovese-syrah) and woodsy all-sangiovese "Vigna al
Cavaliere" remain relative values in comparison to some of
their Bolgheri brethren. The brisk and briny "Costa di
Giulia," a vermentino-sauvignon blend, is a terrific seafood
white. Try the "Costa di Giulia" with the octopus salad ap-
petizer, then uncock the "Piastraia" for a char-grilled steak.

Scacciadiavoli UMBRIA

Cantinone 31, 06036 Montefalco (PG)
Tel.: 0742237210/Fax: 0742378272
DOC(G)s: Montefalco
  Solid producer of the Umbrian specialty Sagrantino di
Montefalco. Theirs is a well-priced introduction, a spicy
and smoky style with a firm tannic bite.

Scagliola PIEMONTE

Frazione San Siro 42, 14052 Calosso (AT)
Tel.: 0141853183

DOC(G)s: Barbera d'Asti; Moscato d'Asti; Langhe; Piemonte

Dense and chunky barrique-aged Barbera d'Asti is a specialty here (the "SanSi" in particular is a big wine). The diverse production also includes a plush Langhe Chardonnay and a highly regarded Moscato d'Asti.

Scarbolo FRIULI–VENEZIA GIULIA

Viale Grado 4, 33050 Pavia di Udine (UD)

Tel.: 0432675612

DOC(G)s: Friuli Grave

Valter Scarbolo's vineyards are at the eastern edge of the Grave DOC, just on the fringe of the Colli Orientali and Collio zones, and his wines can easily compete with their more celebrated neighbors, without the accompanying price tags. Scarbolo is best known for his big-boned tocai friulano, which combines juicy fruit extract with a sharp mineral-tinged finish. He makes an unoaked (and very refreshing) chardonnay, among the other well-priced varietal whites, and his reserve red refosco, called "Campo del Viotto," captures well the smoky, tarry intensity of the grape.

Scarzello PIEMONTE

Via Alba 29, 12060 Barolo (CN)

Tel.: 017356170

DOC(G)s: Barolo; Barbera d'Alba; Langhe Nebbiolo

A "traditional" Barolo producer (wines are aged only in large casks and are styled to have a firm tannic structure) whose wines nevertheless have a "modern" sheen: that is, they are lean and angular, leathery and rosy, without being dirty or defective. The Scarzello take on Barolo is fine and fragrant; the wines have a pinot noir–ish feel but plenty of acid and tannin for long aging. Drink their luscious Langhe Nebbiolo while you wait.

SCAVINO, PAOLO PIEMONTE

Via Alba-Barolo 33, 12060 Castiglione Falletto (CN)

Tel.: 017362850/Fax: 017362850

DOC(G)s: Barolo; Barbera d'Alba; Dolcetto d'Alba; Langhe

Winemaker/proprietor Enrico Scavino's Barolos are some of the most distinctive and powerful available. His cru wines include the sinewy "Bric del Fiasc," the tiny-production "Cannubi," and the rarer still "Rocche dell'Annunziata." Scavino also markets the more plush and accessible "Carobric," an assemblage of grapes from the above crus (the name is an assemblage as well). Also worth checking out are his barbera and the dense and chocolaty Langhe Rosso "Corale" (nebbiolo-barbera-cabernet–sauvignon).

SCHIOPETTO FRIULI–VENEZIA GIULIA

Via Palazzo Arcivescovile 1, 34070 Capriva del Friuli (GO)

Tel.: 048180332/Fax: 0481808073/www.schiopetto.it

DOC(G)s: Collio

The late Mario Schiopetto introduced controlled-temperature fermentation to Friuli, and with it the style of clean, high-acid, varietally true white wine Friuli has become famous for. Now run by Mario's twin sons and daughter, Schiopetto is still best known for its flinty, minerally tocai friulano. But the lineup also includes excellent pinot bianco, malvasia, pinot grigio, and the acclaimed "Podere dei Blumeri" Sauvignon. The exotically aromatic white blend "Blanc des Rosis" (tocai–pinot bianco–malvasia–sauvignon) is vinified exclusively in stainless steel.

Schwanburg
See Castello Schwanburg.

Scrimaglio, Franco e Mario PIEMONTE
Strada Alessandria 67, 14049 Nizza Monferrato (AT)
Tel.: 0141721385/www.scrimaglio.it
DOC(G)s: Barbera d'Asti; Monferrato Rosso
Lots of different barbera wines are made here, highlighted by the Barbera d'Asti "Bricco S. Ippolito."

Scubla, Roberto FRIULI–VENEZIA GIULIA
Via Rocca Bernarda 22, 33040 Premariacco (UD)
Tel.: 0432716258/Fax: 048199153
DOC(G)s: Colli Orientali del Friuli
A small producer of rich, well-structured whites (one of many in the Collio DOC). Specialties include a full-bodied pinot bianco and a tocai friulano that has a terrific combination of fruity richness and edgy minerality. The unusual "Pomédes" combines late-harvest tocai, pinot bianco, and partially dried riesling, all aged in barrique for a thick and viscous effect.

Sebaste, Mauro PIEMONTE
Via Garibaldi 222, 12051 Alba (CN)
Tel.: 0173262148/Fax: 0173262954/www.maurosebaste.it
DOC(G)s: Barolo; Barbaresco; Dolcetto d'Alba; Roero Arneis
A solid, wide-ranging lineup that includes leathery, dark-toned Barolo from the Prapò cru in Serralunga (probably their top wine), along with Barbaresco, Roero Arneis, and two well-priced Dolcetto d'Alba bottlings.

★ Seghesio PIEMONTE
Frazione Castelletto 19, 12065 Monforte d'Alba (CN)
Tel.: 017378108/Fax: 017378513
DOC(G)s: Barolo; Barbera d'Alba; Dolcetto d'Alba; Langhe
Perched on a hilltop overlooking Serralunga d'Alba, this winery, run by brothers Aldo and Riccardo Seghesio, is a source of elegant, reliable Barolo. The Barolo "Vigneto La Villa" is their most acclaimed wine: it has a tightly wound structure and a profound spiciness, definitely a wine to hold on to for a while. As with the Barolos, the excellent Barbera d'Alba is aged in new oak barriques.

Sella & Mosca SARDEGNA
Località I Piani, 07041 Alghero (SS)
Tel.: 079997700/Fax: 079951279/www.sellaemosca.com
DOC(G)s: Alghero; Vermentino di Sardegna; Vermentino di Gallura; Cannonau di Sardegna
This huge property, with more than 1,500 acres under vine, a chapel, a museum, a wine shop, and numerous guesthouses, is one of the largest wine estates in Europe. Founded in 1899 by two Piedmontese men who ventured to Alghero on a hunting trip, the estate was a vine nursery in its early years. Commercial wine production commenced in earnest in the 1950s. The Bonomi family acquired the estate in 1978 and revitalized the vineyards and winery, building production to 6 million bottles a year.

And yet the wines, including the fresh and fragrant Vermentino "La Cala," the spicy Cannonau Riserva, and the luscious, elegant "Marchese di Villamarina" Cabernet Sauvignon, do not taste mass-produced.

SELVAPIANA TOSCANA

Località Selvapiana 43, 50065 Pontassieve (FI)
Tel.: 0558369848

DOC(G)s: Chianti Rúfina; Vin Santo

This estate has a long history in the tiny Rúfina zone. The wines here are great bargains, packed with ripe and savory fruit flavor. The "Riserva Bucerchiale" and "Fornace" bottlings are billed as the top wines, but it is hard to beat the straight Chianti Rúfina for pure enjoyment. There's also some excellent Vin Santo.

Serafini & Vidotto VENETO

Via Arditi 1, 31040 Nervesa della Battaglia (TV)
Tel.: 0422773281/www.serafinievidotto.com

This boutique estate is trying to emulate the great châteaus of Bordeaux with its tarry, spicy reds based on cabernet sauvignon and merlot. "Il Rosso dell'Abbazia," so named for the historic abbey in which the winery is housed, is deeply colorful and well structured, a consistent favorite of the Italian wine cognoscenti. "Phigaia" is a fruity and simple "second" wine.

Serègo Alighieri

See Masi.

Serenelli, Alberto MARCHE

Via Bartolini 2, 60129 Ancona (AN)
Tel.: 07135505

DOC(G)s: Rosso Cònero

Alberto Serenelli is going for a luxurious style of Rosso Cònero, pushing the montepulciano grape to inky, toasty extremes and packaging the wines in burly bottles. There are a number of selections, starting with the great-value "Marro" and climbing up the price (and intensity) ladder from there.

Serra dei Fiori

See Braida di Giacomo Bologna.

★ Sertoli Salis LOMBARDIA

Piazza Salis 3, 23037 Tirano (SO)
Tel.: 0342710404/www.sertolisalis.com

DOC(G)s: Valtellina; Valtellina Superiore; Valtellina Sforsato

Housed in the Palazzo Salis, built by Swiss nobles in the 1700s, this winery was one of the first commercial bottlers in Italy, with labels going back to the mid-1800s. However, winemaking ceased here in 1908 and wasn't revived until 1989, when descendants of the founding family and private investors restarted the operation. Winemaker Claudio Introini, a Valtellina veteran, emphasizes fresh berry fruit in his nebbiolos, preferring shorter aging periods in oak and a longer rest in bottle before release. The *sfursat* wine called "Canva" is one of the best examples of that style, with a fantastic mix of juicy fruit extract and bright, exotic aromas.

Sette Ponti

See Tenuta Sette Ponti.

Settimo, Aurelio PIEMONTE

Frazione Annunziata 30, 12064 La Morra (CN)
Tel.: 017350803/Fax: 0173509318
DOC(G)s: Barolo; Langhe Nebbiolo

A great traditional style of Barolo at a great price. Check out the "Rocche" bottling, from the famed Rocche dell' Annunziata vineyard in the village of La Morra: it has all the bright, plush fruit typical of wines from this vineyard. The Langhe Nebbiolo is a great pinot noir substitute and a bargain at that.

Sinfarosa PUGLIA

c/o Accademia dei Racemi, 74020 Avetrana (TA)
DOC(G)s: Primitivo di Manduria

This primitivo specialist plays up the genetic relationship between primitivo and zinfandel by labeling one of its primitivo wines "Zinfandel." It's a rich and chocolaty red in an American mode, as is its Primitivo di Manduria sibling. Old-vine concentration at a reasonable price.

Solaria TOSCANA

Podere Capanna 102, 53024 Montalcino (SI)
Tel.: 0577849426
DOC(G)s: Brunello di Montalcino; Rosso di Montalcino

Excellent Brunello wines in a chunky, cocoa-rich style. The Rosso di Montalcino is notable for its heft as well.

Soldera

See Case Basse di Soldera.

Soletta SARDEGNA

Via Sassari 77, 07030 Florinas (SS)
Tel.: 079438160
DOC(G)s: Cannonau di Sardegna; Vermentino di Sardegna

A dynamic and growing estate whose vineyards are in northern Sardinia near Sassari. The specialty is wine from cannonau, best exemplified by the smooth, smoky Cannonau di Sardegna "Firmadu." The wines are well made across the board, from the powerfully aromatic Vermentino di Sardegna to the Cannonaudi Sardegna *riserva*.

Solo Arte

See Castellani.

Solo Maremma

See Fattoria Le Pupille.

Sopra La Ripa TOSCANA

Località Podere Sopra Ripa, 58010 Sorano (GR)
Tel.: 0564616885/www.sopralaripa.com

Well-regarded in Italy (if perhaps impossible to find here), this southern Tuscan estate specializes in bright, tangy reds combining sangiovese and ciliegiolo grapes. There are two blends, the fruity "Ea" and the richer, more oak-influenced "Ripa," which includes some alicante as well.

Sordo, Giovanni PIEMONTE

Strada Barolo 38, 12060 Castiglione Falletto (CN)
Tel./Fax: 017362853
DOC(G)s: Barolo; Barbaresco; Barbera d'Alba; Dolcetto d'Alba

An inexpensive introduction to old-school Barolo. A spicy, tart, brick-colored style, with some decent depth.

Sorelle Bronca VENETO

Frazione Colbertaldo, Via Martiri 20, 31020 Vidor (TV)
Tel.: 0423987201/www.sorellebronca.com

DOC(G)s: Prosecco di Valdobbiadene; Colli di Conegliano
This estate's "extra dry" version of prosecco is a
noteworthy bottle at a great price: a substantial Veneto
sparkler with more structure than most.

Sorì Paitin

See Paitin.

★ Sottimano PIEMONTE

Località Cottà 21, 12057 Neive (CN)
Tel.: 0173635186/Fax: 0173635186

DOC(G)s: Barbaresco; Barbera d'Alba; Dolcetto d'Alba
Massive, inky, supercharged Barbaresco is the calling
card of this boutique estate in the village of Neive. The
wines here are often compared to the extract-rich
Barbarescos of nearby La Spinetta. In all there are four
single-vineyard bottlings, three of them from southwest-
facing Neive crus (Cottà, Currà, and Fausoni), the fourth
from Pajorè in Treiso. Currà is probably the densest,
followed closely by the other two Neive wines, while
Pajorè, which sees no new wood during aging, leans a
little more toward the traditional in style. Then there's the
monster barrique-aged Barbera d'Alba "Pairolero," and
several fruit-rich dolcettos to boot. No power shortage
here: grill a steak, braise some beef . . . or simply leave
some cellar time to tame these mighty beasts.

★ Spadafora SICILIA

Via Ausonia 90, 90144 Palermo (PA)
Tel.: 091514952/Fax: 0916703322/www.spadafora.com

DOC(G)s: Alcamo
This winery is located in Monreale, just south of
Palermo. The young winemaker, Francesco Spadafora,
has made great strides with each recent vintage. "Rosso
Virzí" (nero d'avola–syrah) is a juicy value red, and the
similarly cheap "Don Pietro Bianco" (inzolia-grillo-
catarratto) is a fresh, clean white to have with *pesce spada*
(swordfish) with lemon and capers. Reds from the
"Schietto" line (both cabernet and syrah) are serious, if
pricey, as is the hulking "Sole di Padre" syrah.

Speri VENETO

Via Fontana 14, 37020 San Pietro in Cariano (VR)
Tel.: 0457701154/Fax: 0457704994/www.speri.com

DOC(G)s: Valpolicella; Amarone della Valpolicella; Recioto
della Valpolicella
Amarone "Monte Sant'Urbano" is a single-vineyard wine
aged for 4 years in small oak casks, which helps preserve
its color intensity and add toasty flavors. The well-
structured Valpolicella "La Roverina" is also a single-
vineyard wine, aged a year in oak, and the "Sant'Urbano"
Valpolicella is like a mini-Amarone, employing the *ripasso*
method to add depth and complexity.

Spinelli ABRUZZO

Via Piana la Fara 90, 66041 Atessa (CH)
Tel.: 0872897916/Fax: 0872897813

DOC(G)s: Montepulciano d'Abruzzo
Supercheap Abruzzo wines. The "Terra d'Aligi" line isn't
bad.

Spoletoducale UMBRIA

Località Petrognano 54, 06049 Spoleto (PG)
Tel.: 074356224

A rustic, earthy, darkly spicy Sagrantino di Montefalco heads the list of solid wines from this cooperative winery in Spoleto. Pricing is competitive.

Sportoletti UMBRIA

Via Lombardia 1, 06038 Spello (PG)
Tel.: 0742651461/Fax: 0742652349/www.sportoletti.com
DOC(G)s: Assisi

The "Villa Fidelia" line is the stuff to look for: the Bianco, a blend of grechetto and chardonnay, has some creamy depth from fermentation and aging in barrique, as does the sappy Rosso, which combines cabernet sauvignon, cabernet franc, and merlot in an inky, gently tannic package.

Strólogo, Silvano MARCHE

Via Osimana 89, 60021 Camerano (AN)
Tel.: 071732359/Fax: 071731104
DOC(G)s: Rosso Cònero

Over-the-top Rosso Cònero that has received much critical attention: the montepulciano grape pushed to its chocolaty, extracted extreme. The "Julius" bottling is a little more restrained than the "Traiano."

Strozzi, Guicciardini

See Guicciardini Strozzi (Fattoria Cusona).

Struzziero CAMPANIA

Via L. Cadorna 214/216, 83030 Venticano (AV)
Tel.: 0825965065/Fax: 0825965067
DOC(G)s: Fiano di Avellino; Taurasi

The Fiano di Avellino is crisp and spicy, while the Taurasi captures the smoky rusticity of aglianico. Hard-edged, traditionally styled wines.

Suavia VENETO

Frazione Fittà, Via Centro 14, 37038 Soave (VR)
Tel.: 0457675089
DOC(G)s: Soave Classico

In the top rank of Soave producers, with a base bottling that emphasizes freshness and minerality and two more plush and powerful single-vineyard wines, "Monte Carbonare" and "Le Rive," both of which see some barrel fermentation. Clean and stylish whites at fair prices.

Subida di Monte FRIULI–VENEZIA GIULIA

Località Monte 9, 34071 Cormons (GO)
Tel.: 048161011
DOC(G)s: Collio

More good, clean, varietally correct white wine from the prestigious Collio DOC zone: Subida di Monte's tocai friulano is minerally, floral, and substantial, as are the equally fine and fragrant whites from pinot bianco, sauvignon, etc. The reds have that green-bell-pepper edge of the more old-school northeastern wines.

Svetoni, Gracciano

See Folonari, Tenute Ambrogio e Giovanni.

TALENTI TOSCANA

Località Pian di Conti, 53020 Montalcino (SI)

Tel.: 0577844064

DOC(G)s: Brunello di Montalcino; Rosso di Montalcino

The late Piero Talenti was a giant in Montalcino, having crafted the wines at Il Poggione for decades. He also made his own wines at his tiny Podere Pian di Conte, which is now run by his son, Roberto. Talenti Brunello di Montalcino has traditionally been one of the more aristocratic, finely structured styles of Brunello, favoring acidity, aromatics, and angularity over dense extract. Talenti wines are elegant, woodsy, powerfully built expressions of the sangiovese grape, and remain reasonably priced. Evocative, well-balanced Tuscan reds with a hint of rusticity.

Tamellini VENETO

Via Tamellini 4, 37038 Costeggiola Soave (VR)

Tel./Fax: 0457675328

DOC(G)s: Soave; Recioto di Soave

An excellent Soave producer, known for wines with crisp acidity and bright aromas. Great values.

TASCA D'ALMERITA (REGALEALI) SICILIA

Contrada Regaleali, 90029 Vallelunga Pratameno (CL)

Tel.: 0921544011/Fax: 0921542522

Along with Duca di Salaparuta, this is the best-known wine house on Sicily, a sprawling farm owned by the Tasca d'Almerita family. Count Lucio Tasca and son Giuseppe continue to produce one of southern Italy's greatest reds in the rich, fragrant, nero d'avola–based "Rosso del Conte," as well as a good cabernet and a spicy rosato that has become a cult favorite (among many others). The estate is also home to Anna Tasca Lanza's acclaimed cooking school.

TAURINO PUGLIO

Strada Statale 605, 73010 Guagnano (LE)

Tel.: 0832706490

DOC(G)s: Salice Salentino

The late Cosimo Taurino was a legend in Puglia—the producer who put Puglian wines on the map. Taurino's superripe Salice Salentino and the rich and tarry "Notarpanaro" (mostly negroamaro) are well known to American consumers and continue to be consistent values. The pricier "Patriglione," a negroamaro–malvasia nera blend that incorporates some dried fruit like Amarone, is one of Puglia's highest-regarded reds.

Tavignano MARCHE

Località Tavignano, 62011 Cingoli (MC)

Tel.: 0733617303/Fax: 0733617320

DOC(G)s: Verdicchio dei Castelli di Jesi; Rosso Piceno

Good verdicchio wines, particularly the superaromatic "Misco" bottling.

Tedeschi VENETO

Via G. Verdi 4, 37020 San Pietro in Cariano (VR)

Tel.: 0457701487/www.tedeschiwines.com

DOC(G)s: Valpolicella Classico; Amarone della Valpolicella; Recioto della Valpolicella

One of the most consistent (and technologically advanced) wineries in the Valpolicella zone, turning out excellent reds year after year. Tedeschi's Amarone "Monte Olmi" is one of the best values in the category, a complex and flavorful wine in a medium-bodied style. The "La Fabriseria" Amarone is richer and more extracted, a better choice for cheese. The "Capitel S. Rocco" Valpolicella Ripasso is a spicy everyday quaffer.

Tenimenti Angelini TOSCANA

Via della Stella 3, 53045 Valiano di Montepulciano (SI)
Tel.: 0578724018/Fax: 0578724103
DOC(G)s: Vino Nobile di Montepulciano

This Tuscan firm owns estates in each of the Tuscan "big three": Chianti Classico (San Leonino); Montepulciano (Tenuta TreRose); and Montalcino (Val di Suga—see separate listing). Consistency and value are trademarks: the San Leonino Chiantis are plush and full bodied, highlighted by the barrique-aged, single-vineyard "Monsenese," while the wines of TreRose are similarly deep and modern in style. TreRose's Vino Nobile "Simposio" may well be the most impressive wine in the whole Angelini portfolio, in fact, with a deep, coffee-rich texture and lots of smoky sangiovese aromas.

★ Tenimenti D'Alessandro TOSCANA

Via Manzano 15, Camucia, 52044 Cortona (AR)
Tel.: 0575618667/Fax: 0575618411
DOC(G)s: Cortona

Massimo d'Alessandro's estate is in Cortona, just north of Montepulciano, where a number of Tuscan wine estates have taken larger stakes in recent years. Cortona's open, gently rolling hills and hotter climate (relative to Chianti, anyway) have attracted producers looking to make fat, ripe reds, and D'Alessandro's "Il Bosco," made from 100% syrah, is an early leader of the pack: it is warm, rich, and round, a New World–style syrah that can be uncorked on release. There's also a rich, barrel-fermented chardonnay called "Fontarca."

Tenuta di Montecucco

See Montecucco.

Tenute Ambrogio e Giovanni Folonari

See Folonari.

Tenuta Belguardo TOSCANA

Frazione Montebottigli, 58100 Grosseto (GR)
Tel.: 057773571/www.fonterutoli.com
DOC(G)s: Morellino di Scansano

The Mazzei family (of Castello di Fonterutoli in Chianti) are among the many big names who've snapped up property in the Tuscan Maremma, and their Tenuta Belguardo has quickly become one of the leading producers of Morellino di Scansano. In particular, Belguardo's "Poggio Bronzone" exemplifies what everyone is looking for from the Maremma terroir: richness, roundness, immediate drinkability.

Tenuta Beltrame FRIULI–VENEZIA GIULIA

Località Antonini 4, 33050 Bagnaria Arsa (UD)
Tel.: 0432923670/Fax: 0432920054

DOC(G)s: Friuli Aquilea

Sauvignon is a specialty here—both steely, aromatic sauvignon blanc and the peppery red cabernet sauvignon. The latter shows better-than-average depth in an area infamous for thin, weedy reds. Beltrame is the best-regarded winery in the Aquilea DOC, and the wines are relative bargains.

Tenuta Bonzara EMILIA-ROMAGNA
Via S. Chierlo 37/A, 40050 Monte San Pietro (BO)
Tel.: 0516768324/Fax: 051225772/www.bonzara.it
DOC(G)s: Colli Bolognesi

The hills south of Bologna, or Colli Bolognesi, are known for cabernet sauvignon, at least locally. But for a good cabernet value, Tenuta Bonzara's "Bonzarone" is a serious, substantial choice, with soft tannins and good cassis aromatics.

TENUTA CAPARZO TOSCANA
Strada Provinciale del Brunello, Km. 1,700, 53024 Montalcino (SI)
Tel.: 0577848390/Fax: 0577849377
DOC(G)s: Brunello di Montalcino

Always reliable, Tenuta Caparzo wines are all about great balance and pure sangiovese flavors. They're rich but not overblown, and aromatic in a way many Brunellos are not—that is to say, fruity and fresh. The Brunello "La Casa," if you can find (and afford) it, is the wine to collect.

Tenuta Castellino LOMBARDIA
Via San Pietro 46, 25030 Coccaglio (BS)
Tel.: 0307721015
DOC(G)s: Franciacorta; Terre di Franciacorta

Good Franciacorta sparklers, including an all-chardonnay, barrel-fermented Satén. Also notable is a thick and inky red named "Capineto," crafted by consulting enologist Luca D'Attoma. It's a classic Bordeaux blend that's considerably bolder than your typical Terre di Franciacorta Rosso—a real eye-opener from an area known for lean and green reds.

Tenuta Cisa Asinari dei Marchesi di Grésy
See Marchesi di Grésy.

Tenuta del Portale BASILICATA
Contrada Le Querce, 85022 Barile (PZ)
Tel.: 0972724691
DOC(G)s: Aglianico del Vulture

An estate founded by the D'Angelo family of Rionero, and a great-value option for aglianico wines of great character. The basic Aglianico del Vulture DOC is a consistently appealing choice, relatively smooth and medium-bodied but still possessing the wild, smoky, black berry fruit that characterizes aglianico. The top wine of the estate is the richer, darker "Vigne a Capanno."

Tenuta del Terriccio TOSCANA
Via Bagnolii 20, 56040 Castellina Marittima (PI)
Tel.: 050699709

A boutique winery not far from Pisa. Geared toward the international market, it is known for the potent super-Tuscans called "Lupicaia" (barrique-aged cabernet sauvignon and merlot) and "Tassinaia" (a shorter-aged blend of cabernet, merlot, and sangiovese). Serious wines, for sure, but be prepared to pay up.

Tenuta di Ghizzano TOSCANA

Frazione Ghizzano, Via della
Chiesa 1, 56030 Peccioli (PI)
Tel.: 0587630096/www.tenutadighizzano.com

Situated between Florence and Pisa, in the Colline Pisane DOC zone, Ghizzano is best known for its powerful merlot-cabernet blend called "Nambrot." Thick and palate-coating, framed with toasty oak notes, it's the kind of polished and potent red the Tuscan superconsultant Carlo Ferrini is known for. "Veneroso" (sangiovese-cabernet) is another critically acclaimed offering.

★ Tenuta di Salviano UMBRIA

Loc. Salviano 44, 05020 Baschi (TR)
Tel.: 0744950459/www.titignano.it
DOC(G)s: Orvieto

The deep, dark, and delicious red "Solideo," a blend of 60% syrah and 40% cabernet sauvignon, is the headliner at this noble estate outside Orvieto. Crafted by enologist Giorgio Marone (with the help of Tuscan legend Giacomo Tachis), it is meaty and savory yet sweetly fruity at the same time. It's a hefty red (aged a year and a half in barriques) but it carries its weight well. The Salviano Orvieto is round, a touch creamy, and a fantastic value, as is the white "Salviano di Salviano" (a bright and substantial mix of grechetto, sauvignon, and chardonnay). "Turlo" (sangiovese-cabernet) is a smooth red to snap up by the case. A slick and well-priced lineup.

Tenuta di Trecciano TOSCANA

Località Trecciano, 53018 Sovicille (SI)
Tel.: 0577314357

Here is a terrific Tuscan find just outside Siena, with a series of Chiantis from the Colli Senesi that can compete with those of the Classico: Trecciano makes wines with great sangiovese character and smooth textures, and all are reasonably priced. The chunky, fruity "I Campacci" is a sangiovese-merlot blend, while the top-of-the-line "Danielo" is cabernet-based.

Tenuta di Trinoro TOSCANA

Via Ribattola 2, 53047 Sarteano (SI)
Tel.: 0578267110

An out-of-the-way estate owned by Baron Andrea Franchetti, a self-taught winemaker who, having spent lots of time in Bordeaux, planted the cabernets, merlot, and petit verdot when he returned to Tuscany. The two reds are intense, thanks to rigorous vineyard selection and a good dose of French oak: "Tenuta di Trinoro" (cabernet franc–merlot–cabernet sauvignon–petit verdot) is the flagship; "Le Cupole" (both cabernets, merlot, and the Lazio oddity cesanese) is the "second" wine.

Tenuta di Valgiano TOSCANA

Via di Valgiano 7, 55010 Valgiano (LU)
Tel./Fax: 0583402271/www.valgiano.it
DOC(G)s: Colline Lucchesi

A biodynamic farm just outside of Lucca and a great little

find. There are three well-concentrated reds, the best overall value being the dark and spicy "Palistorti," a blend of sangiovese, syrah, and merlot. Big but balanced, it is the little brother to the estate's top wine, labeled simply "Tenuta di Valgiano" and containing a greater percentage of syrah than the Palistorti. Thick, black, stylish reds.

Tenuta Dettori
See Dettori.

Tenuta di Montecucco
See Montecucco.

Tenuta Friggiali
See Centolani.

Tenuta Giuncheo LIGURIA
Località Giuncheo, 18033 Camporosso (IM)
Tel.: 0184288639/www.tenutagiuncheo.it
DOC(G)s: Riviera Ligure di Ponente
Savory, structured, briny whites from the vermentino grape. The basic bottlings are classy wines for seafood; "Eclis" pumps up the variety with barrel fermentation. There's also the spicy red Rossese di Dolceacqua.

TENUTA GUADO AL TASSO TOSCANA
Loc Belvedere 140, 57020 Bolgheri (LI)
Tel.: 0565749735/www.antinori.it
DOC(G)s: Bolgheri
The Antinori family's longtime Bolgheri getaway, now a prized vineyard and state-of-the-art subterranean winery. "Guado al Tasso," a velvety blend of cabernet sauvignon, merlot, and syrah, is one of the elite super-Tuscans and tops a portfolio that includes bright and refreshingly herbaceous vermentino and a tangy, sangiovese-based *rosato* called "Scalabrone."

Tenuta Il Fagetto
See Il Faggeto.

Tenuta Il Greppo
See Biondi-Santi.

Tenuta La Badiola TOSCANA
Località Badiola, 58043 Castiglione della Pescaia (GR)
Tel.: 0155341614/www.andanahotel.com
Not yet an established commercial wine brand but notable because of its size (more than 1,200 acres), its proprietor (Vittorio Moretti, of Bellavista winery fame), and its game plan (a 33-room luxury hotel, with an Alain Ducasse restaurant, is already in operation on the estate). As with many of the other big names who have acquired large tracts of land in the Maremma, Moretti is doing everything on a grand scale.

Tenuta La Fuga
See Folonari, Tenute Ambrogio e Giovanni.

Tenuta Le Querce BASILICATA
Via Appia 123, 85100 Potenza
Tel.: 0971470709/Fax: 0971470856
www.tenutalequerce.com
DOC(G)s: Aglianico del Vulture
The Le Querce wines have a more fruit-driven personality than many of their Vulture peers, particularly the soft,

steel-aged "Il Viola," the estate's base wine. Bigger, blacker, and sweetened by barrique aging are the special selection "Rosso del Costanza" and the single-vineyard "Vigna della Corona." The house style calls for softer tannins and more sweet extract to counterbalance the spicy, smoky notes of the aglianico grape.

Tenuta Mazzolino LOMBARDIA

Via Mazzolino 26, 27050 Corvino San Quirico (PV)
Tel.: 038387612280/www.tenuta-mazzolino.com

Another of many Oltrepò Pavese producers making good wine under the radar. There's a brisk, perfumy pinot noir, called "Noir," and a spicy red bonarda, among other wines. Like most Oltrepò reds, these wines have some edges, and a touch of rusticity, but they are undoubtedly unique and full of character.

Tenuta Oliveto TOSCANA

Località Oliveto, 53020 Montalcino (SI)
Tel./Fax: 0577807170

DOC(G)s: Brunello di Montalcino; Rosso di Montalcino

One of a number of new, boutique-scale estates in Montalcino, and one of a number under the watchful eye of flying winemaker Roberto Cipresso. The small plot of south-facing vines, in the village of Castelnuovo dell'Abate, was purchased by Florentine entrepreneur Alademaro Marchetti in 1993, and since then he's set about making rich, unfiltered Brunello di Montalcino and uncommonly weighty Rosso di Montalcino.

Tenuta Rocca PIEMONTE

Località Ornati 19, 12065 Monforte d'Alba (CN)
Tel: 017378412/Fax: 0173789742/www.tenutarocca.com

DOC(G)s: Barolo; Barbera d'Alba; Dolcetto d'Alba; Langhe; Nebbiolo d'Alba

Purchased by its current owners in 1986, this estate previously sold grapes to other wineries but has since distinguished itself for its own production. All of its nebbiolo-based wines, from the well-priced Nebbiolo d'Alba "Sorì Ornati" to the beefier Barolo, have an elegant combination of dark, smoky power and ethereal aromas. Rocca's is a fine, fragrant style of Barolo — sleek but not overblown. Other highlights include a ripe and tangy Barbera d'Alba, "Roca Neira," which is aged a year in barrique but maintains its bright fruitiness.

Tenuta Roccaccia TOSCANA

Poggio Cavalluccio, 58017 Pitigliano (GR)
Tel.: 0564617978/Fax: 0564617978

DOC(G)s: Bianco di Pitigliano

Located in Pitigliano, in extreme southern Tuscany near its border with Lazio. Topping this winery's offerings is its bright, berried blend of sangiovese and ciliegiolo called "Fontenova," which is aged in barrique.

Tenuta RoncAlto

See Livón.

Tenuta Roveglia LOMBARDIA

Località Roveglia 1, 25010 Pozzolengo (BS)
Tel.: 030918663/Fax: 0309916800/www.tenutaroveglia.it

★ RISING STAR ⊛ VALUE 🍾 AVAILABILITY € PRICING

DOC(G)s: Lugana

A leading producer of the aromatic white Lugana. Sharp minerality and bright, appley aromatics.

TENUTA SAN GUIDO TOSCANA

Località Capanne 27, 57020 Bolgheri (LI)
Tel.: 0565762003
DOC(G)s: Bolgheri Sassicaia

Mario Incisa della Rochetta first planted cabernet sauvignon at the Tenuta San Guido in the late 1940s, intending to make some Bordeaux-style wine for his own consumption, but by the early 1970s "Sassicaia" was an international phenomenon. This is probably the most sought-after collector's wine in Italy, as it is known to age exceptionally well. Sassicaia is made primarily from cabernet sauvignon but includes a little-mentioned proportion of cabernet franc that gives it a gamy, green-pepper edge reminiscent of certain Bordeaux wines. Finely structured as opposed to monolithic, it is a powerful yet restrained red with a beguiling mix of aromas: coffee, cassis, eucalyptus . . . the list goes on and on, as does the list of accolades for the wine. Should you not wish to pay the premium to get some of this highly allocated wine, consider San Guido's new "second" wine, "Guidalberto," a blend of cabernet, merlot, and sangiovese. Though not sourced from the Sassicaia vineyard, it offers up some Sassicaia-esque nobility at a fraction of the price.

TENUTA SAN LEONARDO TRENTINO

Località San Leonardo 3, 38060 Avio (TN)
Tel.: 0464689004/www.sanleonardo.it
DOC(G)s: Trentino

Call it the Sassicaia of the north: Tenuta San Leonardo's estate wine, called simply "San Leonardo," has some of the stately manners of a great Bordeaux. A blend of 60% cabernet sauvignon, 30% cabernet franc, and 10% merlot, San Leonardo most definitely needs time to reveal its charms. It is a cool-climate red, tightly wound and a little "green" on release, but, in good vintages, it is blessed with more than enough fruit intensity to grow into something special. It's safe to say that this stuff rivals many great Bordeaux and yet, since it's from Trentino, it remains at an accessible price. The genteel Marchese Carlo Guerreri Gonzaga and his family run this beautiful estate, which tends to fly a little under the radar — all the better for a lover of great red wine in search of a value.

★ Tenuta Sant'Antonio VENETO

Via Ceriani 23, 37030 San Zeno di Cologna ai Colli (VR)
Tel.: 0457650383/Fax: 0456150913
www.tenutasantantonio.it
DOC(G)s: Valpolicella; Amarone della Valpolicella

This relatively new winery near Illasi has fast become a big name in Valpolicella, thanks to its big, slick wines. The Valpolicella "Monti Garbi" incorporates a touch of Amarone for body, while the newer Valpolicella "La Bandina" achieves its depth without the use of any dried fruit. The Amarone "Campo dei Gigli" is a good example of the "modern" take on Amarone: superrich and chocolaty, with a sheen of vanilla from its aging in small oak barrels.

★ Tenuta Sette Ponti TOSCANA

Frazione San Giustino Valdarno, Località Oreno, 52020
Terranuova Bracciolini (AR)
Tel.: 055977443/www.tenutasetteponti.com

Based not far from Arezzo and named for the seven bridges (*sette ponti*) that span the Arno River between Florence and Arezzo, this estate only recently began bottling wine—but started with a bang. Right out of the gate they've received lots of press for the luscious "Oreno," a blend of sangiovese, cabernet, and merlot crafted by consultant Carlo Ferrini. Superdense but softly tannic, it's an unabashedly drink-now red, as is its little brother, "Crognolo," which is predominantly sangiovese.

Tenute Ambrogio e Giovanni Folanari

See Folonari, Tenute Ambrogio e Giovanni.

Tenute Rapitalà SICILIA

Contrada Rapitalà, 90141 Camporeale (PA)
Tel.: 092437233/Fax: 092437494

Part of the Gruppo Italiano Vini (GIV), this winery not far from Palermo has a great-value offering in "Nuhar," a warm and richly textured blend of nero d'avola (70%) and cabernet sauvignon.

TENUTE SILVIO NARDI TOSCANA

Località Casale del Bosco, 53024 Montalcino (SI)
Tel.: 0577808269

DOC(G)s: Brunello di Montalcino; Rosso di Montalcino

The first Silvio Nardi wines were made back in the 1950s, making this one of the longer-established wineries in the zone. Nardi can still be depended on for stylish and reasonably priced Brunello and Rosso di Montalcino. The base Brunello is sourced from the estate's Casale del Bosco property, in the northwestern part of the Montalcino zone, and has an elegant, fragrant personality; the beefier "Manachiara," from a smaller holding at the southeastern end of Montalcino, is thick-textured and decadent.

Terlano

See Cantina Terlano.

★ Terrabianca TOSCANA

San Fedele a Paterno 17, 53017 Radda in Chianti (SI)
Tel.: 0577738544/Fax: 0577738623/www.terrabianca.com
DOC(G)s: Chianti Classico

Owners Robert and Maja Guldener continue to raise the profile (and expand the product line) of their stylish Tuscan estate. Terrabianca is consistently praised for its luxurious wines, which include the wildly popular "Campaccio" (a silken blend of 70% sangiovese and 30% cabernet) and the luxurious "Ceppate" (cabernet-merlot) and "Piano del Cipresso" (all sangiovese). Perhaps overlooked among all these slick, barrique-aged super-Tuscans are the Chianti wines, sourced from vineyards in Radda and no slouches in terms of concentration and style (check out the Chianti Classico "Croce" in particular). More recently the Guldeners added a new estate in the south of Tuscany, Il Tesoro, which not only houses a restaurant and inn but has already released two softly contoured reds: "Il Tesoro" (merlot) and "La Fonte" (sangiovese). Soft, sweet, drink-now reds.

Terra di Lavoro
See Galardi.

Terrale
See Calatrasi.

Terre Bianche LIGURIA

Località Arcagna, 18035 Dolceacqua (IM)
Tel.: 018431426/Fax: 01843230
DOC(G)s: Riviera Ligure di Ponente; Rossese di Dolceacqua

A leading western Ligurian producer. Solid examples of the briny whites pigato and vermentino, as well as the light red Rossese di Dolceacqua, which has an earthy, spicy tang.

Terre de' Trinci UMBRIA

Via Fiamenga 57, 06034 Foligno (PG)
Tel.: 0742320165/Fax: 0742320243
www.terredetrinci.com
DOC(G)s: Montefalco

For a good bargain in Sagrantino di Montefalco, try the robust and slightly rustic version from this estate. Lots of brambly blackberry fruit. There's also a plush blend called "Cajo," from sagrantino, cabernet, and merlot.

Terre degli Svevi BASILICATA

Località Pian di Camera, 85029 Venosa (PZ)
Tel.: 0972374175/www.giv.it
DOC(G)s: Aglianico del Vulture

Now owned by the Veneto firm Gruppo Italiano Vini (GIV), this is not a new property (the vineyards in Venosa have been there for decades), but it is a new brand. Look for the smoky, tarry Aglianico del Vulture "Re Manfredi," which has burst on the scene to great critical praise.

Terre del Sillabo TOSCANA

Via per Camaiore, 55060 Ponte del Giglio (LU)
Tel.: 0583394487; 03484450984/Fax: 0583395800
DOC(G)s: Colline Lucchesi

Once known as Le Murelle, this small estate in the hills outside Lucca is focused on international varieties. The red blend "Niffo" is a plush, perfumed blend of sangiovese, cabernet, and merlot — a super-Tuscan of medium weight and considerable class. A fresh and fragrant sauvignon (no oak) carries the Colline Lucchesi DOC. Tiny production.

★ Terredora CAMPANIA

Via Serra, 83030 Montefusco (AV)
Tel.: 0825968215/Fax: 0825963022/www.terredora.com
DOC(G)s: Fiano di Avellino; Greco di Tufo; Taurasi

The product of a split of the Mastroberardino family holdings (one side of the family got the brand name, the other got the vineyards). Terredora, run by Walter, Paolo, Lucio, and Daniela Mastroberardino, is a new brand sourcing grapes from prized old vines. The plush yet smoky Taurasi is a standout, as is the IGT aglianico "Il Principio," which softens out the sharp edges of the grape without losing its characteristic savor. Greco di Tufo is also a particular strength of this estate—check out the "Terre degli Angeli" bottling in particular.

Terriccio
See Tenuta del Terriccio.

Teruzzi & Puthod TOSCANA
Via Casale 19, 53037 San Gimignano (SI)
Tel.: 0577940143/Fax: 0577942016
DOC(G)s: Vernaccia di San Gimignano

This estate's melony, fragrant white "Terre di Tufi" may be the best-known white wine in Italy. A blend of vernaccia (80%), chardonnay, malvasia, and vermentino, it is certainly clean and crisp. Enrico Teruzzi and Carmen Puthod started out back in the early seventies with about 2 acres, but have grown their holdings considerably and now turn out more than 100,000 cases a year, mostly light whites such as Vernaccia di San Gimignano. Some spicy, light reds from sangiovese as well.

Thurnhof (Andreas Berger) ALTO ADIGE
Via Castel Flavon 7, 39100 Bolzano (BZ)
Tel.: 0471288460/www.thurnhof.com
DOC(G)s: Alto Adige

This small estate's quirky production includes two unusually aromatic whites from goldmuskateller (golden muscat): there's a crisp, piercingly acidic basic version (a cult hit with sommeliers) and a richer, late-harvest wine called "Passaurum," which is oily, floral, and smoky from botrytis. Also worth a try is the funky red lagrein.

Tiamo PUGLIA/VENETO
c/o Winesellers Ltd., 9933 N. Lawler Avenue Suite 230, Skokie, IL 60077
Tel.: 847-679-0121/Fax: 847-679-2017
www.winesellersltd.com

A value line of wines created by restaurant impresario Melvyn Master (owner of Mel's Restaurant in Denver, Colorado), who sources fruit from several Puglian wineries to create a soft and surprisingly substantial blend of sangiovese and primitivo from Puglia. A lot of wine for $8.

TIEFENBRUNNER ALTO ADIGE
Via Castello 4, 39040 Cortaccia/Kurtatsch (BZ)
Tel.: 0471880122/Fax: 0471880433
www.tiefenbrunner.com
DOC(G)s: Alto Adige

Among the best-known wineries in the Alto Adige, with a typically large product line. The cabernet sauvignon "Linticlarus" is one of several critically acclaimed cabernets being grown in the Alto Adige, but it, like most of its peers, has a green, bell-peppery character that may be off-putting to California cabernet fans. More interesting is the "Linticlaus" lagrien, with all of its dark, meaty flavors, and of course the clean, precise Tiefenbrunner whites, including the pinot grigio, pinot bianco, sauvignon blanc, and "Linticlarus" Chardonnay.

Toffoli, Vincenzo VENETO
Via Liberazione 26, 31020 Refrontolo (TV)
Tel.: 0438894240
DOC(G)s: Colli di Conegliano; Prosecco di Conegliano

Are there really distinctions to be made among $12

bottles of prosecco? They are subtle, to be sure, but here's another name to look for with wines that rise above the pack. Crisp, fragrant, sparklers.

Tollo
See Cantina Tollo.

Tolloy
See MezzaCorona.

Tommasi VENETO
Via Ronchetto 2, 37020 San Pietro in Cariano (VR)
Tel.: 0457701266/Fax: 0456834166/www.tommasiwine.it
DOC(G)s: Valpolicella; Amarone della Valpolicella;
Recioto della Valpolicella

One of the classic Amarone makers, known for a more traditional house style that favors long aging in large oak, resulting in a more leathery, spicy, earthy style.

★ Tormaresca PUGLIA
Via Maternità ed Infanzia 21, 72027 San Pietro
Vernotico (BA)
Tel.: 0805486943/www.tormaresca.it
DOC(G)s: Castel del Monte

Antinori owns this massive estate in Puglia, with some 1,200 acres of vineyards in both Brundisi and Castel del Monte, and the product line continues to grow broader and more impressive. The first Tormaresca wines, crafted by Antinori enologist Renzo Cotarella, debuted in 1999, and included the deep and well-balanced Tormaresca Rosso, a blend of negroamaro and cabernet sauvignon retailing for about $10. Since then the line has expanded to include the silky Castel del Monte DOC "Bocca di Lupo" and the 100% negroamaro "Masseria Maime," a wine that captures the grape's black fruit intensity without being cooked to death in the Puglian sun. There's a clean and fruity chardonnay as well.

Toros, Franco FRIULI–VENEZIA GIULIA
Via Novali 12, 34071 Cormons (GO)
Tel.: 048161327
DOC(G)s: Collio

A perennially acclaimed white-wine master in Friuli, although as yet these wines remain an Italian phenomenon. The tiny-production Toros winery is a boutique to rival that of Miani, with a range of viscous, exceptionally intense whites that includes a luscious pinot bianco and a round and exotic tocai friulano. The chardonnay and sauvignon are similarly concentrated and precise.

Torre dei Beati ABRUZZO
Via Adriatica Svd 89, 66023 Francavilla al Marc (CH)
Tel.: 0854916069/Fax: 06233218468
DOC(G)s: Montepulciano d'Abruzzo

A small estate of recent creation, with some very good Montepulciano d'Abruzzo (look for the inky "Coccia-pazza") and a rich rosé.

Torre Fornello EMILIA-ROMAGNA
Località Fornello, 29010 Ziano Piacentino (PC)
Tel.: 0523861001/www.torrefornello.it
DOC(G)s: Colli Piacentini

An eclectic lineup of wines from Piacenza, in the

northwestern corner of Emilia-Romagna. The Gutturnio (a blend of barbera and bonarda) is characteristically tangy and robust, with a good, spicy balance of acidity and dark fruit (go for the bottling called "Diacono Gerardo Riserva"). On the white side, there's an unusually aromatic white from malvasia called "Donna Luigia."

Torre Quarto PUGLIA

Contrada Quarto 5, 71042 Cerignola (FG)
Tel.: 0885418453
DOC(G)s: Castel del Monte

A winery with a fairly long history in the Castel del Monte area of northern Puglia, although it was only recently restored to past glory by proprietor Stefano Cirillo Farussi. The historic Puglian grape uva di troia (also called nero di troia) is a specialty here—check out the tangy, dark-toned "Bottaccia" for a taste of something completely different. The sweetly fruity primitivo is also good.

Torre Rosazza FRIULI–VENEZIA GIULIA

Località Poggiobello 12, 33044 Manzano (UD)
Tel.: 042751444/Fax: 042750840
DOC(G)s: Colli Orientali del Friuli

One of the better-known names in Friuli, producing a wide range of wines (more than a dozen) at affordable prices. The reds are especially well regarded, particularly the "L'Altromerlot" Merlot. All the crisp, fragrant Friulian whites are represented, all of them good values.

Trabucchi VENETO

Località Monte Tenda, 37031 Illasi (VR)
Tel.: 0457833233/www.trabucchi.it
DOC(G)s: Valpolicella; Amarone della Valpolicella

Located at the eastern edge of the Valpolicella zone, this estate makes Amarone in an intense, tannic style.

Travaglini PIEMONTE

Via delle Vigne 36, 13045 Gattinara (VC)
Tel.: 0163833588/Fax: 0163826482
www.travaglinigattinara.it
DOC(G)s: Gattinara

The Gattinara producer best known to Americans; its rustic nebbiolo in the odd-shaped bottles is still a reliable standard. Check out the new "Tre Vigne" Gattinara, crafted from fruit selected from three choice vineyards; the Gattinara Riserva is also worth a try. In either case, don't expect a fruit-bomb; instead, the wine seems to have drawn flavor out of the ground it comes from.

Travaglino LOMBARDIA

Località Travaglino 6, 27025 Calvignano (PV)
Tel.: 0383872222/www.travaglino.it
DOC(G)s: Oltrepò Pavese

Tangy Oltrepò Pavese reds from bonarda and pinot nero, as well as a *Champenoise* sparkler from pinot nero. The top wine is the lush red blend "Boccanera," an interesting barrique-aged blend of cabernet, pinot nero, merlot, and barbera.

Trecciano

See Tenuta di Trecciano.

★ Tre Monti EMILIA-ROMAGNA

Via Lola 3, 40026 Imola (BO)
Tel.: 0542657116/Fax: 0542657122/www.tremonti.it
DOC(G)s: Albana di Romagna; Colli d'Imola; Sangiovese di
Romagna; Trebbiano di Romagna

Try the Colli d'Imola "Boldo," a blend of sangiovese and
cabernet sauvignon. It is a rich if slightly mentholated
complement to their Sangiovese di Romagna "Thea,"
which seems like a more complete wine. Both sweet and
dry whites from albana are also offered, along with the
light Trebbiano di Romagna. The Albano Passito is an
excellent sweet wine.

Trevisiol VENETO

Via Mazzini 23, 31049 Valdobbiadene (TV)
Tel.: 0423972094/Fax: 0423905567
DOC(G)s: Prosecco di Valdobbiadene

An excellent prosecco for the money. Clean and fragrant.

Trexenta

See Cantina Sociale della Trexenta.

★ Triacca LOMBARDIA

Via Nazionale 121, 23030 Villa di Tirano (SO)
Tel.: 0342701352/Fax: 032704673/www.triacca.com
DOC(G)s: Valtellina; Valtellina Superiore; Valtellina Sforsato

Domenico Triacca is an energetic viticulturist and
technician: he creates his unique "Prestigio" wine by
cutting the cordons of select nebbiolo vines and leaving
the grapes to dry on these cut branches for a good month
after the normal harvest. The nebbiolo and his more
traditional *sforsato* are wines that combine fruity richness
with the aromatic complexity typical of the region.

Trinoro

See Tenuta di Trinoro.

Tua Rita TOSCANA

Località Notri 81, 57028 Suvereto (LI)
Tel.: 0565829237/Fax: 0565827891/www.tuarita.it

A relatively recent arrival on the Tuscan wine scene, but
one that has made a big splash. Located in the red-hot
Suvereto area, south of Livorno on the Tuscan coast, the
small estate named for proprietor Rita Tua has definitely
gotten a good read on the international market. The most
sought-after wine is the "Redigaffi," a sappy yet structured
100% merlot that the wine critics have gone crazy for (and
of which very little is made). Other offerings include the
more affordable "Giusto di Notri" (65% cabernet, 30%
merlot, 5% cab franc) and "Perlato del Bosco" sangiovese
blends. All are fairly pricey but offer plenty of intensity for
the money.

★ Uccelliera TOSCANA

Frazione Castelnuovo Abate, 53020 Montalcino (SI)
Tel.: 0577835729/Fax: 0577835729
DOC(G)s: Brunello di Montalcino

A tiny and very well-run farm in Montalcino owned by
Andrea Cortonesi. Forwardly fruity Brunello and Rosso di
Montalcino make up the estate's lineup. Limited
production.

Umani Ronchi MARCHE

60027 Osimo (AN)

Tel.: 0717108019/Fax: 0717108859/www.umanironchi.it

DOC(G)s: Verdicchio di Castelli di Jesi; Rosso Cònero

When it comes to brand recognition and sheer output, this is the most important estate in the Marche, with an ever-expanding array of good, well-priced wines. The Verdicchio dei Castelli di Jesi "Casal di Serra" is a ripe and unusually powerful expression of the grape, while the "Le Busche" combines verdicchio with chardonnay to interesting effect. Among the many reds, the top wines are the luscious Rosso Cònero "Cúmaro" and the even more luscious red blend "Pélago." The basic Rosso Cònero "San Lorenzo" is one of the great values in Italian wine and very consistent from year to year.

Vajra, G. D. PIEMONTE

Via delle Viole 25, 12060 Barolo (CN)

Tel.: 017356257/Fax: 017356345

DOC(G)s: Barolo; Barbera d'Alba; Dolcetto d'Alba; Langhe

Vajra wines blend modern and traditional winemaking techniques, and are typically readily accessible as young wines, broad and somewhat Burgundian (i.e., earthy, smoky) in their flavor profile. The winery has holdings in three Barolo commune vineyards: Le Coste, Fossati, and Bricco delle Viole. This last seems to make the most consistently good Barolo.

Valle delle Rose

See Cecchi.

Val di Suga (Tenimenti Angelini) TOSCANA

Località Val di Cava, 53024 Montalcino (SI)

Tel.: 057780411

DOC(G)s: Brunello di Montalcino

Good Brunello di Montalcino, particularly the ink-rich "Vigna del Lago" bottling.

★ Valdicava TOSCANA

Località Val di Cava, 53024 Montalcino (SI)

Tel.: 0577848261

DOC(G)s: Brunello di Montalcino; Rosso di Montalcino

Expensive Brunello di Montalcino, and it tastes it: big and round, with rich black cherry fruit and silty, velvety tannins Valdicava Brunellos always seem ready to go on release, although there's plenty under the hood for aging. The Rosso di Montalcino has a rich, oaky texture and plenty of weight (it has the heft of many Brunellos, in fact). These are luxurious wines for special occasions.

★ Valdipiatta TOSCANA

Via della Ciarliana 25/A, 53040 Montepulciano (SI)

Tel.: 0578757930

DOC(G)s: Vino Nobile di Montepulciano

Great value in Vino Nobile. The wines are rich and accessible, fruity and modern, and are now joined by several super-Tuscans: "Tre Fonti" is an interesting blend of cabernet, sangiovese (prugnolo), and canaiolo, while the voluptuous "Trincerone" combines canaiolo with merlot. Topping the list, however, is the Vino Nobile "Vigna Alfiero," a seductive and dark-toned beauty with enough structure for short-term aging.

Valditerra PIEMONTE

Strada Monterotondo 75, 15067 Nove Ligure (AL)
Tel./Fax: 0143321451

DOC(G)s: Gavi

Some of the better Gavi wines around, with great minerality and aromatics.

VALENTINI, EDOARDO ABRUZZO

Via del Baio 2, 65014 Loreto Apruntino (PE)
Tel.: 0858291138

DOC(G)s: Trebbiano d'Abruzzo; Montepulciano d'Abruzzo

The reclusive Edoardo Valentini has developed a reputation as one of the most uncompromising artisans in the world of Italian wine. His wines generally receive considerable bottle age before they go on sale, and it's not uncommon for Valentini to hold back the release of certain vintages if he doesn't think they're ready. Valentini Trebbiano d'Abruzzo is intense, long-lived; it really has no peer in the category. The Montepulciano d'Abruzzo is as deep and fruity as any while also boasting an earthy, smoky complexity. The pink Cerasuolo is also a standout. All are rare and pricey, but unquestionably unique.

Valfieri PIEMONTE

Strada Loreto 5, 14055 Costigliole d'Asti (AT)
Tel.: 0141966881

DOC(G)s: Barolo; Barbaresco; Barbera d'Asti; Dolcetto d'Alba; others

An Asti-area producer with a broad and well-priced line. The Barolo and Barbaresco wines are serviceable, but the specialty here is barbera: try the Barbera d'Asti "I Filari Lunghi" or the plush and sexy nebbiolo-barbera blend called "Cassabò." The latter in particular is a great buy.

Valgiano

See Tenuta di Valgiano.

Vallarom TRENTINO

Via Masi 21, 38063 Avio (TN)
Tel.: 0464684297/Fax: 0464687032

DOC(G)s: Trentino

Owned by the family of Professor Attilio Scienza of the University of Milan, this winery has a deft touch with both whites and reds. The Bordeaux blend "Campi Sarni" is a typically savory, spicy Trentino red, the pinot noir is crisp and aromatic, the marzemino is more exotically fruity. On the white side, a fleshy chardonnay is a specialty.

★ Valle dell'Acate SICILIA

Contrada Bidini, 97011 Acate (RG)
Tel.: 0932874166/Fax: 0932875114/
www.valledellacate.com

DOC(G)s: Cerasuolo di Vittoria

The up-and-coming Valle dell'Acate estate focuses considerable attention on the frappato grape, not only blending it with the richer nero d'avola for Cerasuolo di Vittoria but also bottling it on its own to showcase its bright, fresh, cherry-scented character. Also worth checking out is the "Poggio Bidini" Nero d'Arola, a deeply fruity southern red.

Vallerosa Bonci
See Bonci.

Vallona EMILIA-ROMAGNA
Frazione Fagnano, Via Sant'Andrea 203, 40050 Castello di
Serravalle (BO)
Tel.: 0516703058
DOC(G)s: Colli Bolognesi
  If you love cabernet sauvignon but not its ever-escalating
price, check out this estate just south of Bologna. There
are two cabernets from the Colli Bolognesi that offer good
varietal character and concentration for short money. You
might as well pay a little more for the cabernet "Selezione," a reserve selection aged 18 months in barrique.

Vallone PUGLIA
Via XXV Luglio 5, 73100 Lecce (LE)
Tel.: 0832308041
DOC(G)s: Brindisi; Salice Salentino
  In addition to superripe, supersoft Salice Salentino, the
Vallone estate is known for the VdT "Gratticciaia," a
negroamaro-malvasia blend that incorporates some
semidried fruit to give it an Amarone-like richness. The
Brindisi Rosso DOC "Vigna Flaminio" is dark and juicy.

Varaldo PIEMONTE
Via Secondine 2, 12050 Barbaresco (CN)
Tel./Fax: 0173635160
DOC(G)s: Barbaresco; Barbera d'Alba; Dolcetto d'Alba;
Langhe
  A producer of outstanding wines across the board,
highlighted by powerful yet accessible Barbarescos such
as the "Bricco Libero," Varaldo's top wine. Good barbera,
dolcetto, and freisa complement the powerhouse
Barbarescos.

Varramista TOSCANA
Località Varramista, Via Ricavo, 56020 Montpoli in Val
d'Arno (PI)
Tel.: 0571468121/Fax: 0571468122/www.varramista.it
  A massive, meaty syrah is the main wine of this boutique
estate near Pisa.

Vecchie Terre di Montefili TOSCANA
Via San Cresci 45, 50022 Panzano (FI)
Tel.: 055853739
DOC(G)s: Chianti Classico
  An always reliable estate producing fine and fruity
Chianti Classico, along with the sangiovese-cabernet blend
"Bruno di Rocca." There's also a weird white blend called
"Vigna Regis" (a fruit cocktail of chardonnay, sauvignon,
and gewürztraminer).

Vega (D'Antiche Terre) CAMPANIA
Via Toppole 16, 83030 Manocalzati (AV)
Tel.: 082530777
DOC(G)s: Greco di Tufo; Fiano di Avellino; Taurasi
  Good (and cheap) examples of the spicy, savory inland
Campania DOC wines: Greco di Tufo, Fiano di Avellino,
and especially Taurasi, which here is vinified in an earthy,
traditional style.

Veglio, Mauro PIEMONTE

Frazione Annunziata 50, 12064 La Morra (CN)
Tel./Fax: 0173509212

DOC(G)s: Barolo; Barbera d'Alba; Dolcetto d'Alba; Langhe
A range of top-flight Barolo is made at this artisanal estate, with three cru wines from La Morra ("Arborina," "Gattera," and "Rocche") and one from Barolo ("La Villa"). The wines are fruit-driven and powerfully structured, as are the excellent barberas and dolcettos.

Velenosi

See Ercole Velenosi.

Venegazzù VENETO

Frazione Venegazzù, 31040 Volpago del Montello (TV)
Tel.: 0423870024/www.venegazzu.com

DOC(G)s: Montello e Colli Asolani
Venegazzù is headquartered near Treviso and produces a range of inexpensive Veneto wines. A cut above the otherwise simple lineup is "Capo di Stato," a Bordeaux-inspired blend of cabernets sauvignon and franc, merlot, and malbec.

VENICA FRIULI–VENEZIA GIULIA

Via Mernico 42, 34070 Dolegna del Collio (GO)
Tel.: 048161264/Fax: 0481639906/www.venica.it

DOC(G)s: Collio
The wide range of crisp, varietally precise wines includes excellent chardonnay, pinot grigio, tocai, and especially sauvignon, most notably the single-vineyard "Ronco delle Mele"—a powerful sauvignon redolent of mandarin oranges and wild herbs. "Tre Vignis" is a creamy blend of tocai, chardonnay, and sauvignon, and the tarry, spicy "Rosso delle Cime" (cabernet-merlot-refosco) is among the better Friulian reds. Also worth checking out is the "Bottaz" refosso, loaded as it is with black fruit and peppery spice. A great red for steak.

Venosa

See Cantina di Venosa.

Venturini VENETO

Via Semonte 20, 37020 San Pietro in Cariano (VR)
Tel.: 0457701331; 0457703320

DOC(G)s: Valpolicella; Amarone della Valpolicella; Recioto della Valpolicella
Venturini Amarone is moderate in scale, deeply flavorful without being sappy and sweetish. It's a brighter, lighter take on the style—a good "table" Amarone instead of one to be saved for the cheese course.

Vercesi del Castellazzo LOMBARDIA

Via Aureliano 36, 27040 Montù Beccaria (PV)
Tel.: 038560067

DOC(G)s: Oltrepò Pavese
The tarry, black fruit–flavored bonarda grape is a specialty (try the "Fatila" bottling), and there's also a high-acid, leathery pinot nero (pinot noir) called "Luogo dei Monti." Interesting artisan estate.

Verdi, Bruno LOMBARDIA

Via Vergomberra 5, 27044 Canneto Pavese (PV)
Tel.: 038588023/Fax: 0385241623
DOC(G)s: Oltrepò Pavese

Bruno Verdi's wide range of Oltrepò Pavese DOC wines
are interesting and good. Among the whites, the steely
riesling "Vigneto Costa" is a highlight, while the reds are
headlined by a dense and tarry bonarda (try "Cavariola"
Riserva). Fruity, high-acid barbera is another specialty.

Verrazzano

See Castello di Verrazzano.

Vestini-Campagnano CAMPANIA

Via Barracone 5, 81013 Caiazzo (CE)
Tel.: 0823862770

Part commercial winery and part viticultural research
project, this property—owned by two lawyers—has
enlisted the help of Professor Luigi Moio to create wines
from two ancient local varieties: palagrello (both red and
white versions) and casavecchia. The pallagrello bianco is
pretty interesting, with some piney aromatics typical of
Campanian whites.

Vetusto

See Consorzio Viticoltori Associati del Vulture.

Viberti, Eraldo PIEMONTE

Borgata Tetti dei Turchi 53, 12064 La Morra (CN)
Tel.: 017350308
DOC(G)s: Barolo; Barbera d'Alba; Dolcetto d'Alba

A good, small Barolo estate also known for ripe, oak-
kissed barberas. The Barbera d'Alba "Vigna Clara" has
some stuffing.

Viberti, Osvaldo PIEMONTE

Borgata Tetti dei Turchi 53, 12064 La Morra (CN)
Tel.: 017350374
DOC(G)s: Barolo; Barbera d'Alba; Dolcetto d'Alba; Langhe

A solid range of Langhe wines includes a smoky, tightly
wound Barolo from the Bricco delle Viole cru and well-
priced barbera and dolcetto.

Vicara PIEMONTE

Cascina Madonna delle Grazie 5, 15030 Rosignano
Monferrato (AL)
Tel.: 0142488054/www.vicara.it
DOC(G)s: Barbera del Monferrato; Monferrato

Good Monferrato DOC wines, including a sleek blend of
barbera, cabernet, and nebbiolo called "Rubello." Also
noteworthy is the Barbera dell'Monferrato "Cantico della
Crosia," a clean and fruit-rich red.

Vicchiomaggio

See Castello Vicchiomaggio.

Vie di Romans FRIULI–VENEZIA GIULIA

Località Vie di Romans 1, 34070 Mariano del Friuli (GO)
Tel.: 048169600
DOC(G)s: Friuli Isonzo

` Another star winery from the Isonzo DOC, and one of
Friuli's best. Powerfully aromatic sauvignon (try the fruity
"Vieris" or the woodier "Piere"). The white blend "Flors di

Uis" is one of the top super-whites, a viscous but aromatic blend of malvasia, chardonnay, and riesling vinified in stainless steel. "Ciampagnis Vieris" Chardonnay is also excellent, as is the full-bodied, barrel-fermented "Dessimis" Pinot Grigio.

VIETTI PIEMONTE

Piazza Vittorio Veneto 5, 12060 Castiglione Falletto (CN)
Tel.: 017362825/Fax: 017362941/www.vietti.com
DOC(G)s: Barolo; Barbaresco; Dolcetto d'Alba; Barbera d'Alba; Roero Arneis

Nearly 20 different wines are produced at this landmark estate, which sources grapes from estate-owned vineyards (about 80 acres) and contract growers. Vietti does everything well, from lively Moscato d'Asti to fragrant Roero Arneis to the benchmark Barbera d'Alba "Tre Vigne" and beyond. The specialty is long-lived Barolo from a range of great crus, including Rocche (Castiglione Falletto), Brunate (La Morra), Lazzarito (Serralunga) and, in select vintages, Villero (Castiglione Falletto again). Superpowerful Barolos that will reward long aging.

Vigna Rionda (Massolino)
See Massolino.

★ Vignalta VENETO
Via dei Vescovi 5, 35038 Torreglia (PD)
Tel.: 0499933105; 0429777225
DOC(G)s: Colli Euganei
This Padova-area winery is known for "Gemola," a chunky, savory blend of cabernet sauvignon and merlot.

Vignamaggio TOSCANA
Via di Petriolo 5, 50022 Greve in Chianti (FI)
Tel.: 055854661/www.vignamaggio.com
DOC(G)s: Chianti Classico; Vin Santo
Good Chianti Classico, particularly the "Monna Lisa" Riserva, complemented by some super-Tuscans: "Obsession," a meaty blend of cabernet, merlot, and syrah, and "Vignamaggio," which is based on cabernet franc.

Vignavecchia TOSCANA
Sdrucciolo di Piazza 7, 53017 Radda in Chianti (SI)
Tel.: 0577738090/Fax: 0577738326
www.vignavecchia.com
DOC(G)s: Chianti Classico
Rich and round Chianti Classico dosed with a fair amount of merlot, as well as the intense, all-sangiovese "Raddese" and the barrique-aged "Titanium" chardonnay.

Vigne Regali PIEMONTE
Via Vittorio Veneto 22, 15019 Strevi (AL)
Tel.: 0144363485/Fax: 0144363777
DOC(G)s: Asti; Brachetto d'Acqui; Dolcetto d'Acqui; Gavi
The Piedmont arm of Banfi, which makes fun and fizzy wines such as the unusual red sparkler Brachetto d'Acqui and classic Asti Spumante. The best-known wine here is the superclean, steely Gavi "Principessa Gavi."

Villa Aba FRIULI–VENEZIA GIULIA

Banear, Via Cocul 2, 33010 Treppo Grande (UD)
Tel.: 0432961016
DOC(G)s: Grave del Friuli

Consistent and extremely affordable varietal whites are the specialty: the pinot grigio, tocai, and other whites all have substance and precise aromas at a true bargain price. Great by-the-case wines that will class up a picnic.

Villa Cafaggio TOSCANA

Via S. Martino in Cecione 5, 50020 Panzano in Chianti (FI)
Tel.: 055852949/Fax: 0558549096
DOC(G)s: Chianti Classico

Great-value Chiantis are the trademark of this large Panzano estate, which packs a lot of smoky fruit flavor into all of its wines, whether they are *riservas* or not. A basic *annata* Villa Cafaggio Chianti Classico is an excellent choice for a picnic or a pasta dinner, while the *riserva* "Solatio Basilica" is a more serious and structured bottling. The "Cortaccio" cabernet has gotten its share of high marks, as has the varietal sangiovese "San Martino." You really can't go wrong here.

Villa Chiopris

See Livón.

Villa Forano MARCHE

Contrada Forano 40, 62010 Appignano (MC)
Tel.: 073357102
DOC(G)s: Rosso Piceno

Silky montepulciano at a by-the-case price. Look for the soft and fleshy "Bulciano" in particular.

Villa Giada PIEMONTE

Regione Ceirole 4, 14053 Canelli (AT)
Tel.: 0141831100
DOC(G)s: Barbera d'Asti

Juicy, tangy reds from the friendly barbera grape are the specialty here. The "Suri Russ" bottling is an appealing bargain, but you're better off with the more concentrated "Ajan" or "Vigneto La Quercia" selections.

Villa Girardi VENETO

Via Villa Girardi 1, 37029 San Pietro in Cariano (VR)
Tel./Fax: 0457701063/www.tommasiwine.it
DOC(G)s: Bianco di Custoza; Lugana; Valpolicella; Amarone della Valpolicella

Supercheap Veronese whites (from leased vineyards) are complemented by several old-school Amarones (meaning that they are long-aged in large oak casks for more moderated sweetness and a spicier, dried-fruit character). "Bure Alto" is a silky *ripasso*-style Valpolicella at a bargain price. Also worth checking out is the great-value Mastino Amarone, which is marketed as a stand-alone brand.

Villa La Selva TOSCANA

Località Montebenichi, 52021 Bucine (AR)
Tel.: 055998203

Situated at the southeastern edge of the Chianti Classico zone, Villa La Selva has two sleek "monovarietal" reds that remain within reach of the common man: "Felciaia," a sangiovese aged in barrique, is a consistently smooth and aromatic expression of the grape, while the "Selvamaggio" cabernet sauvignon offers even more extraction and aromatic intensity at a similarly low price. Also some good Vin Santo wines.

★ Villa Matilde CAMPANIA

Strada Statale Domitiana 18, 81030 Cellole (CE)
Tel.: 0823932088/Fax: 0823932134
www.fattoriavillamatilde.com
DOC(G)s: Falerno del Massico

Located on Campania's north coast, where the ancient Romans once cultivated vineyards, this winery produces some great reds from the aglianico grape. Its basic Falerno del Massico DOC Rosso is one example, spicy and rich and well priced, but the "Vigna Camarato" is the wine to track down. It's deep, dark, chocolaty aglianico, a powerful southern red that stands with Campania's best.

Villa Novare

See Bertani.

Villa Petriolo TOSCANA

Via di Petriolo 7, 50050 Cerreto Guidi (FI)
Tel.: 0571509491
DOC(G)s: Chianti; Vin Santo

A Florence-area estate with the plump sangiovese-merlot blend "Golpaja" and a gamy Chianti.

Villa Pillo TOSCANA

Via Volterrana 24, 50050 Gambassi Terme (FI)
Tel.: 0571680212/Fax: 0571680216/www.villapillo.com

An American-owned estate not far from San Gimignano, making varietal wines from international varieties. The style is fruit-driven. The most noteworthy wine is the syrah, though there's also a merlot, a cabernet sauvignon, and a blend called "Vivaldia."

Villa Raiano CAMPANIA

Via Pescatore 19, 83028 Serino (AV)
Tel.: 0825592826/Fax: 0825595781/www.villaraiano.it
DOC(G)s: Fiano di Avellino; Greco di Tufo; Taurasi

Founded in 1996, this relative newcomer to our market is a noteworthy one. It is among a number of new-generation estates (others include Caggiano and Molettieri) that are revitalizing the once-moribund Taurasi DOCG. The Villa Raiano Taurasi is made in a fruit-driven, more gently tannic style—it can be drunk on release, and yet it isn't so overextracted that it loses its smoky, spicy, tobacco-y aglianico character. Also notable is the clean and rather rich "Fiano di Avellino," which boasts terrific ripeness.

★ Villa Russiz FRIULI–VENEZIA GIULIA

Via Russiz 6, 34070 Capriva del Friuli (GO)
Tel.: 048180047/www.villarussiz.it
DOC(G)s: Collio

This estate produces some of the best white wines in Friuli, preferring a lean, firmly structured, assertively aromatic style. "Graf de la Tour" Sauvignon is one of the most intensely flavored sauvignon blancs you'll ever taste, and winemaker Gianni Menotti's tocai, riesling, ribolla, malvasia istriana, pinot grigio, and pinot bianco are all similarly assertive yet elegant. On the red side, Menotti has gained fame for his deep and structured "Graf de la Tour" Merlot, which drinks like a Bordeaux.

Villa Sant' Anna TOSCANA

Frazione Abadia, 53040 Abbadia di Montepulciano (SI)
Tel.: 0578708017/Fax: 0578707577/www.villasantanna.it
DOC(G)s: Chianti Colli Senesi; Vino Nobile di Montepulciano

Damn good Vino Nobile di Montepulciano for the money. Lots of black cherry fruit and good structure.

Villa Simone LAZIO

Via Frascati Colonna 29, 00040 Monteporzio Catone (RM)
Tel.: 069449717/Fax: 069448658/www.pierocostantini.it
DOC(G)s: Frascati

Piero Costantini's Frascati estate is one of the best (he also owns a beautiful *enoteca* in Rome). Check out the oily single-vineyard Frascati "Vigneto Filonardi" and the rich and tangy red "Ferro e Seta," a unique and pretty powerful blend of sangiovese and cesanese.

★ Villa Sparina PIEMONTE

Frazione Monterotondo 36, 15066 Gavi (AL)
Tel.: 0143633835/www.villasparina.it
DOC(G)s: Gavi di Gavi; Dolcetto d'Acqui; Barbera del Monferrato

A destination winery in Gavi. The flagship is the Gavi di Gavi "Monterotondo," a wine that incorporates some late-harvested cortese to lend it an almost tropical richness. The Gavi di Gavi "La Villa" is cleaner and more traditional but still has more depth than most of the Gavi you're likely to come across. On the red side, the proprietors, the Moccagatta family, enlist consultant Beppe Caviola to make inky-black dolcettos and barberas with loads of sappy black fruit flavors. These wines are fat, fun, and over the top, not unlike Stefano Moccagatta himself.

Villa Terlina PIEMONTE

Regione Dani 82, 14041 Agliano Terme (AT)
Tel./Fax: 0141964121/www.villaterlina.com
DOC(G)s: Barbera d'Asti

A barbera specialist near Asti (yes, another one) with two excellent selections: the restrained and brightly fragrant "Gradale" (a terrific, softly contoured value) and the richer "Monsicuro."

Villanova FRIULI–VENEZIA GIULIA

Via Contessa Beretta 29, 34070 Farra d'Isonzo (GO)
Tel.: 0481888013/Fax: 0481888593
DOC(G)s: Collio; Friuli Isonzo

A sleeper in the top rank of Friulian wineries. The whites from the "Monte Cucco" line (sauvignon, ribolla, chardonnay) are all bigger and bolder than the average Friulian varietal white, and the white blend "Menj" has great aromas and brisk acidity.

Vinicola Savese PUGLIA

Via Ippollita Prato 3, 74028 Sara (TA)
Tel./Fax: 0999721964/www.vinipichierri.com
DOC(G)s: Primitivo di Manduria

A Primitivo specialist. "Terrarossa" is superripe and cheap.

Virna

See Borgogno, Lodovico.

Vistorta FRIULI–VENEZIA GIULIA

Via Vistorta 82, 33077 Sacile (PN)

Tel.: 043471135

DOC(G)s: Friuli Grave

An estate focused almost exclusively on merlot. The Vistorta Friuli Grave Merlot is a classic Friulian red, a warm and savory wine that won't challenge the super-Tuscans but has its own spicy personality.

Viticcio TOSCANA

Via San Cresci 12/A, 50022 Greve in Chianti (FI)

Tel.: 055854210/www.fattoriaviticcio.com

DOC(G)s: Chianti Classico

Alessandro Landini's small estate above Greve is unabashedly modern, liberally blending cabernet and merlot into its Chianti Classico wines to give them a roundness and fruitiness not often found in the Greve area, which is known for smoky, more angular wines. In addition to rich, barrique-aged Chianti (check out the massive "Lucius"), Landini offers "Prunaio," an evocative varietal sangiovese, and "Monile," a superripe cabernet-based blend.

Viviani VENETO

Località Mazzano 8, 37024 Negrar (VR)

Tel./Fax: 0457500286

DOC(G)s: Valpolicella; Amarone della Valpolicella; Recioto della Valpolicella

Good, spicy Valpolicella and Amarone from high-altitude vineyards in Mazzano, toward the northern edge of Valpolicella Classico. The Amarones are well balanced and vinous, with nice aromatics.

Voerzio, Gianni PIEMONTE

Strada Loreto 1, 12064 La Morra (CN)

Tel./Fax: 0173509194

DOC(G)s: Barolo; Barbera d'Alba; Dolcetto d'Alba; Langhe; Roero Arneis

Gianni Voerzio and his brother, Roberto (see below), parted ways some years ago because Gianni prefers a more traditional approach to making Barolo. The Gianni Voerzio wines have the delicacy and bright perfume traditionally associated with the vineyards of La Morra.

VOERZIO, ROBERTO PIEMONTE

Località Cerreto 1, 12064 La Morra (CN)

Tel.: 0173509196

DOC(G)s: Barolo; Barbera d'Alba; Dolcetto d'Alba; Langhe

Roberto Voerzio heads the "modernist" camp in Piedmont. His densely extracted, barrique-aged Barolos are tightly allocated, expensive, and highly sought after. These powerful wines—the more rounded "La Serra," the fruit-driven "Brunate," and the brooding "Cerequio"—are considered some of the best Barolos made today. Similarly luxurious is the intense Barbera d'Alba "Vigneto Pozzo dell'Annunziata," bottled only in magnums from the cru in La Morra.

Volpe Pasini FRIULI–VENEZIA GIULIA

Via Cividale 16, 33040 Torreano (UD)
Tel.: 0432715151/www.volpepasini.net
DOC(G)s: Colli Orientali del Friuli

A prolific, high-tech winery with consultancy from Riccardo Cotarella. The broad range includes varietal whites with the designation "Zuc di Volpe," all of which are plumped up by barrel fermentation and aging. The creamy, almondy pinot bianco is a favorite.

Volpi PIEMONTE

Strada Statale 10, Km. 72, 15057 Tortona (AL)
Tel.: 0131861072/Fax: 0131815748/www.cantinevolpi.it
DOC(G)s: Barbera d'Asti; Gavi

More luscious, immediately pleasurable barbera from southeast Piedmont, most notably the extremely well-priced "Vobis Tua." Also worth checking out is the chunky (and also well-priced) "Su Su," a blend of barbera and cabernet. The crisp, citrusy Gavi "Vobis Mea" is solid and cheap as well.

WALCH, ELENA (CASTEL RINGBERG) ALTO ADIGE

Via A. Hofer 1, 39040 Termeno/Tramin (BZ)
Tel.: 0471860172
DOC(G)s: Alto Adige

Rich and exotically aromatic gewürztraminer is a specialty at Elena Walch's winery, although she does everything well. Check out any of the varietal whites from the "Kastelaz" or "Castel Ringberg" lines: cool, rich pinot grigio, oily and powerful pinot bianco—the list goes on, with all of the whites showing great varietal character in a firm, fine package. These wines demonstrate how a wine can be deeply flavorful without being oaky or heavy. There's also a delicious gewürztraminer *passito*.

Wandanna TOSCANA

Frazione San Salvatore, Via del Molinetto, 55015
Montecarlo (LU)
Tel.: 0583228989/Fax: 0583228226
DOC(G)s: Montecarlo
Some interesting reds from the Montecarlo DOC, though the top wine remains the IGT-designated "Virente," a rich and funky syrah.

Zaccagnini ABRUZZO

Contrada Pozzo, 65020 Bolognano (PE)
Tel.: 0858880195
DOC(G)s: Montepulciano d'Abruzzo; Trebbiano d'Abruzzo

Zaccagnini montepulcianos are rich and rustic reds (look for the "San Clemente" designation). There's also a chardonnay and a Trebbiano d'Abruzzo.

Zamò

See Le Vigne di Zamò.

Zardetto VENETO

Via Marcorà 15, 31015 Conegliano (TV)
Tel.: 0438208909/www.bibbly.it
DOC(G)s: Prosecco di Conegliano; Colli di Conegliano

A well-known name in prosecco, with fresh, fine sparklers at very reasonable prices.

Zemmer, Peter ALTO ADIGE

Strada Statale del Vino, Km. 24, 39040 Cortina/Kurtinig (BZ)

Tel.: 0471817143/Fax: 0741817743/www.zemmer.com

DOC(G)s: Alto Adige

A solid and attractively priced lineup of crisp, aromatic Alto Adige varietal wines, including standards such as pinot bianco, pinot grigio, lagrein, and pinot nero.

ZENATO VENETO

Via San Benedetto 8, 37019 Peschiera del Garda (VR)

Tel.: 0457550369/Fax: 0456400449/www.zenato.it

DOC(G)s: Valpolicella; Soave; Lugana

Another of Verona's large wine houses, Zenato has an excellent reputation for quality and consistency across a broad range of different products: there's excellent white Lugana, as exemplified by the great-value "San Benedetto" bottling; tasty, tangy Valpolicella, as evidenced by the benchmark "Ripassa"; and fat, flavorful Amarone, especially the "Sergio Zenato Riserva." These are serious wines made on a large scale, easy to find and always reliable.

Zeni, F.lli VENETO

Via Costabella 9, 37011 Bardolino (VR)

Tel.: 0457210022/Fax: 0456212702/www.zeni.it

DOC(G)s: Bardolino; Bianco di Custoza; Valpolicella; Amarone della Valpolicella; Soave

Everything from this large firm is consistent and well made; standouts include the bright, berried "Vigne Alte" Valpolicella Classico and the Amarone. In general, look for wines with the "Vigne Alte" for a step up from the norm. Bargain prices.

Zeni, Roberto TRENTINO

Via Stretta 2, 38010 Grumo San Michele all'Adige (TN)

Tel.: 0461650456/Fax: 0461650748/www.zeni.tn.it

DOC(G)s: Trentino

A Trentino winery notable for making interesting wines from the region's unusual native grapes: a flinty nosiola, a plump and peachy müller thurgau; a black currant–scented Teroldego Rotaliano, and a rosy, berried sweet wine from moscato rosa.

Zidarich FRIULI–VENEZIA GIULIA

Località Prepotto-Prapro 23, 34011 Duino Aurisina (TS)

Tel./Fax: 040201223/www.zidarich.it

DOC(G)s: Carso

Unique Friulian varietals at a somewhat lofty price. A minerally and aromatic vitovska is reminiscent of Austrian grüner; "Prulke" is a plumper, more intense blend; and a red from the Carso's high-acid terrano grape will take the enamel off your teeth without food to tame it.

Zonin VENETO

Via Borgolecco 9, 36053 Gambellara (VI)

Tel.: 0444640111/Fax: 0444640204/www.zonin.it

DOC(G)s: Gambellara; Valpolicella; Amarone della Valpolicella; Friuli Aquilea

Zonin is a many-tentacled operation, with holdings in Piedmont (Castello del Poggio), Tuscany (Castello d'Albola), Friuli (Ca' Bolani), Lombardia (Tenuta Il Bosco), and Sicily (Feudo Principi di Butera). In the Veneto, Zonin makes various DOC wines, most of them decent if not especially memorable. There's also a supercheap line of varietal wines for supermarkets.

★ RISING STAR ⓐ VALUE 🍾 AVAILABILITY € PRICING

CELLAR SELECTIONS: GREAT ITALIAN WINES FOR ANY OCCASION

HERE, WE OFFER almost 250 Italian wine recommendations for any occasion, budget, or taste. Although vintage variations are likely, we've selected these wines based on their proven quality and consistency from year to year. Selections were also based, as much as possible, on availability. Regions of origin and grape varieties (where appropriate) are included in parentheses.

CHAMPAGNE-METHOD SPARKLERS
- Franciacorta "Gran Cuvée Brut," Bellavista (Lombardia)
- Franciacorta Brut, Ca' del Bosco (Lombardia)
- Franciacorta Brut "Collezione Rosé," Cavalleri (Lombardia)
- Trento Brut "Giulio Ferrari." Ferrari (Trentino)
- "Valentino Brut Zero," Rocche dei Manzoni (Piemonte)

PROSECCO & OTHER BUBBLY
- Asti, F.lli Bera (Piemonte)
- Prosecco Brut "Rustico," Nino Franco and Figli (Veneto)
- Prosecco di Valdobbiadene "Crede," Desiderio Bisol (Veneto)
- Prosecco di Valdobbiadene Extra Dry "Gold Label," Ruggeri (Veneto)
- Prosecco "Sergio," Mionetto (Veneto)

TEN GREAT INDIGENOUS WHITES
- Fiano di Avellino "Terre di Dora," Terredora (Campania; Fiano grape)
- Gavi di Gavi "Etichetta Gialla," Villa Sparina (Piemonte; Cortese)
- Golfo del Tigullio Pigato, Enoteca Bisson (Liguria; Pigato)
- Orvieto Classico "Terre Vineate," Palazzone (Umbria; blend)
- Roero Arneis, Bruno Giacosa (Piemonte; Arneis)
- Taburno Falanghina, Cantina del Taburno (Campania; Falanghina)
- Trebbiano d'Abruzzo Riserva "Bacco," Bruno Nicodemi (Abruzzo; Trebbiano)
- Verdicchio dei Castelli di Jesi "Villa Bucci," Bucci (Marche; Verdicchio)
- Vermentino di Sardegna "Cala Silente," Cantina Sociale di Santadi (Sardegna; Vermentino)

- Vernaccia di San Gimignano "Vigna ai Sassi," Le Calcinaie (Toscana; Vernaccia)

FRIULI'S FAVORITE SON: TOCAI
- Colli Orientali del Friuli Tocai Friulano "Vigne Cinquant'Anni," Le Vigne di Zamò
- Colli Orientali del Friuli Tocai Friulano, Livio Felluga
- Collio Tocai Friulano, Villa Russiz
- Collio Tocai Friulano, Schiopetto
- Friuli Isonzo Tocai Friulano, Ronco del Gelso

FRIULIAN "SUPER-WHITE" BLENDS
- "Bianco della Castellada," La Castellada (Tocai–Pinot Grigio–Chardonnay–Sauvignon)
- "Flor di Uis," Vie di Romans (Chardonnay-Malvasia-Riesling)
- "Sacrisassi Bianco," Le Due Terre (Ribolla Gialla–Tocai–Sauvignon)
- "Vespa Bianco," Bastianich (Chardonnay-Sauvignon-Picolit)
- "Vintage Tunina," Jermann (Chardonnay-Sauvignon-Picolit)

ITALY TAKES ON THE WORLD,
PART I: CHARDONNAY
- Alto Adige Chardonnay "Cornell," Colterenzio (Alto Adige)
- Isonzo Chardonnay "Sant' Jurosa," Lis Neris (Friuli–Venezia Giulia)
- Isonzo Chardonnay "Vie di Romans," Vie di Romans (Friuli–Venezia Giulia)
- Piemonte Chardonnay "Monteriolo," Coppo (Piemonte)
- Sicilia Chardonnay, Planeta (Sicilia)

MORE "INTERNATIONAL" WHITES
- "Almabruna," I Campetti (Toscana; Viognier)
- Alto Adige Pinot Bianco "Kastelaz," Elena Walch (Alto Adige; Pinot Blanc)
- Alto Adige Gewürztraminer "Sanct Valentin," San Michele-Appiano (Alto Adige)
- Collio Sauvignon "Ronco delle Mele," Venica (Friuli–Venezia Giulia)
- Trentino Müller Thurgau "Vigna Palai," Pojer & Sandri (Trentino)

TEN GREAT WHITES YOU'VE NEVER HEARD OF
- Albana di Romagna, Tre Monti (Emilia-Romagna; Albana grape)
- Carso Vitovska, Edi Kante (Friuli–Venezia Giulia; Vitovska)
- Collio Ribolla Gialla, La Castellada (Friuli–Venezia Giulia; Ribolla Gialla)
- Erbaluce di Caluso, Luigi Ferrando (Piemonte; Erbaluce)

- Grechetto "Poggio della Costa," Sergio Mottura (Lazio; Grechetto)
- Moscato Giallo, Manincor (Alto Adige; Moscato Giallo)
- Nuragus di Cagliari "Sélegas," Argiolas (Sardegna; Nuragus)
- Pallagrello Bianco, Vestini-Campagnano (Campania; Pallagrello Bianco)
- Trentino Nosiola, Cesconi (Trentino; Nosiola)
- Valle d'Aosta Petite Arvine, Les Crêtes (Valle d'Aosta; Petite Arvine)

CULT WHITES
- "Batàr," Querciabella (Toscana; Chardonnay–Pinot Bianco)
- Colli Orientali del Friuli Tocai Friulano, Miani (Friuli–Venezia Giulia; Tocai)
- Collio Bianco "Breg," Gravner (Friuli–Venezia Giulia; blend)
- Langhe Chardonnay "Gaia & Rey," Gaja (Piemonte; Chardonnay)
- Trebbiano d'Abruzzo, Edoardo Valentini (Abruzzo; Trebbiano)

TWENTY GREAT WHITES UNDER $20
- Alto Adige Chardonnay, Lageder (Alto Adige)
- Alto Adige Pinot Bianco, Elena Walch (Alto Adige)
- Collio Pinot Grigio, Marco Felluga (Friuli–Venezia Giulia)
- Frascati Superiore, Villa Simone (Lazio)
- Gavi di Gavi "La Meirana," Broglia (Piemonte)
- Grave Tocai Friulano, Scarbolo (Friuli–Venezia Giulia)
- Langhe Bianco "Il Fiore," Braida (Piemonte; Chardonnay-Riesling)
- Lugana "San Benedetto," Zenato (Lombardia; Trebbiano)
- Orvieto Classico "Torricella," Bigi (Umbria; blend)
- Riviera Ligure di Ponente Pigato, A Maccia (Liguria)
- Roero Arneis "San Michele," Deltetto (Piemonte)
- Sicilia Bianco "Anthìlia," Donnafugata (Sicilia; Inzolia-Catarratto)
- Soave Classico Superiore, Leonildo Pieropan (Veneto; Garganega)
- Taburno Falanghina, Cantina del Taburno (Campania)
- Terre di Franciacorta "Curtefranca Bianco," Ca' del Bosco (Lombardia; Chardonnay–Pinot Bianco)
- Trentino Sauvignon di Faedo, Graziano Fontana (Trentino; Sauvignon)
- Verdicchio dei Castelli di Jesi "Casal di Serra," Umani Ronchi (Le Marche)
- Verdicchio di Matelica, Bisci (Le Marche)
- Vermentino di Gallura "Funtanaliras," Cantina Sociale del Vermentino (Sardegna)
- Vermentino "Costamolino," Argiolas (Sardegna)

RELIABLE ROSÉS
- Alto Adige Lagrein Rosato, Muri-Gries (Alto Adige)
- Montepulciano d'Abruzzo Cerasuolo, Cataldi Madonna (Abruzzo)
- Rosé di Regaleali, Regaleali (Sicilia)
- Salento Rosato, Rosa del Golfo (Puglia)
- Toscana Rosato, Castello di Ama (Toscana)

INDIGENOUS REDS I: SPICY SOUTHERNERS
- Aglianico del Vulture "Re Manfredi," Terre degli Svevi (Basilicata; Aglianico)
- Biferno Rosso "Ramitello," DiMajo Norante (Molise; Sangiovese-Aglianico)
- Cannonau di Sardegna "Lillovè," Giuseppe Gabbas (Sardegna; Cannonau)
- Castel del Monte Riserva "Il Falcone," Rivera (Puglia; Nero di Troia–Montepulciano)
- Cerasuolo di Vittoria, COS (Sicilia; Nero d'Avola–Frappato)
- Cirò Rosso Classico, Fattoria San Francesco (Calabria; Gaglioppo)
- Irpinia Aglianico "Il Principio," Terredora (Campania; Aglianico)
- Lacryma Christi del Vesuvio, De Angelis (Campania; Aglianico-Piedirosso)
- Primitivo di Manduria "Archidamo," Pervini (Puglia; Primitivo)
- Salice Salentino "Selvarossa," Cantine Due Palme (Puglia; Negroamaro–Malvasia Nera)

INDIGENOUS REDS II: NOBLE NORTHERNERS
- Alto Adige Lagrein "Porphyr," Cantina Terlano/Terlan (Alto Adige)
- Barbera d'Asti "Bricco dell'Uccellone," Braida (Piemonte)
- Colli Orientali del Friuli Refosco, Ronchi di Manzano (Friuli–Venezia Giulia)
- Colli Orientali del Friuli Schioppettino, Ronco del Gnemiz (Friuli–Venezia Giulia)
- "Coteau La Tour," Les Cretes (Valle d'Aosta; Syrah)
- Dolcetto di Dogliani "Sirì d'Jermu," Pecchenino (Piemonte)
- "Rosso Ca' del Merlo," Giuseppe Quintarelli (Veneto; blend)
- Teroldego Rotaliano, Roberto Zeni (Trentino)
- Valpolicella Superiore "TB," Tommaso Bussola (Veneto; blend)
- Valtellina Sfursat "Canua," Sertoli Salis (Lombardia; Nebbiolo)

TEN GREAT REDS YOU'VE NEVER HEARD OF
- Frappato, Valle dell'Acate (Sicilia; Frappato grape)
- Langhe Freisa, Cavallotto (Piemonte; Freisa)
- Negroamaro, La Corte (Puglia; Negroamaro)
- Nero di Troia "Bottaccia," Torre Quarto (Puglia; Nero di Troia)
- Nieddera, Attilio Contini (Sardegna; Nieddera)

- Oltrepò Pavese Bonarda, Castello di Luzzano (Lombardia/Emilia-Romagna; Croatina)
- Ruché di Castagnole Monferrato "Na'Vota," Cantine Sant'Agata (Piemonte; Ruché)
- Schioppettino, Ronco del Gnemiz (Friuli–Venezia Giulia; Schioppettino)
- Trentino Marzemino, Battistotti (Trentino; Marzemino)
- Rossese di Dolceacqua, Terre Bianche (Liguria; Rossese)

BAROLO and BARBARESCO BARGAINS
- Barbaresco "Ovello," Cantina del Pino
- Barbaresco "Rio Sordo," Walter Musso
- Barbaresco "Torre," Produttori del Barbaresco
- Barbaresco "Faset," La Spinona
- Barolo "Terlo Ravera," Marziano ed Enrico Abbona
- Barolo, Gianfranco Alessandria
- Barolo, Batasiolo
- Barolo "Cannubi," G. B. Burlotto
- Barolo "Ginestra Case Matè," Elio Grasso
- Barolo "Rocche," Aurelio Settimo

OTHER NOTEWORTHY NEBBIOLOS
- Carema di Carema "Selezione," Produttori Nebbiolo di Carema (Piemonte)
- Gattinara "San Francesco," Antoniolo (Piemonte)
- Ghemme, Cantalupo (Piemonte)
- Roero Rosso "Trinità," Malvirà (Piemonte)
- Valtellina Superiore Inferno "Mazér," Nino Negri (Lombardia)

THE CLASS OF CHIANTI
- Castell'in Villa Chianti Classico Riserva
- Castello di Brolio Chianti Classico
- Castello di Fonterutoli Chianti Classico
- Fattoria di Felsina "Vigneto Rancia" Chianti Classico Riserva
- Fontodi "Vigna del Sorbo" Chianti Classico Riserva
- Frescobaldi–Castello di Nipozzano Chianti Rúfina "Montesodi"
- La Massa "Giorgio Primo" Chianti Classico
- Querciabella Chianti Classico Riserva

ELITE BRUNELLOS
- Biondi-Santi (Tenuta Il Greppo)
- Caparzo "La Casa"
- Casanova di Neri "Cerretalto"
- Castello Banfi "Poggio all'Oro"
- Cerbaiona
- Col d'Orcia "Poggio al Vento"
- Gaja–Pieve di Santa Restituta "Sugarille"
- Lisini "Ugolaia"
- Mastrojanni
- Salvioni

VINO NOBILE OF NOTE

- Avignonesi
- Boscarelli "Vigna del Nocio"
- Poliziano "Asinone"
- Salcheto
- Valdipiatta "Vigna d'Alfiero"

TEN GREAT SUPER-TUSCANS UNDER $50

- "Avvoltore," Moris Farms (Sangiovese-Cabernet-Syrah)
- "Badiola," Castello di Fonterutoli (Sangiovese-Cabernet-Merlot)
- "Cabreo il Borgo," Tenute del Cabreo (Sangiovese-Cabernet)
- "Campaccio," Terrabianca (Sangiovese-Cabernet)
- "Cum Laude," Castello Banfi (Cabernet-Merlot-Sangiovese-Syrah)
- "Lucente," Luce della Vite (Sangiovese)
- "Promis," Ca' Marcanda (Merlot-Syrah-Sangiovese)
- "Roccato," Rocca delle Macie (Sangiovese-Cabernet)
- "Sassoalloro," Castello di Montepò–Biondi Santi (Sangiovese)
- "Terre di Galatrona," Petrolo (Merlot-Sangiovese)

AGLIANICO PRIMER: SOUTHERN ITALY'S NOBLE RED

- Aglianico del Vulture, D'Angelo (Basilicata)
- Aglianico del Taburno "Delius," Cantina del Taburno (Campania)
- "Naima," DeConciliis (Campania)
- Taurasi "Vigna Macchia dei Goti," Antonio Caggiano (Campania)
- Taurasi Riserva, DiMeo (Campania)

MONTEPULCIANO GREATS (THE GRAPE, NOT THE PLACE)

- Montepulciano d'Abruzzo "Ursonia," Il Feuduccio (Abruzzo)
- Montepulciano d'Abruzzo "Zanna," Illuminati (Abruzzo)
- Montepulciano d'Abruzzo, Edoardo Valentini (Abruzzo)
- Rosso Cònero "Sassi Neri," Fattoria Le Terrazze (Marche)
- Rosso Cònero "Adeodato," Monte Schiavo (Marche)

ITALY TAKES ON THE WORLD, PART II: MERLOT

- Collio Merlot "Graf de la Tour," Villa Russiz (Friuli–Venezia Giulia)
- "Vigneto L'Apparita," Castello di Ama (Toscana)
- "Masseto," Tenuta dell'Ornellaia (Toscana)
- "Montiano," Falesco (Lazio)
- "Galatrona," Petrolo (Toscana)

ITALY TAKES ON THE WORLD, PART III:
BORDEAUX BLENDS

- "Montsclapade," Dorigo (Friuli–Venezia Giulia)
- "Le Serre Nuove," Tenuta dell'Ornellaia (Toscana)
- "San Leonardo," Tenuta San Leonardo (Trentino)
- Terre di Franciacorta "Capineto," Tenuta Castellino (Lombardia)
- "Vigna del Vassallo," Colle Picchioni (Lazio)

MORE "INTERNATIONAL" REDS

- Alto Adige Pinot Nero "Sant' Urbano," Hofstätter (Alto Adige; Pinot Noir)
- "Campo alle More," Gini (Veneto; Pinot Noir)
- Collio Cabernet Franc, Russiz Superiore (Friuli–Venezia Giulia)
- Lazio Petit Verdot, Casale del Giglio (Lazio)
- Sicilia Rosso "Sole di Sesta," Cottanera (Sicilia; Syrah)
- Toscana Cabernet "Olmaia," Col d'Orcia (Toscana)

BUY AND HOLD: CLASSIC COLLECTOR REDS

- Barbaresco "Santo Stefano Riserva," Bruno Giacosa (Piemonte)
- Barolo "Gran Bussia," Aldo Conterno (Piemonte)
- Barolo "Monfortino," Giacomo Conterno (Piemonte)
- Barolo "Villero," Vietti (Piemonte)
- Bolgheri Sassicaia, Tenuta San Guido (Toscana)
- Bolgheri Rosso Superiore, Tenuta dell'Ornellaia (Toscana)
- Brunello di Montalcino, Case Bass Soldera (Toscana)
- "Cepparello," Isole e Olena (Toscana)
- Langhe Nebbiolo "Sorì San Lorenzo," Gaja (Piemonte)
- "Solaia," Antinori (Toscana)

NEW-GENERATION COLLECTOR REDS

- Amarone, Roccolo Grassi (Veneto; blend)
- Carignano del Sulcis "Terre Brune," Santadi (Sardegna; Carignano)
- Faro, Palari (Sicilia; blend)
- Marche Rosso "Camerte," La Monacesca (Marche; Sangiovese-Merlot)
- Montepulciano d'Abruzzo "Tonì," Cataldi Madonna (Abruzzo; Montepulciano)
- Sagrantino di Montefalco, Paolo Bea (Umbria; Sagrantino)
- Taurasi "Vigna Cinque Querce," Salvatore Molettieri (Campania; Aglianico)
- Teroldego Rotaliano "Granato," Foradori (Trentino; Teroldego)
- "Serpico," Feudi di San Gregorio (Campania; Aglianico)
- "Vigna Custera," Ceuso (Sicilia; Nero d'Avola–Cabernet–Merlot)

CULT REDS

- Amarone della Valpolicella "Monte Lodoletta," Romano Dal Forno (Veneto)
- Cabernet Franc "Alzero," Giuseppe Quintarelli (Veneto)
- Colli Orientali del Friuli Merlot, Miani (Friuli–Venezia Giulia; Merlot)
- "Montevetrano," Montevetrano (Campania; Aglianico-Cabernet-Merlot)
- "Redigaffi," Tua Rita (Toscana; Merlot)
- "Terra di Lavoro," Galardi (Campania; Aglianico-Piedirosso-Cabernet)

TWENTY GREAT REDS UNDER $20

- Barbera d'Alba "Tre Vigne," Vietti (Piemonte)
- Barco Reale di Carmignano, Capezzana (Toscana; Sangiovese-Cabernet-Canaiolo)
- "Brusco dei Barbi," Fattoria dei Barbi (Toscana)
- Cannonau di Sardegna "Firmadu," Soletta (Sardegna)
- Chianti, Giacomo Mori (Toscana)
- Chianti Classico, Viticcio (Toscana)
- Chianti Rúfina, Selvapiana (Toscana)
- Cirò Rosso "Duca San Felice," Librandi (Calabria)
- Falerno del Massico, Villa Matilde (Campania)
- Langhe Nebbiolo, Produttori del Barbaresco (Piemonte)
- Montepulciano d'Abruzzo, Masciarelli (Abruzzo)
- Morellino di Scansano, Fattoria Le Pupille (Toscana)
- Nero d'Avola, Morgante (Sicilia)
- "Palazzo della Torre," Allegrini (Veneto)
- Primitivo, A-Mano (Puglia)
- Rosso Cònero, Lanari (Marche)
- "Rubesco," Lungarotti (Umbria)
- Sangiovese di Romagna "Le More," Castelluccio (Emilia-Romagna)
- Valpolicella Classico, Brigaldara (Veneto)
- "Vitiano," Falesco (Umbria)

"VINI DA MEDITAZIONE": AFTER-DINNER NECTARS

- Colli Orientali del Friuli Picolit "Monasterium," Filiputti (Friuli–Venezia Giulia)
- Loazzolo "Piasa Rischei," Forteto della Luja (Piemonte)
- Malvasia delle Lipari Passito, Carlo Hauner (Sicilia)
- Moscato d'Asti "Nìvole," Michele Chiarlo (Piemonte)
- Moscato d'Asti "Clarté," Elio Perrone (Piemonte)
- "Muffato della Sala," Castello della Sala (Umbria)
- Passito di Pantelleria "Bukkuram," Marco DeBartoli (Sicilia)
- Trentino Moscato Rosa, Zeni (Trentino)
- Vin Santo, Avignonesi (Toscana)
- Vin Santo, Isole e Olena (Toscana)

VINTAGES

THIS IS AN ANNOTATED guide to vintage quality in production zones with established track records for age-worthy reds. Although selected producers in Friuli–Venezia Giulia, Alto Adige, and elsewhere are creating whites with aging potential, no critical mass of such wines yet exists to merit the inclusion of a chart for any one white-wine zone.

Some of the analyses below go back further than others, since reliable information isn't always available for older vintages in certain zones. Unless otherwise indicated, good wines from vintages older than those listed here would be difficult to find, and not necessarily worth the search. Notes on specific vintages are included selectively.

WHAT THE STARS MEAN:
* = poor
** = fair
*** = good
**** = excellent
***** = exceptional

BARBARESCO AND BAROLO

There are certainly some treats to be found from the years preceding 1970, with '58, '61, '64, and '67 topping the list. The assessments below are culled from a variety of sources. Since these zones are so close to each other and their methods of wine production so similar, overall ratings of vintages are the same.

1970: ****
1971: ***** (Vintage of the decade)
1972: (No wine produced)
1973: **
1974: **** (Well structured)
1975: ***
1976: **
1977: *
1978: **** (Powerful; great agers)
1979: **** (Good, but not as concentrated as '78)
1980: ***
1981: **
1982: **** (Very rich, long-lived)
1983: ***
1984: **
1985: ***** (Vintage of the decade; complete wines)
1986: ****

1987: ***
1988: ***** (Superripe, generous wines)
1989: ***** (Rivals '85 in overall structure and power)
1990: ***** (Depth, ripeness, more immediate than '89)
1991: ***
1992: **
1993: *** (Delicate wines, but many surprises)
1994: **
1995: **** (Tannic, more elegant styles)
1996: ***** (The wine drinker's year; maybe the most complete wines of the '90s)
1997: ***** (The critics' year; showy, luxurious wines)
1998: **** (A sleeper; some say 5-star)
1999: **** (Not as hyped as '97 or even '98, but just as good)
2000: ***** (Huge critical acclaim)
2001: ***** (Highly anticipated powerhouse wines)
2002: * (Hail destroyed much of Barolo; spotty production)
2003: **** (Big, potent; short crop due to drought)

MONTALCINO (BRUNELLO DI MONTALCINO)

The producers' association known as the Consorzio del Vino Brunello di Montalcino has a long track record of cataloging vintage quality and is probably most closely identified with the "star" system of rating vintages.

1970: ***** (One of the best of the decade)
1971: ***
1972: (No wine produced)
1973: ***
1974: **
1975: *****
1976: *
1977: ****
1978: **** (Perhaps best of '77–'80)
1979: ****
1980: ****
1981: ***
1982: ****
1983: ****
1984: *
1985: ***** (Vintage of the decade)
1986: ***
1987: ***
1988: *****
1989: **
1990: ***** (Spectacular depth, balance, long life)
1991: ***
1992: **
1993: **** (A sleeper, as in Barolo)
1994: ***
1995: ***** (More angular than '97 but powerful wines)

1996: ***
1997: ***** (Vintage of the decade along with '90)
1998: **** (More drinkable now than '97s)
1999: **** (May come to rival '97)
2000: ***
2001: ****
2002: ** (Difficult weather conditions; spotty production)
2003: *** (Not spectacular; drought-shortened crop)

CHIANTI CLASSICO

Older vintages of Chianti Classico Riserva can be glorious, but in general it isn't worth going too far back. Changes to the Chianti Classico DOCG in 1984 and 1996, however, radically transformed the zone and its wines. Chianti Classico is increasingly ageworthy. Look for vintages such as '97, '99, and '00 to show beautifully in ten, even twenty years' time.

1984: *
1985: ***** (Great vintage throughout Italy)
1986: ****
1987: ***
1988: ****
1989: **
1990: *****
1991: **
1992: *
1993: ***
1994: **
1995: **** (Some say 5-star)
1996: *** (Not as bad as advertised)
1997: ***** (Vintage of the decade)
1998: **** (Also superb)
1999: ***** (Rivals '97)
2000: **** (Right on the heels of '97 and '99)
2001: ****
2002: **
2003: ***

BOLGHERI

Wines such as the great Sassicaia (first commercial vintage: 1968) go much deeper, but here we track vintages since the creation of the Bolgheri DOC in 1984.

1984: **
1985: ***** (All-time greatest Sassicaia so far)
1986: ***
1987: ***
1988: ****
1989: ****
1990: ***** (Benchmark vintage)
1991: ***
1992: *

1993: **
1994: ***
1995: ****
1996: ***
1997: ***** (Superpowerful, tops in decade)
1998: **** (More forward and accessible than '97)
1999: ***** (Rivals '97)
2000: ***** (Rivals '97)
2001: ****
2002: **
2003: ***

VALPOLICELLA
(AMARONE DELLA VALPOLICELLA)

The Bolla family introduced Amarone to the world wine stage in the 1950s. There are some notable years from before 1970, most notably '64, '67, and '68, and there's actually wine to be found from these years that's worth buying.

1970: ***
1971: **** (A great all-around year for Italy)
1972: *
1973: **
1974: ****
1975: ***
1976: ***** (Benchmark vintage)
1977: ***
1978: ***
1979: ****
1980: ***
1981: ***
1982: **
1983: ***** (Perhaps the best of the '80s)
1984: **
1985: ****
1986: ***
1987: **
1988: ***** (Rivals '83)
1989: **
1990: ***** (Huge, long-lived wines: one of Italy's historic years)
1991: ***
1992: **
1993: ***
1994: **
1995: ***** (Might outlast '97)
1996: **
1997: ***** (Powerhouse)
1998: **** (Very solid, silky wines)
1999: ***
2000: ***
2001: **** (A highlight of recent years)
2002: ** (Very difficult weather)

2003: ***** (Short but concentrated crop due to drought;
        early drinking)

TAURASI

Nicknamed "the Barolo of the south," this zone in central Campania boasts a growing number of serious producers. The aglianico grape certainly has the structure for aging, although older vintages of Taurasi are difficult to find.

1985: ***** (Vintage of the decade)
1986: ***
1987: ****
1988: *****
1989: ***
1990: ****
1991: ***
1992: ***
1993: ****
1994: ****
1995: ***
1996: ***
1997: ***** (Barolo-like intensity)
1998: ****
1999: ****
2000: ****
2001: ***
2002: *
2003: ***

MONTEFALCO SAGRANTINO

An emerging category of ageworthy reds from Umbria, crafted from the rare sagrantino grape.

1990: ****
1991: ***
1992: ***
1993: ****
1994: ***
1995: *****
1996: **
1997: *****
1998: ****
1999: **** ('97–'99: Powerful, superb wines like the
        Brunellos and Chiantis of the same years)
2000: ****
2001: ****
2002: **
2003: ***

Appendix II:
GRAPE VARIETIES

ITALIAN VINEYARDS are impossibly diverse. Italy's Ministry of Agriculture has authorized more than 350 grapes for planting and selling as wine, but there are easily hundreds more in regular use. This is an accounting of authorized grapes, as well as some others you might encounter in the market. Included is information about grape type (*w* or *r*); the main region(s) in which the variety is grown; and a description of the variety where appropriate. All grape names are capitalized.

Abbuoto (r)
Lazio.

Aglianico (r)
Campania, Basilicata, and other southern regions. A dark, thick-skinned variety that makes potent, tannic wines with a tobacco edge on finish. Best examples: Taurasi, Aglianico del Taburno (Campania), Aglianico del Vulture (Basilicata).

Albana (r)
Emilia-Romagna. Makes light dry whites and rich, apricot-scented *passito* wines.

Albarola (w)
Liguria. Makes light whites in the Cinque Terre DOC.

Aleatico (r)
Throughout Italy. An unusual red variety that may be a mutation of moscato; it makes sweet, perfumed reds.

Alicante (r)
Sardegna and Toscana. Synonym for Garnacha, or Grenache.

Alicante Bouschet (r)
Various regions. A French cross of Grenache and Petit Bouschet.

Ancellotta (r)
Emilia-Romagna. A deep red variety used in blends with Lambrusco.

Ansonica (w)
Sicilia and Toscana. Synonym for Inzolia. Makes clean, light whites.

Arneis (w)
Piemonte. A floral, smoky white variety native to Roero. Great acid and aroma.

Asprinio Bianco (w)
Campania. A ight white variety used near Naples.

Barbarossa (r)
Emilia-Romagna. A rare native red variety of Romagna.

Barbera (r)
Piemonte, Lombardia, and Emilia-Romagna. A vigorous native of Piedmont known for soft tannins, bright acid, and

rich fruit, it is the second most widely planted red variety in Italy after Sangiovese.

Barbera Bianca (w)
Piemonte, Lombardia, and Emilia-Romagna. A rare white version of Barbera.

Barbera Sarda (r)
Sardegna.

Bellone (w)
Lazio. A blending variety in several Lazio DOC whites.

Biancame (w)
Marche, Umbria, and Abruzzo. Possibly related to Trebbiano. Also known as Passerina and Bianchello.

Bianchetta Genovese (w)
Liguria. An herbal, tangy variety used in Golfo del Tigullio DOC blends.

Bianchetta Trevigiana (w)
Trentino–Alto Adige.

Bianco d'Alessano (w)
Puglia. Used in DOC blends such as Gravina, Locorotondo, and Martina Franca.

Biancolella (w)
Campania.

Blanc de Morgex (w)
Valle d'Aosta. An intensely acidic white variety grown at high altitudes in Valle d'Aosta.

Bombino Bianco (w)
Puglia and Emilia-Romagna. A light white variety, also known as Pagadebit (Romagna) and Campolese (Abruzzo).

Bombino Nero (r)
Puglia.

Bonarda (r)
Piemonte, Lombardia, and Emilia-Romagna. Synonym for the spicy black Croatina used in the Oltrepò Pavese (Lombardia) and Colli Piacentini (Emilia-Romagna). "Bonarda Novarese" in northern Piedmont is actually Uva Rara. The real Bonarda, Bonarda Piemontese, is very rare.

Bosco (w)
Liguria. An herbal, minerally white variety from the Cinque Terre DOC.

Bovale (r)
Sardegna. A deep red variety, of possible Spanish origin, that may be related to Mourvèdre.

Bovale Grande (r)
Sardegna. Synonym for Nieddera. Used for blending.

Brachetto (r)
Piemonte. An exotically aromatic red variety used to make mostly sweet wines, both still and sparkling.

Cabernet Franc (r)
Throughout Italy. An especially prominent variety in Veneto and Friuli, where it makes reds with a peppery, vegetal character.

Cabernet Sauvignon (r)

Throughout Italy. This cassis-scented "French" grape has been in Italy for centuries. Many vintners, especially in the north and northeast, replanted with cabernet and other international grapes after the phylloxera bug ravaged Italian grapevines, often abandoning native varieties to do so.

Cagnina Nera (r)

Emilia-Romagna. Synonym for Refosco.

Calabrese (r)

Sicilia. Synonym for Nero d'Avola.

Canaiolo Bianco (w)

Toscana. A blending white variety, called Drupeggio in Umbria.

Canaiolo Nero (r)

Toscana. A spicy, dark-colored red variety used in some Chianti blends.

Cannonao/Cannonau (r)

Sardegna. Sardinian name for Grenache. Makes plush, smoky reds with red berry flavors.

Carignano (r)

Sardegna. This southern French import makes plump, inky reds.

Carmenère (r)

Northern Italy. Found throughout Veneto and Friuli, where it is often confused with Cabernet Franc. It lends a savory, herbaceous character to a variety of DOC reds.

Carricante (w)

Sicilia. A light, flinty white variety used in the Etna DOC.

Casetta (r)

Veneto. A dark, thick-skinned red variety with marasco cherry notes.

Catarratto Bianco Comune (w)

Sicilia. The most-planted white variety in Italy. It is traditionally used in Marsala but also makes juicy dry whites.

Catarratto Bianco Lucido (w)

Sicilia. Of higher quality than the Comune variety, it is somewhat reminiscent of Viognier.

Cesanese Comune (r)

Lazio. One of several subvarieties used in spicy reds. The larger-berried version is comune.

Cesanese d'Affile (r)

Lazio. This native grape of Lazio is used to make tart, aromatic reds.

Chardonnay (w)

Throughout Italy. Most likely introduced to Italy at the turn of the last century, after a phylloxera infestation. Hugely popular.

Chiavennasca (r)

Lombardia. The name for Nebbiolo in Lombardia's Valtellina.

Ciliegiolo (r)

Toscana. A bright, cherry-scented red variety also grown in Liguria and elsewhere.

Clairette (w)
Sardegna and Toscana. Thought to be native to southeastern France, it is used in blends.

Cococciola (w)
Abruzzo.

Coda di Volpe Bianca (w)
Campania. Given the name "tail of the fox" by the Roman scholar Pliny because of the shape of its grape clusters. Chalky and floral.

Colorino (r)
Toscana. Traditionally used as a blending ingredient in Chianti.

Cornallin (r)
Valle d'Aosta.

Cortese (w)
Piemonte. The base of Gavi DOC whites. Makes flinty, herbal wines.

Corvina (r)
Veneto. This dark and spicy variety is the main red in the Valpolicella DOC blend.

Corvinone (r)
Veneto. Thought to be a subvariety of Corvina, this larger-berried version produces more extract.

Croatina (r)
Emilia-Romagna and Lombardia. A dark, plummy, peppery variety of the Oltrepò Pavese and Colli Piacentini, where it is called Bonarda.

Damaschino (also Damaskino) (w)
Sicilia.

Dolcetto (r)
Piemonte and Liguria. A deeply colored, violet-scented variety that produces well-rounded reds with black fruit flavors. Called Ormeasco in Liguria.

Durella (r)
Veneto and Toscana.

Erbaluce (w)
Piemonte. A high-acid variety grown in northern Piedmont, it makes crisp dry whites and minerally sparklers.

Falanghina (w)
Campania. Thought to have been brought to Italy by the ancient Greeks, this variety makes bright, aromatic whites with chalky notes.

Favorita (w)
Piemonte. A blending grape in Piedmont that may be related to Vermentino.

Fiano (w)
Campania. This honeyed, smoky, and fruity variety is probably the most interesting white in Campania.

Forastera (w)
Campania. A specialty of Ischia.

Fortana (r)
Emilia-Romagna.

Franconia (r)
Friuli–Venezia Giulia.

Frappato (r)
Sicilia. A light, brightly aromatic red variety of southeastern Sicily that is used in Cerasuolo di Vittoria.

Freisa (r)
Piemonte. A light, high-acid variety with an exotic fragrance; it is made mostly into fizzy reds.

Fumin (r)
Valle d'Aosta. A dark and plush, Gamay-like variety with soft tannins.

Gaglioppo (r)
Calabria. A softly tannic, lightly colored red variety used in the Cirò Rosso DOC.

Gamay (r)
Veneto, Tuscany, and Umbria. A plump and purple variety.

Garganega (w)
Veneto. The base of Soave DOC wines.

Girò (r)
Sardegna. Used in rare, Port-style reds made near Cagliari.

Grecanico Dorato (w)
Sicilia. An appley white variety possibly related to Greco.

Grechetto (w)
Umbria, Toscana, and Lazio. Possibly related to Greco, this variety is considered native to Umbria, where it is used in many top whites.

Grechetto Rosso (r)
Umbria, Toscana, and Lazio.

Greco (w)
Campania. An ancient vine that may be the progenitor of Grechetto, Grecanico, and Garganega, as well as Trebbiano. Best known as Greco di Tufo.

Greco Bianco (w)
Calabria. A rare subvariety used in sweet wines.

Greco Nero (r)
Calabria. A dark version of Greco.

Grignolino (r)
Piemonte. A native of Monferrato, it makes light, tangy Beaujolais-style reds.

Grillo (w)
Sicilia. A plump white variety of western Sicily that is used in the Alcamo and Marsala DOCs.

Groppello di Mocasina (r)
Lombardia. Used in the Lake Garda area.

Groppello di San Stefano (r)
Lombardia.

Groppello Gentile (r)
Lombardia. Groppello gives good fruity extract and has bitter chocolate notes.

Guarnaccia (r)
Campania. A subvariety of Grenache found on Ischia. There is also a white version called Guarnaccia Bianca.

Impigno (w)
Puglia. The base of Ostuni DOC whites.

Incrocio Bruni 54 (w)
Marche. *Incrocio* means "cross," in this case of Verdicchio and Sauvignon.

Incrocio Manzoni 2.15 (r)
Veneto and Friuli–Venezia Giulia. A cross of Prosecco and Cabernet Sauvignon.

Incrocio Manzoni 6.0.13 (w)
Veneto and Friuli–Venezia Giulia. A cross of Riesling and Pinot Bianco, it is the most widely planted of Incrocio grapes.

Incrocio Terzi No. 1 (r)
Lombardia. A cross of Barbera and Cabernet Franc.

Kerner (w)
Alto Adige. A cross of Schiava and Riesling.

Lacrima (r)
Marche and Calabria. In Marche, Lacrima is a Gamay-like grape whose skins burst easily and send "tears" (*lacrime*) of juice running down. In Calabria, Lacrima is a synonym for Gaglioppo.

Lagrein (r)
Trentino–Alto Adige. A dark, plump, and oddly flavored (wintry spices, dark chocolate) red variety native to Bolzano.

Lambrusco (r)
Emilia-Romagna, Lombardia, and Trentino. Believed to be a native wild vine *(vitis silvestris),* it has many subvarieties and is typically vinified in a tangy, high-acid *frizzante* style.

Lumassina (w)
Liguria.

Maceratino (w)
Marche. Possibly related to Greco, this variety is used in the Colli Maceratesi DOC.

Magliocco Canino (r)
Calabria. An ancient red variety native to Calabria.

Malbech/Malbec (r)
Throughout Italy. A dark, tannic Bordeaux variety used to beef up blends.

Malvasia (w)
Throughout Italy. Most of the Malvasia family is characterized by an orange-blossom aroma and crisp acidity. Of possible Greek origin, it is one of the most widely planted grapes.

Malvasia Bianca (w)
Lazio, Umbria, and Toscana. Especially popular for Vin Santo.

Malvasia Bianca di Basilicata (w)
Basilicata.

Malvasia Bianca di Candia (w)
Lazio. Makes aromatic dry whites from a variety of DOCs. Often blended with Trebbiano.

Malvasia del Lazio (w)
Lazio. Considered of lesser quality than Candia.

Malvasia di Casorzo (w)
Piemonte.

Malvasia di Lipari (w)
Sicilia. Produces an apricot-scented nectar in the volcanic soils of Lipari.

Malvasia di Sardegna (w)
Sardegna. Used in sweet, apricot-scented whites.

Malvasia di Schierano (w)
Piemonte.

Malvasia Istriana (w)
Friuli–Venezia Giulia. A distinctive subvariety that produces dry whites with hints of white flowers, citrus, and peach.

Malvasia Nera di Basilicata (r)
Basilicata. A dark, tannic red variety for blending.

Malvasia Nera di Brindisi (r)
Puglia. The sweet black fruit offsets the bitter chocolate flavors of Negroamaro in blends such as Salice Salentino.

Malvasia Nera di Lecce (r)
Puglia. A subvariety also used in blends with Negroamaro.

Malvasia Rosa (r)
Trentino–Alto Adige.

Mammolo (r)
Toscana. A violet-scented red variety used as a blending grape in Chianti and Montepulciano.

Marsigliana Nera (r)
Calabria.

Marzemino (r)
Trentino–Alto Adige. A dark, brightly fruity variety that is vinified in both dry and sweet styles.

Merlot (r)
Throughout Italy. Today it is the third most widely planted red grape in Italy behind Sangiovese and Barbera.

Molinara (r)
Veneto. Tart and tannic, it is traditionally the third grape in the Valpolicella DOC blend.

Monica (r)
Sardegna. A light, bright, fragrant red variety of Spanish origin that is widely planted in southern Sardinia.

Montepulciano (r)
Abruzzo and Marche. One of the most widely planted red grapes in Italy, it has a deep, purplish color and soft tannic contours. It is at its deep and fruity best in the Montepulciano d'Abruzzo and Rosso Cònero DOCs.

Montonico Bianco (w)
Calabria. Also known as Mantonico. Used in sweet nectars.

Montù (r)
Emilia-Romagna. Also known as Montuni. Found on the Po plain.

Moscadello (W)
Toscana. A subvariety of Moscato found in Montalcino and used in sweet whites.

Moscatello (W)
Throughout Italy. Large-berried version of Moscato; also known as Muscatel.

Moscato Bianco (W)
Throughout Italy, especially in Piemonte. The most widely planted and best-regarded grape of the Moscato family, which includes dozens of distinct varieties. Synonyms for Moscato Bianco include Moscato Canelli.

Moscato di Scanzo (W)
Lombardia.

Moscato Giallo (W)
Trentino–Alto Adige. Called Goldmuskateller in German, it makes unique dry wines with crisp acidity.

Moscato Nero di Acqui (r)
Piemonte.

Moscato Rosa (r)
Trentino–Alto Adige. A red subvariety of Moscato that produces rose-colored, semisweet wines.

Mostosa (W)
Lazio. A light white variety used in blends. It is also found in Adriatic regions.

Müller-Thurgau (W)
Throughout Italy, especially in Trentino. Though traditionally thought of as a cross between Riesling and Sylvaner, more recent research shows that it may be a subvariety of Riesling.

Nasco (W)
Sardegna. A light white variety of Cagliari.

Nebbiolo (r)
Piemonte, Lombardia, and Valle d'Aosta. Italy's most noble red grape, considered native to Piedmont. Late-ripening and fragile, it produces Italy's most uniquely perfumed (tar, roses, dried cherries) and powerful reds. Called Chiavennasca in Valtellina, Spanna in northern Piedmont, and Picotendro in Valle d'Aosta.

Negrara (r)
Veneto. Garda-area red variety.

Negretto (r)
Italian name for the Négrette grape of southwest France.

Negroamaro (r)
Puglia. One of the most widely planted reds in Italy, it is the base for Salice Salentino and other reds of the Salento peninsula. The name means "black and bitter."

Nerello Cappuccio (r)
Sicilia. A blending variety found mainly in eastern Sicily, near Etna.

Nerello Mascalese (r)
Sicilia. A dark, spicy, earthy red grape used in the Faro DOC blend.

Neretto Cuneese (r)
Piemonte.

Neretto di Bario (r)
Piemonte.

Nero Buono (r)
Lazio. A blending variety in DOCs such as Castelli Romani and Cori.

Nero d'Avola (r)
Sicilia. The most important red variety of Sicily, also called Calabrese. It makes deep, funky, plush reds reminiscent of Australian Shiraz. Some ecologists think it is related to Syrah.

Nero di Troia (see Uva di Troia.)

Neyret (r)
Valle d'Aosta.

Nieddera (r)
Sardegna. Synonym for Bovale. Occasionally made into a varietal wine.

Nieddu Mannu (r)
Sardegna.

Nocera (r)
Calabria and Sicilia. A blending variety found in southeastern Calabria and northeastern Sicily.

Nosiola (w)
Trentino. Used to make flinty, superacidic whites.

Nuragus (w)
Sardegna. Found in the southern plains of Sardinia. Makes fleshy, brightly acidic wines.

Olivella Nera (r)
Campania and Lazio. Synonym for Sciascinoso.

Ortrugo (w)
Emilia-Romagna. Found in the Colli Piacentini.

Oseleta (r)
Veneto. A local vine being revived in Valpolicella that produces dense, dark, perfumed reds.

Ottavianello (r)
Puglia.

Pagadebit (w)
Emilia-Romagana. Synonym for Bombino Bianco.

Pallagrello (w & r)
Campania. Recently revived grapes in vineyards around Caserta. The *bianco* has an odd, tropically fruity flavor; the *rosso* has a very leathery, earthy rusticity reminiscent of Piedirosso.

Pampanuto (w)
Puglia. A light white variety used in the *bianco* of Castel del Monte.

Pascale (r)
Sardegna.

Passerina (w)
Marche. Synonym for Biancame.

Pecorello (w)
Calabria.

Pecorino (W)

Marche and Abruzzo. A firm, minerally white variety.

Pelaverga (r)

Piemonte. A light red variety used in fizzy, berry-scented wines.

Perricone (r)

Sicilia. A popular dark blending grape in Sicily.

Petit Rouge (r)

Valle d'Aosta. A fruity, rose-scented red variety used in wines that tend toward rosé in style.

Petit Verdot (r)

Throughout Italy. Prized for its deep color and tannic structure in blends.

Petite Arvine (W)

Valle d'Aosta. Makes lightly colored, tart dry whites and occasionally sweet wines.

Picolit (W)

Friuli–Venezia Giulia. Famed for rich, honeyed sweet wines, it is also used to round out dry whites.

Picotendro

Valle d'Aosta. Name for Nebbiolo in Valle d'Aosta.

Piedirosso (r)

Campania. Found in a variety of Campania's DOC wines, this rustic and leathery red (so named for its "red feet," or red roots) is mostly used in blends.

Pigato (W)

Liguria. Thought to be of Greek origin, it is largely found in the Riviera Ligure di Ponente DOC of western Liguria. Makes sharp, herbal whites.

Pignola (W)

Lombardia. A white grape of the Valtellina DOC.

Pignoletto (W)

Emilia-Romagna. A pine-scented white variety grown near Bologna.

Pignolo (r)

Friuli–Venezia Giulia. More producers are now reviving and experimenting with this rare grape. Its wines are dense, dark, and tannic when young, but in good vintages the depth is there for long aging.

Pinella (W)

Veneto.

Pinot Bianco (W)

Throughout Italy, especially in the north. Italian name for Pinot Blanc. It has been planted in Italy since the early 1800s. The best versions are from Friuli–Venezia Giulia and Alto Adige.

Pinot Grigio (W)

Throughout Italy. Named for its grayish tint when ripe (*grigio* means gray), it is very productive and highly variable in character. The grape is usually delicate and clean, but many producers, especially those in Friuli, feel that it is harvested too early. When grown and vinified with care, it can produce a more full-bodied wine.

Pinot Nero (r)
Throughout Italy. Italian name for Pinot Noir. Not very interesting in Italy, although it has shown class in isolated instances in Piedmont, Lombardia (Oltrepò Pavese), and Alto Adige.

Pollera Nera (r)
Liguria.

Portoghese (r)
The Italian name for German Portugeiser, or Blauer Portugeiser.

Prie Blanc/Rouge (w, r)
Valle d'Aosta.

Primitivo (r)
Puglia and Campania. Related to California's Zinfandel, it is used in dark, spicy, sun-baked reds from the Salento peninsula.

Procanico (w)
Umbria. A subvariety of Trebbiano.

Prosecco (w)
Veneto and Friuli–Venezia Giulia. Possibly of Friulian origin, this light, peachy white is the base for the sparkling wines of Valdobbiadene.

Prugnolo Gentile (r)
Toscana. A subvariety of Sangiovese unique to Montepulciano (see Sangiovese).

Raboso Piave (r)
Veneto. A dark red variety of the Piave plain.

Raboso Veronese (r)
Veneto. A subvariety of Raboso native to Verona.

Rebo (r)
Trentino. A cross of Marzemino and Merlot.

Refosco dal Peduncolo Rosso (r)
Friuli–Venezia Giulia. "Refosco with the red stalks" is considered the best of the Refosco subvarieties. It produces dark, tarry reds with hints of bitter chocolate.

Refosco Nostrano (r)
Friuli–Venezia Giulia, Veneto, and Emilia-Romagna (where it's called Cagnina).

Ribolla Gialla (w)
Friuli–Venezia Giulia. Makes high-acid, floral whites, although many producers choose to ferment and age it in barrique to give it a deeper structure.

Riesling Italico (w)
Friuli–Venezia Giulia, Veneto, Trentino–Alto Adige, and Lombardia. Not related to German riesling. Makes light, aromatic whites.

Riesling or Riesling Renano (w)
Friuli–Venezia Giulia, Veneto, Trentino–Alto Adige, and Lombardia. The Italian name for Rhine or Johannisberg Riesling.

Rollo (w)
Liguria. May be related to the Rolle of France's Languedoc.

Rondinella (r)
Veneto. One of the three grapes used in the Valpolicella DOC blend to add color and body.

Rossese (r)
Liguria. A savory, spicy red variety native to western Liguria.

Rossignola (r)
Veneto. A minor blending variety in Bardolino and Valpolicella.

Rossola Nera (r)
Lombardia. Also known as Rossara.

Roussanne (w)
Toscana and Liguria. A Rhône native sometimes used in Italian blends and varietal bottlings.

Ruché (r)
Piemonte. Unique to Asti, it makes fruity, floral, sweet-scented reds.

Sagrantino (r)
Umbria. Unique to the area around Montefalco, in central Umbria (only about 250 acres exist), this dark, exotic variety is making a comeback after having all but faded away. It produces one of Italy's most distinctive and powerful reds.

Sangiovese (r)
Throughout Italy. The most widely planted red grape. Considered a native wild vine, first discovered by Etruscans in the Apennines between Tuscany and Romagna, it is the base of Chianti Classico, Vino Nobile di Montepulciano (Prugnolo), Brunello di Montalcino (Brunello), and Morellino di Scansano (Morellino). Characterized by aromas of black cherries, smoke, tar and herbs.

Sauvignon (w)
Throughout Italy. Made in a range of styles. The best versions are found in Friuli–Venezia Giulia, Alto Adige, Trentino, and Tuscany.

Schiava/Vernatsch (r)
Trentino–Alto Adige. The dominant red variety of the Trentino–Alto Adige region used to make light, simple reds often served with a slight chill.

Schioppettino (r)
Friuli–Venezia Giulia. A rare native red of Friuli that is tannic, dark, and violet-scented. Like Pignolo, it is becoming popular again.

Sciascinoso (r)
Campania and Lazio. A blending grape in Campania's Vesuvio DOC and in Lazio.

Semidano (w)
Sardegna. A light white variety of the Cagliari area that is reminiscent of Albariño.

Sémillon (w)
Throughout Italy. A fleshy and oily white variety often used in blends with Sauvignon, à la Bordeaux.

Spanna (r)
Piemonte. Synonym for Nebbiolo.

Susumaniello (r)
Puglia. A blending grape in the Brindisi DOC.

Sylvaner Verde (w)
Trentino–Alto Adige. More associated with Alsace, this aromatic variety makes steely, minerally, petrol-scented whites.

Syrah/Shiraz (r)
Throughout Italy. Gaining popularity, mainly due to its resistance to intense heat, this variety factors prominently in blends and varietal bottlings.

Tannat (r)
A tannic red variety better known in southwestern France.

Tazzelenghe (r)
Friuli–Venezia Giulia. An acidic red variety (the name means "tongue cutter") native to Friuli.

Tempranillo (r)
Toscana. This Spanish import is catching on in the Tuscan Maremma, among other places.

Teroldego (r)
Trentino. Grown mostly on the Campo Rotaliano plain of northern Trentino, this deep purple, tarry red variety has a distinctive personality.

Terrano (r)
Friuli–Venezia Giulia. Synonym for Refosco in the Carso DOC.

Timorasso (w)
Piemonte. An aromatic white variety used for light wines and grappa.

Tocai Friulano (w)
Friuli–Venezia Giulia. The premier native white grape of Friuli, not to be confused with the Tokay of Alsace or Tokaji of Hungary. This unique variety is a distant relation of Sauvignon Blanc.

Tocai Rosso (r)
Veneto.

Torbato (w)
Sardegna.

Traminer (w)
Friuli–Venezia Giulia, Veneto, and Trentino–Alto Adige. The name may be derived from the town of Termeno/Tramin in Alto Adige, where the variety is believed to have originated. Traminer is considered the parent of Gewürztraminer.

Traminer Aromatico (w)
Friuli–Venezia Giulia, Veneto, and Trentino–Alto Adige. The Italian name for Gewürztraminer.

Trebbiano (w)
Throughout Italy. The largest family of white grapes in Italy. Known as Ugni Blanc in France, it is prolific and usually produces minerally, light whites.

Trebbiano di Soave (W)
Veneto and Lombardia. Also called Trebbiano di Lugana, it is considered the best of the Trebbiano subvarieties, adding distinction to whites in Lugana and Soave.

Trebbiano Giallo (W)
Subvariety in Lazio.

Trebbiano Modenese (W)
Subvariety in Emilia-Romagna.

Trebbiano Romagnolo (W)
Subvariety in Emilia-Romagna.

Trebbiano Spoletino (W)
Subvariety in Umbria.

Trebbiano Toscano (W)
Toscana. The most widely planted Trebbiano subvariety. It factors into countless DOC blends throughout Italy.

Uva di Troia (r)
Puglia. Also known as Nero di Troia. This native grape of northern Puglia with a tangy, meaty flavor is thought to have been brought to Italy by the ancient Greeks, thus the name *Troia* (Troy). It is the base of Castel del Monte DOC reds.

Uva Rara (r)
Lombardia. Synonym for Piedmontese Bonarda.

Veltliner (W)
Trentino–Alto Adige. Makes an occasional appearance in Italian wines, particularly those of the Alto Adige.

Verdea (W)
Emilia-Romagna. A white grape of the Colli Piacentini.

Verdeca (W)
Puglia. A tart white found in DOC wines such as Locorotondo and Gravina.

Verdello (W)
Sicilia and Umbria. A high-acid blending white variety.

Verdicchio (W)
Marche. One of Italy's better-regarded native grapes, it produces crisp, full-flavored white wines with distinctive aromas of pine and herbs. May be related to either Greco or Trebbiano.

Verdiso (W)
Veneto. A brightly aromatic white variety found in several DOC zones around Treviso.

Verduzzo Friulano (W)
Friuli–Venezia Giulia. A unique white variety native to Friuli that produces both dry and sweet wines.

Verduzzo Trevigiano (W)
Veneto. A subvariety of Verduzzo found on the Piave plain of Veneto.

Vermentino (W)
Liguria, Toscana, and Sardegna. One of Italy's most distinctive native whites, this savory, herb-scented grape captures some of the flavor of the Mediterranean.

Vermentino Nero (r)

A red version of Vermentino.

Vernaccia di Oristano (w)

Sardegna. Used to make Sherry-style wines in the town of Oristano.

Vernaccia di San Gimignano (w)

Toscana. A delicately aromatic white grape.

Vernaccia Nera (r)

A dark version of Vernaccia.

Vernatsch (r)

See Schiava.

Vespaiola (w)

Veneto. Best known for the Torcolato sweet wines made from it in the Breganze DOC.

Vespolina (r)

Piemonte and Lombardia. A blending variety found in northern Piedmont.

Vien de Nus (r)

Valle d'Aosta.

Viognier (w)

Throughout Italy. A plump, waxy, aromatic French native.

Vitovska (w)

Friuli–Venezia Giulia. A chalky, aromatic white variety native to the Carso region.

Zibibbo (w)

Sicilia and Calabria. The Italian name for the Muscat/Moscato of Alexandria. Juicier, more alcoholic, and less aromatic than Moscato Bianco. Best known in the *passito* wines of the island of Pantelleria.

Appendix III:
APPELLATIONS (DOCG, DOC)

LISTED BELOW, in alphabetical order within their respective categories, are the DOCG and DOC wine classifications as of 2003. Existing classifications are often revised, and new classifications are constantly under consideration, so it is possible that there are more recently created DOCGs and DOCs not included here.

Each listing includes the region and approximate location of the appellation; the grape(s) used in the production of the wine and in which proportions; aging requirements, when appropriate; and the types of wine allowed under the appellation (see key). Abbreviations within the text include "max." and "min." (maximum, minimum), "bet." (between), "nr." (near), "hl." (hectoliters), "hrs." (hours), and "mos." (months).

KEY TO WINE TYPES:
Whites
dw = dry, still white wine
spdw = sparkling dry white
spsw = sparkling sweet white
sw = sweet white
fw = fortified white

Rosés:
ros = dry, still rosé
spros = sparkling dry rosé
sros = sweet rosé

Reds:
dr = dry, still red
spdr = sparkling dry red
spsr = sparkling sweet red
sr = sweet red
fr = fortified red

Others:
abboccato = semisweet
frizzante = semisparkling white, rosé, or red
novello = new, or nouveau, wine

DENOMINAZIONE DI ORIGINE CONTROLLATA E GARANTITA (DOCG)

ALBANA DI ROMAGNA
Region: Emilia-Romagna, east of Bologna. **Grapes:** Albana 100%. **Aging:** Passito released Apr. 1 of the year after vintage. **Wine Types:** dw; sw

ASTI
Region: Southeastern Piemonte, nr. Asti. **Grapes:** Moscato Bianco 100%. **Wine Types:** sw (frizzante); spsw

BARBARESCO
Region: Southeastern Piemonte, nr. Alba. **Grapes:** Nebbiolo 100%. **Aging:** Min. 2 yrs. (min. 1 yr. in wood); Riserva min. 4 yrs. **Wine Types:** dr

BARDOLINO CLASSICO / BARDOLINO CLASSICO SUPERIORE
Region: Veneto, the southern shores of Lake Garda. Classico designation reserved for wines from part or all of the following communes: Bardolino, Garda, Lazise, Affi, Costermano, Cavaion. **Grapes:** Corvina 35%–65%; Rondinella 10%–40%; Molinara 10%–20%; Negrara max. 10%; Rossignola, Barbera, Sangiovese, and/or Garganega max. 15%. **Aging:** Min. 1 yr. **Wine Types:** dr (also novello and frizzante); ros; spros

BAROLO
Region: Southeastern Piemonte, nr. Alba. **Grapes:** Nebbiolo 100%. **Aging:** Min. 3 yrs. (min. 2 yrs. in wood); Riserva min. 5 yrs. **Wine Types:** dr

BRACHETTO D'ACQUI/ACQUI
Region: Southeast Piemonte, nr. Asti. **Grapes:** Brachetto 100%. **Wine Types:** sr (also frizzante); spsr

BRUNELLO DI MONTALCINO
Region: Southern Toscana, the village of Montalcino. **Grapes:** Sangiovese Grosso 100%. **Aging:** Min. 2 yrs. in oak barrels; total of 4 yrs., 5 for Riserva, including 6 mos. in bottle. Wine released Jan. 1 of the year 5 yrs. from vintage year, or 6 yrs. for Riserva. **Wine Types:** dr

CARMIGNANO
Region: Central Toscana, west of Florence. **Grapes:** Sangiovese min. 50%; Canaiolo Nero up to 20%; Cabernets Franc and Sauvignon 10%–20%; Trebbiano Toscano, Canaiolo Bianco, and Malvasia max. 10%; others max. 10%. **Aging:** Min. 8 mos. in wood, 12 mos. for Riserva. Wine not released until June of the year 2 yrs. from vintage; Riserva not released until Sept. 29 of the third year after harvest. **Wine Types:** dr

CHIANTI
Region: Central Toscana. *Subzones:* Chianti Colli Aretini, Chianti Colli Fiorentini, Chianti Colli Senesi, Chianti Colline Pisane, Chianti Montalbano, Chianti Rúfina, Chianti Montespertoli. **Grapes:** Sangiovese 75%–100%; Canaiolo Nero max. 10%; Trebbiano Toscano/Malvasia del Chianti max. 10%; others max. 10%. **Aging:** Chianti, Chianti Colli Aretini, Colli Senesi, Colline Pisane, and Montalbano released March 1 of the year after vintage; Chianti Colli Fiorentini, Rúfina, Montespertoli, and Superiore released June of the year after vintage; Riserva min. 2 yrs. **Wine Types:** dr

CHIANTI CLASSICO
Region: Central Toscana, bet. Florence and Siena. **Grapes:** Sangiovese 75% to 100%; Canaiolo Nero max. 10%; Trebbiano Toscano and/or Malvasia Bianca 0%–6%; others max. 15%. **Aging:** Min. 1 yr.; Riserva, min. 2 yrs. plus 3 mos. in bottle. **Wine Types:** dr

FIANO DI AVELLINO
Region: Central Campania, the village of Avellino. **Grapes:** Fiano min. 85%; Greco, Coda di Volpe, and/or Trebbiano max. 15%. **Wine Types:** dw

FRANCIACORTA
Region: Lombardia, bet. Bergamo and Brescia. **Grapes:** Chardonnay, Pinot Nero and/or Pinot Bianco (min. 15% Pinot Nero for Rosato; "Satèn" is *crèmant*-style wine from 100% Chardonnay). **Aging:** Min. 18 mos. in bottle; wine released 25 mos. after vintage; vintage-dated wines min. 30 mos. in bottle, released 37 mos. from vintage. **Wine Types:** spdw

GATTINARA
Region: Northern Piemonte, nr. Vercelli. **Grapes:** Nebbiolo min. 90%; Vespolina max. 4%; Bonarda max. 10%. **Aging:** Min. 3 yrs. (min. 1 yr. in wood); Riserva min. 4 yrs. (min. 2 yrs. in wood). **Wine Types:** dr

GAVI/CORTESE DI GAVI
Region: Southeastern Piemonte, the village of Gavi. **Grapes:** Cortese 100%. **Aging:** Superiore 1 yr. **Wine Types:** dw (also frizzante); spdw

GHEMME
Region: Northern Piemonte, the village of Ghemme. **Grapes:** Nebbiolo min. 75%; Vespolina and/or Uva Rara max. 25%. **Aging:** Min. 3 yrs. (min. 20 mos. in wood, 9 mos. in bottle); Riserva min. 4 yrs. (25 mos. in wood, 9 mos. in bottle). **Wine Types:** dr

GRECO DI TUFO
Region: Central Campania, the village of Tufo. **Grapes:** Greco 85%–100%; Coda di Volpe max. 15%. **Wine Types:** dw; spdw

MONTEFALCO SAGRANTINO
Region: Central Umbria, the village of Montefalco. **Grapes:** Sagrantino 100%. **Aging:** Secco 30 mos. (min. 12 mos. in wood); Passito 30 mos. **Wine Types:** dr; sr

MONTEPULCIANO DI ABRUZZO COLLINE TERAMANE
Region: Northeastern Abruzzo, centered on the city of Teramo. **Grapes:** Montepulciano min. 90%; Sangiovese max. 10%. **Aging:** Riserva min. 3 yrs. **Wine Types:** dr

RAMANDOLO/RAMANDOLO CLASSICO
Region: Friuli–Venezia Giulia, nr. Tarcento. **Grapes:** Verduzzo 100%. **Aging:** Riserva min. 2 yrs. **Wine Types:** dw; sw

RECIOTO DI SOAVE
Region: Veneto, east of Verona in the commune of Soave. **Grapes:** Garganega min. 70%; Pinot Bianco, Chardonnay, and/or Trebbiano di Soave max. 30%. **Aging:** Wines released Sept. 1 of the year after vintage. **Wine Types:** sw; spsw

TAURASI
Region: Central Campania, the village of Taurasi. **Grapes:** Aglianico min. 85%; other reds max. 15%. **Aging:** Min. 3 yrs. (min. 1 yr. in wood); Riserva min. 4 yrs. (18 mos. in wood). **Wine Types:** dr

TORGIANO ROSSO RISERVA
Region: Central Umbria, southeast of Perugia. **Grapes:** Sangiovese 50%–70%; Canaiolo 15%–30%; Trebbiano Toscano max. 10%; others max. 10%. **Aging:** Min. 3 yrs. **Wine Types:** dr

VALTELLINA SFORSATO/SFURSAT
Region: Northern Lombardia, the town of Sondrio. **Grapes:** Chiavennasca (Nebbiolo) min. 80%; other max. 20%. Grapes dried before pressing. **Aging:** Min. 2 yrs. **Wine Types:** dr

VALTELLINA SUPERIORE
Region: Northern Lombardia, the town of Sondrio. *Subzones:* Sassella, Grumello, Inferno, Valgella. **Grapes:** Chiavennasca (Nebbiolo) min. 90% **Aging:** Min. 2 yrs. (1 yr. in wood); Riserva min. 3 yrs. **Wine Types:** dr

VERMENTINO DI GALLURA
Region: Northeastern Sardegna. **Grapes:** Vermentino min. 95%. **Wine Types:** dw

VERNACCIA DI SAN GIMIGNANO
Region: Central Toscana, the commune of San Gimignano. **Grapes:** Vernaccia min. 90%. **Aging:** Reserva min. 12 mos., including 4 in bottle. **Wine Types:** dw

VINO NOBILE DI MONTEPULCIANO
Region: Toscana, the village of Montepulciano. **Grapes:** Sangiovese min. 70%; Canaiolo Nero max. 20%; others max. 20%, no more than 10% white varieties. **Aging:** Min. 2 yrs., starting Jan. 1 after vintage. *Options:* (1) 24 mos. in wood; (2) 18 mos. min. in wood, remainder in other container; (3) 12 mos. min. in wood + 6 mos. min. in bottle, remainder in another container. Riserva min. 3 yrs. (6 mos. in bottle); wood-aging options apply. **Wine Types:** dr

DENOMINAZIONE DI ORIGINE CONTROLLATA (DOC)

AGLIANICO DEL TABURNO/TABURNO
Region: Campania, around the village of Benevento. **Grapes:** *Aglianico del Taburno:* Aglianico. *Taburno Bianco:* Trebbiano 40%–50%, Falanghina 30%–40%, others max. 30%. *Taburno Rosso:* Sangiovese 40%–50%, Aglianico 30%–40%, others max. 30%. *Varietal Wines:* Falanghina, Greco, Coda di Volpe, Piedirosso. **Aging:** Rosso 2 yrs (Riserva 3 yrs.) **Wine Types:** dw; spdw; ros; dr

AGLIANICO DEL VULTURE
Region: Northern Basilicata. **Grapes:** Aglianico 100%. **Aging:** 1 yr.; Vecchio 3 yrs. (min. 2 in wood); Riserva 5 yrs. (min. 2 yrs. in wood). **Wine Types:** dr; sr; spr

ALBUGNANO
Region: Central Piemonte, bet. Turin and Asti. **Grapes:** Nebbiolo min. 85%; Freisa, Barbera/ Bonarda max. 15%. **Aging:** Superiore 1 yr. **Wine Types:** dr; ros

ALCAMO
Region: Western Sicilia, village of Alcamo. **Grapes:** *Bianco, Spumante, and Vendemmia Tardiva:* Catarratto min. 60%. *Classico:* Catarratto min. 80%. *Rosato and Rosato Spumante:* Nerello Mascalese, Nero d'Avola, Sangiovese, Frappato, Perricone, Cabernet Sauvignon, Merlot, and/or Syrah. *Rosso Novello and Rosso Riserva:* Nero d'Avola min. 60%. *Varietal Whites:* Catarratto, Inzolia, Grillo, Grecanico, Chardonnay, Müller-Thurgau, Sauvignon. *Varietal Reds:* Nero d'Avola, Cabernet Sauvignon, Merlot, Syrah. **Aging:** Rosso Riserva 2 yrs. **Wine Types:** dw; spdw; sw; ros; spros; dr

ALEATICO DI GRADOLI
Region: Northern Lazio, nr. Lago di Bolsena. **Grapes:** Aleatico 100%. **Aging:** Liquoroso min. 6 mos. Liquoroso Riserva min. 3 yrs. (2 yrs. in wood). **Wine Types:** sr; fr

ALEATICO DI PUGLIA
Region: Puglia. **Grapes:** Aleatico min. 85%; Negroamaro, Malvasia Nera, and/or Primitivo max. 15%. **Aging:** min. 6 mos; Riserva 3 yrs. **Wine Types:** sr; fr

ALEZIO
Region: Southwestern Puglia, nr. Alezio and Gallipoli. **Grapes:** Negroamaro min. 80%; Malvasia Nera, Sangiovese, and/or Montepulciano max. 20%. **Aging:** Rosso Riserva min. 2 yrs. **Wine Types:** ros; dr

ALGHERO
Region: Northwestern Sardegna, bet. Alghero and Sassari. **Grapes:** *Bianco, Rosato, and Rosso:* any authorized grapes. *Varietal Whites:* Chardonnay, Sauvignon, Torbato, Vermentino. *Varietal Reds:* Cabernet Sauvignon, Cabernet Franc, and/or Carmenère, Sangiovese. **Aging:** Liquoroso min. 3 yrs.; Riserva 5 yrs. **Wine Types:** dw; spdw; sw; ros; dr; spdr; sr

ALTO ADIGE/SÜDTIROL
Region: Alto Adige. **Grapes:** *Varietal Wines:* Malvasia, Moscato Giallo (Goldmuskateller), Pinot Bianco (Weissburgunder), Pinot Grigio (Rülander), Chardonnay, Riesling Italico (Welschriesling), Riesling, Müller-Thurgau, Sylvaner, Sauvignon, Traminer/Gewürztraminer, Moscato Rosa (Rosenmuskateller), Lagrein, Merlot, Cabernet Franc, Cabernet Sauvignon, Cabernet-Lagrein, Cabernet-Merlot, Lagrein-Merlot, Pinot Nero (Blauburgunder), Schiava (Vernatsch). *Spumante:* Pinot Bianco, Pinot Nero, and/or Chardonnay. *Bianco/Weiss:* Chardonnay, Pinot Bianco, and/or Pinot Grigio min. 75%. **Aging:** Spumante 20 mos. (Riserva 42 mos.); Riserva reds 2 yrs. **Wine Types:** dw; sw; spw; ros; dr; sr; spsr

ALTO ADIGE COLLI DI BOLZANO/SÜDTIROL BOZNER LEITEN (SUBZONE)
Region: Alto Adige, Bolzano area. **Grapes:** Schiava min. 90%. **Wine Types:** dr

ALTO ADIGE LAGO DI CALDARO/SÜDTIROL KALTERERSEE (SUBZONE)
Region: Alto Adige, around Lago di Caldaro. **Grapes:** Schiava min. 85%; Pinot Nero and/or Lagrein max. 15%. **Wine Types:** dr

ALTO ADIGE MERANESE/SÜDTIROL MERANER (SUBZONE)
Region: Northwest Alto Adige, nr. Merano. **Grapes:** Schiava 100%. **Wine Types:** dr

ALTO ADIGE SANTA MADDALENA/SÜDTIROL ST. MAGDALENER (SUBZONE)
Region: Alto Adige, Bolzano area. **Grapes:** Schiava min. 90%; Lagrein and/or Pinot Nero max. 10%. **Wine Types:** dr

ALTO ADIGE TERLANO/SÜDTIROL TERLANER (SUBZONE)
Region: Alto Adige, nr. Terlano. **Grapes:** *Bianco:* Pinot Bianco and/or Chardonnay min. 50%; Riesling Italico, Riesling, Sauvignon, Sylvaner, and/or Müller-Thurgau max. 50%. *Varietal Whites:* Pinot Bianco, Chardonnay, Riesling Italico, Riesling, Sauvignon, Sylvaner, Müller-Thurgau. **Wine Types:** dw

ALTO ADIGE VALLE D'ISARCO/SÜDTIROL EISACKTALER (SUBZONE)
Region: Alto Adige, bet. Bolzano and Bressanone. **Grapes:** *Varietal Whites:* Traminer Aromatico (Gewürztraminer), Pinot Grigio (Rülander), Veltliner, Sylvaner, Müller-Thurgau, Kerner. *Klausner Laitacher:* Schiava, Portoghese, Lagrein, Pinot Nero. **Wine Types:** dw; dr

ALTO ADIGE VALLE VENOSTA/SÜDTIROL VINSCHGAU (SUBZONE)
Region: Alto Adige, bet. Merano and Naturno. **Grapes:** *Varietal Whites:* Chardonnay, Kerner, Müller-Thurgau, Pinot Bianco (Weissburgunder), Pinot Grigio (Rülander), Riesling, Traminer Aromatico (Gewürztraminer). *Varietal Reds:* Pinot Nero, Schiava. **Wine Types:** dw; dr

ANSONICA COSTA DELL'ARGENTARIO
Region: Southern coast of Toscana. **Grapes:** Ansonica (Inzolia) min. 85%. **Wine Types:** dw

APRILIA
Region: Southern Lazio, bet. Nettuno and Aprilia. **Grapes:** *Varietal White:* Trebbiano. *Varietal Reds:* Sangiovese, Merlot. **Wine Types:** dw; dr

ARBOREA
Region: West-central Sardegna. **Grapes:** *Trebbiano:* Trebbiano min. 85%. *Sangiovese Rosso and Rosato:* Sangiovese min. 85%. **Wine Types:** dw (also frizzante); sw; ros; dr

ASSISI
Region: Eastern Umbria, nr. Assisi. **Grapes:** *Bianco:* Trebbiano 50%–70%, Grechetto 10%–30%, others max. 40%. *Grechetto:* Grechetto min. 85%. *Rosso and Rosato:* Sangiovese 50%–70%, Merlot 10%–30%, others max. 40%. **Wine Types:** dw; ros; dr (novello)

ATINA
Region: Southern Lazio, nr. the village of Atina. **Grapes:** *Rosso:* Cabernet Sauvignon min. 50%; Syrah min. 10%; Merlot min. 10%; Cabernet Franc min. 10%; others max. 20%. *Cabernet:* Cabernets Sauvignon and Franc min. 85%. **Aging:** Rosso and Cabernet Riserva min. 2 yrs. (min. 6 mos. in wood). **Wine Types:** dr

AVERSA
Region: Campania coast, north of Naples. **Grapes:** *Aversa Asprinio:* Asprinio min. 85%. *Aversa Asprinio Spumante:* Asprinio 100%. **Wine Types:** dw; spdw

BAGNOLI DI SOPRA/BAGNOLI
Region: Veneto, nr. the city of Padova. **Grapes:** *Spumante Bianco and Rosato:* Chardonnay min. 20%; Raboso min. 40%. *Bianco:* Chardonnay min. 30%; Tocai and/or Sauvignon min. 20%; Raboso (vinified as white) min. 10%; others max. 10%. *Rosato:* Raboso Piave and/or Raboso Veronese min. 50%; Merlot max. 40%; others max. 10%. *Rosso:* Merlot 15%–60%; Cabernet Franc, Carmenère, and/or Cabernet Sauvignon min. 15%; Raboso Piave/Veronese min. 15%; other max. 10%. *"Friularo" Rosso:* Raboso Piave and/or Raboso min. 90%; others max. 10%. Merlot and Cabernet: Varietal wines with min. 85% of said variety. *Rosso Passito:* Raboso Piave and/or Raboso Veronese min. 70%. **Aging:** Rosso, Friularo, and Varietal Red Riserva: min. 2 yrs. (1 yr. in oak); Passito min. 2 yrs. in oak. **Wine Types:** dw; spdw; ros; spros; dr; sr

BARBERA D'ALBA
Region: Piemonte, Alba area. **Grapes:** Barbera 100%. **Aging:** Superiore min. 1 yr. in wood. **Wine Types:** dr

BARBERA D'ASTI
Region: Piemonte, nr. Asti, north and east of the Alba designation. **Grapes:** Barbera 85%–100%; Freisa, Grignolino, and/or Dolcetto max. 15%. **Aging:** Superiore min. 1 yr. (min. 6 mos. in wood). **Wine Types:** dr

BARBERA DEL MONFERRATO
Region: Piemonte, bet. Asti and Alessandria. **Grapes:** Barbera 85%–100%; Freisa, Grignolino, and/or Dolcetto max. 15%. Superiore

min. 1 yr. (min. 6 mos. in wood). **Wine Types:** dr (also frizzante and abboccato)

BARCO REALE DI CARMIGNANO/CARMIGNANO
Region: Toscana, the town of Carmignano, west of Firenze. **Grapes:** *Barco Reale, Carmignano, and Rosato di Carmignano:* Sangiovese min. 50%; Canaiolo Nero max. 20%; Cabernet Franc and/or Sauvignon 10%–20%; Trebbiano Toscano, Canaiolo Bianco. and/or Malvasia max. 10%; others max. 10%. *Vin Santo di Carmignano:* Trebbiano Toscano and/or Malvasia Bianca min. 75%; other whites max. 25%. *Vin Santo di Carmignano Occhio di Pernice:* Sangiovese min. 50%; others max. 50%. **Aging:** Vin Santo min. 3 yrs. (Riserva 4 yrs.) in wood barrels no larger than 3 hl. **Wine Types:** dr; ros; Vin Santo

BARDOLINO
Region: Veneto, the southern shores of Lake Garda. **Grapes:** Corvina 35%–65%; Rondinella 10%–40%; Molinara 10%–20%; Negrara max. 10%; Rossignola, Barbera, Sangiovese, and/or Garganega max. 15%. **Wine Types:** dr (also novello and frizzante); ros; spros

BIANCHELLO DEL METAURO
Region: Northern Marche. **Grapes:** Bianchello (Biancame) min. 95%. **Wine Types:** dw

BIANCO CAPENA
Region: Lazio, just north of Rome. **Grapes:** Malvasia max. 55%; Trebbiano min. 25%; Bellone and/or Bombino max. 20%. **Wine Types:** dw; sw

BIANCO DELL'EMPOLESE
Region: Toscana, west of Florence along the Arno River. **Grapes:** Trebbiano Toscano min. 80%; other whites max. 20% (Malvasia del Chianti max. 8%). **Aging:** Vin Santo min. 3 yrs. in wood barrels no larger than 5 hl. **Wine Types:** dw; Vin Santo

BIANCO DELLA VALDINIEVOLE
Region: Toscana, bet. Pistoia and Lucca. **Grapes:** Trebbiano Toscano min. 70%; Malvasia del Chianti, Canaiolo Bianco and/or Vermentino up to 25%; other white grapes up to 5%. **Aging:** Vin Santo della Valdinievole min. 3 yrs. in wood barrels no larger than 2 hl. **Wine Types:** dw; Vin Santo

BIANCO DI CUSTOZA
Region: Veneto, west and southeast of Lake Garda. **Grapes:** Trebbiano Toscano 20%–45%; Garganega 20%–40%; Tocai Friulano 5%–30%; Cortese, Malvasia, Riesling Italico, Pinot Bianco, and/or Chardonnay 20%–30%. **Wine Types:** dw; spdw

BIANCO DI PITIGLIANO
Region: Southern Toscana, nr. the Lazio border. **Grapes:** Trebbiano Toscano 50%–80%; Greco, Malvasia Bianca, and/or Verdello max. 20%; Grechetto, Chardonnay, Sauvignon Blanc, Pinot Bianco, and Riesling Italico individually max. 15%, together max. 30%; other whites max. 10%. **Wine Types:** dw; spdw

BIANCO PISANO DI SAN TORPÉ
Region: Western Toscana, bet. Empoli and Pisa. **Grapes:** Trebbiano Toscano min. 75%; other whites max. 25%. **Aging:** Bianco released Jan. 31 of the year after harvest. Vin Santo min. 3 yrs. (4 yrs. for Riserva) in wood barrels no larger than 2 hl. **Wine Types:** dw; Vin Santo

BIFERNO
Region: Eastern Molise. **Grapes:** *Bianco:* Trebbiano Toscano 65%–70%; Bombino Bianco 25%–30%; Malvasia Bianca 5%–10%. *Rosso and Rosato:* Montepulciano 60%–70%; Trebbiano Toscano 15%–20%; Aglianico 15%–20%; others max. 5%. **Aging:** Rosso Riserva min. 3 yrs. **Wine Types:** dw; ros; dr

BIVONGI
Region: Southern Calabria. **Grapes:** *Bianco:* Greco Bianco, Guardavalle (Uva Greca), and/or Montonico Bianco 30%–50%; Malvasia Bianca and/or Ansonica 30%–50%; other whites max. 30%. *Rosato and Rosso:* Gaglioppo and/or Greco Nero 30%–50%; Nocera and/or Calabrese (Nero d'Avola) 30%–50%; other reds max. 10%; other whites max. 15%. **Aging:** Rosso Riserva min. 2 yrs. **Wine Types:** dw; ros; dr (also novello)

BOCA
Region: Northern Piemonte. **Grapes:** Nebbiolo 45–70%; Vespolina 20–40%; Bonarda (Uva Rara) max. 20%. **Aging:** Min. 3 yrs. (min. 2 yrs. in wood). **Wine Types:** dr

BOLGHERI/BOLGHERI SASSICAIA
Region: Central coast of Toscana, nr. the village of Bolgheri. **Grapes:** *Bianco:* Trebbiano 10%–70%; Vermentino 10%–70%; Sauvignon 10%–70%; other whites max. 30%. *Sauvignon:* Sauvignon min. 85%. *Vermentino:* Vermentino min. 85%. *Rosato and Rosso:* Cabernet Sauvignon 10%–80%; Merlot max. 70%; Sangiovese max. 70%; other reds max. 30%. *Vin Santo Occhio di Pernice:* Sangiovese 50%–70%; Malvasia Nera 30%–50%; other reds max. 30%. *Bolgheri Sassicaia:* Cabernet Sauvignon min. 80%; other reds max. 20%. **Aging:** Rosso Superiore min. 2 yrs. (1 yr. in wood; 6 mos. in bottle); Vin Santo min. 3 yrs. (Riserva 4 yrs.) in barrels no larger than 5 hl.; Sassicaia min. 18 mos. in 225-liter barrique (6 mos. in bottle). **Wine Types:** dw; dr; Vin Santo

BOSCO ELICEO
Region: Emilia-Romagna, east of Ravenna. **Grapes:** *Bianco:* Trebbiano min. 70%; Sauvignon and/or Malvasia Bianca di Candia max. 30%; other whites max. 5%. *Sauvignon:* Sauvignon min. 85%. *Merlot:* Merlot min. 85%. *Fortana:* Fortana min. 85%. **Wine Types:** dw (also frizzante); sw; dr (also frizzante); sr

BOTTICINO
Region: Lombardia, east of Brescia. **Grapes:** Barbera min. 30%; Schiava min. 10%; Marzemino min. 20%; Sangiovese min. 10%; other reds max. 10%. **Aging:** Riserva min. 2 yrs. **Wine Types:** dr

BRAMATERRA
Region: Northern Piemonte, nr. Gattinara. **Grapes:** Nebbiolo 50%–70%; Croatina 20%–30%; Bonarda and/or Vespolina 10%–20%. **Aging:** Min. 2 yrs. (18 mos. in wood); Riserva min. 3 yrs. (2 yrs. in wood). **Wine Types:** dr

BREGANZE
Region: Veneto, north of Vicenza. **Grapes:** *Bianco:* Tocai Friulano 85%–100%; other whites max. 15%. *Rosso:* Merlot 85%–100%; other reds max. 15%. *Varietal Wines (9):* Min. 85% of variety. Whites (5): Chardonnay, Sauvignon, Vespaiolo, Pinot Grigio, Pinot Bianco. Reds (4): Cabernet, Cabernet Sauvignon, Marzemino, Pinot Nero. *Torcolato:* Vespaiolo 100%, produced as passito. **Aging:** Riserva reds min. 2 yrs.; Torcolato min. 1 yr. **Wine Types:** dw; dr; sw

BRINDISI
Region: Southeastern Puglia (Brindisi). **Grapes:** Negroamaro min. 70%; Malvasia Nera, Sussumaniello, Montepulciano, and/or Sangiovese max. 30%. **Aging:** Rosso Riserva min. 2 yrs. **Wine Types:** ros; dr

CACC'EMMITTE DI LUCERA
Region: Northern Puglia, nr. Foggia. **Grapes:** Uva di Troia 35%–60%; Montepulciano, Sangiovese, and/or Malvasia Nera 25%–35%; Trebbiano Toscano, Bombino Bianco, and/or Malvasia del Chianti 15%–30%. **Wine Types:** dr

CAGNINA DI ROMAGNA
Region: Eastern Emilia-Romagna. **Grapes:** Cagnina (aka Refosco or Terrano) min. 85%. **Wine Types:** sr

CAMPI FLEGREI
Region: Coast of Campania north of Naples. **Grapes:** *Bianco:* Falanghina 50%–70%; Biancolella and/or Coda di Volpe 10%–30%; others max. 30%. *Falanghina:* Falanghina min. 90%. *Rosso:* Piedirosso 50%–70%; Aglianico/Sciascinoso 10%–30%; others max. 30%. *Piedirosso (or Per e Palummo):* Piedirosso min. 90%. **Aging:** Piedirosso Riserva min. 2 yrs. **Wine Types:** dw; spdw; dr (also novello); sr

CAMPIDANO DI TERRALBA/TERRALBA
Region: Southwestern coast of Sardegna. **Grapes:** Bovale min. 80%; Pascale di Cagliari, Greco Nero, and/or Monica max. 20%. **Aging:** Min. 6 mos. **Wine Types:** dr

CANAVESE
Region: Piemonte, northeast of Turin. **Grapes:** *Bianco:* Erbaluce 100%. *Rosso and Rosato:* Nebbiolo, Barbera, Freisa, and/or Neretto min. 60%; others max. 40%. *Varietal Reds:* Min. 85% of variety; wines from Nebbiolo and Barbera. **Wine Types:** dw; ros; dr (also novello)

CANDIA DEI COLLI APUANI
Region: Toscana, north coast nr. Liguria. **Grapes:** Vermentino 70%–80%; Albarola 10%–20%; Trebbiano Toscano and/or Malvasia

Bianca max. 20% (Malvasia max. 5%). **Aging:** Vin Santo min. 3 yrs. in barrels no larger than 5 hl. **Wine Types:** dw; sw; Vin Santo

CANNONAU DI SARDEGNA
Region: Sardegna. *Subzones:* Oliena or Nepente di Oliena reserved for wines from the village of Oliena; Capo Ferrato reserved for wines from the extreme southeast of the island; Jerzu reserved for wines from Jerzu and Cardedu. **Grapes:** Cannonau min. 90%. **Aging:** Riserva min. 2 yrs. (6 mos. in wood); Liquoroso min. 10 mos. (6 mos. in wood). **Wine Types:** dr; ros; sr; fr

CAPALBIO
Region: Southern Toscana, Grosseto province. **Grapes:** *Bianco and Vin Santo:* Trebbiano Toscano min. 50%; other whites max. 50%. *Vermentino:* Vermentino min. 85%. *Rosato, Rosso, and Rosso Riserva:* Sangiovese min. 50%; other reds max. 50%. *Cabernet Sauvignon:* Cabernet Sauvignon min. 85%. *Sangiovese:* Sangiovese min. 85%. **Aging:** Riserva min. 2 yrs. (6 mos. in wood); Cabernet and Sangiovese min. 6 mos.; Vin Santo min. 3 yrs. (2 yrs. in barrels no larger than 3 hl.). **Wine Types:** dw; dr; Vin Santo

CAPRI
Region: Campania, island of Capri. **Grapes:** *Bianco:* Falanghina and Greco, with Greco max. 50% of total. *Rosso:* Piedirosso min. 80%. **Wine Types:** dw; dr

CAPRIANO DEL COLLE
Region: Lombardia, south of Brescia. **Grapes:** *Bianco and Trebbiano:* Trebbiano min. 85%. *Rosso:* Sangiovese min. 40%; Marzemino min. 35%; Barbera min. 3%; Merlot and/or Incrocio Terzi max. 15%. **Aging:** Rosso Riserva min. 2 yrs. **Wine Types:** dw (also frizzante); dr (also novello)

CAREMA
Region: Piemonte, northeast of Turin. **Grapes:** Nebbiolo min. 85%. **Aging:** Min. 3 yrs. (2 yrs. in wood); Riserva min. 4 yrs. (30 mos. in wood; 1 yr. in bottle). **Wine Types:** dr

CARIGNANO DEL SULCIS
Region: Southwestern Sardegna. **Grapes:** Carignano min. 85%. **Aging:** Rosso min. 3 mos. in bottle; Rosso Riserva and Superiore min. 2 yrs. (6 mos. in bottle); Passito min. 6 mos. (3 mos. in bottle). **Wine Types:** dr (also novello); sr; ros

CARSO
Region: Friuli–Venezia Giulia, nr. border with Slovenia. **Grapes:** Terrano min. 70%. *Varietal Wines (11):* Min. 85% of variety. Whites (6): Chardonnay, Malvasia Istriana, Pinot Grigio, Sauvignon, Traminer, Vitovska. Reds (5): Cabernet Franc, Cabernet Sauvignon, Merlot, Refosco dal Peduncolo Rosso, Terrano. **Wine Types:** dw; dr

CASTEL DEL MONTE
Region: North-central Puglia, the village of Castel del Monte. **Grapes:** *Bianco:* Pampanuto up to 100%; Chardonnay up to 100%; Bombino Bianco min. 65%; other nonaromatic whites max. 35%. *Rosso:* Uva di Troia up to 100%; Aglianico up to 100%; Montepulciano up to 100%; other reds max. 35%. *Rosato:* Bombino up to 100%; Aglianico up to 100%; Uva di Troia up to 100%; other reds max. 35%. *Varietal Whites (4):* Min. 90% of variety; wines from Bombino Bianco, Chardonnay, Pinot Bianco, Sauvignon. *Varietal Reds (5):* Min. 90% of variety; wines from Bombino Nero, Uva di Troia, Cabernet, Pinot Nero, Aglianico. *Varietal Rosato (1):* Min. 90% Aglianico. **Aging:** Riserva Reds min. 2 yrs. (1 yr. in wood). **Wine Types:** dw (also frizzante); ros (also frizzante); dr (also novello)

CASTEL SAN LORENZO
Region: Southeastern Campania. **Grapes:** *Bianco:* Trebbiano 50%–60%; Malvasia Bianca 30%–40%; others max. 20%. *Rosso and Rosato:* Barbera 60%–80%; Sangiovese 20%–30%; others max. 20%. *Barbera:* Barbera min. 85%. *Moscato and Moscato Spumante:* Moscato Bianco min. 85%. **Aging:** Min. 2 years for Barbera Riserva. **Wine Types:** dw; dr; ros; spsw; sw

CASTELLER
Region: Trentino. **Grapes:** Schiava min. 30%; Lambrusco max. 60%; Merlot, Lagrein, and/or Teroldego max. 20%. **Wine Types:** dr

CASTELLI ROMANI
Region: Lazio, the Alban hills south of Rome. **Grapes:** *Bianco:* Malvasia/Trebbiano min. 70%; others max. 30%. *Rosso:* Cesanese,

Merlot, Montepulciano, Nero Buono, and/or Sangiovese min. 85%; others max. 15%. *Rosato:* Variable. **Wine Types:** dw (also frizzante); ros (also frizzante); dr (also novello); sw; sr

CELLATICA
Region: Lombardia, just west of Brescia. **Grapes:** Marzemino min. 30%; Barbera min. 30%; Schiava min. 10%; Incrocio Terzi min. 10%; others max. 10%. **Aging:** Superiore 1 yr. **Wine Types:** dr

CERASUOLO DI VITTORIA
Region: Southeastern Sicilia. **Grapes:** Nero d'Avola max. 60%; Frappato min. 40%; Grosseto Nero and/or Nerello Mascalese max. 10%. **Wine Types:** dr

CERVETERI
Region: Lazio, coastal hills northwest of Rome. **Grapes:** *Bianco:* Trebbiano Toscano and/or Trebbiano Giallo min. 50%; Malvasia di Candia and/or Malvasia del Lazio max. 35%; others max. 30%. *Rosso and Rosato:* Sangiovese and Montepulciano min. 60% (min. 25% of each); Cesanese Comune max. 25%; others max. 30%. **Wine Types:** dw (also frizzante); sw; ros (also frizzante); dr (also novello); sr

CESANESE DEL PIGLIO/PIGLIO
Region: Lazio, bet. Rome and Frosinone. **Grapes:** Cesanese min. 90%
Wine Types: dr (also frizzante and spumante); spdr; sr

CESANESE DI AFFILE/AFFILE
Region: Lazio, bet. Rome and Frosinone. **Grapes:** Cesanese min. 90%.
Wine Types: dr; sr

CESANESE DI OLEVANO ROMANO
Region: Lazio, bet. Rome and Frosinone. **Grapes:** Cesanese min. 90%.
Wine Types: dr (also frizzante); sr

CILENTO
Region: Southern coast of Campania. **Grapes:** *Bianco:* Fiano 60%–65%; Trebbiano Toscano 20%–30%; Greco Bianco and/or Malvasia Bianca 10%–15%; others max. 10%. *Rosso:* Aglianico 60%–75%; Piedirosso and/or Primitivo 15%–20%; Barbera 10%–20%; others max. 10%. *Rosato:* Sangiovese 70%–80%; Aglianico 10%–15%; Primitivo and/or Piedirosso 10%–15%; others max. 10%. *Aglianico:* Aglianico min. 85%. **Aging:** Aglianico min. 1 yr. **Wine Types:** dw; dr; ros

CINQUE TERRE/CINQUE TERRE SCIACCHETRÀ
Region: Eastern Liguria. "Sciacchetrà" is a term for sweet wine. **Grapes:** Bosco min. 40%; Albarola and/or Vermentino max. 40%; others max. 20%. **Aging:** Sciacchetrà min. 1 yr. (Sciacchetrà Riserva 3 yrs.). **Wine Types:** dw; sw

CIRCEO
Region: Southern coast of Lazio. **Grapes:** *Bianco (all types):* Malvasia di Candia max. 30%; Trebbiano Toscano min. 60%; others max. 30%. *Rosso and Rosato (all types):* Merlot min. 85%. *Circeo Trebbiano:* Trebbiano min. 85%. *Circeo Sangiovese and Sangiovese Rosato:* Sangiovese min. 85%. **Wine Types:** dw (also frizzante); ros (also frizzante); dr (also novello and frizzante); sw; sr

CIRÒ
Region: Ionian coast of Calabria, the village of Cirò. **Grapes:** *Bianco:* Greco Bianco min. 90%; Trebbiano Toscano max. 10%. *Rosato and Rosso:* Gaglioppo min. 95%; Trebbiano Toscano and/or Greco Bianco max. 5%. **Aging:** Rosso min. 9 mos.; Classico Riserva/Classico Superiore Riserva min. 2 yrs. **Wine Types:** dw; ros; dr

COLLI ALBANI
Region: Lazio, the Alban hills south of Rome. **Grapes:** Malvasia di Candia max. 60%; Trebbiano 25%–50%; Malvasia del Lazio 5%–45%; others (except Moscato) max. 10%. **Wine Types:** dw; spdw; sw

COLLI ALTOTIBERINI
Region: Northern Umbria. **Grapes:** *Bianco:* Trebbiano Toscano 75%–90%; Malvasia max. 10%; others max. 15%. *Rosso and Rosato:* Sangiovese 55%–70%; Merlot 10%–20%; others max. 15%. **Wine Types:** dw; ros; dr

COLLI AMERINI
Region: Southern Umbria, nr. Terni. **Grapes:** *Bianco:* Trebbiano Toscano 70%–85%; Grechetto, Verdello, Garganega, and/or Malvasia max. 30% (Malvasia max. 10%); others max. 15%. *Rosso and Rosato:* Sangiovese 60%–80%; Montepulciano, Ciliegiolo, Canaiolo, Merlot, and/or Barbera max. 35% (Merlot max. 10%); others max. 15%.

Malvasia: Malvasia Toscana min. 85%. **Wine Types:** dw; ros; dr (also novello)

COLLI BERICI
Region: Veneto, west of Vicenza. **Grapes:** All wines except spumante are varietal. Whites (5): *Chardonnay:* Chardonnay min. 85%; Pinot Bianco max. 15%. *Garganega:* Garganega min. 90%; Trebbiano di Soave max. 10%. *Tocai Italico:* Tocai Italico min. 90%; Garganega max. 10%. *Sauvignon:* Sauvignon min. 90%; Garganega max. 10%. *Pinot Bianco:* Pinot Bianco min. 85%; Pinot Grigio max. 15%. *Spumante:* Garganega min. 50%; Pinot Grigio, Pinot Bianco, Chardonnay, and/or Sauvignon max. 50%. Reds (3): *Merlot:* Merlot 100%. *Tocai Rosso:* Tocai Rosso min. 85%; Garganega max. 15%. *Cabernet:* Cabernet Franc and/or Sauvignon 100%. **Aging:** Cabernet Riserva min. 3 yrs. **Wine Types:** dw; spdw; dr

COLLI BOLOGNESE CLASSICO PIGNOLETTO
Region: Emilia-Romagna, south of Bologna. **Grapes:** Pignoletto min. 85%. **Wine Types:** dw

COLLI BOLOGNESI
Region: Emilia-Romagna, south and west of Bologna. *Subzones:* Colline di Riosto, Colline Marconiane, Zola Predosa, Monte San Pietro, Colline di Oliveto, Terre di Montebudello, Serravalle. **Grapes:** *Bianco:* Albana 60%–80%; Trebbiano Romagnolo 20%–40%. *Varietal Whites (5):* Min. 85% of variety; wines from Chardonnay, Pignoletto, Pinot Bianco, Riesling Italico, Sauvignon. *Varietal Reds (3):* Min. 85% of variety; wines from Cabernet Sauvignon, Barbera, Merlot. **Aging:** Barbera and Cabernet Sauvignon Riserva min. 1 yr.; Barbera and Cabernet Riserva with a subzone designation min. 3 yrs. **Wine Types:** spdw; dw (also frizzante); sw; dr (also frizzante)

COLLI D'IMOLA
Region: Emilia-Romagna, east of Bologna. **Grapes:** *Bianco and Rosso:* Variable. *Varietal Whites (3):* Min. 85% of variety; wines from Chardonnay, Pignoletto, Trebbiano. *Varietal Reds (3):* Min. 85% of variety; wines from Barbera, Cabernet Sauvignon, Sangiovese. **Aging:** Riserva reds min. 18 mos. **Wine Types:** dw (also frizzante); sw; dr (also frizzante and novello); sr

COLLI DEL TRASIMENO/TRASIMENO
Region: Umbria, nr. Lake Trasimeno. **Grapes:** *Grechetto:* Grechetto min. 85%. *Merlot:* Merlot min. 85%. *Cabernet Sauvignon:* Cabernet Sauvignon min. 85%. *Gamay:* Gamay min. 85%. *Bianco and Vin Santo:* Trebbiano min. 40%; Grechetto, Chardonnay, Pinot Bianco, and/or Pinot Grigio min. 30%. *Rosso and Rosato:* Sangiovese min. 40%; Ciliegiolo, Gamay, Merlot, and/or Cabernet min. 30%. *Spumante Classico:* Chardonnay, Pinot Grigio, Pinot Bianco, Pinot Nero, and/or Grechetto min. 70%. *Bianco Scelto:* Vermentino, Grechetto, Chardonnay, Pinot Grigio, Pinot Bianco, Sauvignon, and/or Riesling min. 85%. *Rosso Scelto:* Gamay, Cabernet Sauvignon, Merlot, and/or Pinot Nero min. 85%. **Aging:** Rosso, Rosato, Bianco, and Bianco Scelto min. 6 mos.; Rosso Riserva min. 2 yrs. (4 mos. in wood); Vin Santo min. 18 mos. in wood. **Wine Types:** dw (also frizzante); spdw; ros; dr (also frizzante and novello); Vin Santo

COLLI DELL'ETRURIA CENTRALE
Region: Central Toscana. **Grapes:** *Bianco:* Trebbiano Toscano min. 50%; Chardonnay, Pinot Bianco/Grigio, Vernaccia, Malvasia, and/or Sauvignon max. 50%; other whites max. 25%. *Rosso and Rosato:* Sangiovese, min. 50%; Cabernets Sauvignon and Franc, Merlot, Pinot Nero, and/or Canaiolo Nero max. 50%; other reds max. 25%. *Rosso Novello:* Sangiovese, min. 50%; Canaiolo Nero, Merlot, Gamay, and/or Ciliegiolo max. 50%; other reds max. 25%. *Vin Santo:* Trebbiano Toscano and/or Malvasia min. 70%; other whites max. 30%. *Vin Santo Occhio di Pernice:* Sangiovese min. 50%; others max. 50%. **Aging:** Vin Santo min. 3 yrs. (Riserva 4 yrs.) in barrels no larger than 5 hl. **Wine Types:** dw; ros; dr (also novello); Vin Santo

COLLI DELLA SABINA
Region: Lazio, along right bank of the Tiber River. **Grapes:** *Bianco and Spumante:* Trebbiano Toscano and/or Trebbiano Giallo min. 40%; Malvasia di Candia and/or Malvasia del Lazio min. 40%; other whites max. 20%. *Rosso and Rosato/Novello:* Sangiovese 40%–70%; Montepulciano 15%–40%; other reds max. 30%. **Wine Types:** dw (also frizzante); spdw; spsw; ros (also frizzante); dr (also frizzante and novello)

COLLI DI CONEGLIANO
Region: Northeastern Veneto. "Refrontolo" wines from the communes of Refrontolo, Pieve di Soligo, and San Pietro di Feletto. "Torchiato di Fregona" wines from the communes of Fregona, Sarmede, and Cappella Maggiore. **Grapes:** *Bianco:* Incrocio Manzoni 6.0.13 min. 30%; Pinot Bianco and/or Chardonnay min. 30%; Sauvignon and/or Riesling Renano max. 10%. *Rosso:* Min. 10% each of Cabernet Franc, Cabernet Sauvignon, Marzemino, and Merlot (Merlot max. 40% of total); Incrocio Manzoni 2.15 max. 10%. *Refrontolo Passito:* Marzemino min. 95%. *Torchiato di Fregona Passito:* Prosecco min. 30%; Verdiso min. 30%; Boschera min. 25%; other whites max. 15%. **Aging:** Bianco min. 6 mos.; Rosso min. 2 yrs. (6 mos. in wood); Refrontolo min. 6 mos. (3 mos. in bottle); Torchiato min. 1 yr. (3 mos. in bottle). **Wine Types:** dw; dr; sw; sr

COLLI DI FAENZA
Region: Eastern Emilia-Romagna. **Grapes:** *Bianco:* Chardonnay 40%–60%; Pignoletto, Pinot Bianco, Sauvignon, and/or Trebbiano 40%–60%. *Rosso:* Cabernet Sauvignon 40%–60%; Ancellotta, Ciliegiolo, Merlot, and/or Sangiovese 40%–60%. *Pinot Bianco:* Pinot Bianco 100%. *Trebbiano:* Trebbiano 100%. *Sangiovese:* Sangiovese 100%. **Aging:** Rosso/Sangiovese min. 6 mos. (Riserva 2 yrs.). **Wine Types:** dw; dr

COLLI DI LUNI
Region: Eastern Liguria and northwestern Toscana on Mediterranean coast. **Grapes:** *Bianco:* Vermentino min. 35%; Trebbiano Toscano 25%–40%; others max. 30%. *Vermentino:* Vermentino min. 90%. *Rosso:* Sangiovese 60% 70%; Canaiolo Nero and/or Ciliegiolo min 15%; others max. 25% (Cabernet Sauvignon max. 10%). **Aging:** Rosso Riserva min. 2 yrs. **Wine Types:** dw; dr

COLLI DI PARMA
Region: Emilia-Romagna, nr. Parma. **Grapes:** *Rosso:* Barbera 60%–75%; Bonarda (Croatina) 25%–40%; others max. 15%. *Malvasia:* Malvasia Bianca di Candia 85%–100%. *Sauvignon:* Sauvignon 100%. **Wine Types:** dw (also frizzante); sw; spdw; spsw; dr (also frizzante)

COLLI DI RIMINI
Region: Southeastern Emilia-Romagna. **Grapes:** *Bianco:* Trebbiano 50%–70%; Biancame and/or Mostosa 30%–50%; others max. 20%. *Rebola:* Pignoletto min. 85%. *Rosso:* Sangiovese 60%–75%; Cabernet Sauvignon 15%–25%; others max. 25%. *Cabernet Sauvignon:* Cabernet Sauvignon min. 85%. *Biancame:* Biancame min. 85%. **Aging:** Cabernet Sauvignon Riserva min. 2 yrs. **Wine Types:** dw; sw; dr

COLLI DI SCANDIANO E DI CANOSSA
Region: Emilia-Romagna, bet. Parma and Modena. **Grapes:** *Bianco:* Sauvignon 40%–80%; remainder Malvasia di Candia, Trebbiano Romagnolo, Pinot Bianco, and/or Pinot Grigio (Sauvignon for Classico min. 85%). *Varietal whites (4):* Min. 85% of variety; wines from Sauvignon, Malvasia, Pinot Bianco, Chardonnay. *Varietal Reds (6):* Min. 85% of variety; wines from Lambrusco Grasparossa, Lambrusco Montericco, Cabernet Sauvignon, Marzemino, Malbo, Pinot Nero. *Passito:* Sauvignon min. 90%. **Aging:** Cabernet Sauvignon Riserva min. 2 yrs. (8 mos. in wood). **Wine Types:** dw; spdw; sw; ros; dr (also frizzante)

COLLI ETRUSCHI VITERBESI
Region: Northern Lazio, nr. Lago di Bolsena. **Grapes:** *Bianco:* Malvasia max. 30%; Trebbiano Toscano 40%–80%; others max. 30%. *Rosso and Rosato:* Montepulciano 20%–45%; Sangiovese 50%–65%; others max. 30%. *Varietal Wines (9):* Whites from Procanico; Grechetto; Rossetto; Moscatello. Reds from Greghetto; Sangiovese; Violone; Canaiolo; Merlot. **Wine Types:** dw (also frizzante); sw (frizzante); ros (frizzante); swros (frizzante); dr (novello and frizzante); sr (frizzante)

COLLI EUGANEI
Region: Veneto, southwest of Padova. **Grapes:** *Bianco:* Garganega 30%–50%; Prosecco 10%–30%; Tocai Friulano and/or Sauvignon 20%–40%; Pinella, Pinot Bianco, Riesling Italico, and/or Chardonnay max. 20%. *Rosso:* Merlot 60%–80%; Cabernet Franc, Cabernet Sauvignon, Barbera, and/or Raboso 20%–40%. *Fior d'Arancio:* Moscato Giallo min. 95%. *Serprino:* Prosecco min. 90%. *Varietal Wines (9):* Min. 90% of variety; 95% for Moscato. Whites from

Chardonnay, Moscato, Pinello(a); Pinot Bianco, Tocai. Reds from
Cabernet, Cabernet Franc, Cabernet Sauvignon, Merlot. **Aging:** Riserva
reds min. 2 yrs. (6 mos. in oak); Fior d'Arancio Passito min. 1 yr. **Wine
Types:** dw; spdw; dr (also novello); sw

COLLI LANUVINI
Region: Lazio, the Alban Hills south of Rome. **Grapes:** Malvasia Bianca
di Candia max. 70%; Trebbiano min. 30%; others max. 10%. **Wine
Types:** dw; sw

COLLI MACERATESI
Region: Central Marche, the province of Macerata. **Grapes:** Maceratino
min. 80%; Trebbiano Toscano, Verdicchio, Malvasia Toscana, and/or
Chardonnay max. 20%. **Wine Types:** dw

COLLI MARTANI
Region: Central Umbria, south of Perugia. *Subzone:* Todi, centered on
the commune of Todi. **Grapes:** *Trebbiano:* Trebbiano min. 85%.
Grechetto and Grechetto di Todi: Grechetto min. 85%. *Sangiovese:*
Sangiovese min. 85%. **Aging:** Sangiovese min. 1 yr. (Riserva 2 yrs.,
with 1 in wood). **Wine Types:** dw; dr

COLLI ORIENTALI DEL FRIULI
Region: Eastern Friuli–Venezia Giulia. *Subzones:* Ramandolo, nr.
Tarcento; Cialla, nr. Cividale; Rosazzo, southeast of Udine. **Grapes:**
Bianco, Rosato, and Rosso: Variable. *Varietal Wines (20):* Min. 85% of
variety. Whites from Chardonnay, Malvasia Istriana, Picolit, Pinot
Bianco, Pinot Grigio, Ribolla Gialla, Riesling Renano, Sauvignon, Tocai
Friulano, Traminer Aromatico, Verduzzo Friulano. Reds from Cabernet,
Cabernet Franc, Cabernet Sauvignon, Merlot, Pignolo, Pinot Nero,
Refosco, Schioppettino, Tazzelenghe. *Ramandolo:* Verduzzo 100%.
Cialla: Varietals from Picolit, Ribolla Gialla, Verduzzo, Refosco,
Schioppettino. *Rosazzo:* Varietals from Picolit, Ribolla Gialla, Pignolo.
Aging: Riserva min. 2 yrs. **Wine Types:** dw; sw; ros; dr

COLLI PERUGINI
Region: Umbria, west of Perugia. **Grapes:** *Bianco and Vin Santo:*
Trebbiano Toscano min. 50%; other whites max. 50%. *Spumante:*
Grechetto, Chardonnay, Pinot Bianco, Pinot Nero, and/or Pinot Grigio
min. 80%; other whites max. 20%. *Rosso and Rosato:* Sangiovese
min. 50%; others max. 50%. *Varietal Whites (4):* Min. 85% of variety;
wines from Chardonnay, Grechetto, Pinot Grigio, Trebbiano. *Varietal
Reds (3):* Min. 85% of variety; wines from Cabernet Sauvignon,
Merlot, Sangiovese. **Wine Types:** dw; spdw; ros; dr (also novello); Vin
Santo

COLLI PESARESI
Region: Northeastern Marche. **Grapes:** *Rosso and Rosato:* Sangiovese
min. 70%. *Bianco:* Trebbiano Toscano, Verdicchio, Biancame, Pinot
Grigio, Pinot Nero, Riesling Italico, Chardonnay, Sauvignon, and/or
Pinot Bianco min. 75%. *Varietal Whites (3):* Min. 85% of variety; wines
from Trebbiano, Biancame, Roncaglia. *Sangiovese:* Sangiovese min.
85%. *Focara Rosso:* Pinot Nero, Cabernet Franc, Cabernet Sauvignon,
and/or Merlot min. 50%; Sangiovese max. 50%; others max. 25%;
Focara Pinot Nero: Pinot Nero min. 90%. **Aging:** Riserva reds min. 2
yrs. **Wine Types:** dw; ros; dr (also novello)

COLLI PIACENTINI
Region: Western Emilia-Romagna, south of Piacenza. *Subzones:*
Gutturnio (Tidone River valley), Trebbiano Val Trebbia (Trebbia valley),
Val Nure (Nure valley), Monterosso Val d'Arda (Arda valley). **Grapes:**
Gutturnio: Barbera 55%–70%; Croatina (Bonarda) 30%–45%.
Monterosso Val d'Arda: Malvasia di Candia and Moscato Bianco
20%–50%; Trebbiano Romagnolo 20%–50%; others max. 30%.
Trebbiano Val Trebbia: Ortrugo 35%–65%; Malvasia di Candia and
Moscato Bianco 10%–20%; Trebbiano Romagnolo 15%–30%; others
max. 15%. *Valnure:* Malvasia di Candia 20%–50%; Trebbiano
Romagnolo and Ortrugo 20%–65%; others max. 15%. *Novello:* Pinot
Nero and/or Barbera and/or Croatina (Bonarda) min. 60%; others
max. 40%. *Vin Santo:* Malvasia di Candia, Ortrugo, Sauvignon,
Marsanne, and/or Trebbiano min. 80%. *Vin Santo di Vigoleno:*
Marsanne, Bervedino, Sauvignon, Ortrugo, and/or Trebbiano
Romagnolo min. 60%. *Pinot Spumante:* Pinot Nero min. 85%;
Chardonnay max. 15%. *Varietal Wines (9):* Min. 85% of variety; wines
from Ortrugo, Barbera, Bonarda, Malvasia, Pinot Nero, Pinot Grigio,

Sauvignon, Cabernet Sauvignon, Chardonnay. **Aging:** Gutturnio min. 9 mos.; Gutturnio Riserva min. 2 yrs. (3 mos. in wood); Vin Santo min. 4 yrs. (3 yrs. in wood); Vin Santo di Vigoleno min. 5 yrs. (4 yrs. in wood). **Wine Types:** dw (also frizzante); sw; spdw; ros; spros; dr (also frizzante and abboccato); sr; spdr

COLLI TORTONESI
Region: Easternmost Piemonte. **Grapes:** *Bianco:* Variable. *Rosso:* variable. *Chiaretto (rosé):* Variable. *Cortese and Cortese Spumante:* Cortese min. 85%. *Barbera:* Barbera min. 85%. *Dolcetto:* Dolcetto min. 85%. **Aging:** Barbera Superiore min. 1 yr. (6 mos. in wood). **Wine Types:** dw (also frizzante); spdw; ros; dr (also frizzante and novello)

COLLINA TORINESE
Region: Piemonte, city of Turin. **Grapes:** *Rosso:* Barbera min. 60%; Freisa min. 25%; others max. 15%. *Varietal Reds:* Min. 85% of variety; wines from Barbera, Bonarda, Malvasia di Schierano, Pelaverga (Cari). **Aging:** Min. 3 yrs. (20 mos. in wood, 9 mos. in bottle); Riserva min. 4 yrs. (25 mos. in wood, 9 mos. in bottle). **Wine Types:** dr (also novello and frizzante); ros (also novello and frizzante); sros; sr

COLLINE DI LEVANTO
Region: Eastern Liguria. **Grapes:** *Bianco:* Vermentino min. 40%; Albarola min. 20%; Bosco min. 5%; others max. 35%. *Rosso and Novello:* Sangiovese min. 40%; Ciliegiolo min. 20%; others 20%–40%. **Wine Types:** dw; dr (also novello)

COLLINE LUCCHESI
Region: Northwestern Toscana, nr. Lucca. **Grapes:** *Bianco:* Trebbiano Toscano 45%–70%; Greco, Grechetto, Vermentino, and/or Malvasia max. 45%; Chardonnay and/or Sauvignon max. 30%; others max. 15%. *Vermentino:* Vermentino min. 85%. *Sauvignon:* Sauvignon min. 85%. *Rosso:* Sangiovese 45%–70%; Canaiolo and/or Ciliegiolo max. 30%; Merlot max. 15%; others max. 15% (Aleatico and Moscato max. 5%). *Merlot:* Merlot min. 85% (no Aleatico or Moscato). *Sangiovese:* Merlot min. 85% (no Aleatico or Moscato). *Vin Santo and Vin Santo Occhio di Pernice:* Variable. **Aging:** Rosso, Merlot, and Sangiovese Riserva min. 2 yrs.; Vin Santo min. 3 yrs. in barrels no larger than 5 hl. **Wine Types:** dw; dr

COLLINE NOVARESI
Region: Northeastern Piemonte. **Grapes:** *Bianco:* Erbaluce 100%. *Rosso:* Nebbiolo min. 30%; Uva Rara max. 40%; Vespolina and/or Croatina max. 30%. *Varietal Reds:* Min. 85% of variety; wines from Nebbiolo (Spanna), Uva Rara (Bonarda), Vespolina, Croatina, Barbera. **Wine Types:** dw (also frizzante); dr (also frizzante)

COLLINE SALUZZESI
Region: Central Piemonte, bet. Cuneo and Torino. **Grapes:** *Rosso:* Nebbiolo, Pelaverga, and/or Barbera min. 60%; others max. 40%. *Varietal Reds:* 100% of variety; wines from Pelaverga, Quagliano. **Wine Types:** dr; sr (also frizzante); spsr

COLLIO GORIZIANO/COLLIO
Region: Eastern Friuli–Venezia Giulia. **Grapes:** *Bianco and Rosso:* Variable. *Varietal Wines (16):* Whites (12) from Chardonnay, Malvasia Istriana, Müller-Thurgau, Picolit, Pinot Bianco, Pinot Grigio, Ribolla Gialla, Riesling Renano, Riesling Italico, Sauvignon, Tocai Friulano, Traminer Aromatico. Reds (4) from Cabernet Franc, Cabernet Sauvignon, Merlot, Pinot Nero. **Aging:** Riserva whites min. 2 yrs.; Riserva reds min. 3 yrs. (6 mos. in wood). **Wine Types:** dw; sw; dr

CONTEA DI SCLAFANI
Region: Sicilia, southeast of Palermo. **Grapes:** *Bianco:* Catarratto, Inzolia (Ansonica), and/or Grecanico min. 50%; others max. 50%. *Rosso:* Nero d'Avola and/or Perricone min. 50%; others max. 50%. *Rosato:* Nerello Mascalese min. 50%; others max. 50%. *Varietal Whites (7):* Min. 85% of variety; wines from Inzolia (Ansonica), Catarratto, Grecanico, Grillo, Chardonnay, Pinot Bianco, Sauvignon. *Varietal Reds (7):* Min. 85% of variety; wines from Nero d'Avola (Calabrese), Perricone, Cabernet Sauvignon, Pinot Nero, Syrah, Merlot, Sangiovese. *Spumante:* Variable. *Dolce and Vendemmia Tardiva:* Variable. **Aging:** Riserva reds min. 2 yrs.; Vendemmia Tardiva min. 18 mos. (6 mos. in wood). **Wine Types:** dw; spdw; sw; ros; spros; dr (also novello)

CONTESSA ENTELLINA
Region: Central-west Sicilia. **Grapes:** *Bianco:* Inzolia min. 50%; Catarratto, Grecanico, Chardonnay, Müller-Thurgau, Sauvignon, Pinot Bianco, and/or Grillo max. 50%. *Rosso and Rosato:* Nero d'Avola and/or Syrah min. 50%; others max. 50%. *Varietal Whites (4):* Min. 85% of variety; wines from Chardonnay, Grecanico, Inzolia (Ansonica), Sauvignon. *Varietal Reds (3):* Min. 85% of variety; wines from Cabernet Sauvignon, Merlot, Pinot Nero. *Ansonica Vendemmia Tardiva:* Min. 85% Ansonica (Inzolia). **Aging:** Riserva reds min. 2 yrs. (6 mos. in wood). Vendemmia Tardiva min. 18 mos. (6 mos. in wood). **Wine Types:** dw; sw; ros; dr

CONTROGUERRA
Region: Northernmost Abruzzo. **Grapes:** *Bianco:* Trebbiano Toscano min. 60%; Passerina min. 15%; others max. 25%. *Rosso:* Montepulciano min. 60%; Merlot and/or Cabernet Sauvignon min.15%; others max. 25%. *Spumante:* Trebbiano min. 60%; Verdicchio and/or Pecorino min. 30%; others max. 10%. *Passito Bianco:* Malvasia and/or Passerina min. 60%; others max. 40%. *Passito Rosso:* Montepulciano min. 60%; others max. 40%. *Moscato Amabile:* Moscato min. 85%. *Varietal Whites (4):* Min. 85% of variety; wines from Passerina, Malvasia, Riesling, Chardonnay. *Varietal Reds (4):* Min. 85% of variety; wines from Cabernet, Ciliegiolo, Merlot, Pinot Nero. **Aging:** Rosso Riserva min. 2 yrs. (6 mos. in bottle). **Wine Types:** dw (also frizzante); spdw; sw; dr (also novello); sr

COPERTINO
Region: Southern Puglia, nr. Lecce. **Grapes:** Negroamaro min. 70%; Malvasia Nera, Montepulciano, and/or Sangiovese max. 30% (Sangiovese max. 15%). **Aging:** Rosso Riserva min. 2 yrs. **Wine Types:** ros; dr

CORI
Region: Lazio, the Alban Hills south of Rome. **Grapes:** *Bianco:* Malvasia di Candia max. 70%; Trebbiano Toscano max. 40%; Bellone and/or Trebbiano Giallo max. 30%. *Rosso:* Montepulciano 40%–60%; Nero Buono 20%–40%; Cesanese 10%–30%. **Wine Types:** dw; sw; dr

CORTESE DELL'ALTO MONFERRATO
Region: Southeastern Piemonte, south of Alessandria and Asti. **Grapes:** Cortese min. 85%. **Wine Types:** dw (also frizzante); spdw

CORTONA
Region: Central-east Toscana, nr. Arezzo. **Grapes:** *Rosato:* Sangiovese 40%–60%; Canaiolo Nero 10%–30%; others max. 30%. *Vin Santo:* Trebbiano Toscano, Grechetto, and/or Malvasia min. 80%. *Vin Santo Occhio di Pernice:* Sangiovese and/or Malvasia Nera min. 80%. *Varietal wines* contain min. 85% of variety named. **Aging:** Reds min. 6 mos.; Vin Santo min. 3 yrs. (Riserva 5 yrs., including 6 mos. in bottle; Occhio di Pernice 8 yrs., including 6 mos. in bottle). **Wine Types:** dw; ros; dr; Vin Santo

COSTA D'AMALFI
Region: Campania, Amalfi coast. *Subzones:* "Furore" (villages of Furore, Praiano, Conca dei Marini, and/or Amalfi), "Ravello" (villages of Ravello, Scala, Minori, and/or Atrani), Tramonti (villages of Tramonti and/or Maiori). **Grapes:** *Bianco:* Falanghina and Biancolella min. 60% (Falanghina min. 40%); others max. 40%. *Rosso and Rosato:* Piedirosso min. 40%; Sciascinoso and/or Aglianico max. 60%; others max. 40%. **Aging:** Riserva reds with subzone designation min. 2 yrs. **Wine Types:** dw; dr; ros

COSTE DELLA SESIA
Region: Northern Piemonte, nr. Gattinara. **Grapes:** *Bianco:* Erbaluce 100%. *Rosso and Rosato:* Nebbiolo, Bonarda, Vespolina, Croatina, and/or Barbera min. 50%. *Varietal Reds:* Min. 85% of variety; wines from Nebbiolo (Spanna), Vespolina, Bonarda (Uva Rara), Croatina. **Wine Types:** dw; ros; dr

DELIA NIVOLELLI
Region: Western Sicilia. **Grapes:** *Bianco:* Grecanico, Inzolia (Ansonica), and/or Grillo min. 65%; others max. 35%. *Rosso and Novello:* Nero d'Avola (Calabrese), Perricone (Pignatello), Merlot, Cabernet Sauvignon, Syrah, and/or Sangiovese min. 65%; others max. 35%. *Spumante:* Grecanico, Chardonnay, Inzolia (Ansonica), Damaschino, and/or Grillo 100%; varietal spumante permitted if min. 85% of variety. *Varietal Whites (7):* Min. 85% of variety; wines from Chardonnay, Damaschino, Grecanico, Grillo, Inzolia (Ansonica),

Müller-Thurgau, Sauvignon. *Varietal Reds (6):* Min. 85% of variety; wine from Nero d'Avola (Calabrese), Merlot, Perricone (Pignatello), Cabernet Sauvignon, Syrah, Sangiovese. **Aging:** Riserva reds min. 2 yrs. **Wine Types:** dw; spdw; dr (also novello)

DOLCETTO D'ACQUI
Region: Southeastern Piemonte, nr. Ligurian border. **Grapes:** Dolcetto 100%. **Aging:** Superiore min. 1 yr. **Wine Types:** dr

DOLCETTO D'ALBA
Region: Southeastern Piemonte, nr. Alba. **Grapes:** Dolcetto 100%. **Aging:** Superiore min. 1 yr. **Wine Types:** dr

DOLCETTO D'ASTI
Region: Southeastern Piemonte, nr. Asti. **Grapes:** Dolcetto 100%. **Aging:** Superiore min. 1 yr. **Wine Types:** dr

DOLCETTO DELLE LANGHE MONREGALESI
Region: Southeastern Piemonte, west and south of Dogliani. **Grapes:** Dolcetto 100%. **Aging:** Superiore min. 1 yr. **Wine Types:** dr

DOLCETTO DI DIANO D'ALBA/DIANO D'ALBA
Region: Piemonte, the village of Diano d'Alba, bet. Alba and Barolo. **Grapes:** Dolcetto 100%. **Aging:** Superiore min. 1 yr. **Wine Types:** dr

DOLCETTO DI DOGLIANI
Region: Southeastern Piemonte, due south of Barolo in Dogliani. **Grapes:** Dolcetto 100%. **Aging:** Superiore min. 1 yr. **Wine Types:** dr

DOLCETTO DI OVADA
Region: Southeastern Piemonte, bet. the Dolcetto d'Acqui and Gavi zones. **Grapes:** Dolcetto 100%. **Aging:** Superiore min. 1 yr. **Wine Types:** dr

DONNICI
Region: Eastern Calabria, nr. Cosenza. **Grapes:** *Bianco:* Montonico min. 50%; Greco Bianco, Malvasia Bianca, and/or Pecorello Bianco max. 30%; others max. 20%. *Rosato and Rosso:* Gaglioppo min. 50%; Greco Nero min. 10%; Malvasia Bianca, Greco Bianco, Montonico Bianco, and/or Pecorello Bianco max. 10%; others max. 20%. **Aging:** Rosso Riserva min. 2 yrs. (6 mos. in wood). **Wine Types:** dw; ros; dr (also novello)

ELBA
Region: Toscana, the island of Elba. **Grapes:** *Aleatico:* Aleatico 100%. *Ansonica and Ansonica Passito:* Ansonica (Inzolia) min. 85%. *Bianco, Spumante, and Vin Santo:* Trebbiano Toscano (Procanico) min. 50%; Ansonica and/or Vermentino max. 50%; others max. 20%. *Moscato:* Moscato 100%. *Rosso, Rosato, and Vin Santo Occhio di Pernice:* Sangiovese min. 60%; others max. 40% (white max. 10%). **Aging:** Rosso Riserva min. 24 mos (12 mos. in wood). Vin Santo min. 3 yrs. (Riserva 4 yrs.) in barrels no larger than 5 hl. **Wine Types:** dw; spdw; sw; ros; dr; Vin Santo

ELORO
Region: Southeasternmost Sicilia. **Grapes:** *Rosso and Rosato:* Nero d'Avola (Calabrese), Perricone (Pignatello), and/or Frappato min. 90%. *Varietal Reds (3):* Min. 90% of variety; wines from Nero d'Avola (Calabrese), Perricone (Pignatello), Frappato. *Eloro Pachino:* Nero d'Avola min. 80%; Perricone (Pignatello) and/or Frappato max. 20%. **Aging:** Pachino min. 6 mos.; Riserva reds min. 2 yrs. (6 mos. in wood). **Wine Types:** ros; dr

ERBALUCE DI CALUSO/CALUSO
Region: Piemonte, northeast of Torino. **Grapes:** Erbaluce 100%. **Aging:** Passito min. 4 yrs. (Passito Riserva 5 yrs.). **Wine Types:** dw; spdw; sw

ESINO
Region: Marche. **Grapes:** *Bianco:* Verdicchio min. 50%; others max. 50%. *Rosso:* Sangiovese and/or Montepulciano min. 60%; others max. 40%. **Wine Types:** dw (also frizzante); dr (also novello)

EST! EST!! EST!!! DI MONTEFIASCONE
Region: Northern Lazio, around Lago di Bolsena. **Grapes:** Trebbiano Toscano (Procanico) 65%; Malvasia Bianca Toscana 20%; Rossetto (Trebbiano Giallo) 15%. **Wine Types:** dw; sw

ETNA
Region: Eastern Sicilia, Mt. Etna volcano. **Grapes:** *Bianco:* Carricante min. 60%; Catarratto max. 40%; Trebbiano, Minella, others max. 15%. *Bianco Superiore:* Min. 80% Carricante. *Rosato and Rosso:* Nerello Mascalese min. 80%; Nerello Cappuccio max. 20%; others max. 10%. **Wine Types:** dw; ros; dr

FALERIO DEI COLLI ASCOLANI
Region: Southern Marche. **Grapes:** Trebbiano Toscano 20%–50%; Passerina 10%–30%; Pecorino 10%–30%; others max. 20%. **Wine Types:** dw

FALERNO DEL MASSICO
Region: Northern coast of Campania. **Grapes:** *Bianco:* Falanghina 100%. *Rosso:* Aglianico 60%–80%; Piedirosso 20%–40%; Primitivo and/or Barbera max. 20%. *Primitivo:* Primitivo min. 85%; Aglianico, Piedirosso, Barbera max. 15%. **Aging:** Riserva reds min. 2 yrs. (1 yr. in wood). **Wine Types:** dw; dr

FARA
Region: Northern Piemonte, nr. Novara. **Grapes:** Nebbiolo (Spanna) 30%–50%; Vespolina 10%–30%; Bonarda (Uva Rara) max. 40%. **Aging:** Min. 3 yrs. (2 yrs. in wood). **Wine Types:** dr

FARO
Region: Eastern Sicilia, nr. Messina. **Grapes:** Nerello Mascalese 45%–60%; Nocera 5%–10%; Nerello Cappuccio 15%–30%; Calabrese (Nero d'Avola), Gaglioppo, and/or Sangiovese max. 15%. **Aging:** Min. 1 yr. **Wine Types:** dr

FRASCATI
Region: Lazio, the Alban Hills south of Rome. **Grapes:** Malvasia Bianca di Candia and/or Trebbiano Toscano min. 70%; Greco and/or Malvasia del Lazio max. 30%; others max. 10%. **Wine Types:** dw; sw

FREISA D'ASTI
Region: Piemonte, Asti province. **Grapes:** Freisa 100%. **Aging:** Superiore min. 1 yr. **Wine Types:** dr (also frizzante); sr (also frizzante); spsr

FREISA DI CHIERI
Region: Piemonte, just east of Torino. **Grapes:** Freisa 100%. **Aging:** Superiore min. 1 yr. **Wine Types:** dr (also frizzante); sr (also frizzante); spsr

FRIULI ANNIA
Region: Friuli–Venezia Giulia coast, bet. Aquilea and Latisana. **Grapes:** *Bianco, Rosato, and Rosso:* Variable. *Varietal Wines (12):* Min. 90% of variety. Whites (8): Chardonnay, Malvasia Istriana, Pinot Bianco, Pinot Grigio, Sauvignon, Tocai Friulano, Traminer Aromatico, Verduzzo. Reds (4): Cabernet Franc, Cabernet Sauvignon, Merlot, Refosco del Peduncolo Rosso. **Aging:** Riserva reds min. 2 yrs. (1 yr. in wood). **Wine Types:** dw (also frizzante); spdw; sw; ros; dr

FRIULI AQUILEIA
Region: Friuli–Venezia Giulia, Adriatic coast. **Grapes:** *Bianco:* Variable. *Rosso:* Variable. *Rosato:* Merlot 100%. *Varietal Wines (15):* Min. 90% of variety. Whites (10): Chardonnay, Malvasia Istriana, Müller-Thurgau, Pinot Bianco, Pinot Grigio, Riesling Renano, Sauvignon, Tocai Friulano, Traminer Aromatico, Verduzzo. Reds (5): Cabernet, Cabernet Franc, Cabernet Sauvignon, Merlot, Refosco. **Aging:** Riserva reds min. 2 yrs. **Wine Types:** dw (also frizzante); spdw; ros; dr (also novello)

FRIULI GRAVE
Region: Central plain of Friuli–Venezia Giulia. **Grapes:** *Bianco, Rosato, and Rosso:* Variable. *Varietal Wines (14):* Min. 90% of variety. Whites (8): Chardonnay, Pinot Bianco, Pinot Grigio, Riesling Renano, Sauvignon, Tocai Friulano, Traminer Aromatico, Verduzzo. Reds (6): Cabernet, Cabernet Franc, Cabernet Sauvignon, Merlot, Pinot Nero, and/or Refosco. *Spumante:* Chardonnay, Pinot Bianco min. 75%; Pinot Nero max. 10%; others max. 15%. **Aging:** Riserva min. 2 yrs. **Wine Types:** dw (also frizzante); spdw; ros; dr (also novello)

FRIULI ISONZO
Region: Eastern Friuli–Venezia Giulia. **Grapes:** *Bianco, Rosato, and Rosso:* Variable. *Varietal Wines (20):* 100% of variety. Whites (12): Chardonnay, Malvasia Istriana, Moscato Giallo, Moscato Rosa, Pinot Bianco, Pinot Grigio, Riesling Italico, Riesling Renano, Sauvignon, Tocai Friulano, Traminer Aromatico, Verduzzo. Reds (8): Cabernet, Cabernet Franc, Cabernet Sauvignon, Franconia, Merlot, Pinot Nero, Refosco, Schioppettino. *Vendemmia Tardiva:* Tocai Friulano, Sauvignon, Verduzzo Friulano, Pinot Bianco, Chardonnay. **Wine Types:** dw (also frizzante); sw; ros (also frizzante); dr

FRIULI LATISANA
Region: Southwestern Friuli–Venezia Giulia. **Grapes:** *Bianco and Rosso:* Variable. *Rosato:* Merlot 70%–80%; Cabernet Franc, Cabernet

Sauvignon, and/or Refosco 20%–30%. *Varietal Wines (16):* Min. 90% of variety. Whites (9): Chardonnay, Malvasia Istriana, Pinot Bianco, Pinot Grigio, Riesling Renano, Sauvignon, Tocai Friulano, Traminer Aromatico, Verduzzo. Reds (7): Cabernet, Cabernet Franc, Cabernet Sauvignon, Franconia, Merlot, Pinot Nero, Refosco. *Spumante:* Chardonnay, Pinot Bianco, and/or Pinot Nero min. 90%. **Aging:** Riserva reds min. 2 yrs. **Wine Types:** dw (also frizzante); spdw; sw; ros (also frizzante); dr (also frizzante)

GABIANO
Region: Southeastern Piemonte, north of Asti. **Grapes:** Barbera 90%–95%; Freisa and/or Grignolino 5%–10%. **Aging:** Riserva min. 2 yrs. **Wine Types:** dr

GALATINA
Region: Southern Puglia. **Grapes:** *Bianco:* Chardonnay min. 55%; others max. 45%. *Chardonnay:* Chardonnay min. 85%. *Rosato and Rosso:* Negroamaro min. 65%; others max. 35%. *Negro Amaro:* Negro Amaro min. 85%. **Aging:** Negroamaro Riserva min. 2 yrs. (6 mos. in wood). **Wine Types:** dw (also frizzante); ros (also frizzante); dr (also novello)

GALLUCCIO
Region: Northwestern Campania, nr. Lazio. **Grapes:** *Bianco:* Falanghina min. 70%; others max. 30%. *Rosso and Rosato:* Aglianico min. 70%. **Aging:** Riserva min. 2 yrs. (1 yr. in wood). **Wine Types:** dw; dr; ros

GAMBELLARA
Region: Central Veneto, adjacent to Soave DOC. **Grapes:** Garganega 80%–100%. **Aging:** Vin Santo min. 2 yrs.**Wine Types:** dw; sw; Vin Santo

GARDA/GARDA CLASSICO
Region: Lombardia and Veneto, southern shores of Lake Garda. **Grapes:** *Garda:* Varietal whites and reds with a min. 85% of variety. Whites (9): Garganega, Pinot Bianco, Pinot Grigio, Chardonnay, Tocai Friulano, Riesling Italico, Riesling, Cortese, Sauvignon. Reds (7): Barbera, Cabernet, Cabernet Franc, Cabernet Sauvignon, Corvina, Marzemino, Merlot. *Garda Classico:* 4 wine types: *Bianco:* Riesling min. 70%. *Rosso and Chiaretto:* Groppello min. 30%; Marzemino min. 5%; Sangiovese min. 5%; Barbera min. 5%; others max. 10%. *Groppello:* Groppello min. 85%. **Aging:** Groppello Riserva min. 2 yrs. (3 mos. in bottle). **Wine Types:** dw; dr; spdw; ros; spros

GARDA COLLI MANTOVANI
Region: East Lombardia nr. Mantova. **Grapes:** *Bianco:* Garganega max. 35%; Trebbiano max. 35%; Chardonnay max. 35%; Sauvignon and/or Riesling max. 15%. *Rosato and Rosso:* Merlot max. 45%; Rondinella max. 40%; Cabernet max. 20%. *Varietal Whites (4):* Min. 85% of variety. Wines from Chardonnay; Pinot Bianco; Pinot Grigio; Sauvignon. *Varietal Reds (2):* Min. 85% of variety. Wines from Cabernet (Sauvignon and/or Franc); Merlot. **Aging:** Cabernet and Merlot Riserva min. 2 yrs. (1 yr. in wood) **Wine Types:** dw; ros; dr

GENAZZANO
Region: Lazio, bet. Rome and Frosinone. **Grapes:** *Bianco:* Malvasia di Candia 50%–70%; Bellone and/or Bombino 10%–30%; Trebbiano Toscano, Pinot Bianco, others max. 40%. *Rosso:* Sangiovese 70%–90%; Cesanese 10%–30%; others max. 20%. **Wine Types:** dw; dr; sw; sr

GIOIA DEL COLLE
Region: Central Puglia. **Grapes:** *Bianco:* Trebbiano Toscano 50%–70%; others 30%–50%. *Rosato and Rosso:* Primitivo 50%–60%; Montepulciano, Sangiovese, Negroamaro, Malvasia Nera 40%–50% (Malvasia max. 10%). *Primitivo:* Primitivo 100%. *Aleatico:* Aleatico min. 85%. **Aging:** Aleatico min. 6 mos.; Aleatico Riserva min. 2 yrs. (1 yr. in wood); Primitivo Riserva min. 2 yrs. **Wine Types:** dw; ros; dr; sr; fr

GIRÒ DI CAGLIARI
Region: Southwestern Sardegna. **Grapes:** Girò min. 95%. **Aging:** Wines released July 1 of the year after vintage. Liquoroso Riserva min. 2 yrs. (1 yr. in wood). **Wine Types:** sr; fr

GOLFO DEL TIGULLIO
Region: Liguria, Gulf of Tigullio. **Grapes:** *Bianco:* Vermentino 20%–70%; Bianchetta Genovese 20%–70%; others max. 40%. *Rosso and Rosato:* Ciliegiolo 20%–70%; Dolcetto 20%–70%; others max. 40%. *Bianchetta Genovese:* Min. 85% Bianchetta. *Vermentino:* Min.

85% Vermentino. *Ciliegiolo:* Min. 85% Ciliegiolo. *Moscato and Moscato Passito:* Moscato 100%. *Passito:* Variable. *Spumante:* Variable. **Aging:** Passito min. 1 yr. **Wine Types:** dw (also frizzante); spdw; sw; ros (also frizzante); dr (also frizzante and novello)

GRAVINA
Region: Central Puglia, nr. Gravina. **Grapes:** Malvasia del Chianti 40%–65%; Greco di Tufo and/or Bianco d'Alessano 35%–60%; Bombino Bianco, Trebbiano Toscano, and/or Verdeca max. 10%. **Wine Types:** dw; spdw; sw

GRECO DI BIANCO
Region: Southern Calabria. **Grapes:** Greco di Bianco min. 95%. **Aging:** 1 yr. **Wine Types:** sw

GRIGNOLINO D'ASTI
Region: Southeastern Piemonte, nr. Asti. **Grapes:** Grignolino min. 90%; Freisa max. 10%. **Wine Types:** dr

GRIGNOLINO DEL MONFERRATO CASALESE
Region: Southeastern Piemonte, north of Asti. **Grapes:** Grignolino min. 90%; Freisa max. 10%. **Wine Types:** dr

GUARDIA SANFRAMONDI/GUARDIOLO
Region: Campania, north of Benevento. **Grapes:** *Bianco:* Malvasia Bianca di Candia 50%–70%; Falanghina 20%–30%; others max. 10%. *Falanghina:* Falanghina min. 90%. *Rosso and Rosato:* Sangiovese min. 80%; others max. 20%. *Spumante:* Falanghina min. 70%; others max. 30%. *Aglianico:* Aglianico min. 90%. **Wine Types:** dw; spdw

ISCHIA
Region: Campania, the island of Ischia. **Grapes:** *Bianco:* Forastera 45%–70%; Biancolella 30%–55%; others max. 15%. *Rosso:* Guarnaccia 40%–50%; Piedirosso 40%–50%; others max. 15%. *Forastera:* Forastera min. 85%. *Biancolella:* Biancolella min. 85%. *Piedirosso (or Per e Palummo):* Piedirosso (Per e Palummo) min. 85%. **Aging:** Whites min. 30 days in bottle; reds min. 90 days in bottle. **Wine Types:** dw; spdw; dr

LACRIMA DI MORRO/LACRIMA DI MORRO D'ALBAMARCHE
Region: Central Marche, nr. Ancona. **Grapes:** Lacrima min. 85%. **Wine Types:** dr (also frizzante); sr

LAGO DI CALDARO/CALDARO
Region: Trentino–Alto Adige. **Grapes:** Schiava min. 85%; Pinot Nero and/or Lagrein max. 15%. **Wine Types:** dr

LAGO DI CALDARO/KALTERERSEE
Region: Alto Adige, around Lake Caldaro. Also treated as a subzone of the Alto Adige DOC (see the Alto Adige Lago di Caldaro subzone). **Grapes:** Schiava min. 85%; Pinot Nero and/or Lagrein max. 15%. **Wine Types:** dr

LAGO DI CORBARA
Region: Southwestern Umbria. **Grapes:** *Rosso:* Cabernet Sauvignon, Merlot, and/or Pinot Nero min. 70%; Aleatico, Barbera, Cabernet Franc, Canaiolo, Cesanese, Ciliegiolo, Colorino, Dolcetto, and/or Montepulciano max. 30%. *Varietal Reds (3):* Min. 85% of variety; wines from Cabernet Sauvignon, Merlot, Pinot Nero. **Wine Types:** dr

LAMBRUSCO DI SORBARA
Region: Emilia-Romagna plains north of Modena. **Grapes:** Lambrusco di Sorbara min. 60%; Lambrusco Salamino 40%. **Wine Types:** ros (frizzante); dr (frizzante); sr (frizzante)

LAMBRUSCO GRASPAROSSA DI CASTELVETRO
Region: Emilia-Romagna, plains south of Modena. **Grapes:** Lambrusco Grasparossa min. 85%. **Wine Types:** ros (frizzante); dr (frizzante); sr (frizzante)

LAMBRUSCO MANTOVANO
Region: Southern Lombardia, nr. Mantova. *Subzones:* Viadanese-Sabbionetano and Oltrepò Mantovano. **Grapes:** Lambrusco Viadanese, Lambrusco Maestri, Lambrusco Marani, and/or Lambrusco Salamino min. 85%; Lambrusco di Sorbara, Lambrusco Grasparossa, Ancellotta, and/or Fortana max. 15%. **Wine Types:** dr (frizzante); sr (frizzante); ros (frizzante); sros (frizzante)

LAMBRUSCO SALAMINO DI SANTA CROCE
Region: Emilia-Romagna, plains north of Modena. **Grapes:** Lambrusco Salamino min. 90%. **Wine Types:** ros (frizzante); dr (frizzante); sr (frizzante)

LAMEZIA
Region: Calabria, Mediterranean coast. **Grapes:** *Bianco:* Greco Bianco max. 50%; Trebbiano Toscano max. 40%; Malvasia min. 20%; others max. 30%. *Rosato and Rosso:* Nerello Mascalese and/or Nerello Cappuccio 30%–50%; Gaglioppo and/or Magliocco 25%–35%; Greco Nero and/or Marsigliana Nera 25%–35%; others max. 20%. *Greco:* Grego min. 85%. **Aging:** Rosso Riserva min. 3 yrs. (6 mos. wood, 6 mos. bottle). **Wine Types:** dw; ros; dr

LANGHE
Region: Southeastern Piemonte around Alba. **Grapes:** *Bianco and Rosso:* Variable. *Varietal whites:* 100% of variety; wines from Arneis, Chardonnay, Favorita. *Varietal reds:* 100% of variety; wines from Nebbiolo, Dolcetto. **Wine Types:** dw; dr (also frizzante); sr (also frizzante)

LESSINI DURELLO
Region: Northern Veneto, nr. Trentino. **Grapes:** Durella min. 85%; Garganega, Trebbiano di Soave, Pinot Bianco, Pinot Nero, and/or Chardonnay max. 15%. **Wine Types:** dw; spdw

LESSONA
Region: Northern Piemonte, nr. Vercelli. **Grapes:** Nebbiolo min. 75%; Vespolina and Bonarda max. 25%. **Aging:** Min. 2 yrs. (1 yr. in wood). **Wine Types:** dr

LEVERANO
Region: Southern Puglia. **Grapes:** *Bianco, Bianco Passito, and Vendemmia Tardiva:* Malvasia Bianca min. 50%; Bombino Bianco max. 40%; others max. 30%. *Malvasia Bianca:* Malvasia Bianca min. 85%. *Rosso and Rosato:* Negroamaro min. 50%; Malvasia Nera, Montepulciano, and/or Sangiovese max. 40%; others max. 30%. *Negro Amaro and Negro Amaro Rosato:* Negroamaro min. 85%. **Aging:** Rosso Riserva min. 2 yrs. **Wine Types:** dw; sw; ros; dr (also novello)

LISON-PRAMAGGIORE
Region: Northeastern Veneto, also western Friuli. **Grapes:** *Bianco:* Tocai Friulano 50%–70%; others max. 50%. *Rosso and Rosato:* Merlot 50%–70%; others max. 50%. *Lison and Lison Classico:* Tocai Friulano min. 85%. *Varietal wines (13):* Min. 85% of variety. Whites: Pinot Bianco, Chardonnay, Pinot Grigio, Riesling Italico, Riesling Renano, Sauvignon, Verduzzo. Reds: Merlot, Malbech, Cabernet, Cabernet Franc, Cabernet Sauvignon, Refosco. **Wine Types:** dw (also frizzante); spdw; sw; dr (also novello); ros

LIZZANO
Region: Puglia, south of Taranto. **Grapes:** *Bianco:* Trebbiano Toscano 40%–60%; Chardonnay and/or Pinot Bianco min. 30%; Malvasia Bianca max. 10%; Sauvignon and/or Bianco d'Alessano max. 25%. *Rosso and Rosato:* Negroamaro 60%–80%; Montepulciano, Sangiovese, Bombino Nero, and/or Pinot Nero max. 40%; others max. 10%. *Negro Amaro Rosso and Rosato:* Negro Amaro min. 85%. *Malvasia Nera:* Malvasia Nera min. 85%. **Wine Types:** dw (also frizzante); spdw; ros; spros; dr (also novello)

LOAZZOLO
Region: Piemonte, south of Asti. **Grapes:** Moscato Bianco 100%. **Aging:** Min. 2 yrs. **Wine Types:** sw (passito)

LOCOROTONDO
Region: Southeastern Puglia, the village of Locorotondo. **Grapes:** Verdeca 50%–65%; Bianco d'Alessano 35%–50%; Fiano, Bombino Bianco, and/or Malvasia Toscana max. 5%. **Wine Types:** dw; spdw

LUGANA
Region: Lombardia and Veneto, the southern shore of Lake Garda. **Grapes:** Trebbiano di Lugana min. 90%. **Wine Types:** dw; spdw

MALVASIA DELLE LIPARI
Region: Sicilia, the Aeolian islands of Lipari, Salina, Vulcano, and Stromboli. **Grapes:** Malvasia di Lipari min. 95%. **Aging:** Passito min. 9 mos.; Liquoroso min. 6 mos. **Wine Types:** sw

MALVASIA DI BOSA
Region: Western coast of Sardegna. **Grapes:** Malvasia di Sardegna min. 95%. **Aging:** All versions min. 2 yrs. **Wine Types:** dw; sw; fw

MALVASIA DI CAGLIARI
Region: Southwestern Sardegna. **Grapes:** Malvasia di Sardegna min. 95% **Aging:** Wines released July 1 of the year after vintage. Liquoroso Riserva min. 2 yrs. (1 yr. in wood). **Wine Types:** dw; sw; fw

MALVASIA DI CASORZO D'ASTI
Region: Southeastern Piemonte, bet. Asti and Canale Monferrato.
Grapes: Malvasia di Casorzo min. 90%; Barbera, Freisa, and/or
Grignolino max. 10%. **Aging:** Superiore min. 1 yr. **Wine Types:** ros
(frizzante); sros; spros; sr (frizzante); spsr

MALVASIA DI CASTELNUOVO DON BOSCO
Region: Southeastern Piemonte, nr. Asti. **Grapes:** Malvasia di
Schierano min. 85%; Freisa max. 15%. **Aging:** Superiore min. 1 yr.
Wine Types: ros (frizzante); sros; spros; sr (frizzante); spsr

MANDROLISAI
Region: Central Sardegna. **Grapes:** Bovale Sardo min. 35%; Cannonau
20%–35%; Monica 20%–35%. **Aging:** Rosso Superiore min. 2 yrs.
(min. 1 yr. in wood). **Wine Types:** dr; ros

MARINO
Region: Lazio, the Alban Hills south of Rome. **Grapes:** Malvasia Bianca
di Candia max. 60%; Trebbiano 25%–55%; Malvasia del Lazio
5%–45%; others max. 10%. **Wine Types:** dw; sw

MARSALA
Region: Western Sicilia. **Grapes:** *Oro and Ambra versions:* Grillo,
Catarratto, Ansonica (Inzolia), and/or Damaschino. *Rubino versions:*
Perricone (Pignatello), Nero d'Avola (Calabrese), and/or Nerello
Mascalese min. 70%; other whites max. 30%. **Aging:** Fine min. 1 yr.;
Superiore min. 2 yrs.; Superiore Riserva min. 4 yrs.; Vergine (Soleras)
min. 5 yrs.; Vergine (Soleras) Riserva (Stravecchio) min. 10 yrs. **Wine
Types:** fw; fr

MARTINA/MARTINA FRANCA
Region: Puglia, south of Bari. **Grapes:** Verdeca 50%–65%; Bianco
d'Alessano 35%–50%; Fiano, Bombino Bianco, and/or Malvasia
Toscana max. 5%. **Wine Types:** dw; spdw

MATINO
Region: Southern Puglia, bet. Alezio and Matino. **Grapes:** Negroamaro
min. 70%; Malvasia Nera and/or Sangiovese max. 30%. **Wine Types:**
ros; dr

MELISSA
Region: Ionian coast of Calabria. **Grapes:** *Bianco:* Greco Bianco
80%–95%; Trebbiano Toscano and/or Malvasia Bianca 5%–20%.
Rosso: Gaglioppo 75%–95%; Greco Nero, Greco Bianco, Trebbiano
Toscano, and/or Malvasia Bianca 5%–25%. **Aging:** Rosso Superiore
min. 2 yrs. **Wine Types:** dw; dr

MENFI
Region: Southwestern coast of Sicilia. *Subzones:* Feudo dei Fiori used
for some whites; Bonera used for some reds. **Grapes:** *Bianco:* Inzolia
(Ansonica), Chardonnay, Catarratto, and/or Grecanico min. 75%;
others max. 25%. *Feudo dei Fiori:* Chardonnay and/or Inzolia
(Ansonica) min. 80%; others max. 20%. *Varietal whites (3):* Min. 85%
of variety; wines from Chardonnay, Grecanico, Inzolia (Ansonica).
Rosso: Nero d'Avola, Sangiovese, Merlot, Cabernet Sauvignon, and/or
Syrah min. 70%; others max. 30%. *Bonera:* Cabernet Sauvignon,
Merlot, Nero d'Avola, Sangiovese, and/or Syrah min. 85%. *Varietal
reds (5):* Min. 85% of variety; wines from Nero d'Avola, Sangiovese,
Cabernet Sauvignon, Merlot, Syrah. *Vendemmia Tardiva:* Chardonnay,
Catarratto, Inzolia (Ansonica), and/or Sauvignon 100%. **Aging:** Bonera
min. 1 yr.; Bonera, Rosso, and varietal red Riserva min. 2 yrs. **Wine
Types:** dw; ros; dr

MOLISE/DEL MOLISE
Region: Molise. **Grapes:** *Varietal whites, reds, and rosés:* Whites:
Chardonnay, Falanghina, Greco Bianco, Moscato Bianco, Pinot
Bianco, Sauvignon, Trebbiano. Reds: Aglianico, Cabernet Sauvignon,
Montepulciano, Sangiovese, Tintilia. *Spumante:* Chardonnay, Pinot
Bianco, and/or Moscato. *Varietal Spumante:* Min. 85% of variety.
Aging: Min. 2 yrs. (6 mos. in wood). **Wine Types:** dw; spdw; sw; dr
(novello); sr

MONFERRATO
Region: Southeastern Piemonte, bet. Ast and Alessandria. **Grapes:**
Bianco and Rosso: Variable. *Chiaretto/Ciaret:* Barbera, Bonarda,
Cabernet Franc, Cabernet Sauvignon, Freisa, Grignolino, Pinot Nero,
and/or Nebbiolo min. 85%. *Dolcetto:* Dolcetto min. 85%. *Freisa:*
Freisa min. 85%. *Monferrato Casalese:* Cortese min. 85%. **Wine
Types:** dw (frizzante); ros (frizzante); dr (frizzante)

MONICA DI CAGLIARI
Region: Southwestern Sardegna. Grapes: Monica min. 95%. Aging:
Wines released July 1 the year after vintage. Liquoroso Riserva min. 2
yrs. (1 yr. in wood). Wine Types: dr; sr; fr

MONICA DI SARDEGNA
Region: Sardegna. Grapes: Monica min. 85%. Aging: Wines released
Mar. 31 of the year after vintage. Superiore 1 yr. Wine Types: dr (also
frizzante); sr

MONTECARLO
Region: Western Toscana, bet. Lucca and Pistoia. Grapes: *Bianco and Vin
Santo:* Trebbiano Toscano 40%–60%; Sémillon, Pinot Gris, Pinot Bianco,
Vermentino, Sauvignon, and Roussanne 40%–60%. *Rosso and Vin
Santo Occhio di Pernice:* Sangiovese 50%–75%; Canaiolo Nero
5%–15%; Ciliegiolo, Colorino, Malvasia Nera, Sjriak, Cabernets Franc
and Sauvignon, and/or Merlot 10%–15%; others max. 20%. Aging:
Rosso Riserva min. 2 yrs. (6 mos. in bottle); Vin Santo min. 3 yrs.
(Riserva 4 yrs.) in barrels no larger than 5 hl. Wine Types: dw; dr; Vin
Santo

MONTECOMPATRI-COLONNA/MONTECOMPATRI/COLONNA
Region: Lazio, the Alban hills south of Rome. Grapes: Malvasia max.
70%; Trebbiano min. 30%; Bellone and/or Bonvino max. 10%. Wine
Types: dw; sw

MONTECUCCO
Region: Southern Toscana, nr. Grosseto. Grapes: *Bianco:* Trebbiano
Toscano min. 60%; others max. 40%. *Vermentino:* Vermentino min.
85%. *Rosso:* Sangiovese min. 60%; others max. 40%. *Sangiovese:*
Sangiovese min. 85%. Aging: Rosso/Sangiovese Riserva min. 2 yrs.
(18 mos. in wood). Wine Types: dw; dr

MONTEFALCO
Region: Central Umbria. Grapes: *Bianco:* Grechetto min. 50%;
Trebbiano Toscano 20%–35%; other whites max. 15%. *Rosso:*
Sangiovese 60%–70%; Sagrantino 10%–15%; other reds max.
Aging: Rosso min. 18 mos. (Riserva 30 mos., min. 12 mos. in wood).
Wine Types: dw; dr

MONTELLO E COLLI ASOLANI
Region: Northern Veneto, nr. Treviso. Grapes: Rosso: Merlot
40%–60%; Cabernet Franc 20%–30%; Cabernet Sauvignon
10%–20%; others max. 15%. *Varietal wines (8):* Min. 85% of variety.
Whites: Prosecco, Chardonnay, Pinot Bianco, Pinot Grigio. Reds:
Cabernet, Cabernet Franc, Cabernet Sauvignon, Merlot. Aging:
Superiore reds min. 2 yrs. (6 mos. in wood). Wine Types: dw; spdw; dr

MONTEPULCIANO D'ABRUZZO
Region: All Abruzzo. Grapes: Montepulciano min. 85%. Aging: Rosso
Riserva min. 2 yrs. (6 mos. in wood). Wine Types: dr; ros

MONTEREGIO DI MASSA MARITTIMA
Region: Southern coast of Toscana. Grapes: *Bianco:* Trebbiano
Toscano min. 50%; Vermentino, Malvasia, and/or Ansonica (Inzolia)
max. 30%; others singly (max. 15%) or collectively (max. 30%).
Vermentino: Vermentino min. 90%. *Rosato, Rosso, and Novello:*
Sangiovese min. 80%; others singly (max. 10%) or collectively (max.
20%). *Vin Santo:* Trebbiano Toscano and/or Malvasia min. 70%;
others max. 30%. *Vin Santo Occhio di Pernice:* Sangiovese
50%–70%; Malvasia Nera 10%–50%; others max. 30%. Aging: Rosso
Riserva min. 2 yrs. (6 mos. in wood, 3 mos. in bottle). Vin Santo min.
3 yrs. (Riserva 4 yrs.) in barrels no larger than 5 hl. Wine Types: dw;
ros; dr (also novello); Vin Santo

MONTESCUDAIO
Region: Northern coast of Toscana. Grapes: *Bianco and Vin Santo:*
Trebbiano Toscano min. 50%; others max. 50%. *Varietal whites:* Min.
85% of variety. *Rosso:* Sangiovese min. 50%; others max. 50%.
Varietal reds: Min. 85% of variety. Aging: Rosso Riserva min. 2 yrs. (3
mos. in bottle); Vin Santo min. 4 yrs. (18 mos. in barrels no larger than
5 hl.). Wine Types: dw; dr; Vin Santo

MORELLINO DI SCANSANO
Region: Southern Toscana, around the commune of Scansano. Grapes:
Sangiovese ("Morellino") 85%–100%; others max. 15%. Aging: Rosso
Riserva min. 2 yrs. (1 yr. in wood). Wine Types: dr

MOSCADELLO DI MONTALCINO
Region: Toscana, the commune of Montalcino. Grapes: Moscato

Bianco 85%–100%; others max. 15%. **Aging:** Vendemmia Tardiva min. 1 yr. **Wine Types:** sw; spsw

MOSCATO DI CAGLIARI
Region: Southwestern Sardegna. **Grapes:** Moscato Bianco min. 95%. **Aging:** Wines released Mar. 1 of the year after vintage. Liquoroso Riserva 1 yr. **Wine Types:** sw; fw

MOSCATO DI NOTO NATURALE/MOSCATO DI NOTO
Region: Southeastern Sicilia. **Grapes:** Moscato Bianco 100%. **Aging:** Liquoroso min. 5 mos. **Wine Types:** sw; spsw

MOSCATO DI PANTELLERIA NATURALE/MOSCATO DI PANTELLERIA
Region: Sicilia, the satellite island of Pantelleria. **Grapes:** Zibibbo (Moscato) 100%. **Wine Types:** sw; fw

MOSCATO DI SARDEGNA
Region: Sardegna. *Subzones:* Tempio or Tempio Pausania for wines from that commune and Gallura for wines of the Gallura region. **Grapes:** Moscato Bianco min. 90%. **Wine Types:** spsw

MOSCATO DI SIRACUSA
Region: Southeastern Sicilia. **Grapes:** Moscato Bianco 100%. **Wine Types:** sw

MOSCATO DI SORSO-SENNORI
Region: Northern coast of Sardinia nr. Sassari. **Grapes:** Moscato Bianco min. 95%. **Aging:** Wines released Mar. 1 the year after vintage. **Wine Types:** sw; fw

MOSCATO DI TRANI
Region: North-central Puglia, bet. Foggia and Bari. **Grapes:** Moscato Bianco min. 85% **Aging:** Naturale min. 6 mos.; Liquoroso min. 1 yr. **Wine Types:** sw; fw

MOSCATO PASSITO DI PANTELLERIA/PASSITO DI PANTELLERIA
Region: Sicilia, the satellite island of Pantelleria. Passito-style wine from dried grapes. **Grapes:** Zibibbo (Moscato) 100%. **Aging:** Extra min. 1 yr. **Wine Types:** sw; fw

NARDÒ
Region: Southern Puglia, on the Gulf of Taranto. **Grapes:** Negroamaro min. 80%; Malvasia Nera and/or Montepulciano max. 20%. **Aging:** Rosso Riserva min. 2 yrs. **Wine Types:** ros; dr

NASCO DI CAGLIARI
Region: Southwestern Sardegna. **Grapes:** Nasco min. 95%. **Aging:** Wines released July 1 of the year after vintage. Liquoroso Riserva min. 2 yrs. (1 yr. in wood). **Wine Types:** dw; sw; fw

NEBBIOLO D'ALBA
Region: Southeastern Piemonte, nr. Alba. **Grapes:** Nebbiolo 100%. **Aging:** Secco min. 1 yr. **Wine Types:** dr; sr; spdr

NURAGUS DI CAGLIARI
Region: Southwestern Sardegna. **Grapes:** Nuragus 85%–100%. **Wine Types:** dw (also frizzante); sw

OFFIDA
Region: Southern Marche. **Grapes:** Whites from Pecorino (min. 85% and Passerina (min. 85%); Rosso from Montepulciano (50%) and cabnernet sauvignon (30%). **Wine Types:** dw; jr; Vin Santo

OLTREPÒ PAVESE
Region: Southwestern corner of Lombardia. *Subzones:* Buttafuoco and Sangue di Giuda cover the villages of Broni, Stradella, Canneto Pavese, Montescano, Castana, Cigognola, and Pietra de' Giorgi. **Grapes:** *Spumante:* Pinot Nero min. 70%; Chardonnay, Pinot Grigio, and/or Pinot Bianco max. 30%. *Rosso, Rosato, Buttafuoco, and Sangue di Giuda:* Barbera 25%–65%; Croatina 25%–65%; Uva Rara, Vespolina (Ughetta), and/or Pinot Nero max. 45%. *Bonarda:* Croatina, *Barbera:* Barbera. *Varietal Wines (10):* Min. 85% of variety. Whites (6): Riesling Italico, Riesling Renano, Cortese, Moscato, Pinot Grigio, Chardonnay. *Sauvignon:* Sauvignon min. 85%. *Cabernet Sauvignon:* Cabernet Sauvignon min. 85%. *Liquoroso and Passito:* Moscato min. 85%. *Malvasia:* Malvasia min. 85%. **Aging:** Spumante min. 18 mos. in bottle, released 24 mos. from vintage; Moscato Passito min. 8 mos.; Rosso Riserva min. 2 yrs. **Wine Types:** dw (also frizzante); dr (also frizzante); ros; sw (also frizzante); spdw

ORCIA
Region: Toscana, bet. Montalcino and Montepulciano. **Grapes:** *Bianco:* Trebbiano Toscano min. 50%; others max. 50%. *Rosso and Novello:* Sangiovese min. 60%; others max. 40% (white grapes max. 10%). *Vin Santo:* Trebbiano Toscano and/or Malvasia Bianca min. 50%; others

max. 50%. **Aging:** Bianco and Rosso released Mar. 1 the year after vintage. Vin Santo min. 3 yrs. **Wine Types:** dw; dr (also novello); Vin Santo

ORTA NOVA
Region: Northern Puglia. **Grapes:** Sangiovese min. 60%; Uva di Troia, Montepulciano, Lambrusco, and/or Trebbiano max. 40% (Lambrusco and Trebbiano max. 10%). **Wine Types:** ros; dr

ORVIETO
Region: Southern Umbria and part of northern Lazio. *Subzone:* Classico zone is in the center, closer to village of Orvieto. **Grapes:** Trebbiano Toscano (Procanico) 40%–60%; Verdello 15%–25%; Grechetto, Canaiolo Bianco (Drupeggio), and/or Malvasia Toscana for remainder (Malvasia max. 20%). **Wine Types:** dw; sw

OSTUNI
Region: Adriatic coast of Puglia. **Grapes:** *Bianco:* Impigno 50%–85%; Francavilla 15%–50%; Bianco d'Alessano and/or Verdeca max. 10%. *Ottavianello:* Ottavianello min. 85%; Negroamaro, Malvasia Nera, Notar Domenico, and/or Sussumariello max. 15%. **Wine Types:** dw; dr

PAGADEBIT DI ROMAGNA
Region: Emilia-Romagna, from Bologna to Rimini. *Subzone:* Bertinoro. **Grapes:** Bombino Bianco (Pagadebit) min. 85%. **Wine Types:** dw; sw

PARRINA
Region: Southern coast of Toscana. **Grapes:** *Bianco:* Trebbiano Toscano (Procanico) 30%–50%; Ansonica (Inzolla) and/or Chardonnay 30%–50%; others max. 20%. *Rosato and Rosso:* Sangiovese min. 70%; others max. 30%. **Aging:** Rosso Riserva min. 2 yrs. (1 yr. in wood). **Wine Types:** dw; ros; dr

PENISOLA SORRENTINA
Region: Campania, Sorrento Peninsula. *Subzones:* villages of Gragnano and Lettere. **Grapes:** *Bianco:* Falanghina, Biancolella, and/or Greco Bianco min. 60% (Falaghina min. 40%); other grapes max. 40%. *Rosso:* Piedirosso (Pér e Palummo), Sciascinoso, and/or Aglianico min. 60% (Piedirosso min. 40%); other grapes max. 40%. **Wine Types:** dw; dr (frizzante); sr (frizzante).

PENTRO DI ISERNIA
Region: Central Molise, nr. Isernia. **Grapes:** *Bianco:* Trebbiano Toscano 60%–70%; Bombino Bianco 30%–40%; others max. 10%. *Rosso and Rosato:* Montepulciano 45%–55%; Sangiovese 45%–55%; others max. 10%. **Wine Types:** dw; ros; dr

PIEMONTE
Region: Piemonte. **Grapes:** *Piemonte Moscato and Moscato Passito:* Moscato Bianco 100%. *Varietal Whites:* Min. 85% of variety; wines from Chardonnay, Cortese, Pinot Bianco, Pinot Grigio. *Varietal Reds:* Min. 85% of variety; wines from Barbera, Bonarda, Grignolino, Brachetto, Pinot Nero. **Aging:** Moscato Passito min. 1 yr. **Wine Types:** dw; spdw; sw; spsw; dr (novello); sr; spsr

PINEROLESE
Region: Piemonte, southwest of Turin. **Grapes:** *Rosso and Rosato:* Barbera, Bonarda, Nebbiolo, and/or Neretto min. 50%; others max. 50%. *Pinerolese Ramie:* Avanà 30%; Avarengo min. 15%; Neretto min. 20%; other reds max. 35%. *Varietal Reds and Rosés:* Min. 85% of variety; wines from Barbera, Bonarda, Freisa, Dolcetto, Doux d'Henry. **Wine Types:** dr (frizzante); ros (frizzante); sros

POLLINO
Region: Northernmost Calabria. **Grapes:** Gaglioppo min. 60%; Greco Nero, Malvasia Bianca, and/or Guarnaccia Bianca min. 20% (whites max. 20%). **Aging:** Superiore min. 2 yrs. **Wine Types:** dr

POMINO
Region: Central Toscana, east of Firenze. **Grapes:** *Bianco:* Pinot Bianco and/or Chardonnay 60%–80%; Trebbiano Toscano max. 30%; others max. 15%. *Rosso:* Sangiovese 60%–75%; Canaiolo, Cabernets Sauvignon and Franc 15%–25%; Merlot 10%–20%; others max 15%. *Vin Santo:* Variable. **Aging:** Rosso min. 1 yr. (6 mos. in cask). Vin Santo min. 3 yrs. in casks no larger than 4 hl. **Wine Types:** dw; dr; Vin Santo

PRIMITIVO DI MANDURIA
Region: Southern Puglia, bet. Taranto and Brindisi. **Grapes:** Primitivo 100% **Aging:** Rosso and Dolce Naturale min. 9 mos. Liquoroso min. 2 yrs. **Wine Types:** dr; sr; fr

PROSECCO DI CONEGLIANO-VALDOBBIADENE
Region: Northeastern Veneto. Wines from vineyards in San Pietro di Barbozza, near Valdobbiadene, can take the "Superiore di Cartizze" designation. **Grapes:** Prosecco min. 85%; Pinot Bianco, Pinot Grigio, Chardonnay, and/or Verdiso max. 15% (Verdiso max. 10%). **Wine Types:** dw (frizzante); spdw

REGGIANO
Region: Emilia-Romagna, nr. Reggio Emilia. **Grapes:** *Lambrusco Rosso, Rosato, and Novello:* Lambrusco Marani, Lambrusco Salamino, Lambrusco Montericco, Lambrusco Maestri, and/or Lambrusco di Sorbara min. 85%; Ancellotta max. 15%. *Lambrusco Salamino Rosso:* Lambrusco Salamino min. 85%. *Rosso and Rosso Novello:* Ancellotta 50%–60%; Lambrusco max. 50%. *Bianco Spumante:* Lambrusco (vinified white) 100%. **Wine Types:** spdw; dr (frizzante); ros (frizzante); sr (frizzante); dr (novello)

RENO
Region: Emilia-Romagna, bet. Modena and Imola. **Grapes:** *Bianco:* Albana and/or Trebbiano Romagnolo min. 40%; others max. 60%. *Pignoletto:* Pignoletto min. 85%. *Montuni:* Montuni min. 85%. **Wine Types:** dw (frizzante); sw (frizzante)

RIVIERA DEL GARDA BRESCIANO/GARDA BRESCIANO
Region: Lombardia, on the western shores of Lake Garda. **Grapes:** *Bianco:* Riesling Italico and/or Riesling Renano min. 80%; others max. 20%. *Rosso and Chiaretto:* Groppello 30%–60%; Sangiovese 10%–25%; Marzemino 5%–30%; Barbera 10%–20%; others max. 10%. *Groppello:* Groppello min. 85%. **Wine Types:** dw; spdw; ros; spros; dr (novello)

RIVIERA LIGURE DI PONENTE
Region: Western Liguria. **Grapes:** *Varietal Whites* (Vermentino, Pigato): Min. 95% of variety. *Varietal Reds* (Rossese, Ormeasco): Min. 95% of variety. *Ormeasco Sciacchetrà:* 95% Ormeasco vinified as rosé. **Aging:** Ormeasco Superiore min. 1 yr. **Wine Types:** dw; ros; dr

ROERO
Region: Southeastern Piemonte, west of Alba. **Grapes:** *Roero Arneis:* Arneis 100%. *Roero Rosso:* Nebbiolo 95%–98%; Arneis 2%–5%. **Aging:** Roero released in June of the year after vintage. **Wine Types:** dw; spdw; dr

ROMAGNA ALBANA SPUMANTE
Region: Emilia-Romagna. Same as Albana di Romagna DOCG. The DOC is for spumante only. **Grapes:** Albana 100%. **Wine Types:** spsw

ROSSESE DI DOLCEACQUA/DOLCEACQUA
Region: Westernmost Liguria. **Grapes:** Rossese min. 95%. **Aging:** Superiore min. 1 yr. **Wine Types:** dr

ROSSO BARLETTA
Region: Puglia, Adriatic coastal plains bet. Foggia and Bari. **Grapes:** Uva di Troia min. 70%; Montepulciano, Sangiovese, and/or Malbech max. 30% (Malbech max. 10%). **Aging:** Invecchiato min. 2 yrs. (1 yr. in wood). **Wine Types:** dr

ROSSO CANOSA/CANISIUM
Region: Central Puglia, nr. Castel del Monte DOC. **Grapes:** Uva di Troia min. 65%; Montepulciano and/or Sangiovese max. 35% (Sangiovese max. 15%); others max. 5%. **Aging:** Riserva min. 2 yrs. (1 yr. in wood). **Wine Types:** dr

ROSSO CÒNERO
Region: Central Marche, nr. Ancona. **Grapes:** Montepulciano min. 85%; Sangiovese max. 15%. **Aging:** Riserva min. 2 yrs. **Wine Types:** dr

ROSSO DI CERIGNOLA
Region: Northern plains of Puglia. **Grapes:** Uva di Troia min. 55%; Negroamaro 15%–30%; Sangiovese, Barbera, Montepulciano, Malvasia, and/or Trebbiano Toscano max. 15%. **Aging:** Riserva min. 2 yrs. in wood. **Wine Types:** dr

ROSSO DI MONTALCINO
Region: South-central Toscana (Montalcino). **Grapes:** Sangiovese Grosso 100%. **Aging:** 1 yr. **Wine Types:** dr

ROSSO DI MONTEPULCIANO
Region: Central-east Toscana (Montepulciano). **Grapes:** Sangiovese (Prugnolo Gentile) min. 70%; Canaiolo Nero max. 20%; others max. 20% (whites max. 10%). **Aging:** 6 mos. **Wine Types:** dr

ROSSO ORVIETANO/ORVIETANO ROSSO
Region: Southwestern Umbria, nr. Orvieto. **Grapes:** *Rosso:* Aleatico,
Cabernet Franc, Cabernet Sauvignon, Canaiolo, Ciliegiolo, Merlot,
Montepulciano, Pinot Nero, and/or Sangiovese min. 70%. *Varietal
Reds (9):* Min. 85% of variety; wines from Aleatico, Cabernet Franc,
Cabernet Sauvignon, Canaiolo, Ciliegiolo, Merlot, Montepulciano, Pinot
Nero, Sangiovese. **Wine Types:** dr; sr

ROSSO PICENO
Region: Southern Marche. **Grapes:** Montepulciano 35%–70%;
Sangiovese 30%–50%; others max. 15%. **Aging:** Superiore min. 1 yr.
Wine Types: dr (also novello)

RUBINO DI CANTAVENNA
Region: Southeastern Piemonte, north of Asti. **Grapes:** Barbera
75%–90%; Grignolino and/or Freisa max. 25%. **Aging:** Wine not
released until Dec. 31 of the year after vintage. **Wine Types:** dr

RUCHÈ DI CASTAGNOLE MONFERRATO
Region: Southeastern Piemonte, village of Castagnole Monferrato.
Grapes: Ruchè min. 90%; Barbera and/or Brachetto max. 10%. **Wine
Types:** dr; sr

SANT' ANNA DI ISOLA CAPO RIZZUTO
Region: Calabria, Ionian coast. **Grapes:** *Rosso and Rosato:* Gaglioppo
40%–60%; Nocera, Nerello Mascalese, Nerello Cappuccio, Malvasia
Nera, Malvasia Bianca, and/or Greco Bianco 40%–60% (white max.
35%). **Wine Types:** ros; dr

SAN MARTINO DELLA BATTAGLIA
Region: Lombardia and Veneto, on the southern shores of Lake Garda,
intertwined with Lugana DOC. **Grapes:** Tocai Friulano min. 80%; others
max. 20%. **Wine Types:** dw; sw; fw

SALICE SALENTINO
Region: Southern Puglia, the village of Salice Salentino. **Grapes:**
Bianco: Chardonnay min. 70%; others max. 30%. *Pinot Bianco:* Pinot
Bianco min. 85%. *Rosso and Rosato:* Negroamaro min. 80%;
Malvasia Nera max. 20%. *Aleatico:* Aleatico min. 85%; Malvasia Nera,
and/or Primitivo max. 15%. **Aging:** Aleatico min. 6 mos.; Aleatico
Riserva min. 2 yrs.; Rosso Riserva min. 2 yrs. (6 mos. in wood). **Wine
Types:** dw (frizzante); spdw; spros; ros (frizzante); dr (novello); sr; fr

SAMBUCA DI SICILIA
Region: Southwestern Sicilia. **Grapes:** *Bianco:* Ansonica (Inzolia)
50%–75%; Catarratto and/or Chardonnay 25%–50%; others, except
for Trebbiano, max. 15%. *Rosato and Rosso:* Nero d'Avola (Calabrese)
50%–75%; Nerello Mascalese, Sangiovese, and/or Cabernet Sauvignon
25%–50%; others max. 15%. *Chardonnay:* Chardonnay min. 85%.
Cabernet Sauvignon: Cabernet min. 85%. **Aging:** Rosso min. 6 mos.;
Riserva min. 2 yrs. (6 mos. in wood). **Wine Types:** dw; ros; dr

SAN COLOMBANO AL LAMBRO/SAN COLOMBANO
Region: Southwest Lombardia. **Grapes:** Croatina 30%–45%; Barbera
25%–40%; Uva Rara 5%–15%; others max. 15%. **Wine Types:** dr

SAN GIMIGNANO
Region: Central Toscana. **Grapes:** *Rosso:* Sangiovese min. 50%; others
max. 50%. *Rosato:* Sangiovese min. 60%; Canaiolo Nero max. 20%;
Trebbiano Toscano, Malvasia del Chianti, and/or Vernaccia max. 15%;
others max 15%. *Sangiovese and Sangiovese Rosato:* Sangiovese min.
85%. *Vin Santo:* Malvasia max. 50%; Trebbiano Toscano min. 30%;
Vernaccia max. 20%; others max. 10%. **Aging:** Rosso min. 6 mos.;
Riserva min. 2 yrs.; Vin Santo min. 3 yrs. (4 mos. in bottle). **Wine
Types:** dr (novello); ros; Vin Santo

SAN SEVERO
Region: Northern Puglia, nr. the Molise border. **Grapes:** *Bianco:*
Bombino Bianco 40%–60%; Trebbiano Toscano 40%–60%; Malvasia
Bianca and/or Verdeca max. 20%. *Rosato and Rosso:* Montepulciano
d'Abruzzo 70%–100%; Sangiovese max. 30%. **Wine Types:** dw; ros; dr

SAN VITO DI LUZZI
Region: North-central Calabria. **Grapes:** *Bianco:* Malvasia Bianca
40%–60%; Greco Bianco 20%–30%; others max. 40%. *Rosato and
Rosso:* Gaglioppo min. 70%; Malvasia max. 10%; Greco Nero,
Sangiovese, and others max. 30%. **Wine Types:** dw; ros; dr

SANGIOVESE DI ROMAGNA
Region: Emilia-Romagna, from Bologna to Rimini. **Grapes:** Sangiovese
85%–100%. **Aging:** Riserva min. 2 yrs. **Wine Types:** dr (also novello)

SANNIO
Region: Northern Campania, around Benevento. **Grapes:** *Bianco:* Trebbiano Toscano min. 50%; others max. 50%. *Rosso:* Sangiovese min. 50%; others max. 50%. *Metodo Classico Spumante:* Aglianico, Greco, and/or Falanghina. *Varietal Whites:* Min. 85% of variety; wines from Coda di Volpe, Falanghina, Fiano, Greco, Moscato. *Varietal Reds:* Min. 85% of variety; wines from Aglianico, Barbera, Piedirosso, Sciascinoso. **Aging:** Método Classico Spumante min. 1 yr. **Wine Types:** dw; spdw; sw (frizzante); ros (frizzante); spros; sros (frizzante); dr (frizzante and novello); sr (frizzante); spdr

SANT'AGATA DEI GOTI
Region: North-central Campania, west of Benevento. **Grapes:** *Bianco:* Falanghina 40%–60%; Greco 40%–60%; others max. 20%. *Rosso and Rosato:* Aglianico 40%–60%; Piediresso 40%–60%; others max. 20%. *Varietal Whites:* Min. 90% of variety; wines from Falanghina, Greco. *Varietal Reds:* Min. 90% of variety; wines from Aglianico, Piediresso. **Aging:** Aglianico min. 2 yrs. (Riserva 2 yrs. plus 1 yr. in bottle). Piediresso Riserva min. 2 yrs. **Wine Types:** dw; sw; ros; dr (novello for all types)

SANT'ANTIMO
Region: South-central Toscana, the village of Montalcino. **Grapes:** *Bianco and Rosso:* Variable. *Vin Santo:* Trebbiano Toscano and/or Malvasia min. 70%; others max. 30%. *Vin Santo Occhio di Pernice:* Sangiovese 50%–70%; Malvasia Nera 30%–50%; others max. 30%. *Varietal Whites and Reds:* Min. 85% of variety. **Aging:** Vin Santo min. 3 yrs. (Riserva 4 yrs.) in casks no larger than 4 hl. **Wine Types:** dw; dr; Vin Santo

SANTA MARGHERITA DI BELICE
Region: Southwestern Sicilia. **Grapes:** *Bianco:* Ansonica (Inzolia) 30%–50%; Grecanico and/or Catarratto 50%–70%; others max. 15%. *Rosso:* Nero d'Avola (Calabrese) 20%–50%; Sangiovese and/or Cabernet Sauvignon 50%–80%; others max. 15%. *Varietal Whites (3):* Min. 85% of variety; wines from Catarratto, Grecanico, Ansonica (Inzolia). *Varietal Reds (2):* Min. 85% of variety; wines from Nero d'Avola (Calabrese), Sangiovese. **Wine Types:** dw; dr

SARDEGNA SEMIDANO
Region: Sardegna. *Subzone:* Mogoro for communes between Cagliari and Oristano. **Grapes:** Semidano min. 85%; others max. 15%. **Wine Types:** dw; spdw; spsw; sw

SAVUTO
Region: Calabria, Mediterranean coast. **Grapes:** *Rosso and Rosato:* Gaglioppo 35%–45%; Greco Nero, Nerello Cappuccio, Magliocco Canino, and/or Sangiovese 30%–40% (Sangiovese max. 10%); Malvasia Bianca and/or Pecorino max. 25%. **Aging:** Superiore min. 2 yrs. **Wine Types:** ros; dr

SCAVIGNA
Region: Calabria, central Mediterranean coast. **Grapes:** *Bianco:* Trebbiano Toscano max. 50%; Chardonnay max. 30%; Greco Bianco max. 20%; Malvasia Bianca max. 10%; others max. 35%. *Rosso and Rosato:* Gaglioppo max. 60%; Nerello Cappuccio max. 40%; others max. 40%. **Wine Types:** dw; ros; dr

SCIACCA
Region: Southwestern coast of Sicilia. **Grapes:** *Bianco:* Inzolia (Ansonica), Grecanico, Chardonnay, and/or Catarratto min. 70%. *Riserva Rayana:* Inzolia and/or Catarratto min. 80%. *Varietal Whites (3):* Min. 85% of variety; wines from Inzolia, Grecanico, Chardonnay. *Rosato and Rosso:* Merlot, Cabernet Sauvignon, Nero d'Avola, and/or Sangiovese min. 70%. *Varietal Reds (4):* Min. 85% of variety; wines from Merlot, Cabernet Sauvignon, Nero d'Avola, Sangiovese. **Aging:** Riserva Rayana and Rosso Riserva min. 2 yrs. (6 mos. in wood). **Wine Types:** dw; ros; dr

SIZZANO
Region: Northern Piemonte. **Grapes:** Nebbiolo (Spanna) 40%–60%; Vespolina 15%–40%; Bonarda (Uva Rara) max. 25%. **Aging:** Min. 3 yrs. (2 yrs. in wood). **Wine Types:** dr

SOAVE
Region: Veneto, nr. Verona. *Subzone:* Classico, bet. villages of Soave and Monteforte d'Alpone. **Grapes:** Garganega min. 70%; Pinot Bianco, Chardonnay, and/or Trebbiano di Soave max. 30% (15% can be other

types of Trebbiano). **Aging:** Superiore released March 1 of the year after vintage. **Wine Types:** dw; spdw

SOLOPACA
Region: North-central Campania. **Grapes:** *Bianco:* Trebbiano Toscano 40%–60%; Falanghina, Coda di Volpe, Malvasia Toscana, and/or Malvasia di Candia max. 60%. *Falanghina:* Falanghina min. 85%. *Rosso and Rosato:* Sangiovese 50%–60%; Aglianico 20%–40%; others max. 30%. *Aglianico:* Aglianico min. 85%. *Spumante:* Falanghina min. 60%; others max. 40%. **Aging:** Aglianico min. 10 mos.; Rosso Superiore min. 1 yr. in wood. **Wine Types:** dw; spdw; ros; dr

SOVANA
Region: Southernmost Toscana. **Grapes:** *Rosso and Rosato:* Sangiovese min. 50%; others max. 50%. *Varietal Reds:* Min. 85% of variety. **Aging:** Varietal reds Riserva min. 24 mos. (6 mos. in bottle). **Wine Types:** ros; dr

SQUINZANO
Region: Southern Puglia, bet. Lecce and Brindisi. **Grapes:** Negroamaro min. 70%; Malvasia Nera and/or Sangiovese max. 30% (Sangiovese max. 15%). **Aging:** Rosso Riserva min. 2 yrs. (6 mos. in wood). **Wine Types:** ros; dr

TARQUINIA
Region: Northern coast of Lazio. **Grapes:** *Bianco:* Trebbiano Toscano (Procanico) and/or Trebbiano Giallo min. 50%; Malvasia di Candia and/or Malvasia del Lazio max. 35%; others (except Pinot Grigio) max. 30%. *Rosso and Rosato:* Sangiovese and Montepulciano min. 60% (min. 25% of either); Cesanese Comune max. 25%; other reds max. 30%. **Wine Types:** dw; sw; ros; dr (also novello); sr

TEROLDEGO ROTALIANO
Region: Northern Trentino. **Grapes:** Teroldego 100%. **Aging:** Riserva min. 2 yrs.. **Wine Types:** dr; ros

TERRE DI FRANCIACORTA
Region: Central Lombardia. Same as Franciacorta DOC. The Terre di Franciacorta designation is reserved for still wines. **Grapes:** *Bianco:* Chardonnay and/or Pinot Bianco and/or Pinot Nero up to 100%. *Rosso:* Cabernet Sauvignon and Cabernet Franc min. 25%; Barbera min. 10%; Nebbiolo min. 10%; Merlot min. 10%; others max. 10%. **Wine Types:** dw; dr

TORGIANO
Region: Umbria, just southeast of Perugia. **Grapes:** *Bianco:* Trebbiano Toscano 50%–70%; Grechetto 15%–40%; others max. 15%. *Rosso:* Sangiovese 50%–70%; Canaiolo 15%–30%; Trebbiano Toscano max. 10%; others max. 15%. *Rosato:* Sangiovese 50%–70%; Canaiolo 15%–30%; Trebbiano Toscano max. 10%; others max. 15%. *Varietal Whites (3):* Min. 85% of variety; wines from Chardonnay, Pinot Grigio, Riesling Italico. *Varietal Reds (2):* Min. 85% of variety; wines from Cabernet Sauvignon, Pinot Nero. *Spumante:* Chardonnay 40%–50%; Pinot Nero 40%–50%; others max. 15%. **Wine Types:** dw; spdw; ros; dr

TREBBIANO D'ABRUZZO
Region: Abruzzo. **Grapes:** Trebbiano d'Abruzzo and/or Trebbiano Toscano min. 85%. **Wine Types:** dw

TREBBIANO DI ROMAGNA
Region: Emilia-Romagna, from Bologna to Rimini. **Grapes:** Trebbiano Romagnolo 85%–100%. **Wine Types:** dw (also frizzante); spdw; spsw

TRENTINO
Region: Trentino, province of Trento. More than 20 wine types. **Grapes:** *Bianco:* Chardonnay and/or Pinot Bianco, min. 80%; Sauvignon, Müller-Thurgau, and/or Incrocio Manzoni max. 20%. *Rosato (Kretzer):* Schiava, Teroldego, and/or Lagrein, with no one exceeding 70% of total. *Rosso:* Cabernet Franc and/or Cabernet Sauvignon, Merlot. *Varietal Wines:* Min. 85% of variety. Whites: Chardonnay, Moscato Giallo, Müller-Thurgau, Nosiola, Pinot Bianco, Pinot Grigio, Riesling Italico, Riesling Renano, Sauvignon, Traminer Aromatico. Reds: Moscato Rosa, Cabernet, Cabernets Sauvignon and Franc, Lagrein, Marzemino, Merlot, Pinot Nero, Rebo. *Vin Santo:* Nosiola 100%. **Aging:** Reds min. 6 mos.; Bianco, Rosso, Chardonnay, Pinot Bianco, Riesling, Sauvignon, Cabernet Franc, Cabernet Sauvignon, Merlot, Pinot Nero, Lagrein, and Marzemino min. 2 yrs. for Riserva; Vin Santo min. 3 yrs. **Wine Types:** dw; dr; ros; Vin Santo

TRENTINO SORNÌ (SUBZONE)
Region: Trentino, the communes of Lavis, Giovo, and San Michele all'Adige. **Grapes:** *Bianco:* Nosiola, Müller-Thurgau, Sylvaner, Pinot Bianco, Pinot Grigio, and/or Chardonnay. *Rosso:* Teroldego, Schiava, and/or Lagrein. **Wine Types:** dw; dr

TRENTO
Region: Trentino. Used specifically for sparkling wines made in the *metodo classico* (Champagne method). **Grapes:** Varying percentages of Chardonnay, Pinot Bianco, Pinot Nero, and/or Pinot Meunier. **Aging:** Min. 15 mos. on the lees in bottle; 24 mos. for vintage-dated wines; Riserva 36 mos. **Wine Types:** spdw; spros

VAL D'ARBIA
Region: Central Toscana, nr. Siena; follows Arbia River. **Grapes:** Trebbiano Toscano and Malvasia del Chianti 70%–90%; Chardonnay 10%–30%; others max. 15%. **Aging:** Vin Santo min. 3 yrs. in casks no larger than 2 hl. **Wine Types:** dw; Vin Santo

VAL DI CORNIA/VAL DI CORNIA SUVERETO
Region: Southern coast of Toscana. *Subzone:* Suvereto, centered on town of same name, from which producers make 4 varietal reds. **Grapes:** *Bianco:* Trebbiano Toscano min. 50%; Vermentino max. 50%; others max. 20%. *Rosso and Rosato:* Sangiovese min. 50%; Cabernet Sauvignon and/or Merlot max. 50%; others max. 20%. *Varietal Whites and Reds:* Min. 85% of variety. *Aleatico Passito:* Aleatico 100%. *Ansonica Passito:* Ansonica (Inzolia) 100%. **Aging:** Sangiovese, Merlot, Cabernet Sauvignon, and Rosso Superiore min. 18 mos. (6 mos. in wood); Riserva min. 24 mos.; Suvereto reds min. 26 mos. (15 mos. in casks no larger than 30 hl., min. 6 mos. in bottle). **Wine Types:** dw; sw; dr; sr

VAL POLCÈVERA
Region: Liguria, north of Genova. *Subzone:* Coronata for whites from a specific part of zone. **Grapes:** *Bianco (also spumante, passito, and Coronata):* Vermentino, Bianchetta Genovese, and/or Albarola min. 60%; Pigato, Rollo, and/or Bosco max. 40%. *Bianchetta Genovese:* Bianchetta Genovese min. 85%. *Vermentino:* Vermentino min. 85%. *Rosso and Rosato:* Dolcetto, Sangiovese, and/or Ciliegiolo min. 60%; Barbera max. 40%. **Wine Types:** dw (frizzante); spdw; sw; ros (frizzante); dr (novello and frizzante)

VALCALEPIO
Region: Central Lombardia, nr. Bergamo. **Grapes:** *Bianco:* Pinot Bianco and Chardonnay 55%–80%; Pinot Grigio 20%–45%. *Rosso:* Cabernet Sauvignon 25%–60%; Merlot 40%–75%. *Moscato Passito:* Moscato di Scanzo and/or Moscato 100%. **Aging:** Rosso min. 1 yr. (3 mos. in wood). Rosso Riserva min. 3 yrs. (1 yr. in wood); Moscato Passito min. 2 yrs. **Wine Types:** dw; dr; sw

VALDADIGE/ETSCHTALER
Region: Parts of Veneto, Trentino, and Alto Adige, along the Adige River. **Grapes:** *Bianco:* Pinot Bianco, Pinot Grigio, Riesling Italico, Müller-Thurgau, and/or Chardonnay min. 20%; max. 80% Bianchetta Trevigiana, Trebbiano Toscano, Nosiola, Vernaccia, and Garganega. *Rosato and Rosso:* Schiava and/or Lambrusco min. 30% (Schiava min. 20%); max. 70% Merlot, Pinot Nero, Lagrein, Teroldego, Negrara. *Pinot Grigio:* Pinot Grigio min. 85%. *Pinot Bianco:* Pinot Bianco min. 85%. *Chardonnay:* Chardonnay min. 85%. *Schiava:* Schiava min. 85%. **Wine Types:** dw; ros; dr

VALDICHIANA
Region: Eastern Toscana, nr. border with Umbria. **Grapes:** *Bianco and Bianco Vergine:* Trebbiano Toscano min. 20%; Chardonnay, Pinot Bianco, Grechetto, and/or Pinot Grigio max. 80%; others max. 15%. *Chardonnay:* Chardonnay min. 85%. *Grechetto:* Grechetto min. 85%. *Rosso and Rosato:* Sangiovese min. 50%; Merlot and/or Syrah max. 50%; others max. 15%. *Sangiovese:* Sangiovese min. 85%. *Vin Santo:* Trebbiano Toscano and/or Malvasia Bianca min. 50%; others max. 50%. **Aging:** Vin Santo min. 3 yrs. (Riserve 4 yrs.) with min. 2 yrs. in casks no larger than 5 hl. **Wine Types:** dw; spdw; dr; Vin Santo

VALLE D'AOSTA
Region: Valle d'Aosta. *Subzones:* Morgex et La Salle, Enfer d'Arvier, Torrette, Nus, Chambave, Arnad-Monjovet, Donnaz/Donnas. **Grapes:** *Bianco/Blanc, Rosso/Rouge, and Rosato/Rosé:* Variable. *Varietal Wines:* Min. 90% of variety. Whites: Müller-Thurgau, Pinot Grigio,

Chardonnay, Petit Arvine, Pinot Noir. Reds: Gamay, Pinot Nero, Premetta, Fumin, Petit Rouge. *Blanc de Morgex et de La Salle:* Blanc de Morgex 100%. *Chambave:* Moscato Bianco (Muscat Blanc) 100%. *Chambave Rouge:* Petit Rouge 60%; Dolcetto, Gamay, and/or Pinot Nero min. 25%; other reds max. 15%. *Nus/Nus Malvoisie:* Pinot Grigio (Pinot Gris/Malvoisie) 100%. *Nus Rosso/Rouge:* Vien de Nus min. 50%; Petit Rouge and/or Pinot Nero min. 30%; others max. 20%. *Arnad-Monjovet:* Nebbiolo (Picotendro) min. 70%; Dolcetto, Vien de Nus, Pinot Nero, Neyret, and/or Freisa max. 30%. *Torrete:* Petit Rouge min. 70%; others max. 30%. *Donnas/Donnaz:* Nebbiolo (Picotendro) min. 85%; Freisa and/or Neyret max. 15%. *Enfer d'Arvier:* Petit Rouge min. 85%; others max. 15%. **Aging:** Bianco/Rosso/Rosato: 3 mos.; Varietal Whites: 3 mos.; Varietal Reds: 6 mos.; Blanc de Morgex: 3 mos.; Chambave Muscat: 3 mos.; Chambave Rouge: 6 mos.; Nus Malvoisie: 3 mos.; Nus Rosso: 6 mos.; Arnad-Monjovet: 8 mos. (Superiore [12 mos.); Torrette: 6 mos. (Supeiore 8 mos.); Donnas: 24 mos.; Enfer d'Arvier: 6 mos. **Wine Types:** dw (also frizzante); sw; ros (also frizzante); dr (also frizzante)

VALPOLICELLA/RECIOTO DELLA VALPOLICELLA
Region: Veneto, north of Verona. Valpantena designation for wines from eastern part of zone. **Grapes:** Corvina 40%–70%; Rondinella 20%–40%; Molinara 5%–25%; Rossignola, Negrara Trentina, Barbera, and/or Sangiovese max. 15%; other red max. 5%. **Aging:** Superiore min. 1 yr.; Amarone min. 2 yrs. **Wine Types:** dr; sr; spsr

VALSUSA
Region: Piemonte, west of Torino. **Grapes:** Avanà, Barbera, Dolcetto, and/or Neretto min. 60%; others max. 40%. **Wine Types:** dr

VALTELLINA
Region: Northern Lombardia. Valtellina Superiore DOCG reserved for 4 specific subzones. **Grapes:** Chiavennasca (Nebbiolo) min. 80%; others max. 20%. **Aging:** Min. 6 mos. **Wine Types:** dr

VELLETRI
Region: Lazio, Castelli Romani, nr. Rome. **Grapes:** Bianco and Spumante: Malvasia max. 70%; Trebbiano Toscano min. 30%; Bellone, Bonvino, and other whites max. 20%. *Rosso:* Sangiovese 10%–45%; Montepulciano 30%–50%; Cesanese Comune and/or Cesanese d'Affile min. 10%; others max. 30%. **Aging:** Rosso Riserva min. 2 yrs. **Wine Types:** dw; spdw; sw; dr; sr

VERBICARO
Region: Northern Mediterranean coast of Calabria. **Grapes:** *Bianco:* Greco Bianco min. 30%; Malvasia Bianca max. 40%; Guarnaccia Bianca max. 30%; others max. 30%. *Rosso and Rosato:* Gaglioppo and/or Greco Nero 60%–80%; Malvasia Bianca, Guarnaccia Bianca, and/or Greco Bianco min. 20%; others max. 20%. **Aging:** Rosso Riserva min. 3 yrs. **Wine Types:** dw; ros; dr

VERDICCHIO DEI CASTELLI DI JESI
Region: Central Marche. **Grapes:** Verdicchio min. 85% for all types. **Aging:** Riserva min. 2 yrs. (min. 6 mos. in bottle). **Wine Types:** dw; spdw; sw

VERDICCHIO DI MATELICA
Region: Central Marche, nr. the village of Matelica. **Grapes:** Verdicchio min. 85%. **Aging:** Riserva min. 2 yrs. (min. 4 mos. in bottle). **Wine Types:** dw; spdw; sw

VERDUNO PELAVERGA/VERDUNO
Region: Southeastern Piemonte, nr. Barolo DOCG, the village of Verduno. **Grapes:** Pelaverga min. 85%; others max. 15%. **Aging:** Min. 6 mos. **Wine Types:** dr (frizzante)

VERMENTINO DI SARDEGNA
Region: Sardegna. **Grapes:** Vermentino min. 85%. **Wine Types:** dw; spdw; sw

VERNACCIA DI ORISTANO
Region: West coast of Sardegna, the town of Oristano. **Grapes:** Vernaccia di Oristano 100%. **Aging:** Min. 2 yrs. in wood; Superiore min. 3 yrs. in wood; Riserva min. 4 yrs. in wood. **Wine Types:** fw

VERNACCIA DI SERRAPETRONA
Region: Central Marche, nr. the village of Macerata. **Grapes:** Vernaccia Nera min. 85%. **Wine Types:** spdr; spsr

VESUVIO

Region: Campania, Mount Vesuvius. Lacryma Christi designation given to whites, reds, and rosés, sparkling, still, and sweet, of superior alcohol content. **Grapes:** *Bianco (also Lacryma Christi):* Coda di Volpe and/or Verdeca min. 80% (Coda di Volpe min. 35%); Falanghina and/or Greco max. 20%. *Rosso and Rosato (also Lacryma Christi):* Piedirosso and/or Sciascinoso min. 80% (Piedirosso min. 50% of total); Aglianico max. 20%. **Wine Types:** dw; spdw; sw; ros; spros; dr; spdr; sr.

VIGNANELLO

Region: Northern Lazio, nr. Viterbo. **Grapes:** *Bianco:* Trebbiano 60%–70%; Malvasia Bianca 20%–40%; others max. 10%. *Greco:* Greco min. 85%. *Rosso and Rosato:* Sangiovese 40%–60%; Ciliegiolo 40%–50%; others max. 20%. **Aging:** Rosso Riserva min. 2 yrs. (1 yr. in bottle). **Wine Types:** dw; spdw; ros; dr

VIN SANTO DEL CHIANTI

Region: Toscana. Corresponds to Chianti DOCG. **Grapes:** *Vin Santo:* Trebbiano Toscano and/or Malvasia min. 70%; others max. 30%. *Vin Santo Occhio di Pernice:* Sangiovese min. 50%; others max. 50%. **Aging:** Vinification and aging done in wood casks *(caratelli)* of no more than 5 hl.; min. 3 yrs. (Riserva 4 yrs.). **Wine Types:** Vin Santo

VIN SANTO DEL CHIANTI CLASSICO

Region: Toscana. Corresponds to Chianti Classico DOCG. **Grapes:** *Vin Santo:* Trebbiano Toscano and/or Malvasia min. 70%; others max. 30%. *Vin Santo Occhio di Pernice:* Sangiovese min. 50%; others max. 50%. **Aging:** Vinification and aging done in wood casks *(caratelli)* of no more than 5 hl.; min. 3 yrs. (Riserva 4 yrs.). **Wine Types:** Vin Santo

VIN SANTO DI MONTEPULCIANO

Region: Toscana. Corresponds to Vino Nobile di Montepulciano DOCG. **Grapes:** *Vin Santo:* Malvasia Bianca, Grechetto (Pulcinculo), and/or Trebbiano Toscano min. 70%; others max. 30%. *Vin Santo Occhio di Pernice:* Sangiovese min. 50%; others max. 50%. **Aging:** Vinification and aging done in wood casks *(caratelli)* of no more than 3 hl. (smaller for Riserva and Occhio di Pernice); min. 3 yrs. (Riserva 5 yrs.; Occhio di Pernice 8 yrs.). **Wine Types:** Vin Santo

VINI DEL PIAVE/PIAVE

Region: Northeastern Veneto. **Grapes:** *Varietal Wines (10):* Min. 95% of variety. Whites: Chardonnay, Pinot Grigio, Pinot Bianco, Tocai Italico, Verduzzo. Reds: Cabernet, Cabernet Sauvignon, Merlot, Pinot Nero, Raboso. **Aging:** Cabernet and Cabernet Sauvignon Riserva min. 2 yrs. (min. 1 yr. in wood); Merlot and Pinot Nero Riserva min. 2 yrs. (min. 6 mos. in wood); Raboso Riserva min. 3 yrs. (min. 1 yr. in wood). **Wine Types:** dw; dr

ZAGAROLO

Region: Lazio, nr. Rome. **Grapes:** Malvasia max. 70%; Trebbiano min. 30%; Bellone and/or Bonvino max. 10%. **Wine Types:** dw; sw

Appendix IV:
GUIDE TO BAROLO AND BARBARESCO VINEYARDS

ALTHOUGH "SINGLE-VINEYARD" wines are made throughout Italy, the practice of vineyard designation defines the culture of Barolo and Barbaresco. Barolo and Barbaresco are part of the Langhe hills, in southeastern Piedmont, where the undulating topography creates a variety of exposures, soils, and microclimates. Therefore, anyone in search of a deeper understanding of Barolo and Barbaresco wines must consider the effects of vineyard location on style.

Producers have come to equate a vineyard's position with a certain type of wine. Vineyards with a *sorì del mattino* (southeastern, or "morning," exposure) see intense sunlight in the morning hours, when the vine is most productive; these vineyards have long been thought to produce plusher, softer wines. Vineyards with a *sorì mezzogiorno* (southern, or "noontime," exposure) were thought to produce the ripest, biggest-boned wines because they caught the most intense sunlight of the day. And vineyards with a *sorì d'la serra* (western, or afternoon, exposure) were thought to yield leaner, more tannic wines, since they saw the weaker afternoon sun. This being Italy, however, the myriad sites were never rated, as in France—they were just given fanciful names and the rest was left to debate.

BAROLO, VILLAGE BY VILLAGE

The Barolo DOCG covers all or part of eleven villages south and west of the town of Alba: Barolo, Castiglione Falletto, Cherasco, Diano d'Alba, Grinzane Cavour, La Morra, Monforte d'Alba, Novello, Roddi, Serralunga d'Alba, and Verduno. The key villages are La Morra, Barolo, Castiglione Falletto, Serralunga, and Monforte. La Morra produces about 30 percent of all Barolo wine, Monforte and Serralunga about 16 percent each. There are about 3,100 acres of vines in production in the zone.

Barolo
The best-known vineyard here is Cannubi. The well-regarded Cerequio and Brunate crus are shared (and more associated) with La Morra. Calcareous clays dominate, and in general the wines of Barolo are said to combine the finesse of La Morra with the depth of Monforte.

Castiglione Falletto

Vineyards here cover a ridge that runs north-south, spilling down both sides. The majority face west or southwest. Conventional wisdom says the west-facing vineyards (Villero, Monprivato, Bricco Boschis) produce more alcohol-rich, structured wines, while those facing east-southeast (Pernanno, Rocche di Castiglione) produce rounder, more elegant wines. On west-facing slopes such as Meriondino and Villero, there's more limestone, whereas east-facing crus like Rocche contain more sandstone. Classic assemblages often contain grapes from both sides.

La Morra

The village of La Morra sits at one of the highest altitudes in the Barolo zone (about 500 meters) and offers a dramatic panorama. Vineyards are mostly south- and southeast-facing, producing what have traditionally been considered the most elegant and early-maturing Barolos. Average altitudes in La Morra are the highest of the key villages, but the south-southeast orientation of the vineyards gives La Morra wines more *morbidézza* (softness).

Monforte d'Alba

Along with neighbor Serralunga d'Alba, this commune is home to the richest, most tannic, most potent Barolos. This is the southern edge of the Barolo DOCG, with more than its share of famous vineyards, including Ginestra, Bussia, Santo Stefano di Perno, Gramolere, and Dardi. Several small streams subdivide the zone, with a number of vineyards oriented toward Serralunga, to the east, and others oriented toward Barolo and Novello, to the west.

Serralunga d'Alba

This commune lies at the eastern edge of the Barolo zone. As in Castiglione, the Serralunga vineyards run along a spine going north-south. Vineyards have predominantly southern exposures, with some hedging west and some east. Overall, Serralunga wines are considered the most tannic and intense.

BARBARESCO, VILLAGE BY VILLAGE

The Barbaresco DOCG includes all or part of four towns—Barbaresco, Neive, Treiso, and San Rocco Seno d'Elvio—which lie north and east of Alba. There are 1,200 acres of vines in production in the zone, and again, not all are Nebbiolo vines. The vineyards within the commune of Barbaresco account for about 50 percent of all Barbaresco production.

Barbaresco

Here in the namesake village are most of the more famous vineyards, including Asili, Rabajà, and the Secondine vineyard, home to Angelo Gaja's Sorì San Lorenzo. Of the Barbaresco communes, Barbaresco itself is the source of the roundest, most immediately accessible wines, although there are exceptions.

Neive

Said to have a sandier soil composition than those of Barbaresco, Neive vineyards also tend to sit at marginally higher altitudes—both possible explanations for the more austere and tannic wines turned out by Neive producers.

San Rocco Seno d'Elvio

A small sliver of this commune is considered part of the Barbaresco zone, although no major vineyards are located there. In all, the commune's grapes comprise about 5 percent of total Barbaresco production.

Treiso

Situated south of Barbaresco and Neive, Treiso is the least known of the four villages. Most of the vineyard sites have a southwest orientation. Stylistically, these wines lean more toward those of Barbaresco than those of Neive.

Ultimately, however, it is difficult to generalize about vineyard character, since winemaking techniques vary widely. Two wines from the same vineyard may, in fact, be very different in style, but overall some patterns do emerge. The chart that follows is not only an accounting of key vineyards in Barolo and Barbaresco but also an assemblage of conventional wisdom on the styles of wine they produce. At the very least, it should help you to join the debate.

DECODING CRUS
SINGLE VINEYARDS OF BAROLO AND BARBARESCO

ALT = approximate avg. altitude

ASP = vineyard orientation

BAROLO DOCG

Vineyard	Village	Key Producer(s)
Arborina	La Morra	Altare, Bovio, Corino, Veglio
Boscareto	Serralunga	Batasiolo; Principiano
Bricco Boschis	Castiglione Falletto	Cavallotto
Bricco Rocche–Serra	Castiglione Falletto	Ceretto
Bricco Viole	Barolo	Vajra, O. Viberti
Brunate	Barolo	Borgogno, F. Rinaldi, Marchesi di Barolo
Brunate	La Morra	Boglietti, Ceretto, Chiarlo, Marcarini, Vietti, R. Voerzio
Bussia Soprana	Monforte	A. Conterno, F.lli Giacosa, Oddero, Prunotto
Ca' Nere / Case Nere	La Morra	Boglietti
Cannubi	Barolo	Chiarlo, Damilano, E. Pira, Prunotto, Scavino
Cannubi Boschis	Barolo	Sandrone
Capalotti	La Morra	Viberti; R. Voerzio
Cerequio	La Morra	Chiarlo, Contratto, R. Voerzio
Cerequio*	Barolo	
Cerretta	Serralunga	Baudana, Ca'Rome, Ettore Germano
Cicala	Monforte	A. Conterno
Colonnello	Monforte	A. Conterno, Bussia Soprana
Conca dell'Annunziata	La Morra	Renata Ratti
Dardi	Monforte	A & G Fantino, Poderi Colla
Falletto	Serralunga	B. Giacosa
Fiasco/Fiasc	Castiglione Falletto	Azelia, Paolo Scavino
Fossati	La Morra	Boglietti
Fossati*	Barolo	
Francia	Serralunga	G. Conterno
Gabutti	Monforte	
Gabutti	Serralunga	Boasso, Cappellano, G. Sordo
Gancia-Luciani	La Morra	S. Grasso, M. Molino

ASP	ALT	Characteristics
ESE	270	Good up-front fruit; floral aromatics
SSW	400	Extracted and very tannic
WSW	300	Perfumed; high-toned acidity; nervous, fine
WSW	370	Firm tannins, lean and superpowerful
SSE	400	One of the highest altitude sites; great perfume
SE	270	La Morra's portion more famous
SSE	300	Broad and bold but balanced wines; readily drinkable
SSE–SW	400	Amphitheater with full southern orientation; full and sharp wines
SSE	300	Soft and generous
SE	250	Big, open vineyard; generous and soft but concentrated
SSE	250	aka Monghisolfo; same ridge as Cannubi; plush wines
SE	325	Voerzio bottles a rare and intense wine from here
SSE	340	Wines more tannic and intense than neighbor Brunate's
SE	270	See Cerequio of La Morra
SSE	350	Dense and tannic in true Serralunga style
SW	420	More west and slightly higher than Bussia Soprana
SW	420	More west and slightly higher than Bussia Soprana
		See Marcenasco
SW	350	Rich and powerfully built wines
S	400	One of the most pure southern exposures; supple wines
SW	260	Well-structured, moderated tannins
ESE	350	High-altitude fineness and aromatics
SSE	270	See Fossati of La Morra
WSW	400	Western exposure; long-aging, intense; Monfortino is from here
WSW	375	Powerful, tannic (less known than Gabutti in Serralunga)
SSW	320	Big southern exposure; full, rich wines
SSW	250	Gentle and aromatic; Molino's "Vigna Gancia" good example

Barolo DOCG (continued)

Vineyard	Village	Key Producer(s)
Gattera (Monfalletto)	La Morra	Bovio, Cordero di Montezemolo, Revello, Veglio
Giachini	La Morra	Corino, Revello
Ginestra	Monforte	Clerico, Conterno Fantino, E. Grasso, P. Conterno
Gramolere	Monforte	Manzone
La Rosa	Serralunga	Fontanafredda
La Serra	La Morra	Marcarini, G. Voerzio, R. Voerzio
La Villa	Monforte	Seghesio
Lazzarito	Serralunga	Fontanafredda, Porro, Vietti
Le Coste	Barolo	Grimaldi
Le Coste	Monforte	Principiano
Luciani	La Morra	
Marcenasco	La Morra	Ratti
Marenca	Serralunga	L. Pira
Margaria/Margheria	Serralunga	L. Pira, Massolino
Massara	Verduno	Burlotto, Castello di Verduno
Mariondino	Castiglione Falletto	Parusso
Monfalletto	La Morra	
Monprivato	Castiglione Fallettp	G. Mascarello
Monvigliero	Verduno	Castello di Verduno, Burlotto, Mauro Sebaste
Mosconi	Monforte	Bussia Soprana, Rocche dei Manzoni
Munie	Monforte	Batasiolo, Parusso
Ornato	Serralunga	Pio Cesare
Pajana	Monforte	Clerico
Parafada/Delizia	Serralunga	Fontanafredda, Massolino
Pernanno	Castiglione Falletto	Bongiovanni
Pira	Castiglione Falletto	Roagna
Pra di Po/Prapo	Serralunga	Ceretto, Ettore Germano, Mauro Sebaste
Ravera	Monforte	
Ravera	Novello	Marziano Abbona, Elvio Cogno
Rivera	Castiglione Falletto	F.lll Giacosa, F.lli Oddero

ASP	ALT	Characteristics
SWS	270	Higher part considered Monfalletto; firm and well structured
SE	250	Lush and aromatic; luxurious
SSE	350	Big, broad, potent, long-lived wines
WSW	400	Fine, firm, intense
SW	300	Legendary vineyard; huge longevity; impenetrable on release
SSE	400	Intense aromas from a vineyard up above Brunate and Cerequio
SSE	350	Richly perfumed, with a strong backbone of tannin
SSW	375	Bowl-shaped vineyard produces long-lived, powerful wines
SSE	300	Predominantly full southern exposure; round wines
SSE	375	Ultrapowerful; vineyard is at southern edge of Barolo DOCG
		See Gancia-Luciani
SSW	250	Fine and perfumed, with high notes like Arborina's wines
SWS	350	Plush and powerful wine from Pira
WSW	350	More western orientation than Marenca; harder tannins
SE	300	Generous and soft
W	300	Rich and viscous
		See Gattera (Monfalletto)
SW	300	Very high-toned acidity and firm structure, like Cavallotto's wines
S	300	Generous and soft
S	400	Rich, powerfully built; Manzoni's "Vigna Big" from here
WSW	300	Elegant; maybe a little toned down for Monforte
SW	350	Superpowerful perfume and tannin; long ager
SE	350	Slightly north and east of Ginestra cru, facing Serralunga
SSW	350	Parafada directly south; Delizia more southwest
ESE	275	Rare morning exposure in Castiglione; elegance and aroma
SSE	250	Roagna's "La Rocca e La Pira" a great, plump example
SE	350	Rich yet more generous than many Serralunga wines
SSE	400	See also Ravera of Novello
SSW	350	Broad and smooth like Barolos from the Barolo commune
SSE	300	South-facing; more generous and Monforte-like

Barolo DOCG (continued)

Vineyard	Village	Key Producer(s)
Rocche dell'Annunziata	La Morra	Corino, Ratti, P. Scavino, Settimo, Veglio
Rocche di Castiglione	Castiglione Falletto	Brovia, F.lli Oddero, Vietti
Romirasco	Monforte	A. Conterno
San Rocco	Serralunga	
San Rocco (Costabello)	Serralunga	Azelia
Santo Stefano di Perno	Monforte	Rocche dei Manzoni, G. Mascarello
Sarmassa	Barolo	Marchesi di Barolo, Scarzello, Brezza
Serra	Castiglione Falletto	
Via Nuova	Barolo	L. Einaudi
Vigna Rionda	Serralunga	G. Anselma, Chiarlo, Flli Oddero, Massolino, L. Pira
Vignolo	Castiglione Falletto	Cavallotto
Villero	Castiglione Falletto	Brovia, Cordero di Montezemolo, B. Giacosa, Vietti
Voghera/Brea	Serralunga	Brovia

*bottled wines more associated with La Morra

BARBARESCO DOCG

Vineyard	Village	Key Producer(s)
Asili	Barbaresco	Produttori del Barbaresco, Chiarlo, Ceretto
Basarin	Neive	Moccagatta, Pelissero
Bernardot	Treiso	Ceretto
Bricco	Neive	Cigliutti
Bricco di Treise	Treiso	Pio Cesare
Camp Gros	Barbaresco	Marchesi di Grésy
Canova	Neive	Cascina Vano
Castellizzano	Treiso	Pertinace
Cole	Barbaresco	Moccagatta
Costa Russi	Barbaresco	Gaja
Cottà	Neive	Sottimano, Vietti
Curra	Neive	Sottimano
Faset	Barbaresco	Abbona, Ceretto
Gaiun	Barbaresco	Marchesi di Gresy
Gallina	Neive	B. Giacosa, La Spinetta, Ugo Lequio

ASP	ALT	Characteristics
SSW	350	Warm and welcoming, but with considerable power
SE	325	More perfumed, less alcohol; morning-sun softness
WSW	450	Tannic, long-aging; this cru is principal source of A. Conterno's "Gran Bussia"
		See San Rocco (Costabello)
SSW	300	Dark-toned wines
WSW	360	Dense and superpowerful
SE	270	Very sunny, heavy limestone content; perfumed, soft wines
		See Bricco Rocche-Serra
E	350	Einaudi's silky "Costa Grimaldi" is from here
S	325	Full southern exposure; gigantic wines
SW	270	Same ridge as Monprivato; intensely perfumed wine
SSW	300	Big but welcoming; often compared to Monprivato
SE	360	Brovia's "Ca' Mia" from here

ASP	ALT	Characteristics
SSW	250	Elegance, balance, depth; a great introduction to Barbaresco
SSE	275	Softly contoured, with bright fruit and aromas
SSW	360	Good southern exposure; generous and silky wines
WSW	340	High-altitude site, austere
S	350	Pio Cesare's "Il Bricco" a powerhouse
SW	240	More austere and tannic than sibling Gaiun; part of Martinenga
WSW	300	East of Serraboella; fine and firm, smooth
ESE	300	Potent, tightly wound, darker tones
SE	260	Moccagatta estate's top cru; depth and power
WSW	250	Part of Roncagliette; most west-facing; wines of more finesse
SSW	260	Big, tannic, Barolo-like
SW	270	More aromatic than Cotta's wines; potent
SSW	260	Great aromatics; relatively soft
S	240	Part of Martinenga; deep and densely aromatic wine
SSW	250	Mostly southern-facing; fruity, round style; broad and aromatic

BARBARESCO DOCG (continued)

Vineyard	Village	Key Producer(s)
Loreto	Barbaresco	DeForville, Albino Rocca, Varaldo
Marcarini	Treiso	Pertinace
Martinenga	Barbaresco	Marchesi di Gresy
Masseria	Neive	Vietti
Moccagatta	Barbaresco	Produttori del Barbaresco
Montefico	Barbaresco	La Ca' Nova, C. Giacosa
Montestefano	Barbaresco	Produttori del Barbaresco, Prunotto, Mauro Sebaste
Nervo	Treiso	Pertinace
Ovello	Barbaresco	Cantina del Pino, Cascina Morassino, Produttori del Barbaresco
Paglieri/Pajé	Barbaresco	Roagna, Produttori del Barbaresco
Pajoré	Treiso	Sottimano
Pora	Barbaresco	Produttori del Barbaresco, Walter Musso
Rabajà	Barbaresco	B. Rocca, B. Giacosa, Chiarlo, Castello di Verduno, Cascina Luisin
Rio Sordo	Barbaresco	Produttori del Barbaresco, Ca' Rome, Brovia, Walter Musso
Rombone	Treiso	Fiorenzo Nada
Roncaglie	Barbaresco	Poderi Colla
Roncagliette	Barbaresco	Gaja
Ronchi	Barbaresco	Albino Rocca
Santo Stefano	Neive	B. Giacosa, Castello di Neive
Secondine	Barbaresco	Gaja
Serraboella	Neive	Cigliutti, Paitin
Sorì San Lorenzo	Barbaresco	Gaja
Sorì Tildin	Barbaresco	Gaja
Starderi	Neive	La Spinetta
Valeirano	Treiso	La Spinetta, Ada Nada

ASP	ALT	Characteristics
W	270	aka Casotto; perfumed and austere
SW	320	Fragrant and fine; focus on aromatics
SSW	240	Runs below Asili & Rabajà; includes Camp Gros and Gaiun
		See Cottà
SE	290	Soft, more finesse; early-maturing wines
SSE	250	Smooth and perfumed wines, very approachable
S	260	Borders Cole; big-boned, darker Barbarescos; Barolo-like
S ·	300	Good southern exposure; deeper, more brooding
W	260	Firm, fine, tight structure, high-toned aromas
SSW	240	Fair amount of austerity; bright aromatics
SSW	270	Among the more potent; Gaja sources "Sito Moresco" here
SW	240	Runs below Faset; silky yet deep and firmly structured
SSW	290	Borders Asili; great depth and accessibility
SSW	220	Deeper, darker-toned than wines from Rabajà-Asili
SW	240	Good depth, firm tannins
SW	240	Fine, firm, high-toned wines
SSW	250	North of Roncaglie; includes Costa Russi and Sorì Tildin
E	250	Rare east-facing cru; Rocca's "Brich Ronchi" a dense giant
SSW	230	Perhaps most Barolo-like in Barbaresco zone
SSW	250	Includes Sorì San Lorenzo site
WSW	270	Long-aging, tannic
SSW	250	Part of Secondine; Gaja's most potent, long-aging wine
SW	250	Part of Roncagliette; intense, a notch below San Lorenzo
SW	240	Angular, but with good forward fruit
SW	320	Probably the firmest, most powerful structure of Spinetta wines

GLOSSARY

ABBOCCATO
Semisweet.

ALBERELLO
"Little tree"; a spur-trained bush vine.

AMABILE (ah-MAH-bee-lay)
Semisweet.

AMARO
Bitter.

AMARONE
An intense version of Valpolicella that is made from semidried grapes. The process of drying the grapes concentrates the sugars and creates a superrich wine that, in the case of Amarone, hints at sweetness but is technically dry. *Recioto* is essentially the sweet sibling of Amarone.

ANNATA
Vintage.

APPASSIMENTO (ah-pah-see-MEN-toh)
The process of drying to concentrate sugars. See also *passito*.

ARGILLA (ar-JEE-lah)
Clay.

AZIENDA AGRICOLA (ah-zee-EN-dah ah-GREE-cola)
An estate that produces wines from at least half estate-grown grapes.

BARRIQUE (bar-EEK)
225-liter French oak cask.

BIANCO
White.

BICCHIÈRE (pl. *bicchieri*) (bick-ee-YAIR-ay/ee)
Glass.

BOTRYTIS
Fungus that, in the right conditions, doesn't rot grapes but creates a chemical reaction to create glycerine-rich sweet wines.

BOTTE (pl. *botti*)
Large cask (usually 50 hectoliters) for aging wine. Also called *fusto*.

BOTTIGLIA (boh-TEE-lia)
Bottle.

BRICCO
Piedmontese term for hilltop vineyard. Also called *bric*.

BRUT
Dry. *Extra brut* means very dry. See also *pas dosé*.

CALCAREOUS
Limestone-rich soil.

CANTINA
Winery/cellar.

CARAFFA
Decanter.

CASCINA
Farmhouse.

CAVATAPPI
Corkscrew.

CHIARETTO (key-ah-REH-toe)
Rosé wine.

CHINATO

Bitter digestif made by infusing herbs into a base of Barolo wine.

CLASSICO

Classic, or historic, production area.

COLLE/COLLINA (pl. *colli/colline*)

Hill(s).

CONSORZIO

An association or a consortium.

CORPOSO

Full-bodied.

CRÉMANT

French term for a sparkler made outside Champagne; also used to denote a wine with lower atmospheric pressure than a Champagne.

CRU

Single vineyard.

CUVÉE

Blend.

DEGUSTAZIONE (day-goo-staht-see-OH-nay)

Tasting.

DOC(G)

Denominazione di Origine Controllata (e Garantita), or denomination of controlled (and guaranteed) origin.

DOLCE

Sweet.

ENOLOGO

Winemaker.

ENOTECA

Wine bar/library with bottles for carry-out sale.

ETICHETTA (et-ee-KET-ah)

Label.

ETTARO

Hectare.

EXTRACT

Solids in a wine, including sugars, minerals, and glycerols.

FATTORIA

Central production facility of a large (traditionally feudal) wine estate. The word often appears as a prefix on wine labels, mainly in a nod to the estate's tradition.

FIASCO

Flask.

FORTIFICATO

Fortified, also called *liquoroso*.

FRESCO

Fresh.

FRIZZANTE

Semisparkling.

GIOVANE (JOH-vah-nay)

Young.

GRAPPA

Brandy made from the skins, stems, seeds, and pulp of grapes.

GRAPPOLO

Grape bunch.

GRATICCI

Straw mats used in *appassimento*.

IGT

Indicazione Geografica Tipica, or geographic origin wine.

IMBOTTIGLIATO ALL'ORIGINE
Estate-bottled.
INVECCHIATO
Aged.
MARL
Calcareous clay.
MÉTODO CHARMAT
Charmat, or "tank," method of sparkling winemaking.
MÈTODO CLASSICO
Champagne method, or *mèthode Champenoise,* of sparkling winemaking.
MOSTO
Grape must.
MOSTO COTTO
"Cooked must"; heat-concentrated must used for fortification.
MUFFA NOBILE
Noble rot, or *botrytis cinerea.*
PAS DOSÉ
Very dry.
PASSITO
Sweet wine from dried grapes. See also *appassimento.*
PHYLLOXERA
Aphid that attacks grapevines.
PODERE
Small farm holding, traditionally of a sharecropper. This word is often seen on wine labels, usually as an homage to the property's history.
PROFUMO
Aroma.
RECIOTO
Sweet wine made from dried grapes. See also *Amarone.*
RIPASSO
Term used in Valpolicella to describe a red Valpolicella wine that is given extra strength and depth via a process wherein the wine is put into a tank that contains the solids left over from an Amarone fermentation. This process incites a second fermentation and infuses the wine with some of the Amarone's richness.
RISERVA
Reserve. Used to describe a DOC(G) wine aged for a prescribed length of time.
RONCO (pl. *ronchi*)
Hill, or hillside vineyard.
ROSATO
Rosé.
ROSSO
Red.
ROVERE
Oak.
SATEN
The "idea of silk." Term used in Franciacorta to describe a sparkling wine made with all white grapes and styled with a lower dosage and atmospheric pressure to create a creamy texture.
SECCO
Dry.
SENTORE DI TAPPO
Corked. *Sa di tappo* means "It is corked."

SFURSAT/SFORSATO

Literally, "strengthened." Used in Lombardia's Valtellina to describe a rich yet dry wine made from dried grapes, like Amarone.

SOLERA

System of "topping off" aging wines in barrels by adding fractions of younger wine.

SORÌ

Piedmontese term for vineyard exposition.

SPUMANTE (pl. *spumanti*)

Sparkling.

SUPERIORE

DOC wine of "superior" quality (usually determined by higher natural alcohol).

TAPPO

Cork.

TENUTA

Large (traditionally feudal) wine estate. This word appears often on wine labels, although it has no official significance.

TERROIR

The total natural environment of a vine, including soil, microclimate, and vineyard aspect.

TRANQUILLO

Still.

TUFA

Calcareous rock.

UVA

Grape.

UVAGGIO

Blend.

VECCHIO

Aged.

VENDEMMIA

Harvest.

VENDEMMIA TARDIVA

Late-harvest, as in late-harvested grapes for (mostly) sweet wines.

VIGNA/VIGNETO

Vineyard.

VIN(O) SANTO

"Holy wine"; dessert wine made from dried grapes aged in very small casks.

VINACCIA

Pomace. The stems, seeds, etc., left after grapes are pressed.

VINO DA TAVOLA (VdT)

Table wine.

VINO NOVELLO

New or nouveau wine.

VITIGNO

Vine variety.

VQPRD

Literally, *Vin de Qualité dans une Région Déterminée.* Used throughout the European Union to denote a "quality" wine made within a delimited region.

BIBLIOGRAPHY

Anderson, Burton. *The Wine Atlas of Italy and Travelers Guide to the Vineyards*. London: Mitchell Beazley, 1990.

Atlante delle Vigne di Langa. Bra, Italy: Slow Food Editore, 2000.

Bastianich, Joseph, and David Lynch. *Vino Italiano: The Regional Wines of Italy*. New York: Clarkson Potter, 2002.

Codice Denominazioni di Origine dei Vini 2004. Milan: Unione Italiana Vini, 2003.

Gambero Rosso Vini d'Italia 2003. Rome: Gambero Rosso Editore, 2002.

Garner, Michael, and Paul Merritt. *Barolo, Tar & Roses: A Study of the Wines of Alba*. London: Random Century Group, 1990.

Guy, Patricia. *Amarone*. Sommacampagna, Italy: Morganti Editore, 1999.

Michelin Italy. Paris: Michelin et Cie, 1998.

Plotkin, Fred. *Italy for the Gourmet Traveler*. New York: Little, Brown, 1996.

Robinson, Jancis, ed. *The Oxford Companion to Wine, Second Edition*. New York: Oxford University Press, 1999.

Willinger, Faith. *Eating in Italy*. New York: Hearst, 1989.

ACKNOWLEDGMENTS

The authors would like to thank the following people for their assistance in preparing this book:

Our wives, Josie and Deanna, for putting up with us.

Chris Pavone, Adina Steiman, Jennifer K. Beal, and Marysarah Quinn at Clarkson Potter, also for putting up with us.

Jane Dystel, literary agent extraordinaire.

Mario Batali and Lidia Bastianich, *consiglieri* extraordinaire.

Elizabeth Denver, executive assistant extraordinaire.

Everyone in our New York family of restaurants, particularly the staff at Babbo.

Sergio, Derrick, Rob, Anne, Dixon, Chris, and the rest of the crew at Italian Wine Merchants.

Mark Leinwohl and Mark Coscia of Pasta Resources.

Our many colleagues in the wine trade, too numerous to list here, but especially Robert Chadderdon, Claudia Davis, Lars Leicht, Robert Mackin, Sharron McCarthy, Stacy Sherman, Jodi Stern, and Mary Anne Sullivan.